The Turing Programming Language: Design and Definition

Richard C. Holt

Philip A. Matthews

J. Alan Rosselet

James R. Cordy

Prentice Hall, Englewood Cliffs, New Jersey 07632

Library of Congress Catalog Card Number 87-081455

Editorial/production supervision: Lisa Schulz Garboski
Cover design: Richard C. Holt
Manufacturing buyer: S. Gordon Osbourne

The publisher offers discounts on this book when ordered
in bulk quantities. For more information write:
Special Sales/College Marketing
Prentice Hall
College Technical and Reference Division
Englewood Cliffs, New Jersey 07632

Printed in the United States of America

10 9 8 7 6 5 4 3 2 1

ISBN 0-13-933136-0 025

Prentice-Hall International (UK) Limited, *London*
Prentice-Hall of Australia Pty. Limited, *Sydney*
Prentice-Hall Canada Inc., *Toronto*
Prentice-Hall Hispanoamericana, S.A., *Mexico*
Prentice-Hall of India Private Limited, *New Delhi*
Prentice-Hall of Japan, Inc., *Tokyo*
Prentice-Hall of Southeast Asia Pte. Ltd., *Singapore*
Editora Prentice-Hall do Brasil, Ltda., *Rio de Janeiro*

Preface

This book describes the Turing programming language: what it is, how it was designed, and how it is defined. The material presented here should be of particular interest to people who want in-depth knowledge about Turing. It should also be of interest to those interested in programming language design, methods of language definition, and formal methods of program development. The book may be suitable for use in a graduate or advanced undergraduate course in language design, programming languages, or formal specification of languages.

This book presents a detailed case study of the design of a practical, general-purpose programming language. It is hoped that the lessons learned, the trade offs made and the decisions taken will be of interest to a broad spectrum of computer experts.

This book is unique in that it collects in one place the formal and informal definitions of a practical, general purpose programming language. The formal definition of Turing attempts to cover all relevant aspects of the language, including lexical structure, context free syntax, context conditions (static semantics), and semantics (including input/output).

Some parts of the book have been contributed by individual authors; other parts have been the cooperative efforts of two or more of the authors. Chapters 2 and 3 (language design goals and language features) were written by Holt. Holt and Cordy are the designers of the Turing language, and wrote the Turing Report (Chapter 4). Rosselet and Holt developed the language's formal context conditions (Chapter 8). Holt and Matthews developed the language's formal semantics (Chapter 9), drawing heavily on Hehner's book [Hehner 84]. Matthews wrote the appendix on lexical uniqueness of tokens. Holt wrote the appendices on the genesis of the language and on formal operational semantics. The remaining parts of the book were cooperative efforts.

The cartoon on the cover of this book, drawn by R.C. Holt, shows Turing being rescued from the sharks of ambiguity and omissions. Turing is being saved by completeness and consistency, using the spotlight of clarity. Less fortunates, Ada and PL/I, are sinking into a whirlpool of complexity, under a cloud of confusion.

A number of people have read drafts of various chapters of this book and have contributed valuable suggestions. E.C.R. Hehner in particular has been a constant source of ideas, improvements and corrections. Others who have contributed in essential ways are D.T. Barnard, A.J. Malton, E.S. Lee, T.C.N. Graham, and P.L. Rowley. Others making important contributions to the language or this book include: J.N.P. Hume, M.P. Mendell, S.G. Perelgut, T. Norvell, A.F.X. Curley, T.E. Hull, S.W.K. Tjiang, M. Molle, I.S. Weber, J.W. Wait, C.A.R. Hoare, T.W. Pratt, B.A. Hehner, D. Newton and R.N. Horspool. Suggestions by many teachers or students of Turing, and well as various interested parties have also been important, but are too numerous to mention here. The research leading to this work has been generously supported by the Canadian Natural Sciences and Engineering Research Council and by Bell Northern Research Ltd.

R.C. Holt
P.A. Matthews
J.A. Rosselet
J.R. Cordy

Toronto
January 1987

Table of Contents

1 Introduction 1

1.1 Organization of Book 2
1.2 Purposes of the Definitions 2
1.2.1 Purpose of the Informal Definition 2
1.2.2 Purpose of the Formal Definition 3
1.3 History of Development 4

2 Design Goals for the Turing Programming Language 7

2.1 Generality 8
2.2 Ease of Learning 10
2.2.1 Levels of Mastery 10
2.2.2 Concise, Expressive Notation 11
2.2.3 Traditional Notation 12
2.2.4 Notational Consistency 13
2.2.5 Graceful Treatment of Errors 14
2.2.6 Teaching Experience 16
2.3 Reliability 16
2.3.1 Minimizing Frequency and Severity of Errors 17
2.3.2 Cultural and Psychological Aspects 18
2.3.3 Program Development Cycle 18
2.3.4 Examples of Poor Error Handling 21
2.3.5 Controlling Complexity 24

2.4 Mathematical Precision 26
2.4.1 Promises of the Formal Approach 27
2.4.2 The Three C's of Formal Specification 27
2.4.3 Shortcomings of Pascal 28
2.4.4 Designing Turing for Formalization 29
2.5 Efficiency 31
2.6 Implementation 33
2.7 Global Goals 35

3 Features of the Turing Language 39
3.1 Comparison with Pascal, Modula 2 and Ada 39
3.2 Producing a Triangle of Stars 41
3.3 Searching a File for a Word 42
3.4 Functions and Dynamic Arrays 43
3.5 Strings and Substrings 45
3.6 Assertions 45
3.7 Pointers and Collections 46
3.8 Union Types and Enumerated Types 47
3.9 Bind Declaration 49
3.10 Subprograms as Parameters 50
3.11 Modules and Sets 50
3.12 Nondeterminism and Repeatability 51

4 The Turing Report 55
4.1 Introduction, Terminology, and Notation 55
4.1.1 Terminology and Basic Concepts 56
4.1.2 Identifiers and Explicit Constants 60
4.1.3 Comments and Separators 61
4.1.4 Syntactic Notation 62
4.2 Programs and Declarations 62
4.2.1 Programs 62
4.2.2 Declarations 63
4.2.3 Constant Declarations 63
4.2.4 Variable and Collection Declarations 64
4.2.5 Bind Declarations 65
4.3 Types 66
4.3.1 Types and Type Declarations 66
4.3.2 Type Equivalence and Assignability 71
4.4 Subprograms and Modules 73
4.4.1 Subprograms 73
4.4.2 Modules 79
4.4.3 Restrictions on Constants and Read Only Items 82
4.4.4 Restrictions to Prevent Aliasing 82

4.5 Statements and Input/Output 83
4.5.1 Input and Output 86
4.6 References and Expressions 90
4.6.1 References 90
4.6.2 Expressions 91
4.6.3 Numeric Operators 92
4.6.4 Comparison Operators 93
4.6.5 Boolean Operators 93
4.6.6 String Operators and Substrings 94
4.6.7 Set Operators and Set Constructors 95
4.6.8 Compile-Time Expressions 95
4.6.9 Predefined Functions 96
4.6.10 Attributes 101
4.6.11 Predefined Procedures 102
4.6.12 The Uninitialized Value 103
4.6.13 Character Collating Sequence 104
4.7 Source Inclusion Facility 105
4.8 Short Forms 106
4.9 Collected Keywords and Predefined Identifiers 108
4.10 Collected Operators and Special Symbols 108
4.11 Recognizing Tokens 109
4.12 Implementation Constraints on Integer, String, and Real Types 109
4.13 External Subprograms 111
4.14 Changes in the Turing Language 112

5 Overview of the Formal Definition of Turing 115
5.1 Syntax 115
5.1.1 Lexical Structure 116
5.1.2 Context-Free Structure 117
5.1.3 Context Conditions 118
5.1.4 The Complete Definition of Syntax 119
5.2 Semantics 119
5.2.1 Weakest Preconditions 120
5.2.2 Validity Predicates 121
5.3 Formal Requirements for Implementations 122
5.3.1 Requirement for Compilers 122
5.3.2 Requirements for Run Time 123
5.3.3 Unchecked Execution 124
5.3.4 Requirements for Interpreters 125
5.3.5 Consistency of the Axiomatic Semantics and the Report 125
5.4 Goals and Shortcomings 126
5.4.1 Completeness 126
5.4.2 Consistency 127

5.4.3 Clarity 128
5.4.4 Aids to the Implementor 128
5.5 Problems Exposed by Formal Definition 129

6 Lexical Structure 131
6.1 Notation 132
6.2 Tokens 133
6.3 Maximal Scan 135
6.4 Definition of Syn Function 136

7 Context-Free Syntax 137
7.1 Programs and Declarations 139
7.2 Types 140
7.3 Subprograms and Modules 141
7.4 Statements and Input/Output 143
7.5 References and Expressions 145

8 Context Conditions: Static Legality of Turing Programs 149
8.1 Introduction 149
8.1.1 Overview of the Definition of Context Conditions 150
8.1.2 Novel Aspects 152
8.2 ADL: Axiomatic Denotational Language 153
8.2.1 ADL: Basic Concepts 154
8.2.2 ADL Types 156
8.2.3 Function Notation 159
8.2.4 ADL Rules for Context Conditions 161
8.3 ADL Types to Represent Turing Objects 163
8.3.1 Representing Types 164
8.3.2 Representing Symbols 168
8.3.3 Representing Mode 170
8.3.4 Representing Access 171
8.3.5 Representing Context 171
8.3.6 Representing Formals 177
8.3.7 Representing Import Sets 178
8.3.8 Type Equivalence and Assignability, Parameter Compatibility 182
8.4 Rules Defining Context Conditions 186
8.4.1 Context Conditions for Programs 188
8.4.2 Context Conditions for Declarations 189
8.4.3 Context Conditions for Type Specifications 192
8.4.4 Context Conditions for Statements 194
8.4.5 Context Conditions for Input/Output 196
8.4.6 Context Conditions for Expressions 197
8.4.7 Context Conditions for References 200

8.4.8 Context Conditions for Subprograms 204
8.4.9 Context Conditions for Modules 209
8.4.10 Preventing Aliasing 211
8.4.11 Compile-Time Expressions 213
8.5 Assumptions and Observations 214
8.5.1 Assumptions Made by the Definition 215
8.5.2 Incompleteness of Turing's Formal Context Conditions 215
8.5.3 Observations 216

9 Formal Semantics: The Meaning of Turing Programs 217
9.1 Introduction 217
9.1.1 Organization of the Definition 218
9.1.2 Novel Aspects 219
9.1.3 Notation 220
9.2 Basis Statements 221
9.2.1 Informal Semantics of Basis 221
9.2.2 Formal Semantics of Basis 223
9.3 Semantics of Turing Statements and Declarations 225
9.3.1 Variable and Constant Declarations 225
9.3.2 The Bind Declaration 227
9.3.3 Statements other than Input/Output, Loops and Procedure Calls 228
9.3.4 Loops 230
9.3.5 Procedures 231
9.3.6 Functions 234
9.3.7 Modules 236
9.3.8 Input/Output 237
9.4 Validity Predicates 241
9.4.1 Valid Reference Predicate (REF) 242
9.4.2 Valid Expression Predicate (EXPN) 243
9.4.3 Valid Type Predicate (TYP) 245
9.4.4 Assignable Predicate (ASN) 246
9.4.5 Type Equivalence Predicate (EQV) 247
9.4.6 Disjointness Predicate (DISJ) 247
9.4.7 Distinctness Predicate (DIST) 248
9.5 Axioms Defining Expressions 248
9.5.1 Propositional Calculus 249
9.5.2 Predicate Calculus 250
9.5.3 Integers 250
9.5.4 Real Numbers 250
9.5.5 Enumerated Types 251
9.5.6 Strings 251
9.5.7 Sets 252
9.5.8 Arrays and Records 253

9.5.9 Unions 253
9.5.10 Collections and Pointers 253
9.5.11 Uninitialized Values 254
9.6 Implementation Constraints 254
9.6.1 Axioms for Floating Point 255
9.6.2 Bounded Expression Validity Predicate (BEXPN) 255
9.6.3 Time/Space Usage 256
9.7 Observations about Formal Semantics 257
9.7.1 Shortcomings of this Semantics 257
9.7.2 Correctness Methodology 259

Appendix A: Soul of the Turing Language 261

Appendix B: Theorem about Lexical Sequences 269

Appendix C: Translating Extended Context-Free Syntax 271

Appendix D: Turing's Abstract Context-Free Syntax 273

Appendix E: Formal Operational Semantics 279

Appendix F: Available Implementations of Turing 285

Bibliography 287

Index 293

Chapter 1

Introduction

Turing is a general purpose programming language designed for convenient development of reliable, efficient programs. Its language design goals include: ease of learning, concise and expressive syntax, graceful and effective treatment of errors, control of program complexity, mathematically precise language definition, and small, fast implementations.

Turing is designed for a wide range of applications, which include teaching programming concepts to children (where Turing is an alternative to BASIC) and developing serious software (where Turing is an alternative to languages like Pascal). It is designed for use on a wide class of computers, from microcomputers to main frames.

Many of the ideas in Turing have evolved from the Euclid language, which in turn is based on Pascal. Turing expands the applicability of Pascal by adding such needed features as modules, varying length strings, dynamic arrays, and assertions.

Turing's design supports faithful execution; this means that either a program is executed according to the language semantics or else it is halted with a message describing the nature of the failure. Turing is designed to be amenable to formal semantic definition. To attain this goal, the language imposes syntactic restrictions that eliminate side effects in expressions and prevent aliasing (multiple naming) of variables.

The development of Turing included the creation of the Turing Report (the informal language definition), the Turing textbook (for teaching programming using Turing), a portable Turing compiler and Turing interpreter (as of 1986, running on Digital VAX minicomputers, IBM 370 mainframes, IBM PC compatibles and SUN/68000 workstations), and the formal definition of the language. Programming environments for Turing have also been developed.

1.1 Organization of Book

Chapters 2 and 3 of this book give the design goals of Turing and a description of its features. Chapter 4 contains the informal definition of Turing (the Turing Report). The Report is *informal* in that its description of Turing is largely given in English.

Chapter 5 gives an overview of the methods used in formally defining Turing. The remainder of the book presents the formal definition of Turing. It is *formal* in that it makes extensive use of mathematical concepts to specify the syntax (form) and semantics (meaning) of Turing programs.

Turing's syntax is formally defined in Chapters 6 through 8. These specify Turing's lexical structure, context-free syntax, and context conditions (static semantics). Chapter 9 formally specifies Turing's semantics using weakest preconditions.

1.2 Purposes of the Definitions

The formal and informal definitions provide complementary specifications of Turing from different points of view and with different purposes. Briefly put, the informal definition takes an operational viewpoint and tries to describe Turing clearly and completely to a person with a knowledge of Pascal-like languages.

By contrast, the formal definition takes an mathematical point of view. It assumes that the reader has a reasonable facility with formal logic as well as some acquaintance with techniques for formal specification of languages and programs. It uses mathematical notation to attain a higher degree of definitional precision than is possible with an informal approach.

1.2.1 Purpose of the Informal Definition

The non-mathematical presentation of the Turing Report (the informal definition) allows it to be read easily by most programmers. (Those who are not familiar with Algol-like languages should first read the Turing textbook [Holt 84].) To aid the reader, the Report gives examples and explanations, while defining each language construct.

Although the Report is intended to give a complete and unambiguous definition of Turing, its informal exposition relies to an extent on the background and common sense of the reader. Therefore, some aspects of Turing are not as precisely defined in the Report as in the formal definition. For example, the Report's English description of the visibility of parameter names in parametric subprograms may be subject to misinterpretation; the formal context conditions should eliminate this possibility.

The Report takes an operational point of view; that is, it describes the actions, or changes of state, that occur in the execution of a Turing program. Ideally, this execution is carried out by a mathematical model that never runs out of resources; integers of any size can computed, real numbers are infinitely precise, strings can be arbitrarily long, etc. This model, which can be called the GLM (Good Lord's Machine), implements *Ideal*

Turing, which by definition never runs out of resources. The Report takes the position that resource exhaustion is an inevitable constraint; it defines ''resource limited'' Turing as well as Ideal Turing.

The Report takes an engineering approach. It assumes that Turing is a language for applied programming and that Turing programs are executed on practical computers. It discusses implementation concerns, such as limiting the range of case statement labels. To promote program portability, it recommends minimal standards for various exhaustible resources; for example, it recommends that strings up to 255 characters long should be supported. It recognizes existing standards; for example, it recommends use of the ASCII standard character set (although EBCDIC can also be used).

The Report recommends practical extensions to the language. For example, it states that programs which violate aliasing or side effect restrictions can nonetheless be executed, because these have clear operational semantics, even though they are not defined by the formal axiomatic semantics. It recommends an extension for calling **external** subprograms written in other languages. These extensions are ignored by the formal definition of Turing.

1.2.2 Purpose of the Formal Definition

The formal definition specifies the syntax (form) of Turing programs in terms of lexical structure, context-free syntax (BNF) and context conditions (static semantics). A string of characters is considered to be a Turing program if and only if it satisfies Turing's lexical structure, context-free syntax and context conditions.

The formal specification of context conditions is novel in that it uses Rosselet's ADL (Axiomatic Denotational Language) [Rosselet 84]. ADL specifies such things as type compatibility rules and anti-aliasing rules. Its formal presentation eliminates potential ambiguities in the English presentation of the Turing Report.

The axiomatic semantics of Turing considers that a program is a mathematical entity which defines the relationship between values (variables and files) before and after execution. For example, we can think of the Turing **if** statement

```
if x < 0 then
    y := -x
end if
```

as creating the relationship between x and y defined by the predicate

$$x < 0 \Rightarrow y = -x$$

The basis of the formal semantics is predicate calculus, which defines predicates such as this one.

Each Turing statement S is defined by giving its *predicate transformer*. This is a function that maps a predicate R (called the postcondition) that is to hold after execution of S to a predicate (called the weakest precondition) guaranteeing to establish R. This approach, espoused by Dijkstra[76] and Hehner[84], allows us to take advantage of their rigorous framework for developing correct programs. An alternate method of defining semantics (formal operational semantics) is given in an appendix.

The data types of Turing (integers, booleans, records, arrays, etc.) are defined in terms of axioms. These axioms do not restrict the range of integers, the length of strings, nor the precision of real numbers. In other words, the formal definition is concerned with Ideal Turing rather than "resource limited" Turing. (Note, however, that the chapter on formal semantics provides suggestions for dealing with exhaustion problems on a formal basis.)

Further discussion of the formal definition and its relationship to the informal definition is contained in Chapter 5: Overview of the Formal Definition of Turing. The rest of this chapter recounts the story of the development of the Turing Language.

1.3 History of Development

Turing was born out of an effort to find an acceptable language for instructional computing. In 1982, the Computer Science Department at the University of Toronto was faced with the selection of a programming language to replace PL/I for teaching programming. The PL/I language had been used in the department for a decade. PL/I has the advantages of a varied and powerful set of language facilities, good texts and manuals, efficient compilers (including SP/k and PL/C), and reasonably wide acceptance. However, PL/I suffers from a number of shortcomings: it is a large, clumsy, and sometimes ill-defined language. By contrast, the Pascal language is quite elegant; during the last decade, Pascal compilers and textbooks have become widely available. By 1982, Pascal had become one of the most common languages of instruction in Computer Science departments across North America. Pascal was therefore a prime candidate to succeed PL/I as the Computer Science teaching language at the University of Toronto. However, Pascal suffers its own shortcomings [Kernighan 81]. Compared to PL/I, Pascal has poor character string manipulation, limited numeric facilities, no local scopes (i.e., no declarations in **begin** blocks), and no dynamic arrays. In many ways, PL/I is a more serious language than Pascal in that it supports a number of programming techniques that are not feasible in Pascal. (Note: the "Pascal" being referred to here is the language defined by the International Standards Organization [ISO 80], not one of the many incompatible implementations of that language.)

As of 1982, the Concurrent Euclid (CE) language, developed at the University of Toronto, had experienced considerable use and had gained wide acceptance in systems programming. CE has a precise mathematical foundation; it incorporates up-to-date software concepts (such as modules), and it enhances reliability and efficiency. Because of these advantages, CE became a candidate, along with Pascal, to succeed PL/I. Unfortunately, CE does not have the convenient level of programming facilities needed for introductory programming; its input/output is complex, its string handling is rudimentary, and its syntax is verbose.

After considerable discussion and investigation, the decision was made to develop a new language, based on CE, to be used for instructional computing. Originally the language was called New Euclid, because it borrows heavily from CE and Euclid [Lampson 77].

As the design of the new language evolved, it took on a personality of its own. Consequently, it was given its own name, Turing, in honor of Alan M. Turing, one of the pioneering geniuses of Computer Science.

Hodges[83] has written a highly readable biography of Alan M. Turing. Turing is best known for developing a mathematical model of computation, now known as the Turing machine, in 1937. He used this model to prove that certain well-formed questions are undecidable and that certain well-defined functions are not computable. During World War II, he headed the British code-breaking team that deciphered Nazi radio codes; this work helped win the war by providing information about U-boat locations. After the war, Turing designed one of the first electronic computers. He did early work in artificial intelligence, developing the "Turing test" as a criterion to determine if a computer can be considered intelligent.

From August 1982 through August 1983, an intensive research and development effort brought the Turing language into existence. (See "Soul of the Turing Language" [Holt 84a], included as Appendix A of this book, for an account of the human-interest side of this effort.)

During this period, the notation for the language was designed and polished (by R.C. Holt and J.R. Cordy), a textbook was written (by R.C. Holt and J.N.P. Hume), and Turing compilers were developed for the Digital VAX/11 and the IBM 370. The compiler team consisted of J.R. Cordy, R.C. Holt, M.P. Mendell, S.G. Perelgut, S.W.K. Tjiang and P.A. Matthews, later joined by A.F.X. Curley. The Turing compiler was written in CE.

By Fall 1983, 3,000 University of Toronto students were using Turing on five computers (an IBM 3033 and four VAXes). The language was and is used for both introductory and advanced courses. By Fall 1984, the PC (personal computer) version of Turing was also being used in Computer Science courses.

Further support for the language, including programming environments and interactive interpreters, has been developed at the University of Toronto and Queen's University (Kingston). In addition, Turing has served as the basis for further language design. A compatible superset of Turing called Turing Plus adds features including concurrency, exception handling, separate compilation, generalized input/output, and explicit suppression of type checking. T.E. Hull has developed a version of Turing called Numeric Turing that supports dynamic choice of floating point precision [Hull 85].

Chapter 2

Design Goals for The Turing Programming Language

The design of programming languages remains at best an art, and any attempt to reduce it to a simple, quantitative discipline is bound to fail. At the same time, there are many rules and principles that can help the designer to produce a better language. The design goals for the Turing language will be described, along with how these goals were attained.

There have been various discussions on language design [Weinberg 71, Hoare 73, Wirth 74, Gannon 75], but few designers of languages have attempted to lay out the methods they have used [Wirth 76, Popek 77, Ichbiah 79, Brinch Hansen 82]. This discussion represents such an attempt, and it is hoped that the points raised here will be of interest to students of language design. The reader should be warned that no attempt is made here to list all the sources of information or prejudice that impinged on the design of Turing. One of the most notable sources of inspiration is simply many years of experience in programming language design and implementation, from which certain intuition arises.

One of the key lessons to be learned from this discussion is that language design is extremely complex, that no single rule by itself leads assuredly to good decisions, and that trade offs among competing goals are inevitable. As the designers of Euclid [Popek 77] said, a language's design "represents a compromise among conflicting goals, reflecting the skills, knowledge, and tastes ... of its designers."

If the discussion sometimes seems disjoint, it is likely because rules of thumb for language design have not yet crystallized into accepted principles. It is hoped that this discussion will contribute toward the establishment of such principles.

The reader may choose to study the Turing language and its informal and formal definitions without considering its language design goals. However, in doing so, he or she may find it difficult to understand how features were chosen for inclusion in Turing, and how these features were designed to have their particular form and meaning.

We will list goals for Turing with their major ramifications in sections which concentrate on:

- Generality
- Ease of learning
- Reliability
- Mathematical precision
- Efficiency
- Implementation
- Global goals

We begin by considering the goal of generality.

2.1 Generality

Turing is designed to be a general purpose programming language. This design goal means that Turing should potentially be the language of choice for a wide class of applications.

In the abstract, the concept of generality is difficult or impossible to define, and it is not reasonable to attempt to design a language that is good for all purposes. The approach taken in the design of Turing was to consider the utility of other general purpose languages, such as Pascal and PL/I, and to use this insight to maximize the breadth of application of Turing while maintaining other language goals such as ease of learning and implementability. Turing also seeks to support most of the applications for which BASIC, Logo and Fortran are suitable. In the rest of this discussion, various problems with these existing languages will be pointed out along with corresponding solutions provided by Turing. This is not to imply that these languages are poorly conceived, but rather that Turing's design has attempted to capitalize on their many strengths while avoiding their weaknesses.

The approach to maximizing generality, while keeping the language manageable, is captured in this *rule of elegance*:

Rule. *Maximize utility, minimize complexity.*

One source of experience that influenced the design of Turing was the previous development of SP/k (a PL/I subset) at the University of Toronto in 1972 [Holt 72]. SP/k was a special purpose language, designed for introductory programming. Although SP/k was excellent for teaching, certain people did not wish to use it even for teaching, because it was a "toy." It was resolved early in the design of Turing that Turing was to be a practical, widely usable language and not "just a teaching language."

Because of its widespread acceptance, Pascal's range of applicability is an important basis for comparison. Since many people admire Pascal but hesitate to use it due to its limitations, the Turing design followed:

Rule. *More powerful than Pascal.*

Various shortcomings of Pascal [Kernighan 81] became obvious when questioning Computer Science professors to see what classes of algorithms they expect a general purpose language to handle well. Four areas that are poorly supported by Pascal are:

> *Text manipulation.* A widely voiced opinion was that Pascal's string manipulation is much too clumsy, considerably worse than that of PL/I and BASIC.
>
> *Graph algorithms.* From graph theory came the complaint that Pascal lacks dynamic arrays and local declarations in blocks.
>
> *Numeric algorithms.* From numerical analysis come the opinion that Pascal has an insufficient set of predefined numeric functions and is missing the exponentiation operator.
>
> *Software engineering.* The opinion from software engineering was that modularity and information hiding are poorly addressed by Pascal.

Following the goal of generality, Turing introduces a carefully selected set of features to overcome these shortcomings, while maintaining essentially the full functionality of Pascal.

The desire to maximize generality was tempered by the competing goals of language simplicity, efficiency and implementability. Turing restricts its modules to be scope controlling constructs (as in Modula) rather than parameterized types (as in Euclid and CLU), because experience in implementing Euclid demonstrated the implementation complexity arising in parameterized types [Holt 82a]. Similarly, more general features such as generic functions and automatic garbage collection were considered to entail too much complexity or inefficiency to compensate for their potential benefits.

Many features such as these could be added to the Turing language, because Turing is designed to allow graceful expansion to increase its generality. Turing Plus, a compatible extension, introduces a number of features including concurrency, exception handling, separate compilation, generalized input/output, different sizes of numeric types, and escapes to access details of the underlying implementation. As a result, Turing Plus supports those applications for which C, Modula 2 and Ada were designed. Turing can also be trimmed to a language of the size of BASIC for use on extremely limited hardware, such as hand held computers.

2.2 Ease of Learning

Turing is designed to be easy to learn. This design goal demands simplicity and convenience of use. It requires language features to have short, clear explanations. We will divide this discussion about ease of learning into sections on levels of mastery, conciseness of expression, traditional notation, notational consistency, treatment of errors and teaching experience.

2.2.1 Levels of Mastery

Levels of mastery means that a learner must be able to start with a language subset and then learn increasingly larger subsets. It should not be necessary, for example, to learn details of formatting lines of output before running a program. When teaching Turing, one can introduce the basic **put** statement, then simple variables, then simple selection and looping (**if**, **loop** and **for**), without mentioning other language features. This approach follows the concept of a sequence of increasing language subsets developed in the SP/k language and textbook [Holt 77, Hume 73].

As an example of these levels, consider these increasingly sophisticated versions of the **put** statement for outputting the value of real variable x.

```
put x
put x : 10
put x : 10 : 2
put x : 10 : 2 : 1
```

The first is ideal for the beginner and prints out x with a default number of fractional digits, with suppression of trailing zeros. Successive forms, to be learned as needed, specify field width (10), number of fractional digits (2), and number of exponent digits (1).

BASIC allows a gentle introduction to programming. The level of mastery required to solve small, interesting problems in BASIC is manageable by children. One goal for Turing was to be easier to learn than BASIC.

Rule. *Easier than BASIC.*

The goal is that for concepts and algorithms that BASIC handles well, the corresponding subset of Turing should be easier to learn and use.

BASIC has become the world's most commonly learned programming language. Its success derives largely from two facts: (1) it is easy to learn and use for a simple class of applications and (2) it has widely available interactive interpreters. Unfortunately, BASIC is highly unstructured; it is poor for teaching any but the simplest of programming concepts.

Turing is designed to allow easy learning and use at the level of BASIC, and to allow interactive interpreters. At the same time, Turing is a highly structured language, that provides sophisticated features for solving a rich class of programming problems. So a student can learn Turing a level at a time and will not be forced to switch languages when he or she starts writing larger programs.

In a sense, Turing resembles Logo more than BASIC. Logo's most publicized constructs are its built-in procedures to simulate "turtle geometry" and its easily written procedures. Turing also has convenient procedures, and turtle geometry can easily be incorporated into Turing. With the addition of turtle geometry, Turing offers these same advantages.

2.2.2 Concise, Expressive Notation

Turing's syntax is designed so that the programmer can directly and concisely state his or her intentions. The design goal is:

Rule. *No frills syntax.*

A program should not be peppered with extraneous semicolons and parentheses. Keywords should be short and expressive. Concise, expressive notation helps make programs easier to read and write for the beginner as well as the expert.

As an example that violates this rule, consider the minimal PL/I program to print HI:

```
TEST: PROCEDURE OPTIONS(MAIN);
    PUT LIST('HI');
END;
```

The minimal Pascal program for this purpose is no better:

```
program Test(output);
    begin
        write('HI')
    end.
```

By contrast the corresponding Turing program is simply:

```
put "HI"
```

Isolated examples of syntactic trivia, such as the final period (instead of semicolon) of a Pascal program, are not a great hindrance to an expert. But distractions of this sort focuses the beginner's attention on extraneous verbiage rather than on the real job of learning to program.

The rule for shortening certain constructs while leaving others long, is that often used constructs should be brief. For Turing, we used the rule:

Rule. *Usage shortens form.*

In other words, high frequency constructs should be short. We also favored simplifying the notation of forms that are first encountered by the beginner, the reasoning being that the beginner has a harder time dealing with complex syntax then does the expert. For example, the novice Turing programmer learns concise terms such as **put** to print a line, but later when he or she is more proficient, uses longer terms for less frequently used constructs such as **collections**.

Another way in which Turing has been kept concise is through the use of defaults and options. When there are multiple options, the most common case should occur first, with other options added in decreasing order of use. For example, the **put** statement, discussed in the previous section, provides the power of formatted output while retaining the simplicity of BASIC's free format output, by having optional specifications of field width, fractional digits, and exponent digits.

As mastery increases, the programmer may choose to gain more conciseness by using Turing's short forms; for example, the short form for **put** is ! and the entire Turing program to print HI can be written as:

```
! "HI"
```

These short forms are controversial. Some people feel that short forms are not sufficiently mnemonic; for example, the symbol ! is less suggestive than the keyword **put**. This argument claims that the conciseness of short forms is gained by sacrificing too much readability. Others claim that short forms contribute to both readability and writeability *for the expert* by eliminating clutter and reducing a program to concise, specialized symbols. We will generally ignore short forms, because (1) their use is optional, (2) they introduce no new semantics, and (3) software exists to expand Turing's short forms to their equivalent longer forms.

2.2.3 Traditional Notation

We now turn from the goal of a concise, expressive notation to the closely related goal of using traditional notation. The design of Turing acknowledges the culture or tradition of computer science, mathematics and engineering, by using well known conventions and notations, hence:

Rule. *Cultural recognizability.*

This rule helps make Turing easy to learn by the expert or teacher, as well as by the beginner.

A person who knows a language such as Pascal or PL/I already has a "reading knowledge" of Turing. This means that a Pascal programmer can generally guess the meaning of a Turing program, without having studied the Turing language. After the programmer has been introduced to Turing, he or she will commonly be able to guess the form of features that have not yet been learned. In keeping with this respect for tradition, Turing allows semicolons to appear essentially the same places as in either PL/I or Pascal (but does not require them).

To illustrate violation of tradition in notation, we will give examples from the C and Ada languages. By mathematical tradition, the expression $x---y$ is equal to $x-y$. But in C, the statement

$z = x---y$

means to assign x minus y to z with the unpleasant surprise of decrementing x by one. In Ada, the statement

z := x---y

means to assign x to z and to ignore y. The unpleasant surprise in Ada is that two minus signs together signify that the remainder of the line is a comment, which is to be ignored. Since writing three minus signs in a row is not commonly done, these examples are not particularly serious failures in language design, but they serve to warn that violating traditional notation is confusing to the programmer.

A more interesting example involves precedence in expressions, as illustrated by:

if $x > 1$ **and** $x < 100$ **then** . . .

The precedence rules of Pascal violate tradition by causing this example to be rejected (to satisfy Pascal, each comparison must be parenthesized). Turing's precedence rules correspond to mathematical tradition, so this example is legal in Turing.

2.2.4 Notational Consistency

After a programmer has been introduced to Turing, he or she will (ideally) be able to guess the form of features not yet learned. This is because Turing is designed to have notational consistency, that is:

Rule. *Language features with similar purposes should have similar syntax.*

For example, an **if** statement is terminated by **end if**, so by notational consistency, a **case** statement is terminated by **end case**, and a **record** by **end record**.

Options appended to constructs are consistently indicated using a colon. For example, a colon following **put** indicates the specification of a stream and a colon following an output item indicates a field width.

A star (*) means an obvious default. In a substring, such as *s*(2 .. *), the star means the length of string *s*. In an array parameter declaration, it means the bound of the corresponding argument. In a string input format, it means the rest of the input line.

The **for** statement creates (declares) an index, so the **for** loop header uses a syntax that is notationally consistent with declarations, for example:

```
var i: 1 .. 5   % i is a variable
for j: 1 .. 5   % j is local to the for statement
  put 2*j  % Prints 2, 4, ..., 10
end for
```

Since the range of a **for** counter is written as a subrange (1 .. 5), it is notationally consistent to allow the specification of a **for** index range using named subrange types.

Here is an example of this usage:

```
type fingers: 1 .. 5
var i: fingers
for j: fingers
  put 2*j    % Prints 2, 4, ..., 10
end for
```

Notational consistency is defined by users' perceptions of similarities, so it is reasonable to incorporate *user feedback*, i.e., user expectations, into the process of language design. This feedback occurred a number of times in the design of Turing. For example, user feedback resulted in a generalization of Turing's original substring notation. Consider the substring *s*(2 .. *), which selects the second through the last character of string *s*. Once programmers learned this notation, they expected that it could be used in more general ways than it originally designed; for example, programmers wrote *s*(*−1 .. *) expecting to select the last two characters of *s*. This more general notation was invented by users' expectations and was subsequently incorporated into the language.

We now turn from the goal of notational consistency to treatment of errors.

2.2.5 Graceful Treatment of Errors

Graceful and diagnostic treatment of errors is essential for a language used by beginners. Too often, the beginner is frustrated by incomprehensible program output or error messages, and cannot proceed without the aid of an expert. Good error handling is also essential to the professional programmer, to improve productivity and software reliability. We will concentrate here only on error handling as it affects the beginner and will return to the question of reliability in a later section.

The quality of error handling is determined by both the language design and the implementation. We will be concerned here primarily with questions of language design, rather than implementation.

We have already discussed how the language goals of concise, expressive notation, traditional notation, and notational consistency help the beginner. These goals help to minimize the beginner's errors by making the language easier to learn and harder to forget.

From measurements on usage of the SP/k subset of PL/I [Barnard 81], it is known that among the commonest syntax errors are missing or misplaced semicolons and mismatched parentheses. Semicolon errors are more prevalent in Pascal than PL/I , because Pascal's rule of "semicolon as statement separator" is clumsier than PL/I's rule of "semicolon as statement terminator." Turing cuts the Gordian knot by removing the need for semicolons, so semicolon errors are completely eliminated by language design.

Pascal and PL/I require redundant parentheses in several places, for example, around the arguments of *writeln*:

*writeln('Percentage is ', 100*x/(x+y))*

Doubled final parentheses, as in this example, are commonly written incorrectly as a single parenthesis. Turing reduces the frequency of errors due to mismatched parentheses by eliminating redundant parentheses.

From measurements on SP/k usage, it is known that references to uninitialized variables are among of the commonest run-time errors. Consequently, the Turing language specification requires the automatic detection of these errors (when checking is on, which is the case for introductory programming). By contrast, the Pascal language specification considers a reference to an uninitialized variable to be an "error," but this error is not required to be automatically detected. The result is that most Pascal systems leave this common error undetected. BASIC implementations generally provide a default value of zero or null for uninitialized variables, leaving this class of error undetected.

A number of the essential lessons about error handling learned from Fortran, BASIC and PL/I were incorporated into Pascal and Euclid, and subsequently into Turing. Perhaps the most important of these is the requirement for declaration of variables. The declaration documents the programmer's intentions for use of the variable, thereby allowing these intentions to be automatically checked. The utility of both declarations and checks for variable initialization are illustrated in the following two examples.

Example. Consider this BASIC program, which is intended to print the greeting HI:

```
10 PRINT HI
```

In most BASIC implementations, this prints zero. The trouble is that HI is not quoted, so HI is implicitly considered to be a variable, and the implementation gives this variable the default value of zero. In languages like Pascal and Turing, this kind of error is detected automatically, because HI appears to be a variable, but has no declaration. Since BASIC requires neither declaration nor initialization, the beginner is frustrated by unexpected output and no indication of the source of the problem.

Example. This BASIC program supposedly reads in a weight in pounds and converts it to kilograms:

```
10 INPUT WEIGHT
20 PRINT "In kilograms:", WIEGHT/2.2
```

In most BASIC implementations, line 20 prints a kilogram weight of zero, no matter what is input in line 10. The problem is that WEIGHT in line 10 is spelled differently from WIEGHT (I before E) in line 20. BASIC prints zero because the I-before-E variable is implicitly declared and initialized. Most misspelling errors such as this, which are common in practice, are automatically detected in Turing and Pascal due to the requirement for declaration.

One reason that can be given for not requiring declarations in BASIC, Fortran, and PL/I is that declarations complicate a program by adding extra non-essential notation. There is some justification for this position for very short programs, say at most one page. The counterargument is that even short programs benefit from declarations, as the preceding examples show. For longer programs, the extra checking implied by declarations becomes essential.

We have discussed error handling as it affects the beginning programmer. We will return to the subject of error handling when we consider the question of program reliability. This discussion of the language design goal of ease of learning has been organized around the topics of levels of mastery, concise and expressive notation, notational consistency, traditional notation, and error handling. Before leaving this subject, we will recount experience using Turing in the classroom.

2.2.6 Teaching Experience

By the time of this writing, thousands of students have been taught Turing by dozens of teachers. There has been essentially universal agreement that the language is easier to learn and use than PL/I or Pascal. Teachers have observed that they had considerable time (two to three weeks) left at the end of a one-semester introductory programming course, because Turing is so much easier to teach than Pascal or PL/I. An example Pascal program will be used to illustrate this phenomenon:

```
if n > 0 then                        (* No semicolon *)
  begin                              (* Beware of dangling else *)
    if t/n < 50 then                 (* No semicolon *)
      begin                          (* Begin required *)
        fail := fail + 1;            (* Semicolon required *)
        flag := false                (* Semicolon optional *)
      end                            (* Semicolon optional *)
  end                                (* No semicolon *)
else                                 (* No semicolon *)
  null := true
```

The teacher's explanations of the comments given on the right will take considerable time, and many students will remain confused. By contrast, the explanation for Turing is simply that each **if** statement must be concluded by an **end if** (no need to mention semicolons), so the Turing equivalent is:

```
if n > 0 then
  if t/n < 50 then
    fail := fail + 1
    flag := false
  end if
else
  null := true
end if
```

The Turing equivalent is shorter, easier to write, and easier to read. This concludes the discussion on ease of learning; we now turn to the goal of program reliability.

2.3 Reliability

Turing is designed to promote program reliability [Gannon 75]. This design goal means that Turing should help the programmer in developing software that reliably accomplishes its specified purposes.

As procedural languages have evolved, from Fortran to Algol to Pascal, they have generally improved our abilities to produce reliable software. The Euclid and Concurrent Euclid languages, using Pascal as a basis, and Turing, using Euclid as a basis, have continued the evolution toward aiding program reliability. Unfortunately, some languages, notably PL/I and C, have introduced features that are detrimental to reliability.

Turing is designed to promote reliability in three major ways. The first two ways are discussed in this section. First, Turing is designed so that potentially ill-used constructs cause minimal errors and errors of minimal severity. Second, Turing is designed to help control program complexity and thus to maximize program understandability; increased understandability enhances reliability because a primary source of software failure is our inability to comprehend large programs during program maintenance. Third, as will be discussed in a later section, Turing's formal definition provides a constructive approach to producing correct programs.

2.3.1 Minimizing Frequency and Severity of Errors

In this section, we take it for granted that errors of various kinds can and do occur in programming.

Rule. *To err is human.*

Humans develop software, so software contains errors.

Rule. *Bugs are inevitable.*

Given this inevitability, Turing's design attempts to minimize the frequency and severity of these bugs.

By experience and measurement [Gannon 75], we know that there are certain *high frequency* programming errors. An understanding of methods of handling errors in this class is essential for designing a language to promote reliability. Examples of these errors include forgetting to initialize variables and misspelling of identifiers. These particular examples have been discussed in the section on ease of learning, because they can stand in the way of effective learning. Various other high frequency errors are illustrated later in this section.

Perhaps the most severe type of programming error is the *lurking bug*. This is a bug that remains undetected; in the worst case the bug is present in the production version of the program. Bugs of this type are sometimes not considered to be important, because they may be low frequency errors. This point of view is misguided and leads to unreliable software. Although lurking bugs may be seldom observed, they can lead to disaster in a production program, causing loss of life and property. Examples given later illustrate how Turing is designed to flush out lurking bugs.

We will now give a discussion of various error handling concepts, organized into sections on:

- Cultural and psychological aspects (which lead to errors)
- The program development cycle (its relation to cost of errors)
- Examples of poor error handling (from other languages)

2.3.2 Cultural and Psychological Aspects

To understand how people make certain mistakes, it is necessary to consider the *cultural framework* which surrounds them. For example, people who are fluent in a language like English unconsciously know that the symbol = means "equals," that spaces separate words, and that punctuation, such as semicolons, is rarely essential for understanding prose. From psychological studies, we know that fluent readers do not inspect all the letters and punctuation in English prose; rather they inspect prose only enough to confidently extract its meaning. For example, when reading this fragment,

Paris in the
the spring

many people do not notice that "the" appears twice. People read programs in the same way, with the result that certain errors are often overlooked.

Language design should recognize the psychological aspects that lead to errors and should follow:

Rule. *Easily overlooked errors should not lead to disaster.*

Language design should also recognize people's cultural expectations, and should follow the *no surprise* rule:

Rule. *No unpleasant surprises.*

When a person uses his culture, education and common sense to conclude that a program has a particular meaning, then the language should not surprise him or her with a different meaning. One way Turing recognizes the programmer's cultural framework and minimizes unpleasant surprises is by respecting traditional notation (this was discussed in the section on ease of learning). Examples given below show how violation of these two principles leads to error prone language constructs.

2.3.3 Program Development Cycle

To understand the nature of bugs, we must consider the stages or steps of program development. We will assume that the programmer who is trying to develop reliable software will:

Step 1. Write the program carefully.
Step 2. Read the program carefully.
Step 3. Compile the program.
Step 4. Test the program carefully.
Step 5. Use the program in production.

During program maintenance, the programmer cycles through these steps, improving the program's performance, increasing the functionality of the program, and correcting errors.

Turing is designed to help detect bugs as early as possible in this sequence of steps.

Rule. *Early warning.*

In general, the earlier a bug is detected, the easier and cheaper it is to correct it. For example, an error that is detected by the compiler can typically be corrected much more easily than if the bug remains to be found during testing. A bug that remains undetected until production (a lurking bug) can be disastrous.

When an error is detected, it can generally be easily corrected if it can be isolated:

Rule. *Error isolation.*

For example, if an error is isolated to the extent that it is known to be caused by a missing variable declaration, then it can be immediately corrected. Conversely, the hardest errors to fix are those whose symptoms are remote from their cause. One reason early detection of errors leads to their efficient removal is that early detection effectively isolates the problem. For example, syntax errors are usually automatically isolated to a single source line. By contrast, many run-time errors cause trouble that is observable only after execution has passed well beyond the offending construct, so it is difficult to isolate the source of the difficulty.

Following the *early warning* rule, Turing is designed to maximize the chance that an error is detected early in the development cycle. We will now discuss, for each step in the cycle, ways in which Turing helps detect and eliminate errors.

Step 1: Write the program carefully. All program features are designed to have maximum clarity, and certain program features which would detract from reliability are omitted from Turing. For example, GOTOs, uncheckable variant records, and pointer arithmetic are omitted. This selection of language features helps the programmer to write correct programs.

Step 2: Read the program carefully. Turing is designed to maximize readability, so a person studying a program will have a better chance of understanding it well, and so this person will be able to pick out places where the program fails to meet its specification. The *no frills syntax* rule and the *cultural recognizability* rule require concise, expressive, readable language features. As will be discussed under "Controlling Complexity," Turing has language features that are used to make sure that a large program can be understood one part at a time.

The constructive approach to program correctness, to be discussed later, combines steps one and two (program writing and reading) into a larger step. Ideally, this larger step produces a program which is proven correct, and hence does not contain errors. In practice, this ideal is not necessarily attained and methods for detecting errors in steps three and four (compiling and testing) will remain important for the foreseeable future.

Step 3: Compile the program. Turing is designed to maximize the number of errors that can be automatically detected by a compiler. This means that a number of errors that occur at run time in other languages are detected statically in Turing. Consequently, a programmer using Turing may find that it is is more difficult to satisfy the compiler, but easier to debug the program.

Following the tradition of Pascal, Turing has strong static type checking; this means that generally there is a straightforward static test to determine whether the type of a variable will be appropriate for its run-time use. (In more interpretive languages, such as APL and LISP, it is not generally possible to check types statically because a variable's type can change at run-time.) The type information used for type checking is a form of redundancy [Gannon 75] that is useful for catching errors:

Rule. *Useful redundancy.*

Variable declarations and the requirement to initialize variables are other sources of redundancy that are useful for automatic bug detection.

There are two static checks made by a Turing compiler that go well beyond the checks of Pascal. These checks, inherited from Euclid, determine (1) if a program has *aliasing* and (2) if functions have *side effects*. These checks have been necessitated by Turing's formal requirements (see the section describing the goal of Mathematical Precision). From a reliability point of view, these checks warn against particularly treacherous sources of lurking bugs.

Aliasing and side effects both violate the *no surprise* rule, as will now be shown. To illustrate aliasing, consider the Pascal statements,

$$i := 1;$$
$$j := 2$$

Most programmers would be unpleasantly surprised to learn that this sequence may set both i and j to 2. This violation of the *no surprise* rule occurs in Pascal when i and j represent the same variable, for example, when i and j are formal reference parameters with the same actual parameter. Turing guarantees to detect this anomaly.

To illustrate side effects, consider this statement, which contains a call to function f:

$$x := y + f(5)$$

If function f has the side effect of changing variable y, then it is ambiguous whether the original or final value of y will be used in the expression. This violation of the *no surprise* rule is detected by Turing, because it statically detects all function side effects.

We now turn from automatic detection of bugs by the compiler to testing.

Step 4: Test the program carefully. We now discuss how Turing enhances the programmer's ability to locate errors during testing. Turing's novel contribution towards improving our ability to test programs is:

Rule. *Faithful execution.*

Turing's faithful execution means the program is guaranteed to either run according to the language specification or else to emit a message indicating the location and nature of the failure. In other words, faithful execution supports:

Rule. *Fail-stop implementation of language semantics.*

This rule guarantees that a programmer can always understand what a program is doing by inspecting the program's source code (no need to inspect its implementation in object code). The programmer can be confident that the behavior of a program is not just an accident of the implementation. With faithful execution, many errors are automatically detected the first time an erroneous statement is executed. By contrast, in implementations of Pascal and C, local integer variables in a subprogram commonly have values of zero on the first call. This means a subprogram may accidentally pass a test that should have been failed, as is illustrated below in example 8.

By the *error isolation* rule, run-time errors should be localized as much as possible. To attain this localization, we require:

Rule. *No remote effects.*

This means that a particular statement or declaration can modify only the items (variables), it refers to. For example, consider this assignment to an array element:

$a(i) := 23$

In a language like C, this can modify any variable in the program (and possibly the program itself), depending on the value of *i*, because in general in C it is not possible to check subscripts. With faithful execution, Turing prevents remote effects, using run-time checking to verify that subscript *i* is within the array's bounds.

Step 5: Use the program in production. Once the program has been thoroughly tested, it can be used in production. If the cost of running the program is great enough, we may choose to sacrifice faithful execution, by asking for unchecked execution. When we make this request, we are implicitly asserting to the compiler that the program will not fail (will not divide by zero, will not overflow the run-time stack, etc.). For many programs, this sacrifice is unnecessary. In some applications, such as in highly secure computer systems, this sacrifice is unacceptable; in this type of system, the protection and reliability provided by fail-stop execution is considered essential. Turing is designed to minimize the cost of faithful execution, so that full checking can be used in many production situations.

2.3.4 Examples of Poor Error Handling

We have given language design rules for minimizing the frequency of errors and for detecting errors as early as possible in the program development cycle. In order to show how these rules influenced Turing's design, we will give a series of examples of errors that are handled poorly in Fortran, C, PL/I or Pascal. Each of these examples illustrates a potential lurking bug that is eliminated or automatically detected when using Turing.

Example 1, from Fortran:

```
DO 50 I = K TO 100
```

The intent is to repeat the block of code down to line 50 with I successively taking the values K to 100. The error is that "TO" should have been a comma. Fortran ignores blanks and considers this statement to be:

```
DO50I = KTO100
```

This implicitly declares variables DO50I and KTO100 and assigns the latter to the former. (It is said that a Venus space probe failed due to this sort of Fortran bug.) People do not ignore blanks, and so this is a violation of the *no surprise* rule. Later languages such as PL/I, Pascal and Turing avoid this sort of unpleasant surprise by considering blanks to be significant.

Example 2, from Fortran:

```
X = 2 ** - 3
```

The intent is to set real variable X to 0.125. Fortran considers that 2**-3 is equivalent to 1/8. Unfortunately, Fortran requires 1/8 to be an integer (since 1 and 8 are integers) and arbitrarily truncates 1/8 to zero without warning, so X becomes zero. This is a violation of traditional notation and of the *no surprise* rule. Like Fortran, Turing requires that the expression 2**-3 must evaluate to an integer, but Turing gives a run-time warning that the result is not an integer, rather than leaving a lurking bug undetected.

Example 3, from C:

if (*i* = *3*) ...

The intent is to test to see if *i* equals 3. In C, this assigns 3 to *i* and then tests to see if *i* is non-zero. Our mathematical culture and our years of experience indicate that = means "equals." In Turing, this tradition is respected.

Example 4, from C:

x = *sqrt*(4)

The intent is to find the square root of 4 and assign it to *x*. C does not convert the integer 4 to the floating point number 4.0, because C does not check the types of parameters. The unfortunate result is that the internal form of the integer 4 is passed to *sqrt*, which expects a floating point number. C gives no warning and produces a nonsense result. By contrast, in Turing the analogous program would actually assign the square root of 4 to x, because Turing using strong typing.

Example 5, from PL/I:

```
X = 25 + 1/3;
```

The intent is that X should become approximately 25.333. In Fortran, 1/3 evaluates to zero, and the answer would unfortunately be 25. In PL/I, things are even more bizarre; 1/3 is evaluated to 0.333... using the maximum FIXED DECIMAL precision available in the implementation. When this value is added to 25, PL/I maintains all of a fraction's precision and hence there is an overflow (the 2 of 25 is lost), resulting in approximately 5.333. This is a blatant violation of the *no surprise* rule, which arises due to interactions among PL/I's elaborate rules for precision of expressions. By contrast, in Turing 1/3 is considered to be a real number, so 25+1/3 is evaluated in floating point to be approximately 25.333, satisfying the programmer's expectations.

Example 6, from PL/I:

```
I = J = 0;
```

The intent is to set I and J to zero. In PL/I, this compares J to zero and then sets I to be 1 or 0 depending on the result of the comparison. In mathematics, the notation I=J=0 is widely used to mean that I and J are both zero, so this is another violation of traditional notational causing an unpleasant surprise. Turing avoids this difficulty by using := instead of = to mean assignment.

Example 7, from Pascal:

```
if a < 0 then;
   a := - a
```

The intent is to set *a* to its absolute value. The erroneous semicolon following the keyword **then** causes *a* to always be negated. Turing requires **end if** to terminate each **if** statement and makes all semicolons optional, so the possibility of this error is eliminated syntactically.

Example 8, from Pascal:

```
function sum(a: intarray, n: integer): integer;
   var i, s: integer;
   begin
      for i := 1 to n do s := s + a[i];
      sum := s
   end;
```

The intent is that the function should sum up the first *n* elements of array *a*. The bug is that *s* is not initialized. In testing, this bug may not be detected because zero is a common initial (garbage) value. The bug will show up only when the initial value of *s* does not happen to be zero. Turing's faithful execution will automatically detect this use of an uninitialized variable on the first test that calls this function.

Each of these examples violates the *no surprise* rule, and all except example 8 violate traditional notation. All the errors except those in examples 2 and 8 are either eliminated or are statically detected as a result of Turing's design. Example 8 illustrates how Turing's faithful execution automatically detects errors during testing.

Example 2 illustrates a violation by Fortran of:

Rule. *No information loss.*

The idea is that an executing program should not be allowed to discard information, such as a fraction or the end of a string, except by explicit request. The following two statements illustrate cases in which Turing detects information loss, but PL/I gives no warning. In these statements, *i* is an integer variable and *s* is a string with maximum length 4.

```
i := 7.94          % Prevented statically by Turing
s := "Hello"       % Detected dynamically by Turing
```

By contrast, in PL/I, *i* would be assigned 7 and *s* would be assigned *"Hell"*, with no warning, so these are potential lurking bugs.

This concludes the set of examples illustrating how poor error handling can often be overcome by careful language design. We now consider how Turing improves reliability by improving program understandability.

2.3.5 Controlling Complexity

Turing is designed to promote reliability by controlling program complexity and encouraging understandability.

As programs become large, it becomes difficult to understand them. One of the main causes of programming errors, especially during program maintenance, is that the programmer is not able to understand the interactions among the various parts of the program.

We must recognize that people have a limited ability to comprehend complex objects. We know from psychological studies that human short term memory is capable of retaining only about seven items [Miller 56]. From programming experience has come the *one page rule*, which states that a large program must be understandable in terms of relatively independent program parts, each of which is at most one page of source text. The only hope of understanding large programs is using the divide-and-conquer approach; this approach provides programming techniques to divide a program into understandable parts.

There exist two essential programming language features to help us manage program complexity; these are subprograms and modules. The glaring failure of BASIC is its lack of reasonable support in both of these features. Pascal provides a reasonable form of subprograms, but does not have modules. One of the often repeated complaints about Pascal is that global variables are implicitly visible inside subprogram bodies [Wulf 73]. This visibility means that all these subprograms potentially access and change global variables. With this unconstrained access to global variables, the program's complexity becomes unmanageable.

An important concept for controlling complexity is:

Rule. *Textual isolation.*

This is also called the *principle of locality* [Weinberg 71]. It means that the lines of a source program that record a particular decision should be located contiguously. For example, the constants, variables and subprograms that implement a particular data structure should be adjacent. This adjacency makes it easy to understand and maintain the program. Pascal violates textual isolation by its syntactic requirement that constant declarations must precede variable declarations, which must precede subprogram declarations, which in turn must precede statements. By contrast, Turing allows declarations in any order and allows them to be interspersed with statements. For example, in Turing, a conditional swap of elements *i* and *j* of array *a* can be written as:

```
if a(i) > a(j) then
  const t := a(i)
  a(i) := a(j)
  a(j) := t
end if
```

Pascal causes unnecessary confusion by requiring that the declaration of *t* must be textually removed to the beginning of the containing subprogram or program.

One of the basic concepts for controlling complexity is:

Rule. *Information hiding.*

The idea is that details of a particular program part that is of concern only to that part should not be visible elsewhere [Parnas 71]. Use of global variables in Pascal violates information hiding [Wulf 73]. Turing's module construct, which is similar to modules in Concurrent Euclid and Modula 2, is a simple but powerful feature for supporting information hiding. The form of a Turing module is:

```
module moduleName
  import (...names declared outside the module that are accessed inside it..)
  export (...names declared inside the module that are accessed outside it...)
  ...declarations and statements inside module...
end moduleName
```

The **import** and **export** lists provide controlled visibility (scope control) across the boundary of the module. Each subprogram optionally has an **import** list. The **import/export** lists provide explicit constraints on Turing's scope rules, which are otherwise similar to the scope rules of Algol, PL/I and Pascal. The **import** list limits access to global variables. The **export** list hides information, namely, it keeps implementation details inside the module, by exporting only those local names of interest outside.

Many students are not introduced to basic ideas of textual isolation and information hiding, because they learn programming using languages such as BASIC, Fortran and Pascal. Many professional programmers do not master these ideas because they do not have an appropriate software tool, such as Turing's modules, for controlling visibility.

Turing provides students and professionals with appropriate tools (language features) for controlling this complexity.

One way to manage complexity is to use modules to implement *abstract data types* [Guttag 78]. These types are specified in terms of the observable effects of operators on values of the type. The operators are programmed as subprograms and the values are represented as variables. There are two ways to use Turing's modules to implement abstract data types. The first approach considers the module's exported subprograms to be operators and the module's internal variables to represent a particular value of the type. This approach is used in the example module implementing a stack given in the Turing Report; see the section "Terminology and Basic Concepts." The second approach is to have the module export an *opaque* type, which is a type whose values can be inspected or modified only inside the module. Variables of this opaque type represent values of the abstract data type. The operators on the abstract data type are subprograms exported from the module. An illustration of this approach is given in the Turing Report; see the section "Subprograms and Modules".

Turing provides syntactic tools (subprograms and modules) for dividing a program into manageable parts. Turing's scope control (**import/export** lists) guarantee that program parts only interact in prescribed ways. This syntactic guarantee of information hiding allows separation of concerns, so that a programmer can confidently work on one part of a large program without worrying about unforeseen interactions with other parts. In other words, Turing provides the tools the programmer needs to divide and conquer the complexity of large programs.

This discussion on controlling complexity concludes the section on program reliability. In this section we have concentrated on methods of minimizing errors and their effects. The next section explains how a mathematically precise approach to program correctness holds out the hope for creating programs that are guaranteed to be error-free.

2.4 Mathematical Precision

Turing is designed to have a mathematically precise (formal) definition. A driving force behind Turing's design was:

Rule. *All results follow from the language specification.*

This requires that everything that can be observed about an executing Turing program (except questions of efficiency) should be predictable from the language definition. (This rule leads to the concept of faithful execution.)

One reason Turing was formalized was simply the *intellectual challenge* of doing it. We wanted to demonstrate our ability to produce the mathematization of a convenient, efficient, general purpose programming language. We wanted to set a standard of excellence by doing a better job of specifying a practical language than had previously been accomplished. P.A. Matthews prodded us during the development of Turing with the challenge, which we came to call the Matthews Plan, of providing a formal description of every aspect of Turing.

Aside from this intellectual challenge, one might ask, why bother with mathematical formalisms? After all, many people find these formalisms to be tedious and confusing. Why not just give a clear, English description of the language, which most people will find more comprehensible? The answer to this question has two parts. The first is that clear English descriptions *are* necessary. Informal descriptions of Turing exist and are, we hope, "correct, comprehensible and comprehensive" [Cooper 83]; these are contained in the Turing textbook [Holt 84] and the Turing Report. The second part of the answer is that there is also the necessity for the exactness of description that can be obtained only by using mathematics.

2.4.1 Promises of the Formal Approach

It was our hope to realize the great promises of formal approaches to language specification; these include:

- Formal methods of proving programs correct.
- Formal methods of program development using program specifications.
- Formal methods of proving compilers correct [Polak 81].

The original approach to program correctness assumes that there is a program together with a program specification and that these are to be proven equivalent. Turing's axiomatic semantics supports this approach. A more recently developed approach uses *program calculus*, as described by [Dijkstra 76, Gries 81, and Hehner 84], as a methodology for developing correct programs. Turing's semantics supports this approach.

When using a language without a consistent formalization, the utility of these techniques is doubtful. With the worst of languages, the programmer has no means of confidently reasoning about the program; he or she is reduced to testing each fragment of the program to try to gain some measure of assurance that it has the desired meaning.

2.4.2 The Three C's of Formal Specification

Ideally, the language specification should have the following properties, called here the three C's:

- *Clarity*: a person can easily read and understand the specification.
- *Completeness*: all relevant aspects of the language are defined.
- *Consistency*: each relevant aspect of the language has only one meaning.

The goal of clarity will be discussed first, and then completeness and consistency will be discussed as a unit in terms of the formalizations of Pascal and Turing.

Turing was designed so that its formal definition would be simple. Simplicity is, of course, the key to clarity of the definition. Notable aspects of the Turing design which simplify the formalism are elimination of aliasing and of side effects. In principle these two could be retained and handled by an axiomatic definition, but only at the cost of additional complexity in the formalism. There are more drastic changes that would simplify the formalism, such as banning loops (forcing their replacement by recursive subprograms) and banning variables (forcing their replacement by named constants). These changes were not considered seriously because they impact the goals of efficiency, consistency with tradition and understandability.

Another, less drastic change would be to simplify control constructs to provide only **if** statements and **while** loops or only Dijkstra's guarded commands. These suggestions simplify the formalism, but complicate the form and understandability of many programs. Guarded commands introduce gratuitous non-determinism, which invites unnecessary confusion [Dijkstra 75].

The complexity of a feature's formal specification is a warning sign in language design. For example, PL/I's exception handlers are excessively complex in their formalism and are also excessively complex in their use. However, simplicity of formalism does not guarantee simplicity of use. For example, a Turing machine is the epitome of formal simplicity, but is a monster to program. The loop-with-exit construct of Turing is potentially controversial, because it is formally more complex than alternate constructs such as the while loop, but is more convenient to use [Soloway 83]. The approach taken in designing Turing was to try to simplify the formalism, without heavily sacrificing either efficiency or convenience.

The formal semantics promises a relatively mathematical and mechanical guarantee of program correctness. However, this promise has not yet been demonstrated in practice and remains an idealization of program verification (much as certain laws of physics are idealizations of the motion of bodies of mass). This idealization encourages careful, proficient reasoning by programmers, *even if they choose not to carry out the actual mathematical steps in detail.* When a programmer is convinced a program has a clear meaning, independent of the details of a particular implementation or computer, he or she is able to concentrate on the logic of the program. This concentration, together with formal methods of reasoning about program correctness, provide our most effective approach to developing reliable software.

We now turn from the subject of clarity (hence simplicity) of the formal definition to the pair of subjects: completeness and consistency. We will consider these first in terms of Pascal and then in terms of Turing.

2.4.3 Shortcomings of Pascal

Our design goal was to maximize the degree to which a practical language (Turing) could benefit from these promises and to maximize the completeness and consistency of its formal definition. Our goal was:

Rule. *Minimize the gap between the formal definition and implementations.*

To accomplish this goal, Turing was designed to be amenable to formalization, using existing techniques for formal language definition.

One of the reasons for abandoning Pascal and designing Euclid and then Turing is that Pascal has unacceptably large gaps between its axiomatic semantics [Welsh 77] and its implementations [ISO 81]. For example, Pascal's axiomatic semantics can be used to prove that procedure *p* leaves *i* as 1 and *j* as 2:

```
procedure p(var i, j: integer);
  begin
    i := 1
    j := 2
  end;
p(k, k)     { What does k become? }
```

The proof implies that *k* becomes simultaneously equal to 1 and 2, which is obviously impossible. This particular example of inconsistency between formal specification and implementation arises from aliasing, that is, *i* and *j* are both names for *k*. Turing automatically detects this anomaly and thereby maintains the consistency between its formal specification and its implementations.

As another example of inconsistency in Pascal, consider function *f* which has the side effect of assigning to global variable *g*.

```
function f(i: integer): integer;
  begin
    f := g;
    g := i
  end;
g := 15;
if f(24) = f(24) then ...
```

Pascal's axiomatic semantics can be used to prove that the expression $f(24)=f(24)$ is identically true, although it will not be true under most Pascal implementations. This proof follows from the obvious mathematical rule (called the rule of substitution) that textually identical function calls in an expression have equal values. To preserve this rule and to allow a reasonable axiomatic semantics, Turing detects side effects in expressions in general and in functions in particular.

To respect mathematical tradition and to overcome Pascal's various shortcomings, including these inconsistencies, requires extensive modifications. Instead of attempting to maintain compatibility with Pascal, Turing is designed to incorporate the numerous elegant concepts of Pascal, while avoiding Pascal's shortcomings.

2.4.4 Designing Turing for Formalization

Throughout the design of Turing and its various features, there has been the goal of having a clear, formalizable form and meaning. Much of this approach is based on the design of Euclid. It is only because of the continued attention to this goal that it has been possible to produce a formal definition of Turing.

Conversely, there are languages such as PL/I, Ada and Chill, for which formalization is essentially an afterthought, attempted after the conclusion of language design. In such languages, it is probably impossible to approach the degree of consistency and completeness of formalization that Turing has attained [Bekic 74, Bjorner 80, Branquart 82].

There are two particular Turing features, collections and unions, whose design differs from the corresponding feature in Pascal, largely as a result of the goal of clear formalization. The collection feature, which supports dynamic allocation, will be discussed first.

Turing provides a form of dynamic allocation using pointers that can be implemented in the same manner as Pascal's pointers. Turing adopts Euclid's syntax for pointer usage, in order to avoid the formal intractability of Pascal's pointers. Given a pointer *p* locating a record containing integer field *n* we can write the Pascal statement

$$p\uparrow.n := 5$$

The corresponding Turing statement is:

$$c(p).n := 5$$

where *c* is a collection; a *collection* in Turing can be thought of as an array that initially has no elements, has elements added to it by the **new** statement, and has elements deleted from it by the **free** statement. Collection *c* can be declared by:

```
var c: collection of
  record
    n: int
    ...
  end record
```

Access to elements of collections is syntactically and semantically equivalent to access to elements of arrays. Thus, the formalism for array accesses applies (with modest adaption) to collections. Further formal techniques have been developed to handle the problems of uninitialized and dangling pointers.

A new type called a *union* was invented to replace Pascal's variant records. Although unions and variant records provide the same facilities to the user, unions have the advantage that access to union fields is strictly controlled both in terms of both implementation and formalization. The **tag** statement is the only way to set the tag of a union, other than assignment to the entire union, and provides the basis for this control.

In spite of the attention paid to the formalization of Turing, there remain certain ways in which Turing's implementations will not correspond to Turing's formal specification. One of these is that an implementation may choose to add features that are not defined by the specification. The most notable of these extensions is allowing programs to execute even when they have side effects and aliasing. The Turing Report gives the meaning of these programs, but warns that the formal semantics does not apply to them. A particularly troublesome source of inconsistency arises from basic mathematical properties; in particular, the formal definition of Turing assumes certain types, such as integers, have an infinite range of values, while all computers necessarily have a finite memory. (Actually, the formal definition begins by assuming inexhaustible resources, and then shows how to handle in a formal way most cases of finite resources.) Failing to represent large integers is a case of *resource exhaustion*; which in Turing terminology is said to be a violation of an *implementation constraint*. Turing's faithful execution guarantees that these violations will be reported. (See also the Turing Report section Implementation Constraints on Integer, String, and Real Types.)

Another difficulty is that the formal definition of Turing explicitly omits the definition of certain relatively minor aspects; for example, it assumes that all subprograms use import lists, although these lists are actually optional.

Another difficulty arises from the fact that Turing programs can be directly interpreted, without prior compilation. In the case where the program is syntactically well formed according to the formal specification, the interpreter is required to provide the same semantics as would a compiler. In the case where part of the program is ill formed, the compiler will reject the program, but the interpreter may still execute part of it. Consider this example:

```
put "HI"
?!?!GARBAGE?!?!
```

An interpreter may print HI before diagnosing the second line as being syntactically unacceptable. What this means is that the interpreter may give meaning to source text that the formal specification would not consider to be a Turing program.

This concludes the discussion of the goal of mathematical precision in the specification of Turing. We now turn to the question of efficiency.

2.5 Efficiency

Turing is designed for efficiency. This design goal means that Turing programs should be small and fast, as small and fast as would be possible in lower level languages such as C.

The fundamental fact that leads to efficiency is that Turing is a procedural (imperative) language, in the language family including Fortran and Pascal. As a rule, languages in this family follow:

Rule. *Directly implementable.*

This means that on standard computer architectures, most language features do not require significant run-time support (notable exceptions include input/output facilities, mathematical subprograms and string manipulation). This is in contrast to other languages, such as LISP, SNOBOL, APL and PROLOG, that are generally implemented interpretively, with considerable software support for most of the execution. Procedural languages, and Turing in particular, allow the programmer to exploit in a reasonably direct fashion the raw performance of the underlying hardware.

The features of Turing were designed to meet:

Rule. *Obvious, efficient implementation on existing computer architectures.*

Of course these implementations may only be "obvious" to an expert (a compiler writer). (At the same time, Turing is designed so the programmer can safely ignore implementation details, relying instead on language semantics.) A concept that is closely related to "direct implementability" is the idea that introducing a particular language feature should not increase the cost of others.

Rule. *No general taxation.*

An example of violation of this rule is PL/I's exception handling, which causes all subprogram calls to be less efficient, whether or not they involve exceptions. Another way of stating this rule is: *you pay for what you use* (and not for what someone else might want).

The direct implementability of Turing implies that it is generally straightforward to estimate the time/space cost of particular Turing features:

Rule. *Performance transparency.*

The idea is that for most purposes the professional programmer finds it sufficient to inspect Turing source code (rather than object code) to estimate efficiency.

Performance transparency is sacrificed to a certain degree to attain more convenience and expressiveness. This is illustrated by the Turing statement:

$$s := t + u$$

The cost of this statement is only obvious when the types of s, t and u are known. If their type is integer, then the statement is performed in at most three instructions on most computers. But if the type is character string, then plus (+) means catenation, and the cost may involve dozens of instructions.

Turing specifies two modes of execution: faithful and unchecked. To attain ultimate performance, the checking of faithful execution must be sacrificed. It is tempting to conclude, therefore, that efforts to decrease the cost of checking are unimportant. This conclusion is not warranted; rather, we want to make our safety net (checking) as cheap as possible, so that we can use it as much as possible. If the checking is sufficiently efficient, it can be kept in place in most production programs, at least during their initial use.

Turing's faithful execution demands that all discrepancies between the language definition and its implementation must be detected. Traditional sources of discrepancies, including subscript range, case selector range, arithmetic overflow and stack overflow, have well understood techniques for their detection. Somewhat less well understood are techniques of (1) detecting uninitialized variables, (2) detecting dangling pointers, and (3) detecting illegal access to fields of unions (variant records) [Fischer 77]. Techniques for handling these last three cases will now be briefly explained, because they are needed for implementation of efficient faithful execution.

To detect uninitialized variables, each variable that is not explicitly initialized can be given a value, called *uninit*, outside of its range. For standard architectures, using two's complement number representation, a good choice for *uninit* is the largest negative integer. An efficient check to see if a variable is initialized is to negate its value. For all values except *uninit*, this negation is possible, but since two's complement has no positive number corresponding to the largest negative number, negating *uninit* causes an overflow, which is easily detected. (One difficulty is that the user's program may create the *uninit* value. An implementation must either check at runtime that this does not occur, or may choose to omit these checks. Omitting these checks implies a significant efficiency gain, at the cost of a bogus error message when *uninit* is inadvertently created by the user's program.)

Detecting dangling pointers, without expending a great deal of time or space, is challenging. It can be done by time stamping each allocated item, and repeating this time stamp in pointers locating the item. Each access to the item entails a check to verify that the time stamps of the item and pointer are equal, thereby preventing use of dangling pointers. (While this technique is satisfactory in a statistical sense, it unfortunately permits the use of a dangling pointer in the unlikely event that the pointer's time stamp happens to be identical to the corresponding bit pattern in the heap.)

Access to fields of unions (variant records) is meaningful only when the tag of the union is set to indicate that the field is active. Consider the Turing example:

```
var u:          % t is the tag of u
  union t: 1..2 of
    label 1: s: string
    label 2: i: int
  end union
tag u, 2        % Sets tag t to 2
u.i := 4        % Implicit check that t = 2
if u.i = 7 then % Implicit check that t = 2
```

The only way to change the value of *t* is by using the **tag** statement, which is essentially a special purpose assignment statement. The **tag** statement uninitializes fields of the union (assuming faithful execution). Each access to a union field implicitly checks the union's tag value; in this example, each access to *u.i* involves a check to verify that *u.t* = 2. This check is efficiently performed by generating a table for each union type, in which the tag is mapped to a code representing the active set of fields. The tag name *t* can be omitted from the union's declaration, giving an equivalent to Pascal's notoriously unsafe non-discriminated variant records; however, in Turing, the union remains safe, because the (nameless) tag still exists and still can be checked.

Throughout this section on efficiency, we have assumed that Turing is implemented by a compiler, instead of by an interpreter. This assumption is reasonable, because if efficiency is desired, an interpreter should not be used. However, interpreters for Turing are highly appropriate in some environments, in which performance is not critical. The speed of an interpretive implementation of Turing should be comparable to interpretive implementations of languages such as BASIC.

This concludes the discussion of the goal of efficiency; we now consider the difficulty of implementing Turing.

2.6 Implementation

Turing is designed to have small, fast implementations. These implementations can be compilers or interpreters. Turing can be implemented with existing compilation techniques, such as LR(k), S/SL [Holt 82], and standard code optimization methods.

Turing is designed to be implemented for a range of computers.

Rule. *Micros to main frames.*

A small, fast, portable Turing compiler has been developed at the University of Toronto. It is in use on microcomputers (including the IBM PC), workstations (SUN), minicomputers (VAX) and main frames (IBM 370). Transporting the compiler to each new architecture has taken two to four man-months of effort. Portable interpreters and programming environments have also been developed.

One of the key properties of languages that simplifies implementation is:

Rule. *Feedback-free compilation.*

The idea is that the compiler does not require information from a later part of a Turing program to be able to compile an earlier part. To have feedback-free compilation, Turing requires:

Rule. *Declaration before use (DBU).*

This means that the declaration of an identifier must appear textually before any use of the identifier.

The obvious advantage of the feedback-free property is that it allows the construction of one-pass Turing compilers. However, it provides additional advantages, which we will now list. First, these properties greatly simplify the structure of multi-pass compilers. (Note that the original portable Turing compiler uses multiple passes.) In particular, it allows each pass to complete before the next pass begins, and it allows information to be passed from one pass to the next as a stream rather than as a set of tables. Second, these properties allow an interpreter to begin executing the first part of a Turing program without inspecting the last part. Of course some looking ahead into a program is necessary for interpretation (for example to discover how to skip over an **else** clause of an **if** statement), but this is easy to implement.

It should be noted that DBU implies a certain degree of inconvenience and language complexity. In particular, it requires **forward** subprogram (and collection) declarations to support mutual recursion. Explanation of these **forward** declarations is tedious, their specification is complex and their implementation is error-prone.

The goal of minimizing compiler complexity and maximizing run-time efficiency caused the elimination of several features that otherwise may have been included [Fischer 77]. For example, comparison of records is difficult to implement (due to byte alignment problems and ghost fields), so it is eliminated. A maximum length on character strings (by default at most 255 characters) is imposed to simplify allocation of string temporaries. The language was designed, as was Pascal, to provide no automatic "garbage collection" of data structures; this decision simplifies implementation and increases performance transparency, at a certain loss in language generality.

Although Turing supports dynamic arrays, their use is highly restricted. Dynamic arrays are not allowed to appear in record types, union types or named types. This restriction allows all displacements of fields in records and unions to be statically determined, and thus eliminates the complexity of run-time descriptors to represent field displacements.

These various restrictions are examples in which language design goals such as generality have been traded off to satisfy the competing goal of implementability.

The desire to make Turing amenable to formal description causes certain complexities in the compiler. The most notable of these is the handling of importation of identifiers into scopes and compile-time detection of aliasing. Although the algorithms for handling these items are well understood [Cordy 84], they remain rather complex.

This concludes the discussion of the goal of small, efficient implementation.

2.7 Global goals

There are global goals of language design that cannot be easily categorized, including:

- *Coherence*. The language should fit together into a pleasing entity.
- *Enjoyment*. People should have fun using the language.
- *Acceptability*. People should be willing to try and adopt the language.

The designers of Turing have attempted to meet these goals by constant review of language features, their utility, their simplicity, their acceptability, and their interactions.

Chapter 3

Features of the Turing Language

A general description of Turing is given, with emphasis on those features that distinguish Turing from other Pascal-like languages. Detailed descriptions of these features are given in the Turing Report and in the formal definition of Turing. (A tutorial introduction is provided in the Turing textbook [Holt 84].)

This overview of Turing will be presented primarily in operational terms, i.e., in terms of actions carried out during program execution. Unfortunately, this approach will not clarify the fact that a Turing program can be considered to be a non-operational, mathematical entity. Turing's formal semantics gives a non-operational, axiomatic definition of Turing.

1 Comparison with Pascal, Modula 2 and Ada

In many cases we will compare Turing to Pascal. Pascal is an obvious basis for comparison, because most computer scientists are familiar with it and because most Pascal features have corresponding features in Turing.

Perhaps the briefest general description of Turing is:

> *Turing is a super Pascal with a no-frills syntax and an airtight formal definition.*

Turing is a *super Pascal* in that it contains essentially all the functionality of Pascal, while adding badly needed constructs such as modules, varying length strings, dynamic arrays, and exponentiation. Its *no-frills* syntax eliminates Pascal's wordiness by, for example, omitting program headers and semicolons. Turing's formal definition is *airtight* compared to that of Pascal, in that it eliminates the various inconsistencies and insecurities of Pascal [Habermann 73, Hoare 73, Tennent 77, Welsh 77, Kernighan 81].

Modula 2 and Ada are often mentioned as possible successors to Pascal; since Turing is also a possible successor, we will briefly contrast Turing with those two languages.

Modula 2 is a relatively new language that is attracting an increasing number of users. It supports systems programming by providing various features such as concurrency and suppression of type checking. This class of features was purposely omitted from Turing (although it is included in the Turing Plus superset of Turing).

Modula 2 improves Pascal's syntax by, for example, introducing **end** as a closing for **if** statements. However, its syntax, compared to Turing's, remains verbose and stands in the way of learning. Its syntax is not designed for interactive programming nor for use by children. Like Pascal, it omits many features that are needed to make the language convenient to use and more generally applicable, such as convenient I/O, varying length strings, dynamic arrays, exponentiation, and so on.

Modula 2 was designed without a formal definition and has no concept of faithful execution. Axiomatic semantics could be applied to it only with considerable effort and complexity. Proofs of correctness and applications of formal techniques to Modula 2 programs are therefore doubtful.

Modula 2 is a language whose goals and features are quite similar to those of CE (Concurrent Euclid), except that CE has a formal axiomatic basis. It should be recalled that CE was considered for instructional computing and found to be unacceptable for this purpose. For the same reasons, Modula 2 is a poor choice for instructional computing. Turing has been designed to be superior to languages such as CE and Modula 2 in applications not requiring systems programming features.

Ada is a language designed to satisfy the U.S. Department of Defense. It is particularly targetted for programming software for embedded computers (computers that are part of larger systems such as nuclear missiles). Ada can be thought of as a vastly overblown version of CE or Modula 2. It contains systems programming features, which are omitted from Turing. The most commonly voiced complaint about Ada is that it, like PL/I, is an extremely complex language. Ada shares with PL/I the disadvantage that it is a very difficult language to master and a very difficult language to compile. It adopts several elaborate constructs, such as generic packages, that are well intended, but probably too complex and ill-understood to be suited for incorporation into a programming language.

Ada provides few solutions to the problems that Turing is intended to solve. For example, Ada lacks convenient input/output and has no varying length strings. Like Modula 2 and CE, Ada is ill-suited for teaching children and (compared to Turing) is wordy and inconvenient to use. Although attempts have been made to produce a formal definition of Ada, these formalizations are necessarily either highly incomplete or extremely complex. The Turing Plus extension of Turing can be thought of as an alternative to Ada. We will now introduce the various features of Turing, using a sequence of examples.

3.2 Producing a Triangle of Stars

Our first example is a simple but complete Turing program that prints a triangle of stars:

```
*
**
***
****
*****
...
```

Here is the Turing program to print this pattern:

```
var s: string := "*"
loop
        put s
        s := s+"*"
end loop
```

The first line declares character string variable *s*, initialized to a single star. The statements between **loop** and **end loop** are repeatedly executed. The value of *s* is output by the **put** statement. In the assignment statement, the plus sign catenates a star to the end of *s*.

The loop in this example will eventually create a string whose length exceeds the implementation-defined maximum string length, which is standardized to be (at least) 255 characters. When this happens, execution stops with an error message (assuming run-time checking is enabled).

Turing programs are free-format, so this example could be written all on one line or broken into more lines. Note the absence of a header line such as "**program** *test* (*input*, *output*)" and the absence of semicolons.

The declaration given on the first line can be shortened to:

```
var s := "*"
```

The type, which is **string** in this example, can be omitted from a declaration when initialization is present. Although we do not illustrate it here, nonscalars, including arrays and records, can also be initialized in their declarations.

Turing's *short forms* provide an abbreviated syntax for frequently written constructs. Using these forms, our example can be written as:

```
var s := "*"
{       ! s
        s += "*"
}
```

The reader may choose to ignore short forms, because they introduce no new semantics and can be mechanically expanded to their equivalent longer forms.

3.3 Searching a File for a Word

The following example program reads a file (stream) and outputs all lines containing the string "iron."

```
% Read file, print lines containing "iron"
var line : string
var n := 0
loop
    exit when eof
    n := n + 1
    get line : *
    if index(line, "iron") not= 0 then
        put n : 4, " ", line
    end if
end loop
```

The first line contains a comment, which begins with % and extends to the end of the line. Variable *n* is declared as an integer, taking its type from its initial value (zero).

The loop is repeatedly executed until end of file (*eof*) is reached in the input stream. The **get** statement uses the notation *line* : *, which means that an entire line is to be read into the variable called *line*. There are alternate formatting notations in the **get** statement to read a token (a word) with automatic blank skipping, or to read a specified number of characters.

The function call *index*(*line*, "*iron*") returns zero unless the string "*iron*" appears in the line. Note that the **if** statement ends with **end if**, just as **loop** ends with **end loop**. Similarly, each **case** statement ends with **end case** and each **for** statement ends with **end for**.

When the **put** statement is executed, it prints line number *n* in a field of width 4, then prints a blank, and finally prints the line. For example, lines 8 and 52 might be printed as:

```
   8 and yet iron combines in two
  52 mix carefully with iron filings, then
```

The **get** and **put** statements illustrated here can conveniently be applied to other input/output streams. For example, a file called *master* is read from and a file called *newmaster* is written to as follows:

```
var m, nm : int
open(m, "master", "r")         % Reading = "r"
open(nm, "newmaster", "w")  % Writing = "w"
...
get: m, x
...
put: nm, x
```

For details of the *open* procedure, see the Turing Report.

3.4 Functions and Dynamic Arrays

Turing provides convenient constructs for dealing with arrays whose size is not known until run time, as is illustrated in the following program.

```
% Read and sum a list of numbers
var n: int
get n

var a: array 1 .. n of real   % Run-time upper bound

function sum(b: array 1 .. * of real): real
      var total: real := 0.0
      for j: 1 .. upper(b)   % For each array element
            total := total + b(j)
      end for
      result total
end sum
· · ·   compute elements of array a  · · ·
put "Sum of array:", sum(a)
```

The value of *n* is read by executing a **get** statement, and it determines the size of array *a*. The scope of variable *a* begins with its declaration and lasts to the end of the surrounding block, i.e., to the end of the program. This is exactly as if a **begin** block started just before *a*'s declaration and extended to the end of the current block. In Turing, a declaration can appear wherever a statement can appear. This flexibility helps modularize programs by making it convenient to place declarations where they are actually needed, rather than forcing them to be more globally visible.

The header for the *sum* function declares that its parameter *b* is an array of real numbers whose lower bound is 1 and whose upper bound is determined by the argument to the function. Any array whose lower bound is 1 and whose element type is **real** can be passed as an argument to *b*. Turing's type compatibility rules consider arrays to be of *equivalent* types whenever their bounds are equal and their element types are equivalent. The rule for arrays is *structural equivalence* (based on form) rather than Pascal's rule, which is *name equivalence* (hence Pascal requires identifiers for parameter types).

As in Pascal, parameters in Turing can be declared **var** or non-**var**. Assignments to **var** parameters cause changes to the corresponding argument (actual parameter). In Turing (as opposed to Pascal) non-**var** parameters are considered to be constants, and cannot be assigned to. Since Turing disallows side effects in functions, it bans **var** parameters from functions. Turing generalizes the concept of a *constant* to include values that are computed at run time but cannot be modified. This means that for any particular call to *sum*, the value of *b* necessarily remains unchanged, although another call may have a new value for *b*. Consider the declaration:

```
const answer := sum(a)
```

Like array *b*, *answer* is considered to be a constant. Like *b*, it is a *run-time constant* rather than a *compile-time constant* (because its value is not known until run time).

A **for** loop in Turing creates (declares) a counter, which is *j* in the *sum* example. During each iteration of the loop, *j* is considered to be a constant, and the compiler guarantees that the user cannot modify *j*. Turing's **for** loops, like Pascal's, can be either increasing or decreasing. Turing allows the range to be a subrange type name, as in:

```
type pixelRange : 1 .. 472
var line : array pixelRange of 0..7
for i : pixelRange
    line(i) := 0
end for
```

The value of the *sum* function is given in the **result** statement; this statement is required in a function, to produce the function's value and to cause a return. In Turing, the **return** statement is used for optional, explicit completion of a procedure (not a function) or the main program.

3.5 Strings and Substrings

The following function illustrates the use of string operations. This function accepts integer *i* representing pennies and returns an equivalent dollar string. For example, if *i* is 5 then the dollar string will be $0.05.

```
function intDollar (i : int): string
    % i must be non-negative
    % result is dollar string
    var t := intstr(i)
    if length(t)=1 then
        t := "00" + t
    elsif length(t)=2 then
        t := "0" + t
    end if
    % t is now at least 3 characters long
    result "$" + t(1 .. *-2) + "." + t(*-1 .. *)
end intDollar
```

Function *intDollar* uses *intstr* to convert integer *i* to string *t*. Turing provides a complete set of conversion functions, including *realstr, strint, strreal, floor*, and *ceil*.

This example contains an **elsif** clause, used for cascaded selections. The **if** statement is used to extend *t* on the left to at least three digits long, so if *i* is 5, then *t* becomes "005". The **result** statement uses substrings, written as *t* (*L* .. *R*), where *L* gives the left position of the substring in *t* and *R* gives the right position. The star (*) used in writing *L* and *R* represents the length of *t*. The four strings catenated in the **result** statement are:

1. The dollar sign $
2. The digits of *t* up to but not including the last two digits, written as *t* (1 .. *–2)
3. The decimal point "."
4. The last two digits of *t*, written as *t* (*–1 .. *)

A substring can select a single character (a string of length one) by using a single position; for example, *t* (1) is the first digit of *t* and *t* (*) is the last digit of *t*.

This program illustrates the common Turing style of using upper case to start a word occurring in an identifier, for example, *D* in *intDollar*. Turing, unlike Pascal, is sensitive to capitalization; while Pascal considers *inTDolLar*, *Intdollar*, and *iNtDoLlAr* to be equivalent, Turing considers them to be distinct.

3.6 Assertions

Turing includes a set of assertions (**pre, post, assert** and **invariant**) that specify requirements for programs. We will illustrate assertions by rewriting the *intDollar* example to replace each of its comments by an assertion.

```
function intDollar (i : int) s : string
    pre i ≥ 0
    post s (1) = "$" and s (*–2) = "." and
        i = strint (s (2 .. *–3) + s (*–1 .. *))
    var t : string := intstr (i)
    if length (t) = 1 then
        t := "00" + t
    elsif length (t) = 2 then
        t := "0" + t
    end if
    assert length (t) >= 3
    result "$" + t (1 .. *–2) + "." + t (*–1 .. *)
end intDollar
```

We have declared a name *s* for the result of the function by inserting *s* into the function header preceding the function's result type. The only place *s* can be used is in the **post** condition, because *s*'s value only becomes available when the **result** statement is executed and the function is returning.

The **pre** condition is a requirement that the caller must satisfy; *intDollar* must only be called with a non-negative argument. The **post** condition is a requirement that the subprogram must satisfy; the result *s* of *intDollar* must yield a true **post** condition. Each **assert** statement expresses an assumption about the state of a program. The assumption in this example is that following the **if** statement, *t* contains at least three characters.

By default (i.e., with faithful execution) these assertions are checked at run-time (although the compiler may omit a check if it can prove that the condition can never be violated). We have replaced comments by assertions in our example, and we can think of these assertions as *executable comments*. The compiler generates code to check the assumptions made in these assertions. Note that an error can be in the assumption (the assertion) as well as in the program proper. In a time-critical production program, the programmer can remove these checks and the overhead they imply, by recompiling with a request to remove checking.

Turing's formal semantics defines a precondition for the entire program that must be satisfied by the input data if the program is to meet its specification. If the input data satisfies this precondition, then each assertion will be true when executed. In this case, we do not need to check the assertions at run-time, as they are guaranteed to be true. For example, in the *intDollar* function, if *i* is always non-negative, run-time checks of its **assert** or **post** conditions are unnecessary.

The **post** condition of *intDollar* illustrates an important point about the practical use of assertions. This **post** condition is a *necessary* but not a *sufficient* condition, in that it allows certain pathological function results, such as $000000.05, which presumably are not desired. In practical programming it is commonly inconvenient to specify the exact result that is required. The trouble is that many conditions, such as "the array has been sorted into ascending order," are cumbersome to state. In spite of this difficulty, assertions are still highly effective in improving program reliability.

We will not give examples of **invariant** assertions, which are used to give requirements for loops and modules.

3.7 Pointers and Collections

Turing's version of pointers and dynamic allocation is similar to corresponding features in Pascal. However, in Turing dynamically allocated objects are divided into distinct *collections*. A collection can be thought of as an array that initially has no elements. The **new** statement is used to add elements to the collection and the **free** statement deletes items from it. Given collection *c* with pointer *p*, these two statements have the form:

```
new c, p    % Create new element of c located by p
free c, p   % Delete the element of c located by p
```

After the element has been created, but before deletion, it is referenced as *c* (*p*).

The following example illustrates a singly linked list implemented using a collection called *list*. Each node of the list contains a *name* field and a link to another node. The notation *nil* (*c*) represents a null pointer for a collection called *c*, so *nil* (*list*) is the null pointer in this example.

```
% FIFO, singly linked list of names
var list: collection of
      record
            next: pointer to list
            name: string(30)
      end record
var first, last := nil(list)   % Empty list

procedure append(p: pointer to list)
      if first = nil(list) then
            first := p
      else
            list(last).next := p
      end if
      last := p
      list(p).next := nil(list)
end append
 . . .
var item: pointer to list
new list, item     % Allocate a node
list(item).name := "A.M. Turing"
append(item)              % New node goes onto queue
```

Notice that referencing an element of array *a* with subscript *i*, as in *a* (*i*), is notationally equivalent to *c* (*p*). This is an example of *uniform referents*, which means that analogous ways of accessing data should be notationally equivalent. It allows us to write much of a Turing program without regard for whether a data structure is represented by an array or a collection. The similarity also means that collections can be formally defined in much the same manner as arrays.

3.8 Union Types and Enumerated Types

Turing supports a version of variant records called unions. A union is a type whose selection of active components (alternatives) can be changed during program execution. A union allows sharing storage among the values of these different alternatives. We will now give an example illustrating the use and initialization of unions. (This example also appears in the Turing Report.) This example also introduces enumerated types.

The example concerns information for vehicle registration. The vehicle is a passenger car, a farm vehicle or a recreational vehicle. If it is a passenger car, we need to record its number of cylinders. If it is a farm vehicle, we need to record its class, such as "farm," in a string of length at most 10. Otherwise, it is a recreational vehicle and no further information is recorded. Here is the example.

```
type vehicle: enum (passenger, farm, recreational)
type vehicleRecord:
    union kind: vehicle of
        label vehicle.passenger:
            cylinders: 1 .. 16
        label vehicle.farm:
            farmClass: string(10)
        label:   % No fields for ''otherwise'' alternative
    end union
var v : vehicleRecord := init(vehicle. farm, ''dairy'')
                        % Initialize tag and farmClass
...
v. farmClass := ''vegetable''     % Checks that tag is farm
...
tag v, vehicle.passenger
v.cylinder := 4              % Checks that tag is passenger
```

The first line of this example creates the enumerated type called *vehicle*. This type has three values, each of which is written as the word *vehicle*, then a dot, then the enumerated identifier, as in *vehicle. farm*. By contrast, in Pascal an enumerated value is given simply by its name, e.g. *farm*, and does not require the prepending of *vehicle*. The trouble with Pascal's approach is that the scope of its enumerated identifiers is confusing, especially when the enumerated type is defined inside other types, when there are name conflicts, or when enumerated types are exported from modules. By contrast, Turing's approach treats enumerated types much like records, and access to enumerated values follows the same rules as access to record fields. This reduces confusion and simplifies the implementation.

In the example union type, the tag (*kind*) determines the active alternative of the union. Variable *v* is initialized in its declaration to set its tag to *farm* and its *farmClass* to ''dairy.'' (This initialization is optional.) Any attempt to access the *cylinders* field while the tag is equal to *farm* would be detected at run-time (assuming faithful execution). Changing the tag is considered to destroy the contents of all fields (and actually does so under faithful execution). Note that when *kind* is equal to *recreational*, there are no active fields other than *kind*.

If there are common fields across all alternatives of a union, these fields are declared in a record type that contains the union as one of its fields.

3.9 The Bind Construct

Turing replaces Pascal's **with** construct with a **bind** construct. Consider the declarations:

```
type r:
    record
        s, t: string(10)
        i: int
    end record
var a: array 1 .. 500 of r
...
bind var x to a(j)
x. s := "Hughes"
...
```

The **bind** is a declaration that creates variable x to correspond with the j-th element of array a. We can think of x as a **var** formal parameter whose argument is $a(j)$. Any change to x is a change to $a(j)$. If the keyword **var** is omitted, then x can be inspected but not modified. By comparison, in Pascal we would have:

```
with a[j] do
    begin
        s := "Hughes"
        ...
    end
```

The **with** construct makes the fields of $a[j]$ directly visible.

The **bind** offers several advantages over **with**. The most important is that the name introduced in a **bind** allows more than one set of fields of the same record type to be accessed at once, e.g.,

```
bind var x to a(i), y to a(j)
x. s := y.t
```

In Pascal, we cannot write the corresponding program. We can try:

```
with a[i], a[j] do ···
```

However, the fields of $a[i]$ are hidden by the fields of $a[j]$, so only fields of $a[j]$ are visible.

Since **bind** renames a variable (or a part of a variable), it is a potential source of aliasing. This possibility is prevented by a set of restrictions, the essential one being that the variable bound to is not accessible during the scope of the **bind**. This means array a cannot be accessed during the scope of x.

3.10 Subprograms as Parameters

We will now illustrate parametric subprograms in terms of an algorithm to approximate the definite integral of function *f*.

```
function integrate (function f (x: real): real,
                    left, right: real,
                    n: int): real
    const width := (right–left)/n
    var sum := 0.0
    for i: 1 .. n
        sum := sum + f (left + i *width)
    end for
    result width *sum
end integrate

% Example integration
put "Integral of cos from zero to pi is ", integrate (cos, 0.0, 3.14, 100):4:1
```

When this program is executed, it prints:

Integral of cos from zero to pi is 0.0

The first line declares that parametric function *f* has a real parameter and a real result. The *integrate* function receives as parameters function *f*, the *left* and *right* ends of the range of integration, and number *n* of slices to be used in the approximation. The value of the *width* of a slice is computed as a run-time constant. The type of *sum* is real, because its initial value 0.0 is real. The **put** statement illustrates explicit control over field width (4) and fractional digits (2) to be displayed; the number of exponent digits can also be explicitly controlled.

3.11 Modules and Sets

Perhaps the most important programming construct introduced into programming languages in the last decade is the module, also known as the class, cluster, or package. Modules support information hiding [Parnas 71], by providing a method of controlling access to declared items. The Turing Report gives two examples of modules; one implements a stack and the other uses an **opaque** type to implement complex arithmetic. In this section, we will not discuss **import** lists and **opaque** types because they are described in the Turing Report.

The following is a simple module that exports two subprograms. The first subprogram, called *enter*, is used to add integers to a set of integers. The second, called *member*, determines whether a given integer is in the set. The best data structure and algorithms for implementing *enter* and *member* depend on the range of integers to be entered, as well as the frequency of execution of each of *enter* and *member*. If the range is small—say, zero to twenty—we should use Turing's **set** type to directly implement these subprograms, as is shown here:

```
module intset
    export(enter, member)
    const minval := 0
    const maxval := 20
    type smallset: set of minval .. maxval
    var s := smallset( )   % Empty set

    procedure enter (i: int)
        s := s + smallset (i)
    end enter

    function member (i: int): boolean
        result i in s
    end member
end intset
...
intset.enter (9)   % Add 9 to the set
if intset.member (4) then   % Is 4 is in the set?
...
```

The set types of Turing are like the sets of Pascal, except that Turing set constructors use the name of the set type. For example, the empty set in the above example is written in Turing as *smallset*( ), instead of [ ] as it would be in Pascal. The difficulty with Pascal's notation is that the type of set constructors, such as [ ], is ambiguous.

If the range of integers is increased greatly, say to 0 .. 5000, and yet only a few members are to be entered into *intset*, then our implementation of the *intset* module should be changed to use arrays or collections. This sort of change is typical in program maintenance.

Information about the implementation of *intset* is hidden inside the module (because nothing is exported except the subprograms). We can safely re-implement the module using, for example, collections. We are guaranteed that no other part of the program can be depending on the set type used in the current implementation.

3.12 Nondeterminism and Repeatability

In this section we will discuss the concepts of nondeterminism and repeatability. We say that a specification is *nondeterministic* if it allows more then one outcome. For example, Turing's random number generation procedures are nondeterministic; *randint* is a predefined subprogram that produces an integer in a given range:

randint (i, 1, 10)   *% Set i to value in* 1 .. 10

A specification that requires a unique outcome is said to be *deterministic.*

A closely related concept is *repeatability,* which means that each execution produces the same result. Repeatability is a property of the implementation, while determinism is a property of the specification. A deterministic program clearly has a repeatable execution, because there is only one possible outcome. Some nondeterministic features, such as *randint,* are not (generally) considered to be repeatable. However, there are certain nondeterministic features that either require or allow repeatability. There are then three cases of nondeterminism:

(1) Repeatability is disallowed
(2) Repeatability is required
(3) Repeatability is allowed

The third case is a "don't care," meaning that it is immaterial whether or not the implementation is repeatable.

We will list nondeterministic features of Turing in order according to the above three categories.

Case 1: Disallowed repeatability

The first class of features to be considered has nondeterministic specifications and must not be repeatable. In this class are the predefined random number generation procedures, including *randint* and *rand.* (See Turing Report, "Predefined Procedures.") Ideally, these procedures produce sequences of unpredictable, statistically defined outcomes. In other words, their outcomes should be random. In most implementations, this randomness is approximated by a pseudo-random number generator. It is interesting that these approximations to randomness are repeatable; Turing provides predefined procedures (*randnext* and *randseed*) to take advantage of this repeatability in such applications as simulations. Despite this repeatability, in principle Turing random number generators are considered to be truly random.

Case 2: Required repeatability

The second class of features to be considered has a nondeterministic specification but must be repeatable. This class includes user-written functions. As an example, consider:

```
function flip (i : int) f : 1 .. 2
    post f = 1 or f = 2
    result 1
end flip
```

The specification of this function (its **post** condition) nondeterministically allows a result of either 1 or 2. The body of the function correctly implements this specification, by always returning 1. This function is therefore nondeterministic but repeatable. Throughout Turing, all expressions (and thus all operators and functions) are repeatable, but they may have nondeterministic specifications. We will now explain why this repeatability is necessary and how the Turing language has been designed to guarantee it.

Repeatability in expressions is required because of the *law of substitution*:

Textually identical expressions have equal values.

This assumes, of course, that values of variables in the expressions have not changed. This law is implicit in much of mathematics, and is required by Turing's formal definition; if it were violated, our basis for reasoning about Turing's semantics would collapse. As a simple example, consider:

```
x := f + g
y := f + g
assert x = y
```

Let f and g be arbitrary functions that cannot fail and do not depend on x. We can use Turing's formal semantics to prove the assertion $x = y$. The proof follows from the fact that $x = f + g$, $y = f + g$, and $f + g = f + g$. If function f or g or operator + were not repeatable, this reasoning would be faulty.

We will explain now how Turing guarantees repeatability in expressions. Turing's predefined operators and functions are all repeatable. User-defined functions are prohibited from having side effects and from using any features that are nonrepeatable. Functions are explicitly disallowed from doing input/output and from using the predefined random number generators. Note that these generators are procedures, not functions.

The Turing Report requires each floating point result to lie in a particular range enclosing the true mathematical result. (See the section "Implementation Constraints on Integer, String and Real Types".) In other words, the specification of floating point is nondeterministic. At the same time, floating point operations are required to be repeatable, so that the law of substitution remains valid.

Case 3: Allowed repeatability

In the third class of nondeterminism, we do not care if the outcome is repeatable. This is illustrated by:

```
procedure find (key : int, var i : int)
    post a(i) = key
    ··· body of find ···
end find
```

If array *a* contains several elements equal to *key*, then the specification (**post**) nondeterministically allows *i* to locate any of these. The body of *find* can scan array *a* from small to large (or from large to small) subscript values, setting *i* to the first found element equal to *key*. A scan in either direction satisfies the specification and is repeatable. A different body for *find* starts by generating a random number and uses this number to choose a direction for scanning. This body satisfies the specification, but is not repeatable. This example illustrates the "don't care" case, in which either repeatability or nonrepeatability is acceptable.

There is another nondeterministic Turing feature that is allowed to be repeatable. This is the **new** statement, which dynamically creates a data item, setting a pointer variable to locate the item. (See Turing Report, "Declarations of Variables and Collections".) Eventually, an implementation will exhaust its available space, and a new item cannot be created. When this resource exhaustion occurs, the **new** statement returns a nil pointer. This means that the **new** is nondeterministic, because it may produce either a nil pointer or a pointer to an actual item. To maintain the law of substitution, Turing disallows functions from directly or indirectly executing the **new** statement.

An alternative design of the **new** statement, which has a simpler semantics, would have the program fail on this resource exhaustion, much as arithmetic overflow or excessive recursion cause failure. Turing was designed to avoid this case of failure, to allow the user to write Turing programs that are able to continue even when encountering heap exhaustion.

The set of nondeterministic features in Turing listed in this section consists of: random number generation (ideally requiring nonrepeatability), **post** specification of functions as well as floating point (requiring repeatability), and **post** specification of procedures as well as **new** (allowing but not requiring repeatability).

Dijkstra's version [Dijkstra 75] of **if** statements and loops, which are not present in Turing, are nondeterministic, for example:

```
if  b1⇒s1   {a guarded command}
[]  b2⇒s2
fi
```

If both boolean expressions, *b1* and *b2*, are true, then a nondeterministic choice is made to execute either statement *s1* or *s2*. It is allowed to perform this choice either repeatably (e.g., by always choosing *s1* when *b1* is true) or randomly. By contrast, Turing's **if** and **case** statements are deterministic, and hence can be used without constraint in the bodies of functions.

This completes our brief introduction to the various features of the Turing language.

Chapter 4

The Turing Report

This chapter consists of the Turing Report, which gives the informal definition of the Turing programming language. Since the complete language is defined, there are some repetitions of explanations and examples from preceding chapters.

1 Introduction, Terminology, and Notation

Turing is intended to be a general purpose language, meaning that it is potentially the language of choice for a wide class of applications. Because of its combination of convenience and expressive power it is particularly attractive for learning and teaching. Because of its clean syntax, Turing programs are relatively easy to read and easy to write.

The language enhances reliability by disallowing error-prone constructs. It provides numerous compile-time and run-time checks to catch bugs before they cause disaster. These checks guarantee that each Turing program behaves according to the Turing language definition, or else a warning message is printed.

To support maximal efficiency, there is an option to remove run-time checking. This option allows well-tested, heavily used Turing programs to be extremely efficient. Each construct in Turing is designed to have an obvious, efficient implementation on existing computer hardware.

The design of Turing has eliminated verification and security difficulties of Pascal-like languages. For example, compile-time checks are used to prevent aliasing of variables and side effects in functions. Aliasing due to pointers has been eliminated using the concept of **collections.** Variant records (**unions**) have been made type safe by means of a **tag** statement that explicitly selects among the types of values to be represented.

Perhaps the most important programming construct developed in the last decade is the module or cluster, which enforces information hiding and supports data abstraction. Turing incorporates this feature, with the result that construction of large programs as a set of nearly independent parts is relatively straightforward.

Turing is well suited to interactive programming; it is intended for use on personal computers as well as on traditional main frame computers.

The language is designed to be easily and efficiently implemented. Experience has shown that a production quality portable Turing compiler can be constructed in a few man-months.

4.1.1 Terminology and Basic Concepts

This section informally introduces basic terms, such as ''scope'' and ''constant,'' used in describing the Turing language.

Variables and constants. A *variable* is a named item whose value can be changed by an assignment statement. Example:

```
var i: int   % This declaration creates variable i
i :- 10      % This assignment sets the value of i to 10
```

This example uses comments that begin with a percent sign (%) and are concluded by the end of the line. Various items such as variables are given names; these names are called *identifiers.*

A *named constant* is a named item whose value cannot change. In the following, *c* and *x* are named constants:

```
const c := 25
const x := sin(y)**2        % y is a variable
```

In this example, *c*'s value is known at compile time, so it is a *compile-time* constant (or *manifest* constant). (See also ''Compile-Time Expressions.'') The value of *x* is computed at run-time; it is a *run-time* constant (or *nonmanifest* constant). Since *x*'s value depends on variable *y*, different executions of the construct containing *x*'s declaration may produce different values of *x*. During the lifetime of each *x*, the value of that particular *x* remains constant, even though *y* may change.

An *explicit* constant (or *literal* constant) is a constant that denotes its own value; for example, following are an explicit integer constant, an explicit boolean constant and an explicit string constant:

```
219
true
"Have a nice day"
```

Scope and visibility. The textual lifetime of a named item is called its *scope*. For example, the scope of *z* in the following is the body of the **begin** statement.

```
begin
    var z : real
    ··· body of begin statement ···
end
```

A declared item's scope is begun by its declaration and continues to the end of the construct in which the declaration occurs. An item's declaration textually precedes any use of the item (except in those cases in which the identifier is preceded by the **forward** keyword).

The visibility (scope) rules of Turing are basically the same as those of the Algol/Pascal family of languages. This means that a declared item is visible (can be named) throughout its scope, including in subconstructs of the scope.

Most constructs (variables, types, constants, subprograms and modules) cannot be named by an identifier that is already visible. That is, for most constructs, redeclaration of names is disallowed. (The exceptions are names of parameters, values of enumerated types, and names of record and union fields.)

There is one construct (the module) in an item's scope that does not automatically inherit the ability to access the item. Modules must explicitly import items that are to be accessed in the the module body.

A subprogram may optionally use an **import** list to specify items used in the subprogram's body. Example:

```
1    var i: int
2    procedure increase (increment : int)  % Increase i by increment
3        import(var i)
4        i := i + increment
5    end increase
     ...
6    increase (4)   % Increase i by 4
```

In this example, variable *i* is imported on line 3; *i* is imported **var** (as in **var**iable) indicating that *i* can be changed in the procedure (in line 4). If *i* were imported without the **var** keyword, then *i* could be inspected, but line 4, which changes *i*, would not be allowed. A variable that is imported non-**var** is called a *read-only* variable. If a subprogram does not use an **import** list, it is considered to *implicitly* import any items that it actually references. By contrast, a module is always required to explicitly import any global items that are accessed in the module's body.

Subprograms. Turing has two kinds of *subprograms*; these are *procedures* and *functions*. A procedure is called by a "procedure call statement." Calls to a function occur in expressions and return a value to be used in the expression.

A subprogram header may contain declarations of *formal parameters*, for example, line 2 of the above example declares *increment* as a formal parameter. Each call to the subprogram must supply *actual parameters* corresponding to the formal parameters; for example in line 6 above, 4 is an actual parameter.

Modules. A *module* is a construct used for packaging items including subprograms and variables. Access to these items is controlled by an *export list*. Example:

```
module stack    % Implement a stack of integers
    export(push, pop)  % Entries to stack are push and pop
    var contents: array 1 .. 100 of int
    var top: 0 .. 100 := 0
    procedure push (i : int)
        top := top+1
        contents (top) := i
    end push
    procedure pop (var i : int)
        i := contents (top)
        top := top - 1
    end pop
end stack
  . . .
stack.push (14)  % Push 14 onto the stack
```

Since the module exports only *push* and *pop*, these are the only items in the module that can be accessed outside of the module. To access an exported item, one prefixes its name by the module's name, as in *stack.push*.

Side effects. If executing a construct changes values of items outside of the construct, we say it has *side effects*. For example, the *increase* procedure given as an example above has the side effect of changing the value of variable *i*. Turing prevents functions from having side effects. The method of guaranteeing that functions have no side effects is by disallowing them from having **var** parameters (these are parameters that can be changed), by disallowing them from importing items **var**, and by disallowing them from directly or indirectly importing procedures that import items **var**.

Since expressions cannot have side effects, all calls to a function with the same values of parameters and of imported variables necessarily return the same value. Example:

```
x := f (24) % Call function f with 24 as parameter
y := f (24) % Function f does not import x
```

After the execution of these two Turing statements, it is necessarily true that $x=y$.

Aliasing. Given distinct visible identifiers x and y, *aliasing* is said to exist if a change to the value of x would change the value of y. In the following, suppose i and j are aliases for the same variable.

```
i := 1
j := 2
```

After execution of these statements, i and j (which are actually the same variable) will both have the value 2. Aliasing greatly complicates formal program verification, and confuses the programmer. For these reasons, Turing bans aliasing. This ban is enforced by placing constraints on those language constructs which allow variables to be renamed. In Turing, the only constructs that rename variables are reference parameters to subprograms and the **bind** construct. Constraints on the use of these two constructs guarantee that once the new identifier is visible, either the old identifier is inaccessible or both identifiers are read-only.

Execution with side effects and aliasing. As has just been explained, the Turing language nominally prohibits side effects and aliasing. However, an implementation may extend the language to allow execution of programs violating these restrictions, given that appropriate error messages are issued. Programs with these violations have a well-defined operational (execution) semantics that is described by this Report, but such programs are not defined by the formal semantics of the Turing language.

Dynamic arrays. An array is said to be *dynamic* if its size is not known at compile time, i.e., if its bounds are necessarily computed at run-time. Turing allows dynamic arrays. Example:

```
get n % Read value into variable n
var a: array 1 .. n of real
```

This creates an array (really a vector) called a of n **real** values.

Parameters of subprograms can be dynamic. For example, the following function sums the first i elements of an array.

```
1   function sum(b: array 1 .. * of real, i: int): real
2       var total: real := 0.0
3       for j: 1 .. i
4           total := total + b(j)
5       end for
6       result total
7   end sum
    ...
8   x := sum(a,10)
```

Line 8 calls the *sum* function to add up the first 10 elements of array a. Line 1 uses "*" as the upper bound of parameter b to specify that b's upper bound is inherited from the upper bound of its corresponding actual parameter. The final keyword **real** on line 1 specifies that the function returns a **real** value. Lines 3–5 are a **for** statement; it adds the first *i* elements of array *b* to *total.* Line 6 returns the value of *total* as the value of the function.

Checking and Faithful Implementations. An implementation of Turing is said to be *faithful* if it meets the following criterion: the results of executing any Turing program will be determined by the source program together with the Turing specification (this Report) or else execution will abort with a message indicating (1) the reason for the abortion, and (2) the location in the program where it was executing at the time of abortion. A *checking* implementation guarantees that execution is faithful. Abortion may occur only because of (1) violation of a language defined run-time constraint, such as a subscript out of bounds, or (2) resource exhaustion. Resource exhaustion may occur due to a number of reasons, including lack of memory for calling a procedure, excessive running time, or excessive output.

The *run-time constraints* are categorized as (1) language constraints or (2) implementation constraints. The *language constraints* (or *validity constraints*) disallow those actions that are clearly meaningless, such as division by zero, subscript out of bounds, or a false value in an **assert** statement. *Implementation constraints* disallow actions which have a language defined meaning but which are infeasible due to hardware or efficiency reasons, such as: limited range of **int** and limited exponent range of **real**. Note that there are compile-time as well as run-time implementation constraints; limited range of case statement labels is an example of a compile-time implementation constraint.

A *non-checking* implementation of Turing may omit any or all of the run-time checks required for faithful implementation; this omission of checking allows Turing programs to have execution efficiency comparable to programs written in machine-oriented languages. A non-checking implementation may assume that the user has written his program in such a way that there will be no violations of run-time constraints nor resource exhaustion; these assumptions may be used for improving the quality of generated code. It is recommended that a non-checking implementation should provide documentation of the run-time constraints that are not enforced and of any resource exhaustion that is not detected.

The formal definition of Turing assumes that the **real** type corresponds exactly to the real numbers of mathematics. However, it is expected that implementations of Turing will actually implement **real** as floating point. The section "Implementation Constraints on Integer, String and Real Types" in this Report gives suggested minimum standards for floating point precision and exponent range, as well as standards for implemented ranges of integers and maximum string lengths.

This section has introduced basic terminology and concepts. The remaining sections give the detailed specification of the Turing language.

4.1.2 Identifiers and Explicit Constants

An *identifier* consists of a sequence of at most 50 letters, digits, and underscores beginning with a letter; all these characters are significant in distinguishing identifiers. Upper and lower case letters are considered to be distinct in identifiers and keywords; hence *j* and *J* are different identifiers. The keywords must be in lower case. Keywords and predefined identifiers must not be redeclared (they are reserved words).

An *explicit string constant* is a sequence of zero or more characters surrounded by double quotes. Within explicit string constants, the back slash character (\) is an escape to represent certain characters as follows: \" for double quote, \n or \N for end of line character, \t or \T for tab, \f or \F for form feed, \r or \R for carriage return, \b or \B for backspace, \e or \E for escape, \d or \D for delete, and \\ for back slash. Explicit string constants must not cross line boundaries. Within explicit string constants, the following two characters are disallowed: *eos* and *uninitchar*. The *eos* (end of string) character is an implementation dependent character that an implementation may use to mark the ends of strings. The *uninitchar* is an implementation dependent character that an implementation may use to mark a string that has not been assigned a value. (See "Implementation Constraints on Integer, String and Real Types" for recommended values for *eos* and *uninitchar*.)

Character values are ordered by either the ASCII or EBCDIC collating sequence (see "Character Collating Sequence").

An *explicit integer constant* is a sequence of one or more decimal digits, optionally preceded by a plus or minus sign.

An *explicit real constant* consists of three parts: an optional plus or minus sign, a *significant figures part*, and an *exponent part*. The significant figures part consists of a sequence of one or more digits optionally containing a decimal point. The exponent part consists of the letter *e* (or *E*) followed optionally by a plus or minus sign followed by one or more digits. If the significant figures part contains a decimal point then the exponent part is optional. The following are examples of explicit real constants.

2.0   0.   .1   2e4   −56.1e+27

An explicit integer or real constant that begins with a sign is called a *signed* constant; without the sign, it is called an *unsigned* constant.

The *explicit boolean constants* are **true** and **false**.

4.1.3 Comments and Separators

An *end-of-line comment* begins with the character % and ends at the end of the current line. A *bracketed comment* is any sequence of characters not including comment brackets surrounded by the comment brackets /* and */. Bracketed comments may cross line boundaries. A *separator* is a comment, blank, tab, form feed or end of line.

The *tokens* of the Turing language are the identifiers, keywords, explicit unsigned integer and real constants, explicit string and boolean constants, the operators and the special symbols. (See ''Collected Keywords and Predefined Identifiers'' and ''Collected Operators and Special Symbols''.) Each token in a Turing program can be preceded by any number of separators. Separators must not appear within any tokens, except as characters in explicit string constants. (See also ''Recognizing Tokens.'') Ends of lines must not appear within an explicit string constant; note that long string constants can be broken at line boundaries and connected by the catenation operator (+).

In a Turing program, the sign that begins an explicit signed integer or real constant can have separators between it and the following unsigned constant. The sign and the unsigned constant are considered to form a signed constant only if the sign is a prefix operator, and not an infix operator (according to the syntax of Turing). For example, in the following, –4 is a signed constant, but –7 is not:

if *x*–7 > –4 **then** ...

4.1.4 Syntactic Notation

The following syntactic notation is used:

{item} means zero or more of the item
[item] means the item is optional

Be warned: although this Report uses braces { · · · } and brackets [· · ·] as syntactic notation, another use of braces and brackets appears in the section ''Short Forms''. That section explains the use of braces and brackets as short forms for **loop** and **if** statements.

Keywords and special characters are given in **boldface**. Nonterminals, e.g., *typeSpecification*, are given in *italics*. The following abbreviations are used:

id for *identifier*
expn for *expression*
typeSpec for *typeSpecification*

4.2 Programs and Declarations
4.2.1 Programs
A program consists of a sequence of declarations and statements.

A *program* is:

{*declarationOrStatementInMainProgram*}

A program is executed by executing its declarations and statements. Here is a complete Turing program that prints: Alan Turing.

put ''*Alan Turing*''

A *declarationOrStatementInMainProgram* is one of:

a. *declaration* [;]
b. *statement* [;]
c. *collectionDeclaration* [;]
d. *subprogramDeclaration* [;]
e. *moduleDeclaration* [;]

Each *declaration* or *statement* may optionally be followed by a semicolon.

4.2.2 Declarations
A *declaration* is one of the following:

a. *constantDeclaration*
b. *variableDeclaration*
c. *typeDeclaration*

Each of these declarations creates a new identifier (or identifiers); each new identifier must be distinct from other visible identifiers. That is, redeclaration of visible identifiers is not allowed. The effect of the declaration (its scope) lasts to the end of the construct in which the declaration occurs. This will be the end of the program, the end of a subprogram or module, the end of a **begin, loop** or **for** statement, the end of a **then, elsif** or **else** clause of an **if** statement, or the end of a **case** statement alternative. An identifier must be declared textually preceding any references to it; the exception to this rule is the form ''**forward** *id*'', occurring in **import** lists and in **collection** declarations.

4.2.3 Constant Declarations
A *constantDeclaration* is one of:

a. **const** [**pervasive**] *id* := *expn*
b. **const** [**pervasive**] *id* : *typeSpec* := *initializingValue*

An *initializingValue* is one of:

a. *expn*
b. **init** (*initializingValue* {, *initializingValue*})

Examples:

```
const c := 3
const s := "Hello"   % The type of s is string
const x := sin(y)** 2
const a: array 1 .. 3 of int := init(1,2,3)
const b: array 1 .. 3 of int := a
const c: array 1 .. 2, 1 .. 2 of int := init(1,2,3,4)
     % Assigns: c(1,1) := 1; c(1,2) := 2; c(2,1) := 3; c(2,2) := 4
```

A *constantDeclaration* introduces a name whose value is constant throughout the scope of the declaration. If the *typeSpec* is omitted, the type of the constant is taken to be the (root) type of the *expn*; this *expn* must not be a dynamic array. An initializing expression that does not appear inside an **init** construct may be a compile-time or run-time expression (but not a dynamic array), and must be assignable to the constant's type. Named nonscalar values are always considered to be run-time values. (See also "Compile-Time Expressions" and "Type Equivalence and Assignability.")

The **init** construct is used only to initialize arrays, records and unions. All values in an **init** construct must be compile-time expressions. Note that **init** may be nested inside **init** to initialize records, unions or arrays that contain other records, unions or arrays. The number of elements inside an **init** construct must equal the number of elements of the type being initialized. For a union, the **init** must contain first the tag value and then the field values corresponding to this tag value (see discussion of union types in "Types and Type Declarations").

Constants declared using **pervasive** are visible in all subconstructs of the constant's scope. Such constants need not be explicitly imported.

4.2.4 Variable and Collection Declarations

A *variableDeclaration* is one of:

a. **var** *id* {, *id*} := *expn*
b. **var** *id* {, *id*} : *typeSpec* [:= *initializingValue*]

Examples:

```
var j, k: int := 1   % j and k are assigned initial value 1
var t := "Sample output"   % The type of t is string
var v: array 1 .. 3 of string(6) := init("George", "Fred", "Alice")
```

A *variableDeclaration* creates a new variable (or new variables). In form (a), the variable's type is taken to be the (root) type of the *expn*; this type must not be a dynamic array.

Form (b) allows the declaration of dynamic arrays, whose upper bounds are run-time expressions. However, the lower bounds are constrained to be compile-time expressions. Given that *n* is a variable, here is an example of the declaration of a dynamic array:

var *w*: **array** 1 .. *n*, 1 .. *n* **of real**

Run-time bounds are only allowed as illustrated in this example, i.e., as the upper bounds of an array declared using form (b). Note that dynamic arrays can never appear in records, unions, or collections. Each upper bound must be at least as large as its corresponding lower bound. A dynamic array cannot be initialized in its declaration and cannot be a named type.

A *collectionDeclaration* is one of:

a. **var** *id* {, *id*} : **collection of** *typeSpec*
b. **var** *id* {, *id*} : **collection of forward** *id*

A collection can be thought of as an array whose elements are dynamically created and deleted at run-time. Elements of a collection are referenced by subscripting the collection name with a variable of the collection's pointer type. (See discussion of pointers in "Types and Type Declarations.") This subscripting selects the particular element of the collection located by the pointer variable.

The keyword **forward** is used to specify that the type *id* of the collection elements will be given by a later declaration in the collection's scope. The later declaration must appear at the same level (in the same list of *declarationsAndStatements*) as the original declaration. This allows the declaration of cyclic collections, for example, when a collection contains pointers to another collection which in turn contains pointers to the first collection. A collection whose element type is **forward** can be used only to declare pointers to it until the type's declaration is given. The **forward** type *id* is inaccessible until its declaration is given.

The value *nil* (*C*) is the null pointer for the collection.

Elements of a collection are created and deleted dynamically using the statements **new** and **free**; see "Types and Type Declarations" for an example. The statement "**new** *C*, *p*" creates a new element in the collection *C* and sets *p* to point at it; however, if because of resource exhaustion the new element cannot be created, *p* is set to the value *nil* (*C*). The statement "**free** *C*, *p*" deletes the element of *C* pointed to by *p* and sets *p* to *nil* (*C*). In each case *p* is passed as a **var** parameter and must be a variable of the pointer type of *C*. Suppose pointer *q* is equal to pointer *p* and the element they locate is deleted via "**free** *C*, *p*". We say *q* is a *dangling pointer* because it seems to locate an element, but the element no longer exists. A dangling pointer is considered to be an uninitialized value; it cannot be assigned, compared, used as a collection subscript, or passed to **free**.

Collections cannot be assigned, compared, passed as parameters, bound to, or named by a **const** declaration. Collections must not be declared in subprograms.

4.2.5 Bind Declarations

A *variableBinding* is:

bind [**var**] *id* **to** *variableReference* {, [**var**] *id* **to** *variableReference*}

A *variableBinding* is used to give a new name to a variable (or a part of a variable). This declares an identifier that is itself considered to be a variable. The new variable is considered to be "read-only" unless preceded by **var** (see "Restrictions on Constants and Read Only Items"). Example:

bind var *x* **to** *a*(*i*), *y* **to** *r.j*

This declares *x* and *y*, which are considered to be variables; *x* is essentially an abbreviation for *a*(*i*) and *y* is essentially an abbreviation for *r.j*; *y* is read-only. Changing the value of *i* during the scope of the **bind** does not change the value denoted by *x*. Variable *a* is inaccessible and *r* is read-only until the end of the scope of the **bind**.

A *variableBinding* cannot occur as a declaration in the (main) program, except nested inside constructs, such as subprograms and the **begin** statement. A **module** must not contain as one of its fields a *variableBinding*. (This restriction is made to prevent reentry into the scope of an existing **bind**.)

Turing does not allow aliasing. Hence, the "root" identifier of the *variableReference* (the first identifier in the reference) of a **var bind** becomes inaccessible for the scope of the binding. Even though the root identifier is inaccessible, it cannot be redeclared in its scope. See also "Restrictions Preventing Aliasing". To allow binding to different parts of a variable, each root identifier remains accessible to the end of the list of bindings in the *variableBinding*. The new identifiers do not become visible until the end of this list. Bindings that are **var** to different parts of the same variable must be non-overlapping.

Turing has been designed so that each bind can be implemented "by reference" (by using the address of the target variable). An implementation that allows aliasing should warn when aliasing is present and should implement binds by reference.

4.3 Types

4.3.1 Types and Type Declarations

A *typeDeclaration* is:

type [**pervasive**] *id*: *typeSpec*

A *typeDeclaration* gives a name to a type. The type name can subsequently be used in place of the full type definition.

Named types may optionally be declared **pervasive**. Type names declared using **pervasive** are visible in all subconstructs of the scope in which they are declared. Such types need not be explicitly imported.

A *typeSpec* is one of the following:

a. *standardType*
b. *subrangeType*
c. *enumeratedType*
d. *arrayType*
e. *setType*
f. *recordType*
g. *unionType*
h. *pointerType*
i. *namedType*

A *standardType* is one of:

a. **int**
b. **real**
c. **boolean**
d. **string** [(*compileTimeExpn*)]

The standard types can be used in all scopes and must not be imported.

The optional compile-time expression in a string type is a strictly positive integer value giving the string's maximum length. If the string's maximum length is omitted, the string is (ideally) considered to have no limit on its length. However, it is expected that most implementations will impose a default limit. This limit is recommended to be at least 255. Example:

var *s* : **string** := ''*Hello there*''

Parameters can be declared to be *dynamic* strings, with maximum lengths declared as ''*''; see ''Subprograms''.

A *scalar type* is an integer, real, boolean, enumerated type, subrange or pointer. The *nonscalar types* are: strings, sets, arrays, records, and union types.

An *index type* is a subrange, enumerated type or a named type which is an index type. Index types can be used as array subscripts, as selectors (tags) for **case** statements and **union** types, and for base types of **sets**.

A *subrangeType* is:
compileTimeExpn **..** *expn*

The two expressions give the lower and upper bounds of the range of values of the type. The two expressions must be both integers or both of the same enumerated type. The lower bound must be less than or equal to the upper bound. The second expression must be a compile-time expression in all cases except when it gives the upper bound of a dynamic array being defined in a *variableDeclaration*. (See ''Variable and Collection Declarations''.) Example:

var *i*: 1 .. 10 := 2 % *i can be* 1, 2 ... *up to* 10

An *enumeratedType* is:
enum (*id* {, *id*})

The values of an enumerated type are distinct, contiguous and increasing. See definitions of the *ord*, *succ*, and *pred* functions in ''Predefined Functions.'' Example:

type *color*: **enum** (*red* , *green* , *blue*)
var *c* : *color* := *color.green*
var *d*: *color* := *succ* (*c*) % *d becomes blue*

The values are denoted by the name of the enumerated type followed by a dot followed by one of the enumerated identifiers; for example: *color. green* Enumerated types and their subranges are index types.

An *arrayType* is:
array *indexType* {, *indexType*} **of** *typeSpec*

Each *indexType* must be a subrange type, an enumerated type or a named type which is an *indexType*. Note that variables and parameters can be declared to be *dynamic* arrays, with run-time upper bounds; see ''Subprograms.'' A dynamic array type must not be given a name, and must not occur in a record, union or collection. Each *indexType* gives the range of a subscript. The *typeSpec* gives the type of the elements of the array.

Elements of an array may be referenced using subscripts (see ''Variables and Constants'') and themselves used as variables or constants. Arrays may be assigned (but not compared) as a whole.

A *setType* is:
set of *indexType*

The *indexType* is called the *base type* of the set. An implementation may limit the number of items in the base type; this number will be at least 31. A variable of a set type is assigned as values subsets of the entire set. See ''Set Operators and Set Constructors.''

Example:

> **type** *smallSet*: **set of** 0 .. 2
> **var** *s* : *smallSet* := *smallSet* (0,1) % *s contains* 0 *and* 1

A *recordType* is:

> **record**
> *id* {,*id*} : *typeSpec* [;]
> {*id* {,*id*} : *typeSpec* [;] }
> **end record**

Variables declared using a **record** type have the fields given by the declarations in the *recordType*. Fields of a record may be referenced using the dot operator (see ''Variables and Constants'') and themselves used as variables or constants. Record variables may be assigned (but not compared) as a whole.

A **union** type (or variant record) is like a record in which there is a run-time choice among sets (called alternatives) of accessible fields. This choice is made by the **tag** statement, which deletes the current set of fields and activates a new set.

A *unionType* is:

> **union** [*id*]: *indexType* **of**
> **label** *compileTimeExpn* {, *compileTimeExpn*} : {*id* {, *id*}: *typeSpec* [;] }
> {**label** *compileTimeExpn* {, *compileTimeExpn*} : {*id* {, *id*}: *typeSpec* [;] } }
> [**label** : {*id* {, *id*}: *typeSpec* [;] }]
> **end union**

Example:

```
type vehicle: enum (passenger, farm, recreational)
type vehicleRecord:
        union kind: vehicle of
                label vehicle. passenger:
                        cylinders: 1 .. 16
                label vehicle. farm:
                        farmClass: string(10)
                label:   % No fields for ''otherwise'' alternative
        end union
var v: vehicleRecord := init(vehicle. farm, ''dairy'')
                                % Set tag and farmClass
...
tag v, vehicle. passenger   % Activate passenger alternative
v. cylinders := 6
```

The optional identifier following the keyword **union** is the name of the *tag* of the union type. If the identifier is omitted, the tag is still considered to exist, although a non-checking implementation would not need to represent it at run time.

Each expression following **label** is called a *label value*. These must be distinct compile-time expressions in a given union type. Each label value must be assignable to the tag's type, which is an index type. Each labeled set of declarations is called an *alternative*. The final optional alternative with no label expressions is called the *otherwise alternative*.

An implementation may limit the range of the tag's type; its range, from the minimum label value to the maximum inclusive, will be at least 256.

The fields and tag of a union may be referenced using the dot operator (see "Variables and Constants"), and the fields can be used as variables or constants. Access or assignment to a field of an alternative is allowed only when the tag's value matches one of the alternative's label values (or matches none of the union's label values for the otherwise alternative). A checking implementation must guarantee this match at each access or assignment to a field. A tag cannot be assigned to and must not be the object of a **var bind** nor passed to a **var** parameter. A union's tag value is changed using the **tag** statement (see "Statements"). In a checking implementation, the **tag** statement will actually change (uninitialize) any existing field values. A non-checking implementation will not necessarily change the fields. Note that **union** types under a checking implementation are "type safe"; so, changing the tag will *not* automatically change values of one alternative to be values of another alternative. A union's tag can be changed by assigning to the entire union.

The identifiers declared as fields of a record, tag and fields of a union type, or values of an enumerated type must be distinct from each other. However, they need not be distinct from other visible identifiers. Fields of records and unions must not be dynamic arrays.

A *pointerType* is:

pointer to *collectionId*

Variables declared using a *pointerType* are pointers to dynamically created and deleted elements of the specified collection; see "Variable Declarations." Pointers are used as subscripts of the specified collection to select the element to which they point. The selected element can be used as a variable or constant. Pointers may be assigned, compared for equality and passed as parameters. Example:

```
var list: collection of forward node
type node:
    record
        contents: string(10)
        next: pointer to list
    end record
var first: pointer to list := nil (list)
var another: pointer to list
. . .
new list, another     % Create new list element
```

```
list(another).contents := "Belgium"
list(another).next := first
first := another
```

The **forward** directive can be avoided in self-referencing collections, as this example illustrates:

```
var list: collection of
      record
            contents: string(10)
            next: pointer to list
      end record
```

The name of a collection is visible inside the collection.

A *namedType* is:
 [*moduleId* .] *typeId*

The *typeId* must be a previously declared type name. Type names exported from a module are referenced using the dot operator.

4.3.2 Type Equivalence and Assignability

This section defines the terms *type equivalence* and *type assignability*. Roughly speaking, an actual parameter can be passed to a **var** formal parameter only if their types are equivalent, and a value can be assigned to a variable (or a value passed to a non-**var** parameter) only if the value's type is assignable to the variable's type. Type equivalence can be determined at compile time; assignability sometimes cannot be determined until run time (when the target type is a subrange or a string with a maximum length).

Two types are defined to be *equivalent* if they are

(a) the same standard type,
(b) subranges with equal first and last values,
(c) arrays with equivalent index types and equivalent component types,
(d) strings with equal maximum lengths,
(e) sets with equivalent base types, or
(f) pointers to the same collection; in addition,
(g) a declared type identifier is equivalent to the type it names (and to the type named by that type, if that type is a named type, etc.)

Outside of the exporting module *M* an **opaque** type with identifier *T* is not equivalent to any other type (but *M.T* is equivalent to type identifiers declared outside *M*, naming *M.T*). By contrast, if type *U* is exported non-**opaque** from *M*, then type *M.U* is equivalent to the type that *U* names inside *M*. The parameter or result type of an exported subprogram or an exported constant is considered to have type *M.T* outside *M* iff the item is declared using the type identifier *T*. The **opaque** type *M.T* is distinct from any other type that *M* exports or imports. A value of **opaque** type *M.T* can be assigned, but cannot be compared, subscripted, or field selected, and cannot be an operand to an operator. All that can be done with a value of an opaque type is to assign it or to pass it as a subprogram parameter. These rules for determining if **opaque** type *M.T* is equivalent to another type *U* imply that one never needs to look inside module *M* to see if *M.T* is equivalent to *U*; in other words, **opaque** type *M.T* is a new, distinct type created by module *M*. See "Modules" for an example using **opaque** types.

Each textual instance of a type definition for an enumerated, record or union type creates a new type that is not equivalent to any other type definition.

The **int** type is not considered to be equivalent to any integer subrange. The **string** type without explicit maximum length is not considered to be equivalent to any **string** type having an explicit maximum length.

The *root* type of any integer expression is **int**, that of any enumerated value is the defining enumerated type, that of any string expression is **string** (without specified maximum length), and that of any other value is the value's type. The root type of a named type is the root type of the type that is named. The root type of an integer subrange is **int** and that of an enumerated subrange is the original **enum** type. The root type of **opaque** type *M.T* is *M.T*.

Whenever a named value (variable, constant or function) is used where an expression value is required, the type of the expression is considered to be the root type of the named value. For example,

```
var x: 1 .. 10 := 5
y := x    % The type of expression x is int
```

A value is *assignable* to a type (called the target type) if

(a) the value's root type is equivalent to the target's root type or,

(b) the value is an integer and the target is **real**.

These two requirements can be enforced at compile time. In case (a) there is also a run-time requirement that a value assigned to a target subrange is contained in the subrange, and a value assigned to a target string does not exceed the target's maximum length. In case (b) the integer is implicitly converted to real. Throughout the language, wherever a real expression is required, an integer expression is allowed and is converted to real via an implicit call to the predefined function *intreal*.

The type of a reference passed to a **var** parameter must be equivalent to the formal's type. The type of an expression passed to a non-**var** (constant) parameter must be assignable to the formal's type. A dynamic actual array parameter (a parameter with run-time computed upper bounds) can be passed only to a formal array parameter with * declared for upper bounds. Similarly a dynamic actual string parameter can be passed only to **string**(*). See also the discussion of *parameterType* in "Subprograms". Dynamic strings can be assigned, but dynamic arrays cannot. In an assignment *v* := *e*, a variable initialization, a **const** declaration, or an initialization **init** *v* := *e*, *e* must be assignable to *v* and neither *v* nor *e* can be dynamic arrays. Examples:

```
type smallint: 1 .. 10
var i: smallint
var j: 1 .. 100    % Variable j is assignable to i when in range 1 .. 10

type smallarray: array 1 .. 10 of real
var a: array smallint of real   % Equivalent to smallarray

type rec:
    record
        f: string
        g: real
    end record
var r1: rec
var r2: rec
var r3:        % Not equivalent to r1 and r2
    record
        f: string
        g: real
    end record
```

Variables *i* and *j* have the same root type (**int**), so one can be assigned to the other, given that the assigned value is in the target's declared range. Array *a*'s type is equivalent to the type *smallarray*; so *a* could be assigned to a variable or passed to a formal parameter of type *smallarray*. The types of *r1* and *r2* are equivalent and one can be assigned to the other. However, *r3*'s type is not equivalent to the type of *r1* and *r2*.

Here is an example illustrating the equivalence rules for **opaque** types:

```
type T1: int
module m
    import( T1 )
    export( T2, opaque T3, opaque T4, T5)
    type T2: T1
    type T3: T1
    type T4: T3
    type T5: T4
end m
```

Inside module *M*, types *T1* through *T5* are equivalent, but outside of *M*, types *T1*, *M.T2* and *M.T5* are equivalent but types *M.T3* and *M.T4* are distinct (**opaque**) types.

4.4 Subprograms and Modules

4.4.1 Subprograms

A *subprogram* is a procedure or a function.

A *subprogramDeclaration* is one of:

a. *subprogramHeader*
   [*importList*]
   subprogramBody

b. **forward** *subprogramHeader*
   forwardImportList

c. **body procedure** *id*
   subprogramBody

d. **body function** *id*
   subprogramBody

A *subprogramHeader* is one of:

a. **procedure** *id* [(*parameterDeclaration* {, *parameterDeclaration*})]

b. **function** *id* [(*parameterDeclaration* {, *parameterDeclaration*})]
   [*id*] : *typeSpec*

A procedure is invoked by a procedure call statement, with actual parameters if required. A function is invoked by using its name, with actual parameters if required, in an expression. If a subprogram *P* has no parameters, a call to it does not have any parentheses, i.e., the call is of the form "*P*" and not "*P* ()".

A procedure may return explicitly by executing a **return** statement or implicitly by reaching the end of the procedure body. A function must return via a **result** statement (see "Statements").

Subprograms may optionally take parameters, the types of which are defined in the header. The names of the parameters, as well as the name of the subprogram, are visible inside the subprogram, but not visible in the type specifications of the parameters and function result.

Parameters to a procedure may be declared using **var**, which means the parameter is considered to be a variable inside the procedure. An assignment to a **var** formal parameter changes the actual parameter, as well as the formal parameter. The element of an array passed to a parameter is not affected by changes to the subscript, for example, given the call

p(*a*(*i*))

an assignment to *i* in the body of *p* does not affect *p*'s actual parameter. Parameters declared without using **var** are considered to be constants. Functions are not allowed to have any side effects and cannot have **var** parameters.

The identifiers declared in a parameter list must be distinct from each other, from pervasive identifiers, from the subprogram name, and from the result identifier (if present). However, they need not be distinct from other identifiers visible outside of the subprogram.

A *parameterDeclaration* is one of:

a. [**var**] *id* {, *id*} : *parameterType*

b. *subprogramHeader*

Form (a) is used to declare formal parameters that are **var** (variable) or non-**var** (constant). An actual parameter that is passed to a **var** formal must be a variable (a reference) whose type is equivalent to the formal's type. An actual parameter that is passed to a non-**var** formal parameter must be a value that is "assignable" to the formal's type. (See "Type Equivalence and Assignability".)

A *reference* parameter is any non-scalar or **var** parameter. Parameters that are not reference parameters are called *value* parameters; a value parameter is any scalar non-**var** parameter. See "Restrictions Preventing Aliasing" for constraints on the use of **var** and reference parameters. Example:

```
function odd(i: int): boolean   % i is a value parameter
    result (i mod 2) not= 0
end odd
```

Example:

```
var messageCount: int := 0
procedure putMessage (msg : string)   % msg is a reference parameter
    messageCount := messageCount + 1
    put "Message number ", messageCount, ": ", msg
end putMessage
```

The second kind of *parameterDeclaration*, form (b), specifies a *parametric subprogram*. The corresponding actual parameter must name a subprogram. The actual parameter subprogram must have parameters and result type equivalent to those of the formal parameter. Parametric subprograms are called like other subprograms. Example:

```
% Find zero of parametric function f
function findZero (function f (r : real): real,
        left, right, accuracy : real): real
    pre sign (f (left)) not= sign (f (right)) and accuracy >0
    var L : real := left
    var R : real := right
    var M : real
    const signLeft := sign (f (left))
    loop
        M := (R + L)/2
        exit when abs (R - L) <= accuracy
        if signLeft = sign (f (M)) then
            L := M
```

```
            else
                R := M
            end if
        end loop
        result M
    end findZero
```

A *parameterType* is one of:

a. *typeSpec*
b. **string** (*)
c. **array** *compileTimeExpn* .. * {, *compileTimeExpn* .. *} **of** *typeSpec*
d. **array** *compileTimeExpn* .. * {, *compileTimeExpn* .. *} **of string** (*)

In forms (c) and (d), the upper bounds of the index types of a *dynamic* array parameter are declared as * in which case any array whose element type and index types' lower bounds are equivalent to the parameter's can be passed to the parameter. In forms (b) and (d) the maximum length of a *dynamic* string is declared as *. For **var** parameters or arrays of strings, the maximum length is taken to be that of the actual parameter. For non-array, non-**var** formal parameters, the type **string**(*) is taken to mean simply **string**. Note that multiple parameters declared using one dynamic parameter type do not necessarily have the same upper bounds and string maximum lengths; instead each parameter inherits the sizes of its actual parameter. The upper bounds and maximum lengths of dynamic parameters can be accessed using *upper*; see "Attributes."

The Turing language has been designed so that value parameters can be passed "by value" (by passing expression values to the subprograms) and reference parameters can be passed "by reference" (by passing addresses instead of values). Given that aliasing and side effects are prohibited (as nominally required by this Report), passing parameters by reference or by value-result will be logically equivalent. If an implementation allows aliasing or side effects it should warn that these are present and should use "pass by reference" exactly for those parameters designated as reference parameters in this Report.

An *importList* is:

import ([[**var**] *id* {, [**var**] *id*}])

A *forwardImportList* is:

import ([[*varOrForward*] *id* {, [*varOrForward*] *id*}])

A *varOrForward* is one of:

a. **var**
b. **forward**

If a subprogram has an **import** list, it uses this to specify identifiers visible outside the subprogram that are to be visible in the subprogram's body. Identifiers not in the list will not be visible in the body. Pervasive identifiers need not be imported (they are implicitly imported). If a subprogram does not have an **import** list, it is considered to implicitly import identifiers that textually appear in its body. An implicitly imported identifier is considered to be imported **var** if it is assigned to, bound to **var**, passed to a **var** parameter, or acted on by a **tag**, **new** or **free** statement inside the subprogram. The identifier is also considered to be imported **var** if it is a module's name and a procedure of this module is called in the subprogram.

Note that the subprogram name and the parameter names are always visible inside the subprogram, and must not appear in the import list. By contrast, a module name is not visible inside the module, and must not be imported. Modules have **import** lists, and these have the same meaning as in subprograms with the following difference: a module with no explicit **import** list is considered to have this **import** list:

import ()

Only identifiers that name variables or modules can be imported **var**. (See ''Restrictions on Constants and Read Only Items.'')

Functions are not allowed to have side effects and cannot import anything **var**. This restriction is transitive; hence a function cannot import a procedure that directly or indirectly imports anything **var**. Input/output is considered to be a side effect; hence functions cannot use **get** or **put** statements; they must not directly or indirectly call procedures that use these statements or that call the predefined procedures. A parametric procedure that is passed as an actual parameter to a function must not directly or indirectly import anything **var** or directly or indirectly use the **get** and **put** statements or the predefined procedures. (Note that although Turing nominally prohibits function side effects, an implementation may extend the language to allow them given that appropriate messages are issued.)

An identifier must not be repeated in an **import** list. It is permissible to import pervasive identifiers and predefined identifiers.

When a subprogram *P* is passed as a parametric subprogram to subprogram *Q*, any variables imported **var** directly or indirectly by *P* are considered to be **var** parameters passed to *Q*. Any variables imported directly or indirectly non-**var** by *P* are considered to be read-only reference parameters passed to *Q*. This is done to prevent potential aliasing as a result of the call.

The *result type* of a function is given by the *typeSpec* that follows the function's (optional) parameter declarations. The expression in a function's **result** statement must be assignable to the function's result type. Note that the result type can be a nonscalar, but must not be a dynamic array or dynamic string. The optional identifier preceding this *typeSpec* is the name of the function's result. This identifier can only be referenced in the function's **post** assertion.

A *subprogramBody* is:

> [**pre** *booleanExpn*]
> [**init** *id* := *expn* {, *id* := *expn*}]
> [**post** *booleanExpn*]
> *declarationsAndStatements*
> **end** *id*

The identifier following **end** must be the name of the subprogram. The **pre** expression must be true when the subprogram is called; the **post** expression must be true when returning.

The **init** clause defines constants (the identifiers to the left of each assignment operator :=). These can only be accessed in the **post, assert** and **invariant** constructs.

A **forward** subprogram is a subprogram whose **body** declaration will be given later in its scope. (This is the only situation in which the keyword **body** is used as a prefix for a subprogram declaration.) The **body** declaration must appear at the same level (in the same list of *declarationsAndStatements*) as the **forward** declaration. The prefix **forward** in an **import** list can be applied only to subprograms. The use of **forward** in an **import** list refers to a subprogram declared later at the same level (in the same list of *declarationsAndStatements*). Before a subprogram can be called and before its body appears, and before it can be passed as a parametric subprogram, its header as well as headers of subprograms directly or indirectly imported by it must have appeared. A function must not import a **forward** procedure. (This restriction is imposed to simplify checks for side effects in functions.) **Forward** subprograms allow subprograms to be mutually recursive. Example of mutual recursion:

```
% Evaluate an input expression e of the form t { + t } where
% t is of form p { * p } and p is of form ( e ) or
% is an explicit real constant.
% For example, the value of 1.5 + 3.0 * ( 0.5 + 1.5 ) halt is 7.5

var token: string

forward procedure expn(var eValue: real)
      import(forward term, var token)

forward procedure term(var tValue: real)
      import(forward primary, var token)

forward procedure primary(var pValue: real)
      import(expn, var token)

body procedure expn
      var nextValue: real
      term (eValue )        % Evaluate "t"
```

```
        loop        % Evaluate "{ + t }"
            exit when token not= "+"
            get token
            term (nextValue )
            eValue := eValue + nextValue
        end loop
    end expn

    body procedure term
        var nextValue : real
        primary (tValue )     % Evaluate "p"
        loop        % Evaluate "{ * p }"
            exit when token not= "*"
            get token
            primary (nextValue )
            tValue := tValue * nextValue
        end loop
    end term

    body procedure primary
        if token = "(" then
            get token
            expn (pValue )     % Evaluate "( e )"
            assert token = ")"
        else
            pValue := strreal (token )     % Evaluate "explicit real"
        end if
        get token
    end primary

    get token      % Start by reading first token
    var answer : real
    expn (answer )   % Scan and evaluate input expression
    put "Answer is: ", answer
```

The declaration of a subprogram or module must not appear inside a subprogram or statement. The declaration of a collection must not appear in a subprogram.

4.4.2 Modules

A module defines a package of variables, constants, types, subprograms, and submodules. The interface of the module to the rest of the program is defined by its **import** and **export** clauses.

A *moduleDeclaration* is:

> **module** *id*
>
> [*importList*]
>
> [**export** ([**opaque**] *id* {, [**opaque**] *id*})]
>
> [**pre** *booleanExpn*]
>
> {*declarationOrStatementInModule*}
>
> [**invariant** *booleanExpn*
>
> {*declarationOrStatementInModule*}]
>
> [**post** *booleanExpn*]
>
> **end** *id*

A *declarationOrStatementInModule* is one of:

a. *declaration* [;]
b. *statement* [;]
c. *collectionDeclaration* [;]
d. *subprogramDeclaration* [;]
e. *moduleDeclaration* [;]

A module declaration is executed (and the module is initialized) by executing its declarations and statements. See "Terminology and Basic Concepts" for an example of a module. The identifier following the **end** of a module must be the module's name.

The *importList* gives identifiers visible outside the module that are to be visible inside the module. See the description of **import** clauses in "Subprograms."

Exported identifiers are identifiers declared inside the module which may be accessed outside the module using the dot operator. Unexported identifiers cannot be referenced outside the module. Only subprograms, constants and types can be exported. Variables and modules must not be exported. The **opaque** keyword can be used only to prefix names of types. Outside the module an **opaque** type is distinct from all other types; see "Type Equivalence and Assignability." An identifier must not be repeated in an **export** list. Example:

```
module Complex    % Implements complex arithmetic
    export (opaque value, constant, add, ··· other operations )
    % The "value" type is opaque, so information about the
    % representation of complex values is hidden in this module
    type pervasive value:   % "Value" is visible throughout module
        record
            realPt, imagPt: real
        end record
```

```
        function constant(realPt, imagPt: real): value
            var answer: value
            answer. realPt := realPt
            answer. imagPt := imagPt
            result answer
        end constant

        function add(L, R: value ): value
            var answer: value
            answer. realPt := L. realPt + R. realPt
            answer. imagPt := L. imagPt + R. imagPt
            result answer
        end add

        ··· other operations for complex arithmetic go here ···
    end Complex

    var u, v: Complex.value := Complex.constant(1.0, 2.0)
    var w: Complex.value := Complex.add(u,v)
```

See "Restrictions Preventing Aliasing" for constraints on reference parameters in calls to enter a module.

The module's **pre** expression must be true when execution of the module declaration begins. The **post** expression must be true when the initialization of the module (execution of its declaration) is finished. The initialization of the module must make the **invariant** expression true, and it must be true whenever an exported subprogram is called or returns. The **invariant** clause must appear before the headers of exported subprograms. It is good style to limit each **invariant** expression so it does not refer, directly or indirectly, to imported variables or modules; this style implies that the value of the expression cannot change except when the module is active.

Module declarations may be nested inside other modules but must not be nested inside subprograms. A module must not contain as one of its declarations a *variableBinding*.

4.4.3 Restrictions on Constants and Read Only Items

A variable or module is read-only in a subprogram or module into which it is imported non-**var**. An identifier declared non-**var** in a **bind** construct is also read-only. Exported procedures of a read-only module cannot be referenced (called or passed as parametric procedures).

All components of a constant are considered constant, and all components of read-only variables are considered read-only.

Constants and read-only variables are restricted as follows. They cannot be assigned to, bound to **var**, further imported **var**, or passed to **var** parameters. A constant or read-only union cannot be the object of a **tag** statement. A read-only collection cannot be the object of a **new** or **free** statement.

4.4.4 Restrictions to Prevent Aliasing

Given distinct visible identifiers x and y, *aliasing* is said to exist if a change to the value of variable x would change the value of y. Aliasing is possible only when variables are renamed. In Turing, renaming of variables occurs in only two constructs: reference parameters and **bind**. Aliasing is prevented by placing restrictions on these two constructs.

(Note that variables imported by a parametric subprogram *P* are considered to be parameters to the subprogram to which *P* is passed; see ''Subprograms''.)

To explain these restrictions, we first define the terms ''direct importing.''and ''indirect importing''. A subprogram or module *directly* imports the items in its **import** clause. (A subprogram that does not have an explicit **import** clause is considered to have an implicit **import** clause giving the identifiers it accesses; see ''Subprograms.'') Each item is imported non-**var** (which means read-only for imported variables and modules) or **var**.

A subprogram or module *P indirectly* imports all items that are directly or indirectly imported by items directly imported into *P*. The direct and indirect imports of a read-only module are all considered to be non-**var**.

Note: when procedure *p* exported from module *m* is called from outside the module, we consider that *p* has the same **import** list as *m*. The same is true for exported functions except that all items are considered to be imported non-**var**.

Aliasing due to the first construct (reference parameters) is prevented by restrictions (a) and (b). Restriction (a): a (part of) a variable is not allowed to be passed to a **var** parameter if the called subprogram or module has another means of accessing (the same part of) the variable. This access can occur in two ways. The first is by a direct or indirect import of the variable by the called subprogram or module. The second is by passing (an overlapping part of) the same variable to another reference parameter in the same call. Restriction (b): (part of) a variable is not allowed to be passed to a *reference* parameter if the called subprogram or module has another means of *changing* (the same part of) the variable. The possibility of changing the variable can occur in two ways. The first is by a direct or indirect **var** import of the variable by the called subprogram or module. The second is by passing (an overlapping part of) the same variable to a **var** parameter in the same call.

Aliasing due to the second construct (**bind**) is prevented by restrictions (c) and (d). Restriction (c): a **var bind** of *y* to *x* makes *x* inaccessible for the scope of *y*, and a non-**var bind** of *y* to *x* makes *x* read-only for the scope of *y*. Restriction (d): a **var bind** to *x* disallows calls to subprograms or modules that directly or indirectly import *x*, and a non-**var bind** to *x* disallows calls to subprograms or modules that directly or indirectly import *x* **var**.

Function calls never cause aliasing because functions cannot import variables **var** (either directly or indirectly) and cannot have **var** parameters.

These restrictions to prevent aliasing are necessary for proving the correctness of a Turing program using the formal definition of Turing. However, an implementation may extend the language by allowing violations of these restrictions, given that appropriate messages are issued.

4.5 Statements and Input/Output

DeclarationsAndStatements are:

{*declarationOrStatement*}

A *declarationOrStatement* is one of:

a. *declaration* [;]
b. *statement* [;]
c. *variableBinding* [;]

A *statement* is one of:

a. *variableReference* := *expn*
b. *procedureCall*
c. **assert** *booleanExpn*
d. **return**
e. **result** *expn*
f. *ifStatement*
g. *loopStatement*
h. **exit** [**when** *booleanExpn*]
i. *caseStatement*
j. **begin**
        declarationsAndStatements
    end
k. **new** *collectionId*, *variableReference*
l. **free** *collectionId*, *variableReference*
m. *forStatement*
n. **tag** *variableReference*, *expn*
o. *putStatement*
p. *getStatement*

A declaration inside an **if, loop, case, for** or **begin** statement must not be for a module or subprogram; all other kinds of declarations, including **bind**, are allowed.

Form (a) is an assignment statement. The expression is evaluated and the value assigned to the variable. The *variableReference* is a reference that refers to (part of) a variable; see "References." The expression must be assignable to the variable type; see "Type Equivalence and Assignability."

A *procedureCall* is a:

reference

This reference will have the form [*moduleId.*] *procedureId*[(*expn*{,*expn*})]. An exported procedure is called outside the module in which it was declared using the dot operator. See "Subprograms" and "Modules."

Form (c) is an **assert** statement. The boolean expression must be true whenever the **assert** statement is executed. A checking implementation evaluates the assertion at run-time and aborts the program if it is false.

Form (d) is a **return** statement, which causes immediate return from a program or a procedure. A program or procedure returns either via a **return** statement or implicitly by reaching the end of the program or procedure. Functions and module bodies may not contain **return** statements.

Form (e) is a **result** statement, which can only appear in a function and causes immediate return from the function giving the function's value. The **result** expression must be assignable to the result type given in the function's header. Execution of a function must conclude by executing a **result** statement and not by reaching the end of the function.

An *ifStatement* is:

if *booleanExpn* **then**
    declarationsAndStatements
{**elsif** *booleanExpn* **then**
    declarationsAndStatements}
[**else**
    declarationsAndStatements]
end if

The boolean expressions following the keyword **if** and each **elsif** are successively evaluated until one of them is found to be true, in which case the statements following the corresponding **then** are executed. If none of the expressions evaluates to true then the statements following **else** are executed; if no **else** is present then execution continues following the **end if**.

A *loopStatement* is:

loop [**invariant** *booleanExpn*]
    declarationsAndStatements
end loop

The statements within the loop are repeated until terminated by one of its **exit** statements or an enclosed **return** or **result** statement. The boolean expression in the **invariant** must be true whenever execution reaches it; a checking implementation will abort if it is false.

Form (h) is a loop **exit**. When executed, it causes an immediate exit from the nearest enclosing **loop** or **for** statement. The optional boolean expression makes the exit conditional. If the expression evaluates to true then the exit is executed, otherwise execution of the loop continues. An **exit** statement can appear only inside **loop** and **for** statements.

A *caseStatement* is:

> **case** *expn* **of**
>
> > **label** *compileTimeExpn* {, *compileTimeExpn*} : *declarationsAndStatements*
> > {**label** *compileTimeExpn* {, *compileTimeExpn*} : *declarationsAndStatements*}
> > [**label** : *declarationsAndStatements*]
>
> **end case**

The optional final clause with no expression between **label** and : is called the *otherwise alternative*. The case expression is evaluated and used to select one of the alternatives for execution. The selected alternative is the one having a label whose value equals the case expression. If the case expression value does not equal any of the label values then the otherwise clause is executed. If no otherwise alternative is present, the case expression must equal one of the label values. When execution of the selected alternative is completed, execution continues following the **case** statement.

The root type of each label must be **int** or an index type and must be equivalent to the root type of the case selector expression. Label expressions must be compile-time expressions. Label values in a **case** statement must be distinct. An implementation may limit the range of case label values to insure efficient code; this range, from the minimum label value to the maximum, will be at least 256.

Form (j) is a **begin** statement. **Begin** statements can be used to limit the scope of declarations.

Forms (k) and (l) are **new** and **free** statements for creating and deleting elements of a **collection** (see "Variable and Collection Declarations").

A *forStatement* is one of:

a. **for** [*id*] : *forRange*
   [**invariant** *booleanExpn*]
   declarationsAndStatements
   end for

b. **for decreasing** [*id*] : *expn* .. *expn*
   [**invariant** *booleanExpn*]
   declarationsAndStatements
   end for

The statements enclosed in the **for** statement are repeated for the specified range, or until the loop is terminated by one of its **exit** statements or an enclosed **return** or **result** statement.

A *forRange* is one of:

a. *expn* .. *expn*

b. *namedType*

The *namedType* must be a (non-opaque) subrange or enumerated type, and is not permitted if **decreasing** is present. Form (b) of *forRange* is equivalent to form (a) using the type's lower and upper values. The range is given by the value of the two expressions at the time the **for** statement is entered. The types of the two values must be of the same index type or of type **int**. For the first iteration, *id* has the left expression's value; for successive iterations, *id* is increased by one (or decreased if **decreasing** is present), until in the last iteration *id* equals the right value. If the left value exceeds the right (or is less than the right when **decreasing**), there are no iterations. For each repetition, *id* is set to a new value in the range; these are contiguous values that are increasing, unless **decreasing** is specified in which case they are decreasing. The **for** statement is a declaration for *id*, which must be distinct from other visible identifiers. The scope of *id* is from the beginning to the end of the **for** statement. If the *id* is not present, the **for** statement behaves the same, except that the value corresponding to the *id* cannot be accessed. For each repetition, *id* is a constant and its value cannot be changed. The boolean expression in the **invariant** must be true whenever execution reaches it; a checking implementation will abort if it is false.

Statement form (n) is a **tag** statement. The variable of the statement must be a union. The union's tag is changed to be the value of the expression, which must be assignable to the tag's type. See "Types and Type Declarations" for further description and for an example of usage.

4.5.1 Input and Output

Put and **get** statements are used to read/write items to/from streams (sequential files of characters).

A *putStatement* is:

put [: *streamNumber*,] *putItem* {, *putItem*} [..]

Each *streamNumber* is a non-negative integer expression. Omitting the stream number from these statements results in the default input stream for **get** and the default output stream for **put**. The written or read items must be strings or numbers (integer or real). The default input and output streams cannot be selected using a stream number. There is a run-time constraint that a particular stream can be read from or written to but not both. (See also "Predefined Procedures" for *open* and *close*, which are used to associate streams with stream numbers and which determine when streams can be read or written.)

By convention stream 0 is considered to be a special error output stream. By convention the streams numbered 1 to *n* are attached to files specified externally by the user (e.g., by command line arguments).

Since functions cannot have side effects, they are not allowed to contain **get** and **put** statements or to directly or indirectly call procedures that contain **get** or **put** statements.

A *putItem* is one of:

a. *expn* [: *widthExpn* [: *fractionWidth* [: *exponentWidth*]]]
b. **skip**

From left to right in a **put** statement, either the *expn*'s value of the *putItem* is appended to the output stream, or **skip** starts a new line. A new line is also started at the end of the list of *putItems*, unless the list is followed by ".. ", in which case this new line is not started. The ".. " leaves the current line so it can be completed by other **put** statements.

If the *widthExpn* is omitted, then the value is printed in a field just large enough to hold the value. The *fractionWidth* and *exponentWidth* are allowed only for integer and real values.

For string value *s*, integer value *i* and real value *r*, the *putItems* given on the left are defined by the string *putItems* on the right.

s : *w*	*s*+*repeat* (*blank*, *w*−*length* (*s*))
i	*intstr* (*i*, 0)
i : *w*	*intstr* (*i*, *w*)
r	*realstr* (*r*, 0)
r : *w*	*realstr* (*r*, *w*)
r : *w* : *fw*	*frealstr* (*r*, *w*, *fw*)
r : *w* : *fw* : *ew*	*erealstr* (*r*, *w*, *fw*, *ew*)

See "Predefined Functions" for definitions of the functions used on the right. Following are example **put** statements with their output.

Statement	Output	Notes
put 24	24	
put 1/10	0.1	Trailing zeros omitted
put 100/10	10	Decimal point omitted
put 5/3	1.666667	Assumes *fwdefault* = 6
put sqrt(2)	1.414214	
put 4.86*10**9	4.86e9	Exponent printed for ≥ 1e6
put 121: 5	bb121	Width of 5; "b" is a blank
put 1.37: 6: 3	b1.370	Fraction width of 3
put 1.37: 11: 3: 2	bb1.370e+00	Exponent width of 2
put "O'Brian"	O'Brian	
put "X=", 5.4	X=5.4	

put "XX": 4, "Y" XXbbY Blank shown here as "b"

A *getStatement* is:

get [: *streamNumber* ,] *getItem* {, *getItem*}

A *getItem* is one of:

a. *variableReference*
b. **skip**
c. *variableReference* : *
d. *variableReference* : *widthExpn*

Forms (a) and (b) support *token-oriented* input, (c) supports *line-oriented* input, and form (d) supports *character-oriented* input. In form (a) the *variableReference*'s root type must be integer, real or string, while forms (c) and (d) allow only strings. The value read into a string must not contain an *eos* or *uninitchar* character (see "Identifiers and Explicit Constants").

Form (a) first skips *white space* (defined as the characters blank, tab, form feed, new line, and carriage return); then it reads the next characters as a token. A token consists of either (1) one or more non white space characters, up to but not including either a white space character or end of file, or else (2) if the token's first character is a quote ("), then it is an explicit string constant. (See also "Identifiers and Explicit Constants.") Explicit string constants can only be input for string *variableReferences*. When the *variableReference* is a string, the value of the explicit string constant or else the characters of the token, are assigned to the variable. If it is an integer, the predefined function *strint* converts the token to an integer before assigning to the variable. Analogously for reals, *strreal* converts the token to real before assigning it to the variable. It is an error to use form (a) if no token remains in the stream.

In form (b), the **skip** option skips white space, stopping when encountering non-white space (a token) or end of file. This option is used to detect whether further tokens exist in the input; if no more tokens exist in the input, all characters of the file are skipped and the *eof* predefined function becomes **true**. The following input stream:

Alice 216 "World champion"

is used in this example:

```
var name, fame : string
var time : int
get name, time, fame
% name = "Alice", time = 216 and fame = "World champion"
```

Example:

```
% Read and sum a sequence of numbers
var sum : real := 0.0
var x : real
```

```
loop
    get skip    % Skip to eof or next token
    exit when eof   % eof is explained in ''Predefined Functions''
    get x
    sum := sum + x
end loop
put ''Sum is: '', sum
```

Form (c) reads the rest of the characters of the present line (not including the trailing new line character) and assigns them to the *variableReference*, which must be a string. The trailing new line character is read and discarded. (Note: it may be that the final line of a stream is not terminated by a new line character; in this case form (c) reads the remaining characters.) It is an error to use form (c) if no characters remain in the stream (if *eof* is true for the stream).

Form (d) is similar to form (c) except (1) at most *widthExpn* (a non-negative integer) characters are read, (2) the new line character at the end of a line is part of the string assigned to the *variableReference*, and (3) attempting to read past the end of stream is allowed and returns the remaining characters (if any). Examples:

```
var s, t, u: string
get s: *   % Reads input line, discarding trailing new line character
get t: 20   % Reads at most 20 characters; t may end with ''\n''
get u: 1   % Reads next char (or null string for eof)
```

Example:

```
% Read and print stream a line at a time
var line: string
loop
    exit when eof
    get line: *   % Read line
    put line
end loop
```

Example:

```
% Read and print stream a character at a time
var c: string(1)
loop
    exit when eof
    get c: 1   % ''\n'' is read into c at end of line
    put c ..   % Lines are ended when c=''\n''
end loop
```

4.6 References and Expressions

4.6.1 References

The syntax for a *reference* includes variable references and constant references, as well as procedure statements, function calls, values of enumerated types, attributes and parametric subprograms. A *variableReference* is a *reference* that denotes a variable or part of a variable.

A *variableReference* is a:
    reference

A *reference* is one of:
    a. *id*
    b. *reference componentSelector*

The form of each of these *references* is: [*moduleId.*] *id* {*componentSelector*}.

A *componentSelector* is one of:
    a. (*expn* {, *expn* })
    b. . *id*

Form (a) of *componentSelector* allows subscripting of arrays and collections. The value of each array subscript expression must be in the declared range of the corresponding index type of the array. The number of array subscripts must be the same as the number of index ranges declared for the array. A collection must have exactly one subscript and this must be a pointer to the collection.

Form (a) also allows calls to functions. The number of expressions must be the same as the number of declared parameters of the function. Each expression must be assignable to the corresponding formal parameter of the function.

Form (b) of *componentSelector* allows field and tag selection for records and unions. (Fields of a record or variable and a union's tag are referenced using the dot operator). It also allows access to items exported from a module.

A value of an enumerated type is a special case of form (b), namely, *id.id*, where the first *id* is the name of the type and the second *id* must be one of the identifiers given in the **enum** type definition.

4.6.2 Expressions

An *expn* (expression) represents a calculation that returns a value. A *booleanExpn* is an *expn* whose value is **true** or **false**.

Turing is a strongly typed language, meaning that there are a number of constraints on the ways values can be used. The following sections explain how values are mapped by operators to produce new values.

An *expn* is one of the following:

a. *reference*
b. *explicitConstant*
c. *substring*
d. *setConstructor*
e. *expn infixOperator expn*
f. *prefixOperator expn*
g. (*expn*)

Form (a) includes (1) references to constants and variables including subscripting and field and tag selection, (2) function calls and (3) values of enumerated types. See "References."

Form (b) includes explicit boolean, integer, real and string constants; see "Identifiers and Explicit Constants." Form (c) is a substring; see "String Operators and Substrings." Form (d) is a **set** constructor; see "Set Operators and Constructors."

An *infixOperator* is one of:

a. + (integer and real addition; set union; string catenation)
b. – (integer and real subtraction; set difference)
c. * (integer and real multiplication; set intersection)
d. / (real division)
e. **div** (truncating integer division)
f. **mod** (remainder)
g. ** (integer and real exponentiation)
h. < (less than)
i. > (greater than)
j. = (equal)
k. <= (less than or equal; subset)
l. >= (greater than or equal; superset)
m. **not**= (not equal)
n. **and** (boolean conjunction)
o. **or** (boolean inclusive or)
p. => (boolean implication)
q. **in** (member of set)
r. **not in** (set non-membership)

A *prefixOperator* is one of:

a. + (integer and real identity)
b. – (integer and real negation)
c. **not** (boolean negation)

The order of precedence is among the following classes of the operators, in decreasing order of precedence:

1. **
2. prefix +, –
3. *, /, **div**, **mod**
4. infix +, –
5. <, >, =, <=, >=, **not=**, **in**, **not in**
6. **not**
7. **and**
8. **or**
9. =>

Expressions are evaluated according to precedence, left to right within precedence. Note that exponentiation is grouped from left to right.

For example, each expression on the left is equal to the expression on the right.

$a-b-c$	$(a-b)-c$
$-1**2$	$-(1**2)$
$a+b*c$	$a+(b*c)$
$x<y$ **and** b	$(x<y)$ **and** b
b **or** c **and** d	b **or** $(c$ **and** $d)$

4.6.3 Numeric Operators

The numeric (integer and real) operators are +, –, *, /, **div** (truncating division), **mod** (remainder) and ** (exponentiation).

The **div** operator is defined by:

$$x \textbf{ div } y = trunc(a \div b)$$

where $\div$ means exact mathematical division and *trunc* truncates to the nearest integer in the direction of zero. The result is of type **int**. The operands can be integer or real. Note that with real operands, **div** may produce an integer overflow.

The **mod** operator is defined by:

$$x \textbf{ mod } y = x - y * (x \textbf{ div } y)$$

If x and y are both of root type **int**, the result type is **int**, otherwise the result is **real**. Note that **mod** applied to real operands is useful for range reduction; for example, for $x>0$, $sin(x)$ can be computed as $sin(x \textbf{ mod } (2*pi))$. Note that **mod** with **int** operands never produces an overflow, but with real operands, it may produce a real underflow. The / operator requires real or integer operands and produces a result of type **real**.

Whenever a real value is required, an integer value is allowed and is converted to real by an implicit call to the *intreal* predefined function; see "Predefined Functions". Note that this rule implies the the / operator can accept two integer operands, but both will be converted to real. The operators +, – (infix and prefix), * and ** require integer or real operands; if one or both operands are **real**, the result is **real**, else it is **int**. The right operands of **div** and / must not be zero. If both operands of ** are of root type **int**, the right operand must not be negative. If the left operand is real and the right is of root type **int**, the right operand must be non-zero when the left is negative. If both operands are real, the right operand must be strictly positive when the left is negative and otherwise must be zero or positive. Examples:

7/2 = 3.5	–7/2 = –3.5
7 **div** 2 = 3	–7 **div** 2 = –3
7 **mod** 2 = 1	–7 **mod** 2 = –1
7**2 = 49	–7 **mod** 2 = –1

A checking implementation is expected to detect division and **mod** by zero, zero to the zero power, integer overflow, and **real** overflow and underflow.

4.6.4 Comparison Operators

The comparison operators are <, >, =, <=, >=, and **not**=. These operators yield a boolean result. Operands of a comparison operator must have the same root type; see "Type Equivalence and Assignability." Only strings, sets, and scalars (values whose root type is integer, real, boolean, enumerated or pointer) can be compared. Arrays, records and unions cannot be compared. Booleans and pointers can be compared only for equality (= and **not**=). See "String Operators and Substrings" for a description of string comparison.

4.6.5 Boolean Operators

The boolean operators are **and** (conjunction), **or** (inclusive or), => (implication) and **not**. These require boolean operands and return a boolean result. Note that *a* => *b* has the same meaning as (**not** *a*) **or** *b*. The boolean operators are conditional; that is, if the result of the operation is determined by the value of the left operand then the right operand is not evaluated. In the following, division by zero is avoided, because the right operand of **and** is executed only if the left operand is true:

if *count* **not**= 0 **and** *sum*/*count* >60 **then** · · ·

4.6.6 String Operators and Substrings

The only string operator is + (catenation); it requires string operands and returns a string. An implementation may limit the allowed length of string values; this limit will be at least 255.

The ordering of strings is determined by left to right comparison of pairs of corresponding characters until an end of string or a mismatch is found. See "Character Collating Sequence." The string with the greater of the mismatched characters is considered greater. If no mismatch is found and one string is longer than the other, the longer string is considered greater. Note that strings of differing lengths are never considered to be equal, and there is no implicit "blank padding" of the ends of strings. The following function recursively defines the "greater than" string relation in terms of comparison of strings of length one.

```
function GT (s, t: string): boolean
    if length (s) = 0 or length (t) = 0 then result length (s)>length (t)
    elsif s (1) = t (1) then result GT (s (2 .. *), t (2 .. *))
    else result s (1) >t (1)
    end if
end GT
```

The *length* predefined function returns the number of characters in a string value; see "Predefined Functions."

A substring selects a contiguous sequence of the characters in a string. For example, if $L = 2$, $R = 4$ and *s* = "*bring*", then the substring of *s* from position *L* to position *R*, written *s(L .. R)*, equals "*rin*". A single character can also be selected, for example, *s(L)*="*r*". In general, for any expression *e*

s(e) = *s(e .. e)*

String positions *R* and *L* can be written as * [−*expn*], where the star represents the length of the string, i.e., * [−*expn*] is an abbreviation for: *length(s)*[−*expn*]. For example, if *s* = "*bring*", then *s* (*)="*g*", *s* (3 .. *)="*ing*" and *s* (*−2 .. *−1)="*in*". The general form of a substring is:

reference (*substringPosition* [.. *substringPosition*])

where each *substringPosition* is either an *expn* or else * [−*expn*]. Each *expn* must be of root type **int**. Since one case of string, *reference*(*expn*), is syntactically identical to a *reference*, it is not separately included in the following context-free description of substrings.

A *substring* is one of:

a. *reference* (*substringPosition* .. *substringPosition*)
b. *reference* (* [−*expn*])

A *substringPosition* is one of:

a. $*$ [$-$*expn*]

b. *expn*

The following restriction applies to L and R:

$$L \geq 1 \textbf{ and } R \leq length(reference) \textbf{ and } R-L+1 \geq 0.$$

Note that $length(s(L\ ..R)) = R-L+1$. Note that for $L \geq 1$ and $L \leq length(s)+1$, $s(L, L-1)$ is the null string, i.e., the string of length zero. A substring is an expression (not a variable), and so it cannot be assigned to.

4.6.7 Set Operators and Set Constructors

The set operators are + (set union), – (set difference), * (set intersection), <= and >= (set inclusion), and **in** and **not in** (membership). Sets can also be compared for equality using = and **not**=. The set operators +, – and * take operands of equivalent set types and yield a result of the same type. The set operators <= and >= take operands of equivalent set types and yield a Boolean result. The operators **in** and **not in** take a set as right operand and an expression in the set's base type as left operand. They yield a Boolean result.

A *setConstructor* is one of:

a. *reference* ( )

b. *reference* (**all**)

There is a third form of *setConstructor*, *reference(expn* {,*expn*}); it has the same form as a *reference*. Form (a), which always occurs as [*moduleId*.] *setTypeId*(), represents the empty set. Form (b), which always occurs as [*moduleId*.]*setTypeId*(**all**), represents the complete set. The third form, which always occurs as [*moduleId*.]*setTypeId*(*expn* {,*expn*}), is a set containing the elements specified by the expressions.

4.6.8 Compile-Time Expressions

A *compile-time expression* is an expression whose value can, in principle, be computed at compile time. The following are compile-time expressions:

1. Explicit integer, real, boolean and string constants, as well as enumerated values of the form *id1*.*id2* where *id1* is the name of the enumerated type
2. Set constructors containing only compile-time element values (or **all**)
3. Named constants that name scalar compile-time expressions
4. The result of integer operators prefix + and –, infix + and –, *, **div** and **mod** when the operands are compile-time integer expressions

5. The built-in functions *chr* and *ord* when the actual parameter is a compile-time expression
6. The result of the catenate operator (+) when both operands are compile-time string expressions

Note that a compile-time expression can be invalid, for example, 1/0, and is still considered to be a compile-time expression. Expressions that do not satisfy this definition are called *run-time* expressions.

4.6.9 Predefined Functions

The following are pervasive, predefined functions.

eof (*i*: **int**): **boolean**

Accepts a non-negative stream number (see description of **get** and **put** statements) and returns true if and only if there are no more characters in the stream. This function must not be applied to streams that are written to (via **put**). The parameter and parentheses can be omitted, in which case the parameter is taken to be the default input stream.

pred(expn)

Accepts an integer or an enumerated value and returns the integer minus one, or the previous value in the enumeration. *Pred* must not be applied to the first value of an enumeration.

succ (*expn*)

Accepts an integer or an enumerated value and returns the integer plus one, or the next value in the enumeration. *Succ* must not be applied to the last value of an enumeration.

STRING FUNCTIONS

length (*s*: **string**): **int**

Returns the number of characters in the string. The string must be initialized.

index (*s*, *patt*: **string**): **int**

If there exists an *i* such that *s* (*i* .. *i*+*length* (*patt*)–1) = *patt*, then the smallest such *i* is returned, otherwise zero is returned. Note that 1 is returned if *patt* is the null string.

repeat (*s* : **string,** *i* : **int**): **string**

If $i>0$, returns i copies of s catenated together, else returns the null string. Note that if $j \geq 0$, $length(repeat(t, j)) = j*length(t)$.

MATHEMATICAL FUNCTIONS

abs (*expn*)

Accepts an integer or real value and returns the absolute value. The type of the result is **int** if the *expn* is an of root type **int**; otherwise it is real.

max (*expn* , *expn*)

Accepts two numeric (real or integer) values and returns their maximum. If both are of root type **int**, the result is an **int**; otherwise it is real.

min (*expn* , *expn*)

Accepts two numeric (real or integer) values and returns their minimum. If both are of root type **int**, the result is an **int**; otherwise is is real.

sign (*r* : **real**): –1 .. 1

Returns –1 if $r<0$, 0 if $r=0$, and 1 if $r>0$.

sqrt (*r* : **real**): **real**

Returns the positive square root of *r*, where *r* is a non-negative value.

sin (*r* : **real**): **real**

Returns the sine of *r*, where *r* is an angle expressed in radians.

cos (*r* : **real**): **real**

Returns the cosine of *r*, where *r* is an angle expressed in radians.

arctan (*r* : **real**): **real**

Returns the arctangent (in radians) of *r*.

sind (*r* : **real**): **real**

Returns the sine of *r*, where *r* is an angle expressed in degrees.

cosd (*r* : **real**): **real**

Returns the cosine of *r*, where *r* is an angle expressed in degrees.

arctand (*r* : **real**): **real**

Returns the arctangent (in degrees) of *r*.

ln (*r* : **real**): **real**

Returns the natural logarithm (base e) of *r*.

exp (*r* : **real**): **real**

Returns the natural base *e* raised to the power *r*.

TYPE TRANSFER FUNCTIONS

floor(*r* : **real**): **int**

Returns the largest integer less than or equal to *r*.

ceil (*r* : **real**): **int**

Returns the smallest integer greater than or equal to *r*.

round (*r* : **real**): **int**

Returns the nearest integer approximation to *r*. Rounds to the numerically larger value in case of a tie.

intreal (*i* : **int**): **real**

Returns the real value equivalent to *i*. No precision is lost in the conversion, so *floor*(*intreal* (*j*))=*ceil* (*intreal* (*j*))=*j* . To guarantee that these equalities hold, an implementation may limit the range of *i*.

chr (*i* : **int**): **string**(1)

Returns a string of length 1. The i-th character of the collating sequence is returned, where the first character corresponds to 0, the second to 1, etc. See "Character Collating Sequence." The selected character must not be *uninitchar* (a reserved character used to mark uninitialized strings) or *eos* (a reserved character used to mark the end of a string). See "Identifiers and Explicit Constants."

ord (*expn*)

Accepts an enumerated value or a string of length 1 and returns the position of the value in the enumeration or of the character in the collating sequence. Values of an enumerated type are numbered left to right starting at zero. See "Character Collating Sequence."

intstr (*i* , *width* : **int**): **string**

Returns a string equivalent to *i*, padded on the left with blanks as necessary to a length of *width*; for example, *intstr* (14,4)="*bb* 14" where *b* represents a blank. The width parameter is optional; if omitted, it is taken to be 1. The width parameter must be non-negative. If width is not large enough to represent the value of *i*, the length is automatically increased as needed. The string returned by *intstr* is of the form:

{blank}[–]digit{digits}

The leftmost digit is non-zero, or else there is a single zero digit.

strint (*s* : **string**): **int**

Returns the integer equivalent to string *s*. String *s* must consist of a possibly null sequence of blanks, then an optional plus or minus sign, and finally a sequence of one or more digits. Note that for integer *i*, and for non-negative *w*, *strint* (*intstr* (*i* , *w*))=*i* .

erealstr (*r* : **real**, *width* , *fractionWidth* , *exponentWidth* : **int**): **string**

Returns a string (including exponent) approximating *r*, padded on the left with blanks as necessary to a length of *width*; for example, *erealstr* (2.5e1, 9, 2, 2) = "*b* 2.50*e*+01" where *b* represents a blank. The *width* must be non-negative **int** value. If the *width* parameter is not large enough to represent the value of *r*, it is implicitly increased as needed. The *fractionWidth* parameter is the non-negative number of fractional digits to be displayed. The displayed value is rounded to the nearest decimal equivalent with this accuracy, with ties rounded to the next larger value. The *exponentWidth* parameter must be non-negative and gives the number of exponent digits to be displayed. If *exponentWidth* is not large enough to represent the exponent, more space is used as needed. The string returned by *erealstr* is of the form:

{blank}[–]digit.{digit}e sign digit {digit}

where "sign" is a plus or minus sign. The leftmost digit is non-zero, unless all the digits are zeroes.

frealstr(*r* : **real**, *width* , *fractionWidth* : **int**): **string**

Returns a string approximating *r*, padded on the left with blanks if necessary to a length of *width*. The number of digits of fraction to be displayed is given by *fractionWidth*; for example, *frealstr*(2.5*e*1, 5, 1) = "*b* 25.0" where *b* represents a blank. The *width* must be non-negative. If the *width* parameter is not large enough to represent the value of *r*, it is implicitly increased as needed. The *fractionWidth* must be non-negative. The displayed value is rounded to the nearest decimal equivalent with this accuracy, with ties rounded to the next larger value. The result string is of the form:

{blank} [–] digit{digit}. {digit}

If the leftmost digit is zero, then it is the only digit to the left of the decimal point.

realstr (*r*: **real**, *width*: **int**): **string**

Returns a string approximating *r*, padded on the left with blanks if necessary to a length of *width*, for example, *realstr* (2.5*e*1, 4) = "*bb*25" where *b* represents a blank. The *width* parameter must be non-negative. If the *width* parameter is not large enough to represent the value of *r*, it is implicitly increased as needed. The displayed value is rounded to the nearest decimal equivalent with this accuracy, with ties rounded to the next larger value. The string *realstr* (*r*, *width*) is the same as the string *frealstr*(*r*, *width*, *defaultfw*) when *r*=0 or when $1e{-}3 \leq abs(r) < 1e6$, otherwise the same as *erealstr* (*r*, *width*, *defaultfw*, *defaultew*), with the following exceptions. With *realstr*, trailing fraction zeroes are omitted and if the entire fraction is zero, the decimal point is omitted. (These omissions take place even if the exponent part is printed.) If an exponent is printed, any plus sign and leading zeroes are omitted. Thus, whole number values are in general displayed as integers. *Defaultfw* is an implementation defined number of fractional digits to be displayed; for most implementations, *defaultfw* will be 6. *Defaultew* is an implementation defined number of exponent digits to be displayed; for most implementations, *defaultew* will be 2.

strreal (*s*: **string**): **real**

Returns a real approximation to string *s*. String *s* must consist of a possibly null sequence of blanks, then an optional plus or minus sign and finally an explicit unsigned real or integer constant.

4.6.10 Attributes

There are pervasive attributes that are properties of variables rather than properties of values. For example, the *upper* attribute of a string variable gives its maximum length. Note that assigning a value to a variable does not change the variable's attributes. Example:

> **var** *s*: **string**(10) := "*Eggs*"
> **var** *t*: **string**(6) := "*Bacon*"
> *s* := *t*

At all times, *upper* (*s*)=10 and *upper* (*t*)=6. The available attributes are:

lower (*reference* [, *dimension*])

Accepts an array and returns the lower bound of the array.

upper (*reference* [, *dimension*])

Accepts an array and returns the upper bound of the array; also accepts a string and returns its maximum length.

In *lower* and *upper*, *dimension* is a compile-time integer expression, which is present iff the *reference* is a multi-dimensioned array. It specifies which dimension, where the first is 1, the second is 2 and so on. The *reference* does not need to be initialized.

nil (*collectionId*)

Accepts a collection and returns the collection's null pointer.

4.6.11 Predefined Procedures

The following procedures are pervasive and predefined.

rand (**var** *r* : **real**)

Sets *r* to the next value of a sequence of pseudo random real numbers that approximates a uniform distribution over the range $0<r<1$.

Example:

```
var r : real
loop % Randomly print a sequence of phrases
    rand (r)
    if r >0.5 then
        put "Hi ho, hi ho"
    else
        put "It's off to work we go"
    end if
end loop
```

randint (**var** *i* : **int**, *low*, *high* : **int**)

Sets *i* to the next value of a sequence of pseudo random integers that approximates a uniform distribution over the range $low \le i \le high$. It is required that $low \le high$.

randomize

This is a procedure with no parameters that resets the sequences of pseudo random numbers produced by *rand* and *randint*, so different executions of the same program will produce different results.

randnext (**var** *v* : **real**, *seq* : 1 .. 10)

This is the same as *rand*, except *seq* specifies one of 10 independent and repeatable sequences of pseudo random real numbers.

randseed (*seed*: **int**, *seq*: 1 .. 10)

This restarts one of the sequences generated by *randnext*. Each restart with the same seed causes *randnext* to produce the same sequence for the given sequence.

open (**var** *streamNumber*: **int**, *fileName*: **string**, *mode*: **string**)

The *fileName* gives the name of a file that is to be read from or written to. The *streamNumber* parameter is set to the stream number to be used for the file in **get** or **put**. The *mode* must be *"r"* (for *read*) or *"w"* (for *write*) indicating whether the stream is to be read from or written to. If the *open* fails, *streamNumber* is set to zero.

close (*streamNumber*: **int**)

This dissociates the stream number from the stream it is presently designating.

The predefined procedures (*rand, randint, randomize, randnext, randseed, open* and *close*) have side effects. As a result, functions are not allowed to contain them or to directly or indirectly call procedures that contain them.

4.6.12 The Uninitialized Value

The value of a scalar, string or set that is not initialized must not be used (fetched) in evaluating an expression. For example, before any of the following are executed, variable *x* must have been assigned a value.

```
const c := x
y := x + y
P (x+y)
```

A scalar, string or set need not be initialized before being passed to a **var** parameter, but must be initialized before being passed to a non-**var** parameter. These rules imply that once a particular scalar, string or set variable is initialized, it will stay initialized.

A variable that has been declared and not assigned to (and not initialized in its declaration) is considered to be uninitialized. When an element of a collection is created by the **new** statement, it is uninitialized. Fields of a union become uninitialized when the **tag** statement is applied to the union. Part or all of an array, record or union variable may become uninitialized when the variable is assigned to, according to the initialization of the value being assigned.

When conditional evaluation of an expression does not require the value of a particular variable, the variable need not be initialized. For example, in the following, if i=10 then x need not be initialized:

exit when $i=10$ **or** $x=5$

A nonscalar that is not a string or set can be assigned, used as the value of a **const**, passed to a parameter (**var** or non-**var**) or returned as a function result without being initialized. Note: the nonscalars in question (i.e., nonscalars that are not strings or sets) are arrays, records and unions. Scalar, string or set components of nonscalar types must be initialized before being used (fetched). An initialized component of a nonscalar can become uninitialized due to assigning to the containing nonscalar variable or changing the tag of the containing union.

A checking implementation of Turing is expected to enforce these restrictions on the use of uninitialized values.

4.6.13 Character Collating Sequence

Certain Turing language features, notably string comparison and the *chr* predefined function, depend on the character *collating sequence*. This is the sequence that determines the ordering among character values. There are two widely used collating sequences: ASCII and EBCDIC. A Turing implementation is expected to use one of these, with preference given to ASCII. Note that a Turing program that is correct assuming one of these sequences is not necessarily correct assuming the other.

The *ord* function maps a character value to its corresponding ASCII or EBCDIC value, which will be in the range 0..255. For standard ASCII characters, the range is limited to 0..127. Therefore, subject to limits on the domain of *succ*, the following equation holds.

For all characters c:
$chr(ord(c)) = c$ **and**
$succ(c) = chr(ord(c)+1)$

The ASCII and EBCDIC sequences share the important property that digits are contiguous. Therefore, if s is the string of length 1 corresponding to integer i then $ord(s)-ord(\text{"0"}) = i$, for example, $ord(\text{"3"})-ord(\text{"0"}) = 3$. In ASCII, letter characters are also contiguous:

$ord(\text{"A"}) = ord(\text{"B"})-1$
$ord(\text{"B"}) = ord(\text{"C"})-1$
. . .
$ord(\text{"a"}) = ord(\text{"b"})-1$
$ord(\text{"b"}) = ord(\text{"c"})-1$
. . .

The following function converts a string of digits to an integer.

```
function digitsint (s : string): int
    const L := length (s)
    const digit := ord (s (L))-ord ("0")
    if L=1 then
        result digit
    else
        result 10*digitsint (s (1 .. L-1)) + digit
    end if
end digitsint
```

Unfortunately, in EBCDIC the letters are not contiguous; there are gaps between letters *I* and *J* and between *R* and *S*. The test to see if ASCII character *c* is a capital letter is:

```
"A"≤c and c≤"Z"
```

But for EBCDIC character *c*, we must use:

```
("A"≤c and c≤"I") or
("J"≤c and c≤"R") or
("S"≤c and c≤"Z")
```

Similarly, for lower case letters there are gaps in EBCDIC between *i* and *j* and between *r* and *s*. Consult standard definitions of ASCII and EBCDIC collating sequences for more details.

4.7 Source Inclusion Facility

Other source files may be included as part of a program using the **include** construct.

An *includeConstruct* is:
    include *explicitString*

The *explicitString* gives the name of a source file to be included in the compilation. The **include** construct is *replaced* in the program source by the contents (tokens) of the specified file. **Include** constructs can appear anywhere in a program and can contain any valid source fragment. Included source files can themselves contain **include** constructs.

4.8 Short Forms

The following forms can be used as alternatives for the syntax given in the language specification. These alternatives shorten frequently used constructs.

Long form	Short form
v := *v* + (*expn*) *v* := *v* − (*expn*) *v* := *v* * (*expn*)	*v* += *expn* *v* −= *expn* *v* *= *expn*
if *expn* **then** *statements* **elsif** *expn* **then** *statements* **else** *statements* **end if**	[*expn* : *statements* | *expn* : *statements* | : *statements*]

case *expn* **of**
  label *labels* : *statements*
  . . .
  label : *statements*
end case
	case *expn* **of**
	| *labels* : *statements*
	. . .
	| : *statements*
	end case

union *id*: *typeSpec* **of**
  label *labels* : *statements*
  . . .
  label : *statements*
end union
	union *id*: *typeSpec* **of**
	| *labels* : *statements*
	. . .
	| : *statements*
	end union

loop
  statements
end loop
	{
	  statements
	}

exit	>>
exit when *expn*	>>: *expn*
return	>>>
result *expn*	>>>: *expn*

for *optionalId* : *expn* .. *expn*
  statements
end for
	{+ *optionalId*: *expn* .. *expn*
	  statements
	}

for decreasing *optionalId*: *expn* .. *expn*
    statements
end for
	{− *optionalId* : *expn* .. *expn*
	    statements
	}

and	&
not	~
put	!
get	?
array *indexTypes* **of**	{ *indexTypes* }
procedure	**proc**
function	**fcn**
pervasive	*

Example using short forms.

Long form

```
function GCD (i, j: int): int
    var x: int := i
    var y: int := j
    loop
        exit when x = y
        if x >y then
            x := x−y
        else
            y := y−x
        end if
    end loop
    result x
end GCD
```

Short form

```
fcn GCD (i, j: int): int
    var x := i
    var y := j
    { >>: x=y
        [ x>y:  x −= y
        |     :  y −= x
        ]
    }
    >>>: x
end GCD
```

4.9 Collected Keywords and Predefined Identifiers

Keywords of Turing:

all	**and**	**array**	**assert**	**begin**
bind	**body**	**boolean**	**case**	**collection**
const	**decreasing**	**div**	**else**	**elsif**
end	**enum**	**exit**	**export**	**false**
fcn	**for**	**forward**	**free**	**function**
get	**if**	**import**	**in**	**include**
init	**int**	**invariant**	**label**	**loop**
mod	**module**	**new**	**not**	**of**
opaque	**or**	**pervasive**	**pointer**	**post**
pre	**proc**	**procedure**	**put**	**real**
record	**result**	**return**	**set**	**skip**
string	**tag**	**then**	**to**	**true**
type	**union**	**var**	**when**	

Predefined Identifiers of Turing:

abs	*arctan*	*arctand*	*ceil*	*chr*
close	*cos*	*cosd*	*eof*	*erealstr*
exp	*floor*	*frealstr*	*index*	*intreal*
intstr	*length*	*ln*	*lower*	*max*
min	*nil*	*open*	*ord*	*pred*
rand	*randint*	*randnext*	*randomize*	*randseed*
realstr	*repeat*	*round*	*sign*	*sin*
sind	*sqrt*	*strint*	*strreal*	*succ*
upper				

4.10 Collected Operators and Special Symbols

The operators and special symbols of Turing are:

,   ..   .   :   ;   *   **

/   +   –   <   >   >>   >>>

=   <=   >=   +=   -=   *=   :=

=>   ~   !   ?   &   (   )

{   }   [   ] |

Twelve of these are introduced with short forms:

>> >>> += −= *= ~ ! ? & [ ] |

White space or comments must not appear between characters comprising a special symbol.

4.11 Recognizing Tokens

The tokens of the Turing program are recognized by scanning characters from left to right, skipping white space, until the beginning of a token is found. The token is recognized by *maximal scanning* meaning the token is extended on the right as long as the additional characters (potentially) form more of the token. Then white space, if any, is skipped, up to the beginning of the next token.

In the following fragment, "10" and "**then**" are distinct tokens even though they are not separated by white space:

if *a* > 10**then** % *Acceptable*

In the next example, by maximal scanning "4*e*" is the (ill-formed) initial part of a real constant, so this fragment is not acceptable:

if *a* > 10**then** *x* := 4**else** % *Not acceptable*

Turing has one exception to the maximal scanning rule, and this is: two adjacent dots are always considered to be the ".." token. For example, in

var *a*: **array** 1 .. 10 **of real**

the fragment "1 .. 10" is considered to be the three tokens "1", ".." and "10" and *not* the two tokens "1." and ".10".

4.12 Implementation Constraints on Integer, String, and Real Types

Ideally, there should be no implementation constraints on Turing programs (see description of *language* and *implementation constraints* in "Terminology and Basic Concepts"). If there are no implementation constraints, then we call the language *Ideal Turing*. In Ideal Turing, the **int** type has an infinite range of values, and the **real** type has infinite precision and infinite exponent range; that is, **int** and **real** correspond exactly to the mathematical concepts of the integers and the real numbers. Similarly, in Ideal Turing the type **string** (without an explicit length), comprises all sequences of characters, with no limit on length.

Programs written in Ideal Turing can be thought of as mathematical formulae, rather than as instructions for a computer. For example:

```
function factorial (i: int): int
    pre i ≥ 0
    if i=0 then
        result 1
    else
        result i * factorial (i−1)
    end if
end factorial
```

In Ideal Turing, this function gives a definition of "factorial" for all non-negative integers; but note that in a particular implementation of Turing, integer overflow will occur for large values of *i*.

In most practical implementations of Turing, **int** will be limited to a range of integers: *minint* .. *maxint*, and string lengths will be limited to *maxstr*. To support program portability, it is recommended that in all implementations, $minint \leq -(2^{**}31-1)$, $maxint \geq 2^{**}31-1$, and $maxstr \geq 255$. It is recommended that *eos* and *uninitchar* correspond, respectively, to the characters with ordinals of 0 and 128.

In an implementation, each non-zero **real** *r* may be represented by a floating point number of the form:

$$r = f * radix ** e$$

where:

- f is the significant digits part,
- e is the exponent,
- *radix* is the number base of the representation.

It is assumed that f is *normalized*, i.e., if f is not zero then

$$1/radix \leq abs(f) \textbf{ and } abs(f) < 1.0$$

If f is zero then e is also zero. The number of digits of precision of f (in the given radix) may be limited to *numdigits*.

In most practical implementations, the exponent e will be limited to the range *minexp* .. *maxexp*. To support program portability, it is recommended that the equivalent base 10 range of exponents be at least −38 .. 38, i.e., that $minexp * ln(radix)/ln(10) \leq -38$ and $maxexp * ln(radix)/ln(10) \geq +38$.

Floating point operators provide an approximate but repeatable result corresponding to the exact mathematical result. For operators +, −, * and / with operands x and y, let F be the floating point result and let M be the exact result. For non-zero M the *relative* *round off error* is defined as:

$$abs((M-F)/M)$$

(If M is exactly zero, F should also be zero.) Each implementation of Turing is to specify the value of *rreb* (relative round off error bound) such that the round-off error for +, −, * and / never exceeds *rreb*. To support program portability, it is recommended that *rreb* be at most $1e-14$.

For implementations using rounding floating point operators, such as the Digital VAX, *rreb* is:

$$rreb = 0.5 * radix ** (-numdigits + 1)$$

For implementations using chopping floating point operators, such as the IBM 370, *rreb* can be given as:

$$rreb = radix ** (-numdigits + 1)$$

Unfortunately, there are some implementations of floating point in which neither rounding or chopping is consistently carried out; in this case, *rreb* is larger than would be calculated by these formulas.

Each implementation of Turing will provide a standard **include** file called *limits* which will contain definitions of *minint*, *maxint*, *maxstr*, *radix*, *minexp*, *maxexp*, *numdigits* and *rreb*. This file can be included in a Turing program by writing **include** *"%limits"*. This **include** file will also contain the definition of functions that access and modify exponents of a floating point values:

getexp (*r* : **real**): **real**
Returns exponent *e* of *r*. If *r*=0, then *e*=0.

setexp (*r* : **real**, *e* :**int**): **real**
Returns value of *r* with the exponent changed to *e*.
The value of *e* must be in the range *minexp* .. *maxexp*.

4.13 External Subprograms

There is a language extension which allows Turing programs to call subprograms written in other languages. The syntax for this extension is:

external [*overrideName*] *subprogramHeader*

The optional *overrideName* must be an explicit string constant. When it is omitted, the name used for external linking is the subprogram's identifier. If the *overrideName* is present, it is used as the linking name. An implementation may limit the number of characters in the linking name. Conventions for order of and method of parameter passing are implementation dependent.

4.14 Changes in the Turing Language

The Turing language as defined in this Report is slightly modified from the version of the original Turing Report published as [Holt 83, Holt 84]. These modifications have been made so that certain features are more convenient for the user. This version of the Report is somewhat modified and expanded from the original Report to clarify certain descriptions. The description of Turing constructs, in terms of context-free rules, has been made to satisfy LR(1) requirements. The modifications are:

1. Upper and lower case in identifiers and keywords are now distinct. For example, *r* and *R* are now considered to be distinct identifiers. The keywords must now be given strictly in lower case.
2. Sets are now considered to be nonscalars instead of scalars. This allows efficient implementation of long sets, by allowing passing sets by reference.
3. Collection names are now visible inside their declarations, so self referencing collections need not use the **forward** directive.
4. The definitions of *realstr* and *frealstr* were modified so that with *realstr*, small values do not show their exponents. This means that the *putItem i*:*w*:*f* creates nice columns of numbers even if $i < 10$** −3.
5. The range of an increasing **for** statement can now be given as a named type (subrange or enumerated).
6. In a **for** loop, the (optional) **invariant** now must come before the loop body, instead of after.
7. The substring feature now allows each position to be selected by the form * [− *expn*]. The star represents the length of the string. For example, if *s*=''*abc*'' then *s* (*)=''*c*'' and *s* (1 .. *−1)=''*ab*''.
8. The *round* function now rounds ties to the next larger integer instead of to an even value.
9. The *intstr* function now allows omission of the width parameter, so if *i*=25, then *intstr* (*i*)=''25''. Note that *intstr* (*i*)=*intstr* (*i*, 1).
10. It is now clarified that the dimension parameter of *upper* and *lower* is to be present iff the first parameter is a multi-dimensioned array.
11. The rules restricting use of ** (exponentiation) are clarified to be the following three cases.

    a. *i****j* requires $j \geq 0$, allows $i < 0$
    b. *x****i* allows $x < 0$ and $i < 0$
    c. *x****y*, *i****y* requires $x \geq 0$ and $i \geq 0$, allows $y < 0$

    where *i* and *j* are of root type **int** and *x* and *y* are **real**.
12. Semicolons are now allowed following declarations in records and unions.
13. The restriction that a module's **invariant** must not reference imported variables or modules has been removed.
14. Modules and subprograms can no longer be pervasive.

15. The implication operator is now => instead of ->.
16. A **bind** can no longer be declared in the (main) program (except as nested in constructs such as subprograms and **begin**.)
17. Collections can no longer be declared in subprograms.
18. It is clarified that the **forward** type *id* of a collection is inaccessible until declared.
19. External subprograms are introduced as an extension to Turing.
20. The short form for **import** (:) is no longer defined.
21. Carriage return characters are now considered to be white space.

Chapter 5

Overview of the Formal Definition of Turing

This chapter overviews the formal definition of the Turing language. This includes describing the techniques of specifying the language and the advantages and shortcomings of these techniques. Also included are the requirements that an implementation of Turing must meet to be considered correct.

The definition of Turing has two parts; one defines form (or syntax) while the other defines semantics (or meaning). We will first overview the techniques and concepts used for defining syntax.

1 Syntax

This section explains how Turing's syntax is formally specified. We will not be concerned with questions of implementation. The reader is warned that elsewhere, the term "syntax" sometimes means context-free syntax. This book consistently uses the term syntax to mean the specification of the set of programs in a given language. There is a context-free syntax for Turing but it defines only one aspect (the phrase structure) of the syntax of Turing. Note that all strings satisfying Turing's syntax also satisfy Turing's context-free syntax, but not vice versa.

What we want to specify is a function, call it *syn*, that accepts a string that purports to be a Turing program, and tells us whether the string really is a Turing program. Defining this *syn* function is equivalent to defining the syntax of Turing.

We shall assume that there is a finite set Σ of symbols called the *character set*, which are formed into sequences or strings. For Turing, Σ is defined by the set of ASCII (or EBCDIC) characters. We define Σ^* as the set of all (finite) strings of characters from Σ.

We define the boolean function *syn* to map each string S to true or false:

$$syn: \Sigma^* \rightarrow \text{boolean}$$

We say S is a Turing program iff $syn(S)$ is true. In other words, if T is the set of all Turing programs, then $syn(S)$ is true iff $S \in T$.

The definition of Turing's syntax is broken into three parts; these define lexical structure, context-free syntax and context conditions (context sensitive syntax). Corresponding to these parts we define boolean functions called *lex*, *cfs* and *cc*. We can think of *syn* as being defined in terms of these three functions as follows:

$$syn(S) = (lex(S)\ \&\ cfs(S)\ \&\ cc(S))$$

There is a difficulty with this formulation; the trouble is that although *lex* properly accepts string S in Σ^*, *cfs* actually accepts token sequences rather than character strings, and *cc* accepts a representation of the program in terms of its parsed structure. We can rectify this problem by writing instead:

$$syn(S) = (lex(S)\ \&\ cfs(S')\ \&\ cc(S''))$$

where S' is S as mapped into a sequence of tokens, and S'' is S' as mapped into its parsed structure. We will now consider the lexical structure (defined by the *lex* function).

5.1.1 Lexical Structure

The lexical structure of Turing effectively defines a mapping from a string S of characters to a sequence of tokens (also called *lexemes* or *words*). Each *token* is a keyword (such as **procedure**), an identifier (such as *n* and *incomeTax*), an explicit constant (a manifest constant or literal, such as 29 or *"Hello"*) or a special symbol (such as := or +). For example, the sequence of 7 characters "put x+3" is mapped into a sequence of 4 tokens (the keyword **put**, the identifier *x*, the special symbol + and the explicit constant 3).

This mapping defines how to distinguish where the characters representing one token end and where the characters representing the next token begin. It also defines the language's comment convention (note that comments are not considered to be tokens).

The lexical structure of Turing uses *maximal scan*, meaning that a token is extended on the right as long as following characters are potentially part of the token. For example, *put10* is considered to be one token (the identifier *put10*) rather than two tokens (**put** and *10*). There is one exception to maximal scan, that occurs in subrange specification; for example, the sequence 1..10 is considered to be three tokens (1, "..", and 10) rather than the two tokens (1. and .10) that maximal scan would dictate.

Lexical structure can be defined in many ways, and finite automata or regular expressions are commonly used for this purpose. The formal definition of Turing's lexical structure *lex* uses functions instead.

Traditional compiler structure divides a compiler into a series of phases or modules; the first is a *scanner*, which parcels the incoming sequence of characters into tokens. Using an analogous structure, the *syn* function is divided into the conjunction of subfunctions, the first being *lex*. Just as modularizing a compiler helps to make it more manageable, dividing the *syn* definition into parts makes it more understandable. Besides helping make *syn* more understandable, this splitting off of *lex* also aids the compiler writer, by providing a clear specification of the responsibility of the scanner. There is also the advantage that the lexical structure can be significantly changed without affecting the rest of the definition of *syn*; for example, if a character set containing boldface were available, one might want to modify *lex* to require that keywords are written in boldface.

5.1.2 Context-Free Structure

Turing's context-free constraints are split into a distinct subfunction of *syn*, thereby providing analogous advantages to those accrued by splitting off lexical constraints. By long tradition, Pascal-like languages have had a part of their syntax described by context-free (or BNF) grammars, and Turing follows this tradition. It abandons the ::= notation of BNF and uses instead what is hoped to be a more readable notation. For example, instead of

statement ::= reference := expn

the context-free syntax would be written for Turing as:

A *statement* is:
reference := expn

The context-free grammar that is spread, production by production, through the Turing Report, is collected and given as Turing's formal *cfs* in Chapter 6. The original version of the Turing Report (as it appears in the Turing textbook) contains a context-free syntax that was designed for human readability, without regard for whether it satisfied the LR(k) property [Aho 77]. Turing's formal *cfs* is LR(k). Therefore it can be used for automatically generating a parser, and it is guaranteed to be unambiguous.

Although *cfs* is LR(k), it does not follow that an automatically generated LR(k) style parser is inevitable for implementing Turing. The implementor is free to use a method of his/her choice to enforce the syntactic restrictions implied by *cfs*. In fact, the original Turing compiler uses S/SL [Holt 82] rather than an LR(k) technique for not only *cfs*, but also for *lex*, *cc* and code generation. Turing's *cfs* can as well be implemented by a recursive descent parser written in a high level language such as Turing.

There are certain constraints that can be defined by a context-free grammar, but which would cause considerable complexity in the grammar. For example, the constraint that **exit** statements can appear only inside loops can be encoded in the *cfs*, but to do so requires special productions to describe statement lists inside loops. The approach used in preparing Turing's *cfs* was to try to maximize the number of constraints encoded in the *cfs*, except when significant complexity occurred. To avoid this complexity, the responsibility for enforcing the constraint was transferred to context conditions.

5.1.3 Context Conditions

After the constraints implied by *lex* and *cfs* have been imposed, it remains for *cc* (context conditions or context sensitive syntax) to impose further restrictions, such as type compatibility, to complete the definition of *syn*. Traditionally, the syntax constraints of Pascal-like languages have been given by a context-free grammar together with an informal (English) description defining further restrictions. This is the approach taken in the Turing Report.

In the formal definition of Turing we wanted to do better; we wanted to reduce this English description to an unambiguous mathematical specification. By a happy circumstance, J.A. Rosselet was doing his Ph.D. research on formal specification of context conditions at the time Turing was being developed. This provided Turing with an appropriate notation, ADL as developed by Rosselet, for specifying *cc*. More importantly, Rosselet agreed to describe *cc* in ADL; the result of his work is Turing's formally defined context conditions.

ADL is notable in that it divides the job of specifying context conditions into two parts: a context-free or denotation part and a data or axiomatic part. This is analogous to the split in compilers that separates parsing proper from so-called semantic routines, which in S/SL terminology corresponds to the split between S/SL rules and semantic mechanisms. This split makes *cc* easier to understand because it isolates concerns into readily recognizable units within the *cc* specification.

One disappointment in the design of Turing is that its *cc* definition is so large. It does not appear that ADL is to blame for this complexity. Rather, it appears that the context conditions for a language like Turing are themselves inherently complex. Turing's goals of efficient execution (hence reference parameters), practical and convenient use (hence a rich set of language features), information hiding (controlled scope via import/export), and formalizability (hence anti-aliasing and side effect prevention) dictate a fair degree of complexity in its context conditions.

5.1.4 The Complete Definition of Syntax

When we combine the constraints imposed by *lex, cfs* and *cc* we arrive at the definition of *syn* which tells us which strings are to be considered to be Turing programs.

The three subfunctions *lex, cfs* and *cc* successively impose more constraints, thereby eliminating more and more candidates among strings purporting to be Turing programs. Strings satisfying all these constraints satisfy *syn*, and are deemed to be Turing programs.

Recall that *lex, cfs* and *cc* are considered to be boolean functions and do not necessarily correspond to parts of a compiler. On the other hand it is no accident that a multi-pass compiler for Turing can be constructed using passes corresponding to each of these three functions. Indeed, that is the organization of the original Turing compiler.

5.2 Semantics

Once we have a definition of the syntax of Turing, we need to provide semantics for each string that *syn* accepts. In other words, we want a function *sem* that maps each of these strings (each Turing program) to its meaning. If T is the set of all Turing programs and M is the set of all program meanings, then we want:

$$sem: T \rightarrow M$$

There are a number of distinct approaches that can be used for defining semantics, three of the best known being:

Operational semantics. This gives the meaning of programs in terms of the actions or changes of state in an executing program. The Turing report uses an informal version of operational semantics. To formalize this approach, we can use a mathematical notation to effectively define the "next state" function, which specifies the action of each Turing statement or declaration.

Scott-Strachey denotational semantics. This approach is said to be *denotational* because it attaches semantics directly to the syntactic structure of the program [Scott 72, Tennent 76, Stoy 77]. It gives semantics by mapping the program into a function. This function defines the relationship between initial and final program values.

Axiomatic semantics. This approach directly helps in proving programs correct, by providing *proof rules* for each statement. Taken together, these rules determine how to prove the correctness of a program. This approach defines meaning in terms of predicates relating program variables.

Turing is designed to be amenable to formalization by any of these approaches. Development of a Scott-Strachey denotational definition is a highly desirable undertaking, and it is hoped that someone will take it up as a challenge.

The formalization of Turing semantics uses a set of ten *basis statements*. All Turing statements and declarations are defined in terms of these basis statements. The basis statements are in turn defined in terms of both formal operational semantics and axiomatic semantics. Consequently, Turing's formal semantics can be considered to be both operational and axiomatic.

The strength of the operational approach is that it closely models the steps by which real-world computers execute Turing programs. This means that operational semantics can be used as an aid in designing a compiler and, at least in principle, in proving compiler correctness.

There are several advantages of the axiomatic approach to semantics. The most important of these is that it provides a framework for developing correct programs. So, by developing axiomatic semantics for Turing, we are not only defining the language, we are also providing guidance for writing programs.

Another reason for taking an axiomatic approach was our extensive experience with Euclid and its proof rules. P.A. Matthews had produced proof rules for Concurrent Euclid (CE), together with a CE verification condition generator, which transforms a CE program containing assertions into predicates that, when simplified to true, guarantee program correctness. We had carried out a number of correctness proofs for simple CE programs. J.A. Rosselet had worked out techniques for proving correctness of modules written in CE [Guttag 78].

5.2.1 Weakest Preconditions

We adopted E.C.R. Hehner's style of axiomatic semantics, which is presented elegantly and persuasively in his book *The Logic of Programming* [Hehner 84]. His approach, based on Dijkstra's weakest preconditions, provides carefully worked out solutions to problems such as meaningless constructs (e.g. zero division). (Hehner also contributed directly to the work described here by providing many valuable suggestions during the development of the Turing language and its formal semantics.)

We will use an example to explain how weakest preconditions are used in developing programs. This explanation can be skipped by those readers already familiar with weakest preconditions. Suppose we require a statement or program S to accomplish (part of) a goal called R. R is the specification that the program is to meet. It is a predicate involving the variables of our program, and it is the postcondition that is required to be true after S is executed. Suppose our goal is to set variable A (area) equal to L (length) times W (width) and to set V (volume) to H (height) times A; so R is written as:

$$A = L*W \ \& \ V=H*A$$

We will assume that L, W and H are to remain unchanged. We can write statement S to accomplish part of goal R:

$$V := H*A$$

S sets V to $H*A$, and it remains for a preceding statement to set H to $L*W$. In other words the weakest precondition *wp* of S to establish R is $A=L*W$:

$$wp(S, R) = (A=L*W)$$

If S is preceded by statement U, as in

$$U; S$$

then $A=L*W$ is the postcondition for U. If U is the statement:

$$A := L*W$$

then U discharges our last responsibility, so we have

$$wp(U, A=L*W) = \textbf{true}$$

A true precondition means the post condition is guaranteed to be satisfied, i.e., no further statements are required.

Turing's axiomatic semantics consists of the effective definition of the weakest precondition for every Turing program, statement or declaration.

5.2.2 Validity Predicates

There is a difficulty that we have ignored in our example, and it is the possibility that L, W or H might not have a value. If this were the case, we would be dealing with statements that are not valid.

One of the dangers in defining the formal semantics of a practical programming language is that we may give meaning to constructs that would fail under an actual implementation. For example, faithful (checked) implementations of Turing detect uninitialized variables. It is not considered to be *valid* to use an uninitialized variable; so the statement

$$V := H*A$$

is valid only if H and A have been assigned values.

The formal semantics of Turing defines predicates specifying when constructs are valid. In particular, *EXPN* is a validity predicate that is true iff the expression it is applied to is valid. For example, *EXPN* $(24/n)$ is true for initialized variable n iff $n \neq 0$, i.e.,

$$EXPN\,(24/n) = (n \neq 0)$$

Similarly,

$$EXPN\,(H*A) = (INITIALIZED(H)\ \&\ INITIALIZED(A))$$

where *INITIALIZED*(x) is a predicate that is true iff variable x has a value.

In our previous examples, we have simplified *wp* by ignoring validity predicates. Expanding to include them we get:

$$wp(V := H*A, V=H*A\ \&\ A=L*W) =$$
$$(INITIALIZED(H)\ \&\ INITIALIZED(A)\ \&\ A=L*W)$$

In other words, H and A must be initialized for the statement to be valid. Note that the requirement to be valid is included into preconditions by adding in (conjoining) the *EXPN* predicate.

For any particular statement *S*, we can determine the requirements for it to be valid using **true** as a postcondition. With this postcondition (*R*=**true**), the only goal for *S* is to complete without any possibility of failure. In other words, the statement *S* is guaranteed to complete iff it starts in a state satisfying the predicate *wp(S,* **true***)*.

Validity predicates correspond to what are called run-time language constraints in the Turing Report. For example, the Report states that one of these constraints prohibits zero division. Consequently, any attempt to divide by zero is detected at run-time (assuming faithful execution).

5.3 Formal Requirements for Implementations

We will now give the requirements that an implementation must meet to satisfy the definition of Turing. We will assume that each implementation **I** of Turing consists of a compiler **COM** and a run-time (execution) system **RUN**:

I = (**COM, RUN**)

Implementation **I** is correct iff **COM** and **RUN** are correct.

5.3.1 Requirements for Compilers

To be considered correct, compiler **COM** must complete in a finite time after reading any finite string *S* of characters. After **COM** has completed, we may observe:

CL(S): The compiler issues *language constraint messages*, indicating that the string violates the syntax *syn* of Turing. We also call these *syntax error messages*.

CI(S): The compiler issues an *implementation constraint messages*, indicating that due to resource exhaustion, the compilation cannot be completed. We also call these *resource exhaustion messages*.

We will abbreviate *syn(S)*, *CL(S)* and *CI(S)* to simply *syn*, *CL* and *CI* when *S* is obvious. If the string contains a feature that is an extension to Turing (not defined by *syn*), the compiler is expected to issue a message (*CL*). Note that a compiler may issue other messages as well, for example warning that a construct is likely to cause a run-time failure such as a zero division.

An *ideal* compiler would never run out of resources and would satisfy:

Requirement for ideal compiler:

$(CL \neq syn)$ & $\sim CI$

In other words, an ideal compiler issues syntax error messages for exactly those strings that are not acceptable to Turing's formal syntax, and it never issues a resource exhaustion message. Note that there is no formal requirement to translate a Turing program to, say, machine language, although most practical compilers do so. The requirement simply demands that Turing's syntax be correctly enforced.

In the implementation of an actual compiler, resource exhaustion necessarily occurs for some strings. For a compiler to be *useful*, this should occur rarely for programs of interest. To be considered correct, an implemented compiler must satisfy this condition:

Requirement for implemented compiler:

$\sim CI \Rightarrow (CL \neq syn)$

This requirement specifies that a correctly implemented compiler behaves exactly like an ideal compiler, except when there is a resource exhaustion message.

5.3.2 Requirements for Run Time

The axiomatic semantics of Turing, given by weakest preconditions, determines required properties for execution of Turing programs. Consider Turing program S with postcondition R and precondition $P=wp(S, R)$.

When program S with input data d is executed by run-time system **RUN**, we may observe:

RL(d,S): The run-time system issues *language constraint messages*, indicating that the executing program violates a language defined constraint (a validity predicate), such as dividing by zero. These are also called *semantic error messages*.

RI(d,S): The run-time system issues *implementation constraint messages*, indicating that due to resource exhaustion, the execution cannot continue satisfactorily. These are called *resource exhaustion messages*.

RD(d,S): The run-time system indicates, within a finite time, that the Turing program has completed its execution. (The letters *RD* stand for: *run done*).

We will abbreviate these to simply *RL, RI* and *RD* when d and S are obvious. When completion (*RD*) is observed, then the output from the program is called o.

If data d satisfies precondition P, we write

d **sat** P

Similarly when the output o satisfies postcondition R we write o **sat** R.

An ideal run-time system would never run out of resources and would satisfy:

Requirement for ideal run time:

d **sat** $P \Rightarrow (\sim RL \ \& \ RD \ \& \ o$ **sat** $R \ \& \ \sim RI)$

In other words, in an ideal system, if the data satisfies the precondition then the program will terminate without semantic messages producing an output that establishes the postcondition.

Arbitrarily elaborate optimization techniques may be employeed as long as these requirements are met. Note that there is no mention of the method of implementation, whether it is interpretive or direct execution, and no mention of intermediate states or intermediate versions of the output. It is as if we submit our program S with data d to be executed and are allowed to inspect the output o only after program completion.

In an actual implementation, resource exhaustion may occur, so the requirement is:

Requirement for faithful run time:

$\sim RI \Rightarrow (d$ **sat** $P \Rightarrow (\sim RL \ \& \ RD \ \& \ o$ **sat** $R))$

This is similar to the ideal case, but now an exhaustion message RI may notify us that satisfactory completion is not possible.

5.3.3 Unchecked Execution

The requirements given for run time have assumed faithful execution, which detects run-time resource exhaustion (RI) and semantic errors (RL). Semantic errors are guaranteed to be eliminated in the case where the data satisfies a weakest precondition. In this case, a faithful run-time system can omit semantic checks, but it would still need to check for resource exhaustion.

Unchecked execution does not necessarily check for resource exhaustion. If exhaustion cannot or does not occur, then unchecked execution still satisfies *wp*'s requirements for run-time. However, if exhaustion does occur, the program's execution becomes completely unpredictable *without any warning*. We define:

RJ(d,S): Run-time resource exhaustion occurs, and it may or may not be signaled by a message (RI).

RN(d,S): A run-time language constraint is violated, and it may or may not signaled by a message.

To be considered faithful, an implementation must satisfy:

Requirement for faithful run time:

$(RJ \Rightarrow RI)\ \&\ (RN \Rightarrow RL)$

In other words, violations of either language or implementation constraints must be signaled by corresponding messages.

Unchecked run time does not necessarily produce these messages, but must satisfy:

Requirement for unchecked run time:

$\sim RJ \Rightarrow (d\ \mathbf{sat}\ P \Rightarrow (\sim RN\ \&\ \sim RL\ \&\ \sim RI\ \&\ RD\ \&\ o\ \mathbf{sat}\ R))$

This is the same as the requirement for faithful execution except that if exhaustion (*RJ*) occurs, the computation becomes completely unpredictable. This requirement has the unfortunate shortcoming that it can be trivially satisfied by a run-time system that is always considered to have exhausted its resources. This run-time system correctly satisfies our requirement, but is not very useful. To be considered *useful*, a run-time system must rarely exhaust its resources for programs of interest.

5.3.4 Requirements for Interpreters

An interpreter can be implemented which begins executing a Turing program without inspecting the entire program to see if it is syntactically legal. Consider this string of characters that is not actually a Turing program.

```
put "Start"
put1 + 2    % Programmer intended: put 1 + 2
```

An interpreter might execute this string, outputting "Start" and then reporting that the second line is ill-formed. This output is reasonable, but is not defined by either the Report or the formal definition, because this string is not considered to be a Turing program. Ideally, the interpreter will continue executing until it determines that the program is ill-formed; unfortunately, this determination will depend on the implementation and so will not be formalized. The only formalized requirement imposed on an interpreter is the following: if the interpreter is given a (syntactically correct) Turing program then it must satisfy our previously given requirement for run-time systems. If it is given a string that is not actually a Turing program, then the output is implementation dependent.

5.3.5 Consistency of the Axiomatic Semantics and the Report

The axiomatic semantics of Turing takes the point of view that any requirement for Turing execution, other than the ones it implies (as just given above) are superfluous. This point of view assumes that the operational semantics described in the Turing Report satisfies these requirements. In other words, if the Report explains that Turing program *S* (satisfying *syn*) reads data *d* and produces output *o*, and if $P = wp(S,R)$, then the axiomatic semantics considers that the Report is incorrect unless d and o satisfy the above listed requirements.

Conversely, the Turing Report takes the point of view that it authoritatively defines the Turing language. From this point of view, Turing's axiomatic semantics are simply a formalization of what has already been defined by the Report.

The Report and the axiomatic semantics are intended to satisfy each others' requirements. It is best to consider that these two give complementary definitions of Turing, rather than considering one or the other to be the final authority [Donahue 76].

5.4 Goals and Shortcomings

We have discussed the methods used in defining Turing. This section gives goals (hopes and expectations) for these definitions and discusses ways in which these goals were not wholly fulfilled.

The most important goals for a language definition are the three C's: completeness, consistency and clarity. *Completeness* means that all relevant aspects of the language are defined. (We have arbitrarily considered questions of performance and implementation to be irrelevant.) *Consistency* means that there is only one way to interpret the definition. Turing has two definitions, the formal and the informal, and we expect them to be consistent with each other. We also expect implementations to be consistent with these definitions. *Clarity* means that the definition is easy for a person to read and understand. Turing's definitions satisfy these three C's reasonably well, because the language was designed with them in mind. Even so, these definitions have various shortcomings, which will now be discussed.

5.4.1 Completeness

A language definition is incomplete if it fails to specify a particular aspect of a language construct. This omission may be *accidental* or *purposeful*. Whenever accidental omissions have been noticed, they have been rectified. The purposeful omissions from the Turing definitions include:

> *Predefined subprograms.* The formal semantics is simplified by omitting the specifications of most of these.
>
> *Importing.* The formal definition is simplified by assuming that all subprograms have explicit **import** lists, although these are actually optional. Note that it would be possible to generate these lists automatically. The formal context conditions assume that input/output is performed by a module that is imported wherever **put** or **get** is used.

Nonscalar initialization. The definition of the **init** construct for initializing non-scalars is omitted from the formal definitions.

Besides these purposeful omissions, there are two ways in which the two definitions can be considered to be incomplete; these will now be discussed.

First, the axiomatic semantics can be considered to be less complete than the Report's operational semantics, because it provides little information about certain programs. In particular, the axiomatic approach assigns null semantics (a **false** precondition) to programs that may abort or loop infinitely. For example the following program has null axiomatic semantics:

```
loop
  put "HI"
end loop
```

The Report's semantics provide more information in that it specifies that the program keeps printing HI indefinitely (or until resource exhaustion occurs).

Second, the Report and Turing implementations can be considered to be incomplete because of resource exhaustion. For example, according to the formal definition, this program will read any integer and print its successor:

```
var i: int
get i
put i+1
```

However, when $i = maxint$, an implementation will experience resource exhaustion, so the successor cannot be computed. Both the Report and the formal semantics give methods for dealing with resource exhaustion.

5.4.2 Consistency

A language definition may be inconsistent due to ambiguities allowing different interpretations of a particular explanation or formula. Each of the two Turing definitions (informal and formal) should be self consistent, and they should be consistent with each other. We have just discussed the fact that they differ in the meanings they to give the programs which abort or loop infinitely.

One potential for inconsistency between the definitions and implementations is due to approximation of real arithmetic by floating point. The axiomatic semantics can be used to prove that this program prints "HI".

```
if 1e20 + 1e-20 > 1e20 then
  put "HI"
end if
```

However, due to limited precision, an implementation might not print HI. As suggested in the formal semantics, this inconsistency can be eliminated by replacing the axioms defining real arithmetic by axioms defining floating point.

Language extensions, which are defined as any features not defined by the formal definition, are another source of inconsistency. The extensions suggested by the Report are: **external** procedures, the **include** facility, and execution of programs with aliasing or side effects. A particular implementation may provide additional extensions. A Turing compiler should issue warnings when encountering extensions.

5.4.3 Clarity

The goal of clarity requires that a language definition should be easy to read and difficult to misunderstand. A person should be able to grasp the language quickly by studying the definition. He/she should be able to use the definition to quickly and confidently answer questions. These ideals are not easy to attain even with the simplest of languages, and are particularly elusive for applied, general purpose languages such as Turing.

Turing's design had as a goal the simplification of its language definition, but this goal competed with other goals including generality, ease of learning, reliability and efficiency. The result is a language definition that is reasonably understandable compared with definitions of larger languages like PL/I and Ada, but still is more complex than had been hoped for. This remaining complexity strongly suggests the need for further research in both language design and in techniques for formalizing languages.

We have discussed the three C's of language definition; completeness, consistency and clarity. We will now consider the important but less essential goal of aiding the implementor.

5.4.4 Aids to the Implementor

It is desirable that the language definition should simplify the job of implementation. Ideally, the definition should be constructive, meaning that it can be used to mechanically construct an implementation.

Turing's context-free syntax is constructive, in that it can be used to automatically generate an LR(k) parser. However, no other part of Turing's definition is constructive.

Originally, the context conditions, as written in ADL, were constructive and could be executed directly to check context sensitive syntax. However, it was felt that the context conditions could be made clearer and more concise by presenting them in their present almost but not quite constructive form.

Constructivity provides the obvious advantage of an implementation for free. Even if this implementation is too slow or large to be used for production, it can still be extremely useful. It allows the language designer to try out various language features to verify that they behave as expected. It also provides guidance in constructing and verifying the correctness of a production quality implementation.

Although Turing's lexical definitions and context conditions are not strictly constructive, they still provide guidance to the implementor by suggesting interfaces within a compiler. The axiomatic semantics is not constructive and provides little guidance to the implementor. However, the formal operational semantics can be of direct help to the implementor. The operational descriptions in the Report are not constructive, but they are highly suggestive of methods of implementation.

5.5 Problems Exposed by Formal Definition

An important aspect of the process of language formalization is that it exposes poorly designed language features. The difficulty may be uncovered due to the detailed scrutiny required for formalization. It may also be noticed because of problems in trying to precisely describe the feature.

Since the Turing language design was essentially complete by the time formalization was begun, the formalization did not provoke major language modifications. However, it did expose a number of difficulties including:

(1) omissions from the Report,
(2) vagueness in the Report,
(3) minor errors in the language design, and
(4) sources of language complexity.

Generally, the difficulties were related to relatively obscure language feature, and the Report's description of the features glossed over the problem. The most notable features exhibiting problems were: opaque types, forward subprograms, and anti-aliasing constraints. The formalization effort led directly to clarifications in the Report.

This completes the overview of the methods used in formally defining the Turing language.

Chapter 6

Lexical Structure

A Turing program is a sequence of characters. This sequence is made up of *tokens* and *separators*. Each token is a sequence of characters, while a separator is either a white space character (a blank, tab, newline, formfeed, or carriage return) or a comment. If we remove all the separators from a program and put quotation marks around the tokens, we get the *token sequence* that corresponds to the Turing program. For example, the program

```
const x := 5; put x+3
```

has the corresponding token sequence

"const", "x", ":=", "5", ";", "put", "x", "+", "3"

Note that in this chapter we use ordinary characters instead of **boldface** for keywords, such as const, to emphasize the fact that these characters are not in fact distinct from other character in a source program.

The purpose of a lexical structure definition is to define the correspondence between a sequence of characters (which may or may not be a program) and a sequence of tokens. It defines which sequences of tokens, if any, correspond to a given character sequence. If a sequence of characters *s* has a corresponding sequence of tokens, and if the token sequence satisfies Turing's context-free syntax definition and Turing's context condition definition, then *s* is a program.

A lexical structure definition can be either analytic or generative. If it is *analytic*, it describes how to find the token sequence corresponding to a particular character sequence. If it is *generative*, it describes all the character sequences corresponding to a particular token sequence. Analytic definitions formalize the task of a scanner; generative definitions formalize the task of generating a sequence of characters (a program) from a token sequence.

The definition presented here is generative and defines a correspondence between sequences of tokens and sequences of characters. (The Turing Report states that these characters are defined by either the ASCII or EBCDIC character sets.) It is a formalization of the representation used throughout this book. We do not present an algorithm for finding the token sequence represented by a given character sequence, nor for finding a character sequence representing a given token sequence, but it is not difficult to construct such an algorithm based on the definition presented here.

An essential idea behind our definition is the principle of *maximal scan*. In generative terms it can be described as follows. Two tokens can be juxtaposed in a program if and only if the characters of the first token, when extended by the first character of the second token, do not form the beginning of a longer token. Thus, for example, two identifiers can not be juxtaposed because the result would look like a single longer identifier. Nor can the number "3.14159" be juxtaposed with the keyword "else" because the result would begin "3.14159e · · · ", which looks like the beginning of the token "3.14159e-127". But the number "217" can be juxtaposed with the keyword "then", because "217t · · · " does not begin a token. If the result of extending the characters of the first token by the first character of the second does begin a longer token, then separators must be placed between the two tokens when they appear in a program.

6.1 Notation

The notation we use in presenting this definition is a mixture of Turing and standard mathematical notation. We continue to use Turing's notation for strings, but we use certain mathematical notation for sets. Thus we write $\{a, b, c\}$ to denote the set containing the elements a, b, and c; + for set union; * for set intersection; – for set difference; and $\{s \textbf{ in } T \mid P\}$ for the set of all elements of type T which satisfy P.

In addition, we use the concept of a sequence. We write $\langle a, b, c \rangle$ to denote the sequence of length 3 which has a as its first element, b as its second, and c as its third. We write + to denote sequence concatenation; $s(i)$ for the ith element of s (the numbering begins at one); $s(i\,..\,j)$ for the sequence which contains the ith through jth members of s; and $length(s)$ for the length of the sequence. Finally, * is a Kleene star operator: given a set t of elements of some type, t^* is the set of all sequences that can be constructed from the elements of t. Examples:

$$length(\langle\rangle) = 0$$
$$\langle a, b, c \rangle(2\,..\,3) = \langle b, c \rangle$$

$$(\langle\rangle + \langle c, a\rangle + (\langle a, b, c\rangle(2))) = \langle c, a, b\rangle$$
$$\{a, b\}^* = \{\langle\rangle, \langle a\rangle, \langle b\rangle, \langle a, a\rangle, \langle a, b\rangle, \dots \langle a, a, a\rangle, \dots\}$$

We will use single quotes around character literals, e.g., '*x*' and double quotes around string literals, e.g., "*xyz*".

6.2 Tokens

In this section we define two sets: *tokens* and *lexicalUnits*. The set *tokens* consists of all the possible tokens that can appear in a Turing program. The set *lexicalUnits* consists of all tokens together with all separators. These two sets will be used in the next section to define maximal scan.

Each token of Turing is a string whose characters are chosen from either the ASCII or EBCDIC character sets. We call this set *char*. Example tokens are, "loop" or "<=" or "x". In this chapter we write tokens in roman surrounded by quotes, and in the context-free syntax definition we write them in boldface.

We define *tokens* as the union of sets called *integers*, *reals*, *keywords*, etc. (described below). These are the sets of all strings representing explicit integer constants, explicit real constants, keywords, and so on.

tokens = *integers*+*reals*+*strings*+*keywords*
 +*identifiers*+*specialSymbols*

The definition of these various sets is straightforward. For example, the set *integers* is defined by:

integers = { *s* **in** *digits** | *length*(*s*)>0 }
digits = { '0', '1', '2', '3', '4', '5', '6', '7', '8', '9' }

The definitions of the other sets are given below.

We also define a second set called *lexicalUnits* which includes both tokens and separators.

lexicalUnits = *tokens*+*separators*

Lexical units are important because they represent the intermediate step between a sequence of characters and a sequence of tokens. Conceptually, a scanner first finds the lexical units in its input string, then deletes the separators to leave just the tokens.

Here is the definition of all the sets required to define *tokens* and *lexicalUnits*.

integers = { *s* **in** *digits** | *length*(*s*)>0 }

reals = ({ i+e | i **in** integers & e **in** exponents }
+ { i+'.'+d+e | i **in** integers & d **in** digits*
& (e **in** exponents **or** e=“”) }
+ { d+'.'+i+e | i **in** integers & d **in** digits*
& (e **in** exponents **or** e=“”) })

exponents = { e+s+i | i **in** integers & (e='e' **or** e='E')
& (s='+' **or** s='–' **or** s=“”) }

digits = { '0','1','2','3','4','5','6','7','8','9' }

identifiers = ({ l+ldu | l **in** letters & ldu **in** (letters+digits+'_')* }
–keywords)

letters = {“a”,..., “z”, “A”,...,“Z”}

keywords = { “all”, “and”, “array”, “assert”, “begin”,
“bind”, “body”, “boolean”, “case”, “collection”,
“const”, “decreasing”, “div”, “else”, “elsif”,
“end”, “enum”, “exit”, “export”, “false”, “fcn”,
“for”, “forward”, “free”, “function”, “get”,
“if”, “import”, “in”, “include”, “init”,
“int”, “invariant”, “label”, “loop”, “mod”,
“module”, “new”, “not”, “of”, “opaque”,
“or”, “pervasive”, “pointer”, “post”, “pre”,
“proc”, “procedure”, “put”, “real”, “record”,
“result”, “return”, “set”, “skip”, “string”,
“tag”, “then”, “to”, “true”, “type”,
“union”, “var”, “when” }

specialSymbols = { “.”, “..”, “,”, “:”, “;”, “*”, “**”,
“/”, “+”, “–”, “<”, “>”, “>>”, “>>>”,
“=”, “<=”, “>=”, “+=”, “–=”, “*=”, “:=”,
“=>”, “~”, “!”, “?”, “&”, “(”, “)”, “{”, “}”, “[”, “]”, “|” }

strings = { “"” +s+ “"” | s **in** ((char+escapes) – “"” – '\'–newline)* }

escapes = { “\n”, “\N”, “\t”, “\T”, “\f”, “\F”, “\r”, “\R”, “\b”,
“\B”, “\e”, “\E”, “\d”, “\D”, “\"”, “\\” }

separators = whitespace+comments

whitespace = { blank, tab, formfeed, newline, carriagereturn }

$comments = bracketedComments + endOfLineComments$

$bracketedComments = \{ \text{'/*'} + s + \text{'*/'} \mid$
$\quad s \textbf{ in } char^* \ \& \ \sim contains(s, \text{'/*'}) \ \& \ \sim contains(s, \text{'*/'}) \}$

$contains(s, p) = (length(s) \geq length(p)$
$\quad \& \ (s(1 \,..\, length(p)) = p \textbf{ or } contains(s(2 \,..\, length(s)), p)))$

$endOfLineComments = \{ \text{'\%'} + s + newline \mid s \textbf{ in } (char - newline)^* \}$

Note that these definitions imply that each lexical unit contains at least one character.

6.3 Principle of Maximal Scan

A sequence of lexical units satisfies the principle of maximal scan if any element in the sequence, when extended by the first character of the following element, is not the prefix of any lexical unit. This property is expressed formally by the predicate $maxscan(t)$ which is true iff the sequence t of lexical units obeys the property of maximal scan.

$maxscan(t) = (\forall i \textbf{ in } 1 \,..\, length(t) - 1 : \sim prefix(t(i) + t(i+1)(1)))$
$prefix(u) = (\exists v \textbf{ in } char^* : u + v \textbf{ in } lexicalUnits)$

Here "$t(i)+t(i+1)(1)$" appends to the ith element of t the first character of the i+1st element. It would be nice if we could use this definition directly to define Turing's lexical structure, but unfortunately Turing has one exception to the maximal scan rule. The exception is illustrated by the following string:

"1..5"

According to the maximal scan principle, this string should be composed of the two tokens "1." and ".5". However, the Report says that this string is composed of the three tokens "1", "..", and "5". So we must use a modified version of *maxscan* definition which explicitly recognizes this exception. This modified version is used to specify the *lex* function which defines when a sequence of lexical units satisfies Turing's lexical syntax.

$maxscan(t) = (\forall i \textbf{ in } 1 \,..\, length(t) - 1 :$
$\quad \sim prefix(t(i) + t(i+1)(1))$
$\quad \textbf{or } (t(i) \textbf{ in } integers \ \& \ t(i+1) = \text{".."}))$
$lex(t) = (maxscan(t) \ \&$
$\quad \forall i \textbf{ in } 1 \,..\, length(t) : t(i) \textbf{ in } lexicalUnits)$

The third line above explicitly allows a ".." token to follow immediately after an integer.

6.4 Definition of Syn Function

With these definitions for *tokens, lexicalUnits*, and *lex*, we can formalize the *syn* function described in the formal definition overview (Chapter 5). Recall that *syn* defines what a Turing program is; a string *s* is a Turing program iff *syn*(*s*) is true. Formally, *syn* is defined as follows.

syn(*s*) = (∃*s*′ **in** *lexicalUnits** : *s*=*cat*(*s*′) & *lex*(*s*′) & *cfs*(*s*″) & *cc*(*s*″))
where *s*″ **is** *strip*(*s*′)

This says that *s* is a program if there exists a corresponding sequence *s*′ of lexical units (think of *s*′ as *s* divided into lexical units) such that *s*′ satisfies *lex*, and the result *s*″ of removing the separators from *s*′ satisfies Turing's context-free syntax (*cfs*) and context conditions (*cc*). (The definitions of *strip* and *cat* used here are given below.)

For example, let *s* be the following program.

s: "put 4, 17"

Dividing *s* into lexical units gives the following sequence which satisfies the lexical structure definition.

s′: ⟨"put", " ", "4", ",", " ", "17"⟩

Then removing the separators from *s*′ yields the following sequence, which we will see in the next two chapters satisfies Turing's context-free syntax and context conditions.

s″: ⟨"put", "4", ",", "17"⟩

The *cat* function used above takes a sequence of lexical units *s*′ and produces a corresponding sequence of characters *s* by concatenating all the elements of *s*′ together. Let *s*′ be any sequence of lexical units, and let *a* be any lexical unit.

cat(⟨⟩) = ""
cat(⟨*a*⟩+*s*′) = *a*+*cat*(*s*′)

In the line above, the left + creates a sequence of tokens, the first of which is *a* and the rest of which are the tokens in *s*'. The right + creates a character string which is the catenation of the character string *a* and the character string *cat*(*s*′). The *strip* function removes all separators from *s*′ to get *s*″.

strip(⟨⟩) = ⟨⟩
a **in** *separators* ⇒ *strip*(⟨*a*⟩+*s*′)=*strip*(*s*′)
a **not in** *separators* ⇒ *strip*(⟨*a*⟩+*s*′)=⟨*a*⟩+*strip*(*s*′)

This completes the formal definition of Turing's lexical structure. See also the appendix called "A Theorem about Lexical Sequences" for a proof that there is at most one way to break up a character string into a sequence of Turing tokens.

Chapter 7

The Context-Free Syntax of Turing

The context-free (or phrase-structure) syntax of Turing is described using a variation of Backus-Naur Form (BNF), an idea developed by N. Chomsky to describe the syntax of natural languages, and subsequently used by J.W. Backus to describe the context-free syntax of Algol 60 [Naur 60]. In our notation, *tokens* (also called terminals) such as **loop** and **procedure**, are written in boldface, while *non-terminals* (called *syntactic variables* in the Algol 60 Report), such as *declaration* and *setType*, are written in italics. A set of production rules describes how to replace the non-terminal *program* by zero or more tokens to yield a token sequence that satisfies the context-free syntax of Turing.

A *production rule* consists of a single non-terminal (which names the production) and a list of sequences containing tokens and non-terminals, with the meaning that any occurrence of the non-terminal can be replaced by one of the sequences.

The usual method of presenting a context-free grammar has been extended with conventions for using brackets and braces. A sequence in the production can contain the open and close brackets [and], and the open and close braces { and }, which enclose tokens and non-terminals that are optional (if enclosed in brackets) or can occur zero or more times (if enclosed in braces). That is, if "item" is a sequence of tokens, non-terminals, brackets, and braces, then

[item] means that item is optional, and
{item} means that item can occur zero or more times.

Another extension is the convention that the precedence of Turing operators is given in a separate table (and is not encoded in the productions themselves). An appendix gives a technique for mechanically translating these extensions into the standard form for context-free grammars.

The YACC program of S.C. Johnson [Johnson 76] has been used to confirm that the result of applying this translation to the context-free syntax of Turing given below is a set of LALR(1) production rules.

In this chapter we write all tokens in boldface and non-terminals in italics to make clear what is a token and what is a non-terminal.

Note that this definition of the context-free syntax omits the short forms of Turing described at the end of the Turing Report.

7.1 Programs and Declarations

A *program* is:

{*declarationOrStatementInMainProgram*}

A *declarationOrStatementInMainProgram* is one of:

a. *declaration* [;]
b. *statement* [;]
c. *collectionDeclaration* [;]
d. *subprogramDeclaration* [;]
e. *moduleDeclaration* [;]

A *declaration* is one of the following:

a. *constantDeclaration*
b. *variableDeclaration*
c. *typeDeclaration*

A *constantDeclaration* is one of:

a. **const** [**pervasive**] *id* := *expn*
b. **const** [**pervasive**] *id* : *typeSpec* := *initializingValue*

An *initializingValue* is one of:

a. *expn*
b. **init** (*initializingValue* {, *initializingValue*})

A *variableDeclaration* is one of:

a. **var** *id* {, *id*} := *expn*
b. **var** *id* {, *id*} : *typeSpec* [:= *initializingValue*]

A *collectionDeclaration* is one of:

a. **var** *id* {, *id*} : **collection of** *typeSpec*
b. **var** *id* {, *id*} : **collection of forward** *id*

A *variableBinding* is:

bind [**var**] *id* **to** *variableReference* {, [**var**] *id* **to** *variableReference*}

7.2 Types

A *typeDeclaration* is:

type [**pervasive**] *id* : *typeSpec*

A *typeSpec* is one of the following:

a. *standardType*
b. *subrangeType*
c. *enumeratedType*
d. *arrayType*
e. *setType*
f. *recordType*
g. *unionType*
h. *pointerType*
i. *namedType*

A *standardType* is one of:

a. **int**
b. **real**
c. **boolean**
d. **string** [(*compileTimeExpn*)]

A *subrangeType* is:

compileTimeExpn .. *expn*

An *enumeratedType* is:

enum (*id* {, *id*})

An *arrayType* is:

array *indexType* {, *indexType*} **of** *typeSpec*

A *setType* is:

set of *indexType*

An *indexType* is one of:

a. *subrangeType*
b. *enumeratedType*
c. *namedType*

A *recordType* is:

record
id {, *id*} : *typeSpec* [;]
{*id* {, *id*} : *typeSpec* [;] }
end record

A *unionType* is:

union [*id*] : *indexType* **of**
label *compileTimeExpn* {, *compileTimeExpn*} : {*id* {, *id*} : *typeSpec* [;] }
{**label** *compileTimeExpn* {, *compileTimeExpn*} : {*id* {, *id*} : *typeSpec* [;] }}
[**label** : {*id* {, *id*} : *typeSpec* [;] }]
end union

A *pointerType* is:

pointer to *collectionId*

A *namedType* is one of:

a. *typeId*
b. *moduleId* . *typeId*

A *collectionId*, *moduleId*, or *typeId* is an:

id

7.3 Subprograms and Modules

A *subprogramDeclaration* is one of the following:

a. *subprogramHeader*
[*importList*]
subprogramBody
b. **forward** *subprogramHeader*
forwardImportList

c. **body procedure** *id*
    subprogramBody
d. **body function** *id*
    subprogramBody

A *subprogramHeader* is one of:
a. **procedure** *id* [(*parameterDeclaration* {, *parameterDeclaration*})]
b. **function** *id* [(*parameterDeclaration* {, *parameterDeclaration*})]
    [*id*] : *typeSpec*

A *parameterDeclaration* is one of:
a. [**var**] *id* {, *id*} : *parameterType*
b. *subprogramHeader*

A *parameterType* is one of:
a. *typeSpec*
b. **string** (*)
c. **array** *compileTimeExpn* .. * {, *compileTimeExpn* .. *} **of** *typeSpec*
d. **array** *compileTimeExpn* .. * {, *compileTimeExpn* .. *} **of string** (*)

An *importList* is:
import ([[**var**] *id* {, [**var**] *id*}])

A *forwardImportList* is:
import ([[*varOrForward*] *id* {, [*varOrForward*] *id*}])

A *varOrForward* is one of:
a. **var**
b. **forward**

A *subprogramBody* is:
[**pre** *booleanExpn*]
[**init** *id* := *expn* {, *id* := *expn*}]
[**post** *booleanExpn*]
declarationsAndStatements
end *id*

A *moduleDeclaration* is:

module *id*
[*importList*]
[**export** ([**opaque**] *id* {, [**opaque**] *id*})]
[**pre** *booleanExpn*]
{*declarationOrStatementInModule*}
[**invariant** *booleanExpn*
{*declarationOrStatementInModule*}]
[**post** *booleanExpn*]
end *id*

A *declarationOrStatementInModule* is one of:

a. *declaration* [;]
b. *statement* [;]
c. *collectionDeclaration* [;]
d. *subprogramDeclaration* [;]
e. *moduleDeclaration* [;]

7.4 Statements and Input/Output

DeclarationsAndStatements are:

{*declarationOrStatement*}

A *declarationOrStatement* is one of:

a. *declaration* [;]
b. *statement* [;]
c. *variableBinding* [;]

A *statement* is one of the following:

a. *variableReference* := *expn*
b. *procedureCall*
c. **assert** *booleanExpn*
d. **return**
e. **result** *expn*
f. *ifStatement*
g. *loopStatement*
h. **exit** [**when** *booleanExpn*]
i. *caseStatement*

j. **begin**
   declarationsAndStatements
   end
k. **new** *collectionId* **,** *variableReference*
l. **free** *collectionId* **,** *variableReference*
m. *forStatement*
n. **tag** *variableReference* **,** *expn*
o. *putStatement*
p. *getStatement*

A *procedureCall* is a:
   reference

An *ifStatement* is:
   if *booleanExpn* **then**
      declarationsAndStatements
   {**elsif** *booleanExpn* **then**
      declarationsAndStatements}
   [**else**
      declarationsAndStatements]
   end if

A *loopStatement* is:
   loop [**invariant** *booleanExpn*]
      declarationsAndStatements
   end loop

A *caseStatement* is:
   case *expn* **of**
      label *compileTimeExpn* {, *compileTimeExpn*} **:** *declarationsAndStatements*
      {**label** *compileTimeExpn* {, *compileTimeExpn*} **:** *declarationsAndStatements*}
      [**label :** *declarationsAndStatements*]
   end case

A *forStatement* is one of:

a. **for** [*id*] **:** *forRange*
    [**invariant** *booleanExpn*]
    declarationsAndStatements
  end for

b. **for decreasing** [*id*] **:** *expn* **..** *expn*
    [**invariant** *booleanExpn*]
    declarationsAndStatements
  end for

A *forRange* is one of:

a. *expn* **..** *expn*

b. *namedType*

A *putStatement* is:

put [**:** *streamNumber* **,**] *putItem* {**,** *putItem*} [**..**]

A *putItem* is one of:

a. *expn* [**:** *widthExpn* [**:** *fractionWidth* [**:** *exponentWidth*]]]

b. **skip**

A *getStatement* is:

get [**:** *streamNumber* **,**] *getItem* {**,** *getItem*}

A *getItem* is one of:

a. *variableReference*

b. **skip**

c. *variableReference* **: ***

d. *variableReference* **:** *widthExpn*

A *streamNumber*, *widthExpn*, *fractionWidth*, or *exponentWidth* is an:

expn

7.5 References and Expressions

A *variableReference* is a:

reference

A *reference* is one of:

a. *id*
b. *reference componentSelector*

A *componentSelector* is one of:

a. (*exppn* {, *expn*})
b. . *id*

A *booleanExpn* or *compileTimeExpn* is an:

expn

An *expn* is one of the following:

a. *reference*
b. *explicitConstant*
c. *substring*
d. *setConstructor*
e. *expn infixOperator expn*
f. *prefixOperator expn*
g. (*expn*)

An *explicitConstant* is one of:

a. *explicitUnsignedIntegerConstant*
b. *explicitUnsignedRealConstant*
c. *explicitStringConstant*
d. **true**
e. **false**

An *infixOperator* is one of:

a.	+	(integer and real addition; set union; string catenation)
b.	–	(integer and real subtraction; set difference)
c.	*	(integer and real multiplication; set intersection)
d.	/	(real division)

e. **div** (truncating integer division)
f. **mod** (integer remainder)
g. ** (integer and real exponentiation)
h. < (less than)
i. > (greater than)
j. = (equal to)
k. <= (less than or equal to; subset)
l. >= (greater than or equal to; superset)
m. **not=** (not equal)
n. **and** (boolean and)
o. **or** (boolean inclusive or)
p. => (boolean implication)
q. **in** (set membership)
r. **not in** (set non-membership)

A *prefixOperator* is one of:
a. + (integer and real identity)
b. – (integer and real negation)
c. **not** (boolean negation)

All infix operators (including **) associate left-to-right. The precedence of all the operators is as follows, in decreasing order of precedence (tightest binding to loosest binding):

1. **
2. prefix +, –
3. *, /, **div**, **mod**
4. infix +, –
5. <, >, =, <=, >=, **not=**, **in**, **not in**
6. **not**
7. **and**
8. **or**
9. =>

A *substring* is one of:
a. *reference* (*substringPosition* .. *substringPosition*)
b. *reference* (* [– *expn*])

A *substringPosition* is one of:

a. * [– *exppn*]
b. *expn*

A *setConstructor* is one of:

a. *reference* ( )
b. *reference* (**all**)

Note: a fourth form of a substring, *reference* (*expn*), and a third form of a set constructor, *reference* (*expn* {, *expn*}), cannot be distinguished from a *reference* using context-free productions.

The four non-terminals:

id,
explicitUnsignedIntegerConstant,
explicitUnsignedRealConstant, and
explicitStringConstant

are not defined here. Instead, they should be replaced by any member of the sets *identifiers*, *integers*, *reals*, and *strings* respectively, which are defined by the lexical syntax definition.

Chapter 8

Context Conditions: Static Legality of Turing Programs

1 Introduction

The syntax of the Turing language is formally defined by giving its lexical syntax, its context-free syntax, and its context conditions. The formal definition of Turing's context conditions (or *context sensitive syntax* or *static semantics* or *static legality*) will be given here. These context conditions, together with Turing's lexical syntax and context free syntax, define the set of strings that are considered to be Turing programs. These strings (Turing programs) are given meaning by Turing's formal semantics.

Context conditions define syntactically enforceable rules that cannot reasonably be expressed in a context-free grammar. (Certain of these rules could be specified using a context-free grammar, but only with considerable complication.) For example, context conditions enforce the requirements that variables must be declared before they can be used and that the type of an actual parameter must be compatible with its corresponding formal parameter.

Traditionally, context conditions have been defined in prose, as is the case in the Turing Report, which defines Turing's context conditions informally. By contrast, the definition of Turing's context conditions that will be given here is formal.

This definition is divided into two parts. The first part defines types that are used to represent the objects in a Turing program (the variables, procedures, etc.) These types are defined *axiomatically*. The second part uses these types to give the context conditions of each construct of Turing. For example, there are rules defining the static legality of statements and expressions. These rules are *denotational* in that each is associated with a production of the abstract context-free grammar for Turing. This grammar, which is given in an appendix, is like Turing's standard context-free grammar except for simplifications that omit details that are not of concern to context conditions. The notation used for defining these types and rules is a version of Rosselet's Axiomatic Denotational Language (ADL) [Rosselet 84].

The primary goals for the formal definition of Turing's context conditions are clarity, completeness and consistency. The definition is intended to be easily understood by a Turing programmer or a Turing implementor. Its formalisms are chosen to be of immediate help in the development of correct Turing implementations. By the mathematical nature of this definition, it is independent of any particular implementation of Turing. The definition of Turing's context conditions is complete except for certain omissions listed in the section called Incompleteness of Turing's Formal Context Conditions.

Turing's context conditions have been designed with a number of goals in mind. They have been designed to catch programmer errors early in the software development cycle; in particular, they allow a compiler to detect a number of errors that would not be caught until run-time in other languages. They simplify Turing's semantics; in particular, syntactic elimination of side effects and detection of potential aliasing allow a relatively elegant axiomatic semantics for Turing. They improve run-time efficiency, for example, by enforcing type compatibility that would otherwise need to be checked at run-time. They enforce certain restrictions that simplify implementation; for example, they prevent records from having fields whose size cannot be determined until run-time. This set of goals implies that the definition of Turing's context conditions is not particularly short. Another goal, which is at odds with the preceding goals, has been that it should be straightforward for a compiler to enforce the context conditions. (The part of a compiler that carries out this enforcement has traditionally been called *semantic analysis.*)

In principle, the enforcement of context conditions can be deferred until run-time (or can be incorporated into semantics). When Turing is implemented using an interpreter rather than a compiler, this is what is done. However, we assume here that the enforcement precedes run-time (and hence precedes the act of giving semantics to a program).

8.1.1 Overview of the Definition of Context Conditions

This section gives an overview of the formal definition of Turing's context conditions. The definition consists of two parts. The first part consists of ADL type definitions. The second part gives rules defining the context conditions of each Turing construct.

The first part of the definition consists of seven ADL types that are used to represent objects in Turing programs; these are:

1. **TyDef** (type definition). Values of the *TyDef* type represent types written in Turing programs. For example, the Turing type **string**(27) is represented as the *TyDef* value *StringN*, and the Turing type **enum**(*red*, *yellow*, *green*) is represented as the *TyDef* value *Enum*({"*red*","*yellow*","*green*"}).

2. **SyDef** (symbol definition). Values of the *SyDef* type represent symbols written in Turing programs. For example, the symbol *t* declared by **type** *t*: **string**(27), is represented by the *SyDef* value *Type* (*StringN*).

3. **Mode**. This is effectively an enumerated type with three values: *PERVASIVE, nonPERVASIVE* and *fwdSubPgm*. It is used to record whether an identifier is pervasive, is non-pervasive, or is the name of a forward subprogram.

4. **Access** (accessibility). This is effectively an enumerated type with three values: *inaccessible, readOnly* and *VAR*. It is used to record whether an identifier is *inaccessible* (as is the case when bound to **var**), read-only, or *VAR* (can be modified).

5. **Context**. This is used to define the surrounding environment (or scope) for a particular Turing construct. Each declaration adds a new entry to the existing context.

6. **Formals**. This is used to record the list of formal parameters of a subprogram. It maps each parameter's identifier to its symbol definition and is used to enforce parameter compatibility.

7. **ImportSet**. This is used to record the import list of a subprogram or module. It is used to prevent aliasing and to define the context for the bodies of subprograms and modules. It maps each imported identifier to its symbol definition and accessibility.

Two of these seven types, *Mode* and *Access*, are analogous to enumerated types that could be defined in Turing. Two of them, *TyDef* and *SyDef*, are analogous to union types that could be defined in Turing. Two of them, *Formals* and *ImportSet*, are defined as ADL map types. An ADL map type associates a value, such as an identifier, with another value, such as a symbol definition. The remaining type, *Context*, is the most complex of the seven types; it is used to represent the preceding or surrounding declarations in effect at a particular point in a Turing program.

Besides defining these seven types, the first part of the specification of Turing's context conditions defines functions for checking type equivalence, assignability, and parameter compatibility.

The second part of the context conditions for Turing contains the rules defining the static legality for each syntactic construct of Turing. These rules are divided into the following nine sections:

1. **Programs**. The first rule in this section gives the context conditions of an entire program, using other rules and using ADL types to represent objects in the program. This section contains rules that map a program and the "predefined context" to a boolean value. If the value is true, the program satisfies Turing's context conditions, and hence is a Turing program and not just a string that satisfies Turing's lexical structure and context-free syntax. If the value is false or if no value is produced (because an **assert** fails or an **if** construct produces no value), the string violates Turing's context conditions.

2. **Declarations**. A set of rules maps each Turing declaration together with the current context to a new context which includes the declared item(s). If the declaration is statically illegal (does not satisfy Turing's context conditions), then no context is produced.

3. **Types.** A set of rules maps each type appearing in a Turing program to its representation in terms of *TyDef.* If the type is statically illegal, no type definition is produced.

4. **Statements.** A set of rules maps each Turing statement together with the current context to a boolean value. If the value is true, the statement satisfies Turing's context conditions.

5. **Input/output.** This section is like the section on statements.

6. **Expressions.** A set of rules maps each Turing expression together with the current context to the expression's type definition. If the expression is statically illegal, no type definition is produced.

7. **References.** A set of rules maps each Turing reference together with the current context to the reference's symbol definition. If the reference is statically illegal, no symbol definition is produced. Notice that a reference, such as *x.z* (14), produces a symbol definition, while an expression, such as $5+y$, produces a type definition.

8. **Subprograms.** A set of rules maps each subprogram declaration together with the current context to a new context which includes the declared subprogram. If the declaration is statically illegal, then no context is produced.

9. **Modules.** This section is similar to the section on subprograms.

Besides defining these nine sets of rules, the second part defines functions that are used to prevent aliasing and to determine when an expression is considered to be a compile-time expression.

The two parts of Turing's context conditions (its types and its context condition rules) are defined in ADL. ADL is itself divided into two corresponding parts; the first defines types and the second defines rules.

8.1.2 Novel Aspects

This definition is unusual in that it is more complete and formal than that given for most other languages. Formal definitions are sometimes heavily biased toward implementation rather than comprehension. Most attribute grammar definitions have this characteristic. Clarity was never deliberately sacrificed for implementation concerns in developing this definition.

This definition was designed to cater to understanding in several ways: the organization of contextual information into modular types, the organization of rules by context-free syntax productions and the use of terminology and concepts introduced in the Turing Report.

The use of (modular) types and rules allows separate parts of the language to be studied and understood independently. For example, to understand Turing's type equivalence rules, you need study only the rules for Turing type specifications together with the *TyDef* type equivalence operator. (In other words, determine how type specifications are modelled and then examine the type equivalence operator defined on the model.)

The modular organization of the definition is also important when using the definition as the basis for implementation. The definition immediately suggests a modular decomposition for an implementation. If an implementation is to be verified, the modularity of the specification and implementation will allow the correctness proofs to be broken into a number of small largely independent parts.

The definition uses only familiar concepts from elementary mathematics (such as sets, sequences) and programming (such as conditional expressions). No advanced knowledge of methods such as denotational semantics is required to understand the definition. (But note that the definition has a firm mathematical basis.) The definition uses notation from Turing wherever possible so that the reader's intuition about Turing can be applied to the formal definition.

Although the definition makes use of mathematical notations not usually found in programming languages, such as elision (...) and quantification (∀, ∃), it would not be difficult to transform the definition into a program in a functional language (for example, by using recursion rather than quantification). The advantage in doing so is that an executable definition can be evaluated on test cases to confirm that it behaves in accord with our intuition about the language rules. (Parts of an earlier version of the definition were executed by mechanically translating them to LISP code [Rosselet 84].)

8.2 ADL: Axiomatic Denotational Language

This section presents ADL, which is a notation designed for specifying the context conditions of programming languages [Rosselet 84]. The version of ADL described here is intended to maximize the clarity and conciseness of the specification of programming language context conditions. It has been made to be syntactically similar to Turing, so a person familiar with Turing can more easily read context conditions specified in ADL.

An earlier version of ADL is presented in [Rosselet 84]. Also considered there are questions of validation and implementation of specifications written in ADL as well as an in-depth discussion of the use of ADL for formalizing context conditions.

The basis of ADL is a method of defining operators (functions) in a classical mathematical way, using axioms. In the actual use of ADL, in defining Turing's context conditions, ADL has the appearance of a Turing-like language that has functions, but no assignment statements, no side effects, and no procedures. In other words, ADL has the appearance of a *functional* programming language that is closely related to Turing. The basic difference between ADL and Turing lies in the definition of data structures; in ADL, all data structures are (in principle) defined by axioms written in ADL notation, while in Turing, they are based on predefined types such as arrays. However, this difference can often be ignored, because ADL also provides predefined types, such as sets and sequences.

ADL divides the specification of context conditions into two parts, type definitions and context condition rules (in a way suggested by S/SL [Holt 82]). Each type is defined as a collection of operators whose meaning is given by axioms. Each rule is a function given in terms of these operators.

8.2.1 ADL: Basic Concepts

Defining types using axioms. Data types for programming languages can be defined by giving equational axioms that give the relationship among the values of the type [Guttag 78]. We will illustrate this idea using a simple example type called *Set*, which has three operators. The first operator, called *EmptySet*, takes no arguments and hence is best thought of as a *Set* value. The second, called *Insert*, takes an element value (the element type is not specified here) and a *Set* value and produces a new *Set* value. The third, called *In*, takes an element value and a *Set* value and produces value true iff the element is in the set.

We will define this simple *Set* type by giving two axioms:

$$In(e, EmptySet) = \textbf{false} \qquad \text{(Axiom 1)}$$
$$In(e, Insert(e_1, s)) = ((e = e_1) \textbf{ or } In(e, s)) \qquad \text{(Axiom 2)}$$

The first axiom specifies that no element is in the *Set* denoted as *EmptySet*. The second axiom specifies that an element e is in a *Set* denoted as $Insert(e_1, s)$ iff either e and e_1 are the same element or e is in the set s.

In these axioms, e, e_1, and s are *free variables*. They are considered to be universally quantified, so axiom 2 can be written as:

$$\forall\, e, e_1, s\colon In(e, Insert(e_1, s)) = ((e = e_1) \textbf{ or } In(e, s))$$

In this quantification, e and e_1 range over the element values and s ranges over the *Set* values.

An operator is applied to values, for example, we can apply *Insert* to 5 and *EmptySet* to obtain *Insert(5, EmptySet)*. *EmptySet* and 5 are called *operands* or *parameters*, and the entire expression is called an *operation* (or a *call*).

Proving versus evaluating. The two axioms for the *Set* type define the three operators, *EmptySet*, *Insert* and *In*, by specifying the relationship among them. By using these axioms, one can answer questions such as, is the value 25 in the *Set* denoted as *Insert* (13, *Insert* (5, *EmptySet*))? The following sequence answers this question and is a proof that 25 is not the set:

In (25, *Insert* (13, *Insert* (5, *EmptySet*)))	(Use axiom 2)
(25=13) **or** *In* (25, *Insert* (5, *EmptySet*))	(Use integer axiom)
false or *In* (25, *Insert* (5, *EmptySet*))	(Use boolean axiom)
In (25, *Insert* (5, *EmptySet*))	(Use axiom 2)
(25=5) **or** *In* (25, *EmptySet*)	(Use integer axiom)

false or *In* (25, *EmptySet*)	(Use boolean axiom)
In (25, *EmptySet*)	(Use axiom 1)
false	

This sequence of steps *simplifies* the original expression to false, and hence we say that we have *proven* the original expression to be false. We can also consider that these steps *evaluate* the original expression, producing the **false** value.

In ADL each expression's meaning is determined by axioms, and these axioms allow us to manipulate ADL expressions to produce other equivalent expressions.

When using ADL to define Turing's context conditions, we will write all expressions in such a way that they can be evaluated (much as Turing expressions are evaluated), in spite of the fact that ADL's axiomatic foundations do not directly specify the concept of evaluation. The advantage of this style of presentation is that persons familiar with procedural languages such as Turing can immediately understand our definitions written in ADL, without generally being concerned with their axiomatic nature.

Constructor operators. Of the three operators of the *Set* type, two (*EmptySet* and *Insert*) are considered to be *constructor operators* (or simply, *constructors*), while the other operator (*In*) is a *non-constructor operator*. Constructor operators are sufficient for building up all values of the type; for example, the *Insert* and *EmptySet* operators build up the value *Insert* (5, *EmptySet*). Non-constructor operators, such as *In*, are used to extract information about values of the type.

The if operator. We now introduce the ADL **if** operator, which uses a boolean operand to select among two other operands. Written using prefix notation, the **if** operator has the form **if**(b, x, y) and is defined by these two axioms:

if(**true**, x, y) = x
if(**false**, x, y) = y

Instead of prefix notation we will use this Turing-like notation: **if** b **then** x **else** y **end if**.

The third operand can be omitted. When this is done we have an *unbalanced* **if** operation, defined by these axioms:

if true then x **end if** = x
if false then x **end if** = **undefined**

The second axiom specifies that an unbalanced **if** in which b is **false** has an undefined value. (The **undefined** value is defined to be unique, i.e., distinguished from all other values.) This axiom is not necessary as will now be explained. Without this axiom, an expression of the form **if false then** x **end if** cannot be further simplified (evaluated); this unsimplifiable form provides an alternate representation of an undefined value.

ADL supports **elsif** clauses in **if** operations. The form

if b_1 **then** x_1 **elsif** b_2 **then** x_2 ... [**else** y] **end if**

is defined to mean

if b_1 **then** x_1 **else if** b_2 **then** x_2 ... [**else** y] ... **end if end if**

where the **else** clause is optional.

8.2.2 ADL Types

Defining types using axioms. A type is defined in ADL by giving its operators and the relationship among the operators using axioms. For example, the *Set* type can be defined in ADL this way:

type *Set*
constructors
    EmptySet: *Set*,
    Insert (e : *Element*, s : *Set*): *Set*
nonConstructors
    In (e : *Element*, s : *Set*): *Boolean*
        In (e, *EmptySet*) = **false**
        In (e, *Insert* (e_1, s)) = ((e=e_1) **or** *In* (e, s))
end *Set*

This notation for defining a type is analogous to Turing's notation for modules, in which each entry point to the module is characterized by the types of its formal parameters and its result type (assuming the entry is a function). *EmptySet* is an operator that has no operands and produces (or is) a *Set*. *Insert* takes as operands an *Element* and a *Set* and produces a *Set*. These two operators are constructors, meaning that they are not defined by giving a function or axioms for them; rather, their meaning is determined by the axioms given for the type's non-constructor operators. For the *Set* type, *In* is the only non-constructor operator. Its parameters are an *Element* and a *Set* and it produces a boolean.

Other ways to define ADL types. In principle, all ADL types are (or can be) defined in terms of axioms. However, ADL provides two predefined types, booleans and integers, so their axioms need not be given explicitly. ADL also provides notation for defining commonly used types, such as sets and sequences. This additional notation is not really necessary (and was not present in the original version of ADL), because any type defined using the notation can also be directly defined using axioms. However, it provides a convenient way to specify ADL types that are enumerations, union-like types, sets, sequences, record-like types called tuples, and map types.

Enumerations. If a type has only parameterless constructor operators (and no non-constructors), it can be defined in ADL by simply listing the operators separated by commas, for example:

> **type** *Access* $=_{\text{df}}$ *inaccessible, readOnly, VAR*

This is, in fact, the definition of the *Access* type used in Turing's context conditions. The three operators (*inaccessible, readOnly* and *VAR*) are nullary in that they take no parameters; they each denote a value of the *Access* type. Since these are all constructors, they necessarily produce (denote) a value of the *Access* type, so the notation does not require the specification of this result type. Nullary operators can be thought of as values rather than operators, and the *Access* type is analogous to a Turing enumerated type with three values.

Union-like types. A similar ADL notation allows constructor operators to have operands, as in this example:

> **type** *SyDef*
> **constructors**
>   *Constant* (*tyOf* : *TyDef* , *isCompileTime* : *Boolean*),
>   *Variable* (*tyOf* : *TyDef*),
>   ... (other constructor operators) ...
> **nonConstructor**
>   ... (non-constructor operators with their axioms) ...
> **end** *SyDef*

This is, in fact, an abbreviated version of the *SyDef* type used in defining Turing's context conditions. The operator called *Constant* takes a *TyDef* operand and a boolean operand. These operands or parameters are named *tyOf* and *isCompileTime*. The notation allows field selection; for example, if *sy* is an instance of *SyDef* and is an application of the *Constant* operator then *isCompileTime(sy)* denotes its boolean operand. The *SyDef* type can be thought of as a Turing union type in which the operators (*Constant*, *Variable*, ...) are the labels and the fields are the parameters. This ADL form is more general than Turing's union type, in that it allows fields in different variants to have the same names, and fields can be recursive in that a parameter can have the same type that the operator produces. This recursive nature is exploited in *TyDef* by allowing a type definition (such as an array) to have embedded in it other type definitions (the array's element type and subscript type).

Sets. ADL provides a convenient method of defining sets, using Turing-like notation:

set of T	This is the type that is a set of type T
empty	This is an empty set, also written { }
$\{e_1, \ldots, e_n\}$	This is a set, containing elements e_1 through e_n
$s+t$	This is the union of sets s and t

$s*t$	This is the intersection of sets s and t
$s-t$	This is the subtraction of set t from set s; elements of t are removed from s
e **in** s	This is set membership

As in Turing, operators such as + are *overloaded* in that their meaning depends on the types of operands they are applied to.

Sequences. ADL provides a method of defining sequences, using this notation:

seq of T	This is the type that is a sequence of type T
$\langle\rangle$	This is an empty sequence
$\langle e_1, \ldots, e_n\rangle$	This is a sequence of n elements, e_1 through e_n
$length(s)$	This is the length of sequence s
$s+t$	This is the catenation of sequences s and t

This borrows Turing's notation for length and catenation of strings. (Turing's **string** type is essentially the same as the type **seq of** *char*.)

Tuples. *Tuples*, which are sequences of types with field names, are defined using the notation:

$$\langle fieldName_1 \colon T_1, \ldots, fieldName_n \colon T_n\rangle$$

A tuple is analogous to a record in Turing, and $fieldName_i$ can be used to select the i-th field of a tuple value. The field names can be omitted, in which case field selection is not possible.

For example, the following defines a type that is the pairing of a symbol definition with an accessibility:

$$\langle syOf : SyDef, AccessOf : Access\rangle$$

If p is a value of this type, i.e., if p is an expression of this form

$$\langle syOf : sy_p, AccessOf : access_p\rangle$$

then $syOf(p)$ denotes p's first element sy_p and $AccessOf(p)$ denotes p's second element $access_p$.

Maps. Each value of a map type is a sequence of pairs. Since this value is a sequence, the above notation for sequences applies. The first elements of the pairs must be distinct.

map T **of** U	This is the type that is a map from type T to type U. T is called the domain type and U is called the range type.
$m(e)$	This selects the second element of the pair whose first element is e. If m is the map $\langle\langle e_1, v_1\rangle, \ldots, \langle e_n, v_n\rangle\rangle$, then $m(e_i)$ denotes v_i.
$m-n$	This is map subtraction; elements (pairs) of map n are removed from map m

domain(m)	If m is the map $\langle\langle e_1, v_1\rangle, \ldots, \langle e_n, v_n\rangle\rangle$, then this produces the set $\{e_1, \ldots, e_n\}$
p **in** m	If p is an element (a pair) in m, this produces **true**

The *Formals* and *ImportSet* types used in specifying Turing's context conditions are defined as maps. For example, the *Formals* type represents a list of subprogram formal parameters as a mapping from each parameter's identifier to its symbol definition:

type *Formals* $=_{\text{df}}$ **map** *Ident* **of** *SyDef*

8.2.3 Functional Notation

Defining functions. ADL includes functions that map parameter values to result values. For example, this is the definition of a function in ADL:

max (*i* : *integer* , *j* : *integer*): *integer* $=_{\text{df}}$
  if $i > j$ **then** *i*
    else *j*
  end if

As is done for function definitions in Turing, the types of the parameters and result value are specified. A call to a function is defined to be equivalent to the function's body with actual parameters (parenthesized as needed) textually substituted for formal parameters. For example, the call *max* (i+9, 7) is equivalent to **if** $i+9 > 7$ **then** i+9 **else** 7 **end if**.

Preconditions. An operator or function can have a precondition. For example, the *Declare* operator for the *Context* type used in defining Turing's context conditions has this precondition:

pre ~*Visible* (*c* , *id*)

The operator or function is defined only when its precondition is true.

Where clauses. ADL provides a **where** clause for naming expressions. For example, the expression

sum **div** 4 **where** *sum* **is** $x1+x2+x3+x4$

is equivalent to

($x1+x2+x3+x4$) **div** 4

An identifier defined by a **where** clause is equivalent to the textual substitution of its body (parenthesized as needed).

Matching operators. ADL provides a construct called *OperatorOf* , which extracts the operator of a given operation. For example, *OperatorOf* (*Insert* (5, *EmptySet*)) extracts the *Insert* operator. The operators for each ADL type are implicitly defined to be an enumeration (another type), whose values can be compared for equality. For example, we can write

if *OperatorOf* (*s*) = *Insert* **then** ...

This expression between **if** and **then** is **true** iff *Set* value *s* is equivalent to *Insert* (e, s_1) for some e and s_1. The notation

OperatorOf (*a*) **in** $\{b_1, \ldots, b_n\}$

is used as an abbreviation for

OperatorOf (*a*) = b_1 **or** ... **or** *OperatorOf* (*a*) = b_n

Matching operations. A further ADL construct, which is a generalization of *OperatorOf*, allows matching of the operator together with the operands of an operation. The form of this construct is:

Formal = *Operator* (*Operand*$_1$, ... , *Operand*$_n$)

The *Formal* must be a formal parameter of the function or operator in which this construct appears. The construct has the value **true** iff the *Formal*'s operator is the specified *Operator*, i.e., iff *OperatorOf* (*Formal*) = *Operator*. If this is true, then *Operand*$_i$ takes on the value of the i-th operand of *Formal*. For example, if *Formal* is the value *Insert* (5, *EmptySet*), then in

if *Formal* = *Insert* (*e*, *s*) **then** ...

e takes on the value 5, and *s* takes on the value *EmptySet*.

We will now illustrate the use of functions and matching operations by giving an alternate definition of the previously defined *Set* type:

```
type Set
constructors
        EmptySet: Set,
        Insert (e : Element, s : Set): Set
nonConstructors
        In (e : Element, s : Set): Boolean =df
                if s=EmptySet then false
                elsif s=Insert (e1, s1) then (e=e1) or In (e, s)
                end if
end Set
```

In this definition of *Set*, the *In* operator is defined as a function, rather than by giving axioms for it.

Elision. In the definition of context conditions, there are sometimes sequences or sets of values. To shorten the notation for these cases, elision will sometimes be used. For example, the following

$$max(x_1, ..., x_i, ..., x_n)$$

may be elided to

$$max(x_i)$$

This completes the presentation of ADL notation used for defining types. We will now present ADL notation for specifying context condition rules.

8.2.4 ADL Rules for Context Conditions

In order for a string to be a program in a particular language, it must satisfy the language's lexical structure and context-free syntax. In addition, it must satisfy the language's context conditions. This section presents ADL notation for specifying these context conditions.

Rules for expansions. Each production of the language's context-free syntax specifies the expansion of a non-terminal symbol into a right-hand side. For example, the production *Stmt* ::= *Ref*:= *E* specifies that the *Stmt* non-terminal can be expanded into the sequence of symbols *Ref*:=*E*. An ADL rule is used to specify the static legality (context conditions) for each production in the language's context-free syntax. This is a *denotational* approach to specifying context conditions in that each rule *denotes* (or corresponds to) a particular production [Tennent 76].

Any string satisfying the language's lexical structure and context-free syntax will have a *parse tree*. This tree gives the string's phrase structure. Each non-leaf node in this tree corresponds to a production in the context-free syntax. In the case of Turing, the context conditions and the parse tree are simplified by using Turing's *abstract* context-free grammar, which is given in an appendix.

The static legality of each subtree in the parse tree is determined by the ADL rule that is associated with the subtree's root node. For example, consider a subtree representing a Turing expression (the non-terminal E), which expands to a subtraction (to the right-hand side $E-E$). In other words, the subtree's root node corresponds to the production $E ::= E-E$ in Turing's abstract context-free syntax. The ADL rule for this production requires that the operands of the subtraction (the two right-hand E's) must both have numeric types or else must be of equivalent Turing set types.

Each rule is a function that maps the expansion together with the current environment into a value that determines static legality. In many cases, this value's type is boolean, in which case a value of **true** specifies static legality. In other cases, a different type is returned. For example, the rules for expanding expression E return a value whose type is *TyDef*. This value gives the type of the Turing expression. The expression is considered to be statically legal if the rule actually produces a value. If there is no returned value, i.e., if the result is undefined, the expansion is not legal.

For some rules, we use a special notation to isolate context conditions from rule values. We write a context condition as:

assert E_1

where E_1 must be a boolean expression that is true for the context condition to be satisfied. This is followed by notation giving the rule's value:

result E_2

Together these have the same meaning as the notation:

if E_1 **then** E_2 **end if**

Each rule for *Decl* (Turing declaration) produces a result whose type is *Context*. The result value represents the environment to be used for the following declaration or statement. This value is created by adding the information in the declaration to the current environment.

We will illustrate the format for presenting rules using the first four productions of Turing's abstract context-free syntax:

Program::=*S*	(Production 1)
S::=*Decl S*	(Production 2)
S::=*Stmt S*	(Production 3)
S::=*empty*	(Production 4)

The non-terminal *S* represents a sequence of declarations and statements, and these productions specify that the non-terminal called *Program* expands to such a sequence.

The ADL rules for productions 2 through 4 are given here

(a)	**RHS for**	**Context Condition**
(b)	*S*	*cc* (*RHS* : *S* , *c* : *Context*): *boolean*
(c)	*Decl S*	*cc* (*S* , *cc* (*Decl* , *c*))
(d)	*Stmt S*	*cc* (*Stmt* , *c*) & *cc* (*S* , *c*)
(e)	*empty*	... (all symbols in *c* must be resolved) ...

Lines (a) and (b) are the heading for the rules given in lines (c), (d) and (e). The heading specifies that these rules are for expansions of *S* and that each rule accepts a right-hand side *RHS* for *S* and a context *c* and produces a boolean.

Line (c) is the rule for the production *S*::=*Decl S*. It requires that the expansion of *Decl* must be legal in context *c*, i.e., that *cc* (*Decl* , *c*) must be defined. It also requires that the right-hand side *S* must be statically legal in the context given by *cc* (*Decl* , *c*).

Line (d) is the rule for $S ::= Stmt\ S$. It requires that both *Stmt* and S must be statically legal in context c. Line (e), whose rule is not given here, requires that all symbols declared in c must be resolved, e.g., that bodies must be given for forward procedures.

Rule for entire program. The context conditions for production 1 are specified this way:

RHS for *Program*	**Context Condition** $cc\,(RHS: Program, c: Context)$: *boolean*
S	$cc\,(S, c)$

This requires that S (the declarations and statements making up *Program*) must be statically legal in context c. Context c specifies Turing's predefined subprograms, as will now be explained.

The static legality of an entire program is defined to be:

$$cc\,(Program, c_{prefined})$$

The initial context, $c_{predefined}$, specifies the parameter types and return types of Turing's predefined subprograms. (We will not actually specify the value of $c_{prefined}$ for Turing.) This context is passed down to parameter c in the rule for the first production ($Program ::= S$). In turn, further rules are invoked until the entire tree is checked. The entire *Program* is statically legal (satisfies the language's context conditions) iff a final result of **true** is produced.

Matching productions. ADL provides notation, called *IsProduction*, that produces the value true if a specified non-terminal expands to a given right-hand side. For example, in

if $IsProduction\,(E_1 ::= E_2 - E_3)$ **then** ...

the value between **if** and **then** is true iff non-terminal E_1 expands in the program of interest into the form $E_2 - E_3$. If this is true, E_2 and E_3 subsequently represent elements of this expansion.

This completes the presentation of ADL. ADL will now be used to formalize Turing's context conditions.

8.3 ADL Types to Represent Turing Objects

This section and the next (Sections 8.3 and 8.4) contain the formal specification, written in ADL, of the context conditions of the Turing language. Section 8.3 gives the definition of the seven ADL types (*TyDef, SyDef, Mode, Access, Context, Formals,* and *ImportSet*) used to represent objects in Turing programs. The reader may wish to review the discussion of these seven in "Overview of the Definition of Context Conditions" (Section 8.1.1). Section 8.4 gives rules defining static legality (context conditions) for each production in Turing's abstract context-free syntax. As was explained in Section 8.1.1, these rules are divided into nine sections (on programs, declarations, types, statements, input/output, expressions, references, subprograms, and modules).

In Section 8.4, the rules are presented in such a way that in many cases it is not necessary to know the seven ADL definitions in detail. For example, the rule for the static legality of uses of the **div** operator, given in Section 8.4.6, has this form:

RHS for	**CONTEXT CONDITION**
E	*cc (RHS : E, c : Context): TyDef*
E_1 **div** E_2	**assert** *isNumeric* (ty_1) & *isNumeric* (ty_2) **result** *Int*

Without looking beyond this rule, it is clear that the types of the two operands of **div** must be numeric and that the type of the result is an integer. A more comprehensive interpretation of the rule requires, of course, explicit definition of terms such as ty_1. Each of ty_1 and ty_2 is an abbreviation (see Section 8.4) which expands into an explicit ADL expression. The *isNumeric* function is a non-constructor operator of *TyDef* and *Int* is a constructor operator of *TyDef* (see Section 8.3.1.) The reader may wish to look ahead to the rules (Section 8.4.4 "Statements" and Section 8.4.6 "Expressions" are recommended) to gain some intuition about the use of ADL before studying the present section.

The presentation of the seven ADL types (representing objects in Turing programs) is organized into sections, as listed in this table:

Section	**ADL Type**	**Operator, Function or Constant**
8.3.1	*TyDef*	*Int, Real, Boolean, String, StringN, StringStar, Enum, EnumIds, NameOf, Subrange, Root, isCompileTime, Array, IndexOf, ElementOf, Record, FieldsOf, Union, TagNameOf, TagType, Set, BaseOf, Collection, Pointer, Opaque, Forward, tyTagOf, EquivType, Assignable, RootType, isNumeric, NumericType, isScalar, isIndex, isDynamicType, isDynamicArray, compileTime, dummyTy*
8.3.2	*SyDef*	*Constant, Variable, Type, Procedure, Function, Module, ProcedureCall, syTagOf, compileTime, dummySy*
8.3.3	*Mode*	*PERVASIVE, nonPERVASIVE, fwdSubPgm*
8.3.4	*Access*	*inaccessible, readOnly, VAR,* ≤

8.3.5	*Context*	*EmptyContext, Declare, Close, DecreaseAccess, LocalContext, loopNesting, Visible, AccessOf, syOf, ModeOf, LocallyDeclared, SymbolOfContext, Closed, Resolve, AssertionContext, NestedInLoop*
8.3.6	*Formals*	*DeclareFormals, CompatibleParams, EquivFormals*
8.3.7	*ImportSet*	*ImportContext, MergeImports, TransitiveImports, TransitiveROImports, ResolveFwdImports, SideEffect*

8.3.1 Representing Types

In defining Turing's context conditions, *TyDef* is used to represent a type appearing in a Turing program. The non-terminal *T* expands to produce Turing types. The context condition rule for this expansion produces a value of type *TyDef*, which represents the particular Turing type.

We now give examples of the representations, followed by the definition of *TyDef*. The reader will probably wish to refer to these examples when studying the rules (for *T* as well as for *ForRange* and *ParameterType*) that produce *TyDef*. The types written on the left in Turing are represented as shown on the right:

TYPE IN TURING	REPRESENTATION USING *TyDef*
int	*Int*
real	*Real*
boolean	*Boolean*
string	*String*
string(27)	*StringN* (string length bound is not represented)
string(*)	*StringStar*
enum(*red*, *green*, *blue*)	*Enum*({''*red*'', ''*green*'', ''*blue*''}, *typeId*) (The *typeId* uniquely identifies the type, see below)

1 .. 3	*Subrange* (*Int*, *compileTime*) (Lower, upper bounds are not represented)
array 1 .. 3, 5 .. 7 **of real**	*Array* (⟨*Subrange* (*Int*, *compileTime*), *Subrange* (*Int*, *compileTime*)⟩, *Real*) (An array is *dynamic* if it has a non-compile-time index.)
record *i*, *j*: **int** **end record**	*Record* (⟨⟨"*i*", *Int*⟩, ⟨"*j*", *Int*⟩⟩, *typeId*) (The *typeId* uniquely identifies the record, see below
union *tg*: 1 .. 3 **of** **label** 1: *x*: **real** **label** 3: *s*: **string** **end union**	*Union* (⟨⟨"*x*", *Real*⟩, ⟨"*s*", *String*⟩⟩, *typeId*, "*tg*", *Subrange* (*Int*, *compileTime*)) (Label values are not represented. The *typeId* uniquely identifies the union, see below
set of 1 .. 3	*Set* (*Subrange* (*Int*, *compileTime*))
var *d*: **collection** **of int**	*Collection* (*Int*, "*d*")
pointer to *d*	*Pointer* ("*d*")
export(... , **opaque** *u*, ...)	*Opaque* (*typeId*, *typeDef*) (The *typeId* uniquely identifies the type. The *typeDef* is the definition of type *u*.)
var *d*1: **collection of** **forward** *v*	*Forward* ("*v*") (This represents unresolved type *v*, which is the type of the elements of *d*1. Type *v* must be resolved by a subsequent declaration. Collection *d*1's type is represented as follows.) *Collection* (*Forward* ("*v*"), "*d*1")

These examples illustrate each of the constructor operators of *TyDef*. The non-constructor operators for *TyDef* are used to answer questions such as: is a type numeric, or is one type assignable to another. Enumerated, record and union types definitions are distinguished by unique names. These names consist of the name under which the type was declared, prefixed by the names of all the closed scopes surrounding the declaration. A more complete explanation of unique type naming is given in Section 8.4, where the assumptions made by the definition are discussed. Here is the definition of *TyDef*.

type *TyDef*

constructors

Int, Real, Boolean, String, StringN, StringStar,

Enum (*EnumIds* : **set of** *Ident* , *NameOf* : *Ident*),

Subrange (*Root* : *TyDef* , *isCompileTime* : *Boolean*)
  pre *tyTag* (*Root*) **in** {*Int* , *Enum* },

compileTime $=_{\text{df}}$ **true**, % Constant used in representing subranges

Array (*IndexOf* : **seq of** *TyDef* , *ElementOf* : *TyDef*)
  pre $\forall\, i$: *isIndex* (t_i) **where** $\langle t_1, \cdots, t_n \rangle$ **is** *IndexOf* ,

Record (*FieldsOf* : **map** *Ident* **of** *TyDef* , *NameOf* : *Ident*),

Union (*FieldsOf* : **map** *Ident* **of** *TyDef* , *NameOf* : *Ident* ,
  TagNameOf : *Ident* , *TagType* : *TyDef*),

Set (*BaseOf* : *TyDef*)
  pre *isIndex* (*BaseOf*),

Collection (*ElementOf* : *TyDef* , *NameOf* : *Ident*),

Pointer (*NameOf* : *Ident*),

Opaque (*NameOf* : *Ident*, *tyOf* : *TyDef*),

Forward (*NameOf* : *Ident*)

nonConstructors

tyTagOf (*ty* : *TyDef*) : (*Int* , *Real* , *Boolean* , *String* , *StringN* , *StringStar* ,
  Enum , *Subrange* , *Array* , *Record* , *Union* , *Set* ,
  Collection , *Pointer* , *Opaque* , *Forward*) $=_{\text{df}}$
  OperatorOf (*ty*) % Returns operator that constructed *ty*

EquivType (ty_1: *TyDef* , ty_2: *TyDef*): *Boolean* $=_{\text{df}}$
  % Returns true if the two types are equivalent
  ... Definition given in section "Type Equivalence and Assignability,
  Parameter Compatibility" ...

Assignable (ty_1: *TyDef* , ty_2: *TyDef*): *Boolean* $=_{df}$
    % Returns true if the right type is assignable to the left
    ... Definition given in section "Type Equivalence and Assignability,
    Parameter Compatibility" ...

RootType (*ty* : *TyDef*): *TyDef* $=_{df}$
    % Returns the root type of the given type
    if *tyTag* (*ty*) **in** {*StringN* , *StringStar* } **then** *String*
    elsif *tyTag* (*ty*) = *Subrange* **then** *Root* (*ty*)
    else *ty*
    end if

isNumeric (*ty* :*TyDef*): *Boolean* $=_{df}$
    % Returns true if the type is int or real
    tyTag (*ty*) **in** {*Int, Real*}

NumericType (ty_1: *TyDef* , ty_2: *TyDef*): *TyDef* $=_{df}$
    % Returns the common type for combining the two numeric types
    pre *isNumeric* (ty_1) & *isNumeric* (ty_2)
    if *tyTag* (ty_1) = *Real* **or** *tyTag* (ty_2) = *Real*
    then *Real*
    else *Int*
    end if

isScalar (*ty* : *TyDef*): *Boolean* $=_{df}$
    % Returns true if the type is a scalar
    tyTag (*ty*) **in** {*Int, Real, Boolean, Subrange, Enum, Pointer*}

isIndex (*ty* : *TyDef*): *Boolean* $=_{df}$
    % Returns true if the type is an index type
    tyTag (*ty*) **in** {*Subrange, Enum*}

isDynamicType (*ty* : *TyDef*): *Boolean* $=_{df}$
    % Returns true if the type is a dynamic type
    tyTag (*ty*) = *StringStar* **or** *isDynamicArray* (*ty*)

isDynamicArray (*ty* : *TyDef*): *Boolean* $=_{df}$
    % Returns true if the type is a dynamic array
    tyTag (*ty*) = *Array* & $\exists\, i$: (*tyTag* (t_i) = *Subrange*
    & ~*isCompileTime* (t_i)) **where** $\langle t_1, \ldots, t_n \rangle$ **is** *IndexOf* (*ty*)

dummyTy $=_{df}$ *Int*   % Constant used in *dummySy*

end *TyDef*

8.3.2 Representing Symbols

In defining Turing's context conditions, *SyDef* is used to represent a symbol definition. The non-terminal *Ref* expands to produce a Turing reference. The context condition rule for this expansion produces a value of type *SyDef*, which represents the definition of the reference. Values of type *SyDef* also appear within values of type *Context*, where they represent declared symbols. We now give examples of these representations, followed by the definition of *SyDef*. The reader will probably wish to refer to these examples when studying the rules (for *Ref* as well as for *Decl*) involving *SyDef*. The symbols written on the left in Turing are represented as shown on the right:

TURING CONSTRUCT	REPRESENTATION USING SyDef
var *i* : **int**	*Variable* (*Int*)
var *x*, *z* : **real**	*Variable* (*Real*) (Same for *x* and *z*)
const *j* : **int** := 2	*Constant* (*Int*, *compileTime*)
const *y* :=*sin* (*x*)	*Constant* (*Real*, ~*compileTime*)
type *t* : **real**	*Type* (*Real*)
type *t*2 : **record** *i*, *j* : **int** **end record**	*Type* (*Record* (⟨⟨"*i*", *Int*⟩, ⟨"*j*", *Int*⟩⟩, "*t*2"))
procedure *p* (*k* : **int**, **var** *w* : **real**) **import**(*x*, **var** *z*) ... **end** *p*	*Procedure* (⟨⟨"*k*", *Constant* (*Int*, ~*compileTime*)⟩, ⟨"*w*", *Variable* (*Real*)⟩⟩, ⟨⟨"*x*", ⟨*Variable* (*Real*), *readOnly*⟩⟩, ⟨"*z*", ⟨*Variable* (*Real*), *VAR*⟩⟩⟩)
function *f* (*k* : **int**, *w* : **real**) *r* : **string** **import**(*x*, *z*) ... **end** *f*	*Function* (⟨⟨"*k*", *Constant* (*Int*, ~*compileTime*)⟩, ⟨"*w*", *Constant* (*Real*, ~*compileTime*)⟩⟩, ⟨⟨"*x*", ⟨*Variable* (*Real*), *readOnly*⟩⟩, ⟨"*z*", ⟨*Variable* (*Real*), *readOnly*⟩⟩⟩, "*r*", *String*)

module *m*	*Module* (c_{export},
import(x, **var** z)	⟨⟨"x", ⟨*Variable* (*Real*), *readOnly*⟩⟩,
export(q, **opaque** t)	⟨"z",⟨*Variable* (*Real*), *VAR*⟩⟩⟩)
type t : **int**	**where**
procedure q	c_{export} **is**
(**var** i : **int**)	*Declare* (c_1, "t", *Type* (*Opaque* ("t", *Int*)),
i:=i+1	*nonPERVASIVE*, *readOnly*),
end q	c_1 **is**
end m	*Declare* (*EmptyContext*, "q",
	Procedure (⟨⟨"i", *Variable* (*Int*)⟩⟩, ⟨ ⟩)
	nonPERVASIVE, *readOnly*)
p (5, y)	*ProcedureCall*
	% Note that a function call
	% is represented using *Constant* (...)

These examples illustrate each of the constructor operators of the type called *SyDef*. The only non-constructor operator for *SyDef* is *syTagOf*, which returns the operator used in constructing the symbol definition. Here is the definition of *SyDef*:

type *SyDef*

constructors

Constant (*tyOf* : *TyDef*, *isCompileTime* : *Boolean*),

compileTime $=_{df}$ **true** % value used as parameter to Constant

Variable (*tyOf* : *TyDef*),

Type (*tyOf* : *TyDef*),

Procedure (*FormalsOf* : *Formals*, *ImportsOf* : *ImportSet*),

Function (*FormalsOf* : *Formals*, *ImportsOf* : *ImportSet*,
ResultId : *Ident*, *ResultType* : *TyDef*),

Module (*ExportsOf* : *Context*, *ImportsOf* : *ImportSet*),

ProcedureCall
% This is used to represent a call to a procedure. It is produced
% by the rule for *Ref* when the reference is a procedure call.

nonConstructors

syTagOf (*sy*: *SyDef*) : (*Constant*, *Variable*, *Type*, *Function*,
Procedure, *Module*, *ProcedureCall*) $=_{\text{df}}$
OperatorOf (*sy*) % Operator that constructed *sy*

dummySy $=_{\text{df}}$ *Constant* (*dummyTy*, *compileTime*)

end *SyDef*

8.3.3 Representing Mode

When an identifier is declared, it has associated with it one of three modes. The *PERVASIVE* mode applies to constants and types that are explicitly declared to be pervasive. All other identifiers are considered to be *nonPERVASIVE*, with the exception of the declarations of forward subprograms, whose mode is *fwdSubPgm*. For examples, see the section on Representing Context. The definition of *Mode* is simply:

type *Mode* $=_{\text{df}}$ *PERVASIVE*, *nonPERVASIVE*, *fwdSubPgm*

Note the following use of boldface, lower case and upper case:

pervasive is a Turing keyword.
Pervasive is a non-terminal, which produces **pervasive** or empty.
PERVASIVE is one of the three *Mode* values.

8.3.4 Representing Access

The declarations of variables, modules and **var** binds have *VAR* accessibility. All other declarations have *readOnly* accessibility, with the following exceptions: forward types and forward imported subprograms are *inaccessible*, as are **init** constants in subprogram bodies (they are made *readonly* during the scope of assertions). Note that an identifier can be visible but *inaccessible*. This occurs, for example, when the identifier is the object of a **var bind**; this implies the identifier cannot be redeclared, but neither can it be referenced. The definition of *Access* is simply:

type *Access* $=_{\text{df}}$ *inaccessible*, *readOnly*, *VAR*

Note the following use of bold face, lower case and upper case:

var is a Turing keyword.
Var is a non-terminal, which produces either **var** or empty.
VAR is one of the three *Access* values.

The *LessEq* function determines the ordering among accessibilities.

$$\begin{aligned} &LessEq(access_1: Access, access_2: Access): Boolean =_{df} \\ &\qquad access_1 = inaccessible \\ &\qquad \textbf{or } (access_1 = readOnly \ \& \ (access_2 = readOnly \textbf{ or } access_2 = \text{VAR})) \\ &\qquad \textbf{or } (access_1 = \text{VAR} \ \& \ access_2 = \text{VAR}) \end{aligned}$$

We will use the notation "≤" instead of *LessEq*:

$$access_1 \leq access_2 =_{df} LessEq(access_1, access_2)$$

8.3.5 Representing Context

The context for a particular Turing construct represents the identifiers that the construct is allowed to access together with the attributes of those identifiers. (A context corresponds to a symbol table in a compiler.) The context represents additional information such as identifiers that are hidden due to closed scopes (modules and subprograms). The *Declare* operator creates a new context which includes the new identifier with its symbol definition, mode, and accessibility, as illustrated by the following examples. Many of the Turing constructs shown here have previously been used to illustrate *SyDef* values (see Representing Symbols).

TURING CONSTRUCT	REPRESENTATION IN CONTEXT *c*
var *i* : **int**	*Declare* (*c*, "*i*", *Variable* (*Int*), *nonPERVASIVE*, *VAR*)
const pervasive *x* : **int** := 2	*Declare* (*c*, "*x*", *Constant* (*Int*, *compileTime*), *PERVASIVE*, *readOnly*)
type *t* : **real**	*Declare* (*c*, "*t*", *Type* (*Real*), *nonPERVASIVE*, *readOnly*)
procedure *p* ... **end** *p*	*Declare* (*c*, "*p*", *Procedure* (...), *nonPERVASIVE*, *readOnly*)
module *m* ... **end** *m*	*Declare* (*c*, "*m*", *Module* (...), *nonPERVASIVE*, *VAR*)
forward procedure *q*	*Declare* (*c*, "*q*", *Procedure* (...),

(i: **int**) **import**(i)	*fwdSubPgm*, *readOnly*)
import(**forward** g)	*Declare* (c, ''g'', *Procedure* (...), *fwdSubPgm*, *inaccessible*)
var d : **collection of int**	*Declare* (c, ''d'', *Variable* (*Collection* (*Int*, ''d'')), *nonPERVASIVE*, *VAR*)
var $d1$: **collection of forward** v	*Declare* (c_u, ''$d1$'', *Variable* (*Collection* (*Forward* (''v''), ''$d1$'')), *nonPERVASIVE*, *VAR*) **where** c_u **is** *Declare* (c, ''v'', *Type* (*Forward* (''v'')), *nonPERVASIVE*, *inaccessible*)
bind var j **to** i	*DecreaseAccess* (c_j, ''i'', *inaccessible*) **where** c_j **is** *Declare* (c, ''j'', *Variable* (*Int*), *nonPERVASIVE*, *VAR*)

These examples illustrate use of the *Declare* operator; they may be referred to when reading the rules for declarations. Here is the definition of *Context*:

type *Context*

constructors

EmptyContext: *Context*,
    % The empty context contains no declarations

Declare (c: *Context*, *id*: *Ident*, *sy*: *SyDef*, *mode*: *Mode*, *access*: *Access*)
    : *Context*
    pre ~*Visible* (c, *id*),
    % Creates a new context that includes the identifier with its
    % symbol definition, mode and accessibility. The precondition
    % disallows re-declaration of visible identifiers.

Close (c: *Context*, *sy*: *SyDef*): *Context*,
    % The *Close* operator is used to hide identifiers for a closed scope.
    % It is used to close the context for the bodies of subprograms and
    % modules. Imported identifiers are re-declared using the
    % *ImportContext* operator, defined in "Representing Import Sets."

% The symbol definition *sy* represents the subprogram or
% module; it is retrieved using the *SymbolOfContext* operator.

DecreaseAccess (*c* : *Context*, *id*: *Ident*, *access*: *Access*): *Context*
pre *Visible* (*c* , *id*) & *access* ≤*accessOf* (*c* , *id*,
% The *DecreaseAccess* operator decreases the accessibility of
% the identifier to *access*. This is used to make "bound to"
% identifiers inaccessible, and to define *ImportContext*.

LocalContext (*c* : *Context*, *isInLoop*: *Boolean*): *Context*,
% Marks a context as local. This is used for two purposes. First is to
% specify where forward subprograms and types must be
% resolved. Second is to designate whether the context is in a loop;
% this determines where an **exit** statement can appear.

loopNesting $=_{df}$ **true** % Use as second argument
% in *LocalContext*

nonConstructors

% Note that $Declare_1$, $Close_1$, $DecreaseAccess_1$
% and $LocalContext_1$ are defined in the final
% part of this definition of *Context*

Visible (*c* : *Context*, *id*: *Ident*): *Boolean* $=_{df}$
% Returns true if the identifier is visible
if *c* = *EmptyContext* **then** **false**
elsif $c = Declare_1$ **then** $id = id_1$ **or** $Visible(c_1, id)$
elsif $c = Close_1$ **then** $Visible(c_1, id)$
& $ModeOf(c_1, id) = PERVASIVE$
elsif $c = DecreaseAccess_1$ **then** $id = id_1$ **or** $Visible(c_1, id)$
elsif $c = LocalContext_1$ **then** $Visible(c_1, id)$
end if

AccessOf (*c* : *Context*, *id*: *Ident*): *Access* $=_{df}$
pre *Visible* (*c* , *id*)
% Returns the accessibility of the identifier
if *c* = *EmptyContext* **then undefined**
elsif $c = Declare_1$ **then** **if** $id = id_1$
then $access_1$
else $AccessOf(c_1, id)$
end if
elsif $c = Close_1$ **then** $AccessOf(c_1, id)$

```
    elsif c = DecreaseAccess₁ then  if id = id₁
                                    then access₁
                                    else AccessOf (c₁, id)
                                    end if
    elsif c = LocalContext₁   then  AccessOf (c₁, id)
    end if

syOf (c : Context, id : Ident): SyDef =df
    pre Visible (c, id)
    % Returns the symbol definition of the identifier
    if    c = EmptyContext    then  undefined
    elsif c = Declare₁        then  if id = id₁
                                    then sy₁
                                    else syOf (c₁, id)
                                    end if
    elsif c = Close₁          then  syOf (c₁, id)
    elsif c = DecreaseAccess₁ then  syOf (c₁, id)
    elsif c = LocalContext₁   then  syOf (c₁, id)
    end if

ModeOf (c : Context, id : Ident): Mode =df
    pre Visible (c, id)
    % Returns the mode of the identifier
    if    c = EmptyContext    then  undefined
    elsif c = Declare₁        then  if id = id₁
                                    then mode₁
                                    else ModeOf (c₁, id)
                                    end if
    elsif c = Close₁          then  ModeOf (c₁, id)
    elsif c = DecreaseAccess₁ then  ModeOf (c₁, id)
    elsif c = LocalContext₁   then  ModeOf (c₁, id)
    end if

LocallyDeclared (c : Context, id : Ident): Boolean =df
    % Returns true if the identifier has been declared in
    % the local context; see the LocalContext operator.
    if    c = EmptyContext    then  false
    elsif c = Declare₁        then  id = id₁ or LocallyDeclared (c₁, id)
    elsif c = Close₁          then  false
    elsif c = DecreaseAccess₁ then  LocallyDeclared (c₁, id)
    elsif c = LocalContext₁   then  false
    end if
```

```
SymbolOfContext (c : Context ): SyDef =df
        pre Closed (c )
        % Returns the symbol definition of the closed scope;
        % this symbol definition is a Function, Procedure or Module .
        % This is used to determine a function's result type, which is
        % used in checking result statements. See the Close operator.
        if    c = EmptyContext          then  undefined
        elsif c = Declare_1             then  SymbolOfContext (c_1)
        elsif c = Close_1               then  sy_1
        elsif c = DecreaseAccess_1      then  SymbolOfContext (c_1)
        elsif c = LocalContext_1        then  SymbolOfContext (c_1)
        end if

Closed (c : Context ): Boolean =df
        % Returns true if the context has been closed.
        % See the Close operator.
        if    c = EmptyContext          then  false
        elsif c = Declare_1             then  Closed (c_1)
        elsif c = Close_1               then  true
        elsif c = DecreaseAccess_1      then  Closed (c_1)
        elsif c = LocalContext_1        then  Closed (c_1)
        end if

Resolve (c : Context , id : Ident , sy : SyDef ,
            mode : Mode , access : Access ): Context =df
        pre Visible (c , id )
        % Creates a context in which the identifier's previous declaration is
        % replaced by one with the new symbol definition, mode and access.
        if    c = EmptyContext          then  undefined
        elsif c = Declare_1             then  if id = id_1
                                              % Replace old declaration by new
                                              then Declare (c_1, id, sy , mode , access )
                                              else Declare (c_resolve , id_1, sy_1,
                                                    mode_1, access_1)
                                              end if
        elsif c = Close_1               then  Close (c_resolve , sy_1)
        elsif c = DecreaseAccess_1      then  DecreaseAccess (c_resolve , id_1, access_1)
        elsif c = LocalContext_1        then  LocalContext (c_resolve , isInLoop_1)
        end if
        where c_resolve is Resolve (c_1, id, sy , mode , access )
```

```
AssertionContext (c : Context): Context =df
        % Creates a context to be used by assertions (pre, post and invariant).
        % This context makes init constants be accessible (readOnly);
        % in most contexts these constants are inaccessible,
        if    c = EmptyContext          then  EmptyContext
        elsif c = Declare_1             then  % Inaccessible constants
                                              % become readOnly
                                              Declare (c_assert, id_1, sy_1, mode_1, access)
                                              where access is
                                                 if syTag (sy_1) = Constant
                                                 then readOnly
                                                 else access_1
                                                 end if
        elsif c = Close_1               then  c_1
        elsif c = DecreaseAccess_1      then  DecreaseAccess (c_assert, id_1, access_1)
        elsif c = LocalContext_1        then  LocalContext (c_assert, isInLoop_1)
        end if
        where c_assert is AssertionContext (c_1)

NestedInLoop (c : Context): Boolean =df
        % Returns true if this context is nested in a loop;
        % see the LocalContext operator. This is used to determine where
        % exit statements can appear.
        if    c = EmptyContext          then  false
        elsif c = Declare_1             then  NestedInLoop (c_1)
        elsif c = Close_1               then  false
        elsif c = DecreaseAccess_1      then  NestedInLoop (c_1)
        elsif c = LocalContext_1        then  isInLoop_1 or NestedInLoop (c_1)
        end if

    where
    Declare_1          is Declare (c_1, id_1, sy_1, mode_1, access_1),
    Close_1            is Close (c_1, sy_1),
    DecreaseAccess_1   is DecreaseAccess (c_1, id_1, access_1),
    LocalContext_1     is LocalContext (c_1, isInLoop_1)

end Context
```

8.3.6 Representing Formals

Lists of formal parameters for subprograms are represented using a type called *Formals*. This type maps the identifier of each formal parameter to its corresponding symbol definition. The symbol definition's tag (or operator) will be one of *Variable, Constant, Function* or *Procedure*. For example, the list of formal parameters shown on the left is represented as shown on the right.

TURING CONSTRUCT	REPRESENTATION OF FORMAL PARAMETERS
procedure *p*	
(**var** *x* : **real**,	⟨⟨"*x*", *Variable* (*Real*)⟩,
int *i* : **int**,	⟨"*i*", *Constant* (*Int*, ~*compileTime*)⟩,
procedure *q*	⟨"*q*", *Procedure* (
(**var** *j*, *k* : **int**))	⟨⟨"*j*", *Variable* (*Int*)⟩,
	⟨"*k*", *Variable* (*Int*)⟩⟩,
	empty)⟩⟩ % Empty import set

This example illustrates the use of the *Formals* type in a recursive fashion; one of the formal parameters of *p* is parametric procedure *q*, which in turn has a list of formal parameters. The reason for including parameter names in the representation is that a forward subprogram header (which introduces parameter names) may be given separately from the subprogram body, where the parameter names must be declared in the body scope. Here is the definition of *Formals*:

type *Formals*

constructors

map *Ident* **of** *SyDef*
% A *Formals* value is a sequence of pairs, each of the form ⟨*id*, *sy*⟩.
% An identifier is mapped to its corresponding symbol definition.

nonConstructors

DeclareFormals (*formals* : *Formals*, *c* : *Context*): *Context* $=_{df}$
% Declare each identifier in the list of formals.
% This is used to create the context for a subprogram's body.
Declare (c, id_i, sy_i, *nonPERVASIVE*, $access_i$) % Declare each formal
where $\langle\langle id_1, sy_1\rangle, \ldots, \langle id_n, sy_n\rangle\rangle$ **is** *formals*, % Defines n, id_i, sy_i
$access_i$ **is**
if *syTagOf* (sy_i) = *Variable*
then *VAR*
else *readOnly*
end if

CompatibleParams (*formals* : *Formals*, % Formal parameters
    $\langle E_1, \dots, E_n \rangle$: **seq of** *E*, % Actual parameter expressions
    c : *Context*): *Boolean* $=_{df}$
  % Returns true if each formal's type is compatible with its
  % corresponding actual's type. This function is used in determining
  % if actual parameters can be passed to corresponding formals.
  ... Definition is in the section on Type Equivalence, Assignability
    and Compatibility ...

EquivFormals ($formals_A$: *Formals*, $formals_B$: *Formals*): *Boolean* $=_{df}$
  % Returns true if the types of each pair of formal parameters
  % are equivalent. This function is used by the function
  % *CompatibleParams* in determining if a subprogram
  % can be passed as an actual parameter.
  ... Definition is in the section on Type Equivalence, Assignability
    and Compatibility ...

end *Formals*

8.3.7 Representing Import Sets

The import list for each module or subprogram is represented using the type called *ImportSet*. In the definition of Turing's context conditions, it is assumed that all import lists for Turing subprograms are given explicitly, although the language actually allows the omission (and hence automatic creation) of these lists.

An import list is represented by pairing each imported identifier with its symbol definition and accessibility. The *ImportSet* type is defined as a **map** to allow the identifier to be used as the key for looking up the corresponding symbol definition and accessibility. The following examples illustrate the representation of import lists. It is assumed that the imported identifiers in this example are declared as:

```
var x : int
const j := 2
type t : real
procedure p (var w : real)
        import(x)
        ...
end p
```

TURING CONSTRUCT	**REPRESENTATION USING** *ImportSet*
import(**var** x, j)	$\langle\langle$"x", $\langle sy_x, VAR\rangle\rangle$, $\langle$"j", $\langle sy_j, readOnly\rangle\rangle\rangle$
import(t)	$\langle\langle$"t", $\langle sy_t, readOnly\rangle\rangle\rangle$
import(p, **forward** q)	$\langle\langle$"p", $\langle sy_p, readOnly\rangle\rangle$, $\langle$"q", $\langle sy_q, inaccessible\rangle\rangle\rangle$ % Declaration for q has not yet appeared. % This import list is in a **forward** subpgm header.

where sy_x **is** *Variable* (*Int*),
sy_j **is** *Constant* (*Int*, *compileTime*),
sy_t **is** *Type* (*Real*),
sy_p **is** Procedure(% Params then imports
$\langle\langle$"w", *Variable* (*Real*)$\rangle\rangle$,
$\langle\langle$"x", $\langle$*Variable* (*Int*), *readOnly*$\rangle\rangle\rangle\rangle$,
sy_q **is** *dummySy*

If *imps* is the representation of the first import list above, then *imps* ("x") is the pair $\langle sy_x, VAR\rangle$ and *AccessOf* (*imps* ("x")) is *VAR*. The transitive imports of the third import set given above, i.e.,

TransitiveImports ($\langle\langle$"p", $\langle sy_p, readOnly\rangle\rangle$,
$\langle$"q", $\langle sy_q, inaccessible\rangle\rangle\rangle$, $\langle\,\rangle$)

includes the imports of both p and q; assuming q has no imports, this transitive import set is

$\langle\langle$"p", $\langle sy_p, readOnly\rangle\rangle$,
$\langle$"q", $\langle sy_q, inaccessible\rangle\rangle$,
$\langle$"x", $\langle sy_x, readOnly\rangle\rangle\rangle$.

The definition of the *TransitiveImports* operator is perhaps the most complex part of the formal definition of Turing's context conditions. *ImportSet* is defined as follows:

type *ImportSet*

constructors

map *Ident* **of** $\langle$*syOf* : *SyDef*, *AccessOf* : *Access*$\rangle$

nonConstructors

ImportContext (*imps* : *ImportSet* , *c* : *Context*): *Context* $=_{df}$
% A new context is created by importing the identifiers in *imps*
% from context *c* . After applying the *Close* operator to a context,
% *ImportContext* is used to create the context for the bodies of
% modules and subprograms.
if ∃ *id*, *sy*, *access* : (⟨*id*, ⟨*sy*, *access*⟩⟩ **in** *imps*)
then *ImportContext* (*imps* – ⟨*id*, ⟨*sy*, *access*⟩⟩, *DecreaseAccess* (*c* , *id* , *access*))
else *c* % Case for empty *imps*
end if

MergeImports ($imps_1$: *ImportSet*, $imps_2$: *ImportSet*): *ImportSet* $=_{df}$
% The two import lists are merged, using the maximum of an
% identifier's accessibilities when the identifier appears in
% both lists. *MergeImports* is used in defining *TransitiveImports* .
if ∃ *id*, *sy*, $access_1$, $access_2$:
(⟨*id*, ⟨*sy*, $access_1$⟩⟩ **in** $imps_1$
& ⟨*id*, ⟨*sy*, $access_2$⟩⟩ **in** $imps_2$)
then ⟨⟨*id*, ⟨*sy*, *maxAccess* ⟩⟩⟩
+ *MergeImports* ($imps_1$ – ⟨⟨*id*, ⟨*sy*, $access_1$⟩⟩⟩,
$imps_2$ – ⟨⟨*id*, ⟨*sy*, $access_2$⟩⟩⟩)
else $imps_1$+$imps_2$
end if
where *maxAccess* **is**
if $access_2 \le access_1$ **then** $access_1$ **else** $access_2$ **end if**

TransitiveImports (*imps* : *ImportSet* , *transImps* : *ImportSet*): *ImportSet* $=_{df}$
% This creates a transitive import set, which is the union of all
% direct or indirect imports of *imps*, except that the accessibility of
% each identifier is the maximum of its accessibilities in any of the
% imports. The second parameter, *transImps*, accumulates the
% transitive imports. *transImps* is used in the operator definition
% to handle circular imports among mutually recursive subprograms.
if ∃ *id*, *sy*, *access* : (⟨*id*, ⟨*sy*, *access*⟩⟩ **in** *imps*)
then *TransitiveImports* (*imps* – ⟨*id*, ⟨*sy* , *access* ⟩⟩,
MergeImports (*transImps* , *importsDueToSy*))
else *transImps*
end if
where
importsDueToSy **is**
⟨⟨*id*, ⟨*sy*, *access* ⟩⟩⟩
+ *indirectImportsOfSy* ,

```
indirectImportsOfSy is
        if syTag(sy) in {Function, Procedure}
          or (syTag(sy) = Module & access = VAR)
        then TransitiveImports(newIndirectImports, transImpsWithId)
        elsif syTag(sy) = Module & access = readOnly
        then TransitiveROImports(newIndirectImports, transImpsWithId)
        else ⟨⟩   % Null sequence
        end if,
newIndirectImports is
        % Indirect imports not previously seen
        ResolveFwdImports(ImportsOf(sy)) − transImps,
transImpsWithId is
        MergeImports(transImps,⟨⟨id, ⟨sy, access⟩⟩⟩)

TransitiveROImports(imps: ImportSet, transImps: ImportSet): ImportSet =df
    % This creates a transitive read-only import set. All
    % accessibilities become readOnly. This operator is used
    % when considering read-only modules.
    if ∃ id, sy, access: (⟨id, ⟨sy, access⟩⟩ in imps)
    then TransitiveROImports(imps − ⟨id, ⟨sy, access⟩⟩,
            MergeImports(transImps, ROImportsDueToSy))
    else transImps
    end if
    where
    ROImportsDueToSy is
            ⟨⟨id, ⟨sy, readOnly⟩⟩⟩
            + indirectROImportsOfSy,
    indirectROImportsOfSy is
            if syTag(sy) in {Function, Procedure, Module}
            then TransitiveROImports(newIndirectImports, transImpsWithId)
            else ⟨⟩   % Null sequence
            end if,
    newIndirectImports is
            % Indirect imports not previously seen
            ResolveFwdImports(ImportsOf(sy)) − transImps,
    transImpsWithId is
            MergeImports(transImps,⟨⟨id, ⟨sy, access⟩⟩⟩)

ResolveFwdImports(imps: ImportSet, c: Context): ImportSet =df
    % This creates an import set like imps except that each unresolved
    % forward import (marked as inaccessible) has its symbol
    % definition and accessibility resolved using context c.
    % id must not be inaccessible in context c (indicating that
```

```
% id has not been declared).
if ∃ id, sy, access: (⟨id, ⟨sy, access⟩⟩ in imps)
then resolvedImp+ResolveFwdImports(imps − ⟨id, ⟨sy, access⟩⟩)
else ⟨ ⟩   % Null sequence
end if
where
resolvedImp is
   if access_id ≠ inaccessible then
       if access = inaccessible
       then ⟨⟨id, ⟨syOf(c, id), AccessOf(c, id)⟩⟩⟩
       else ⟨⟨id, ⟨sy, access⟩⟩⟩
       end if
   else undefined
   end if

SideEffect(imps: ImportSet): Boolean =df
   % Returns true if there is VAR accessibility in the import set.
   % When checking for side effects in functions, imps must be the
   % function's transitive import set.
   ∃id in domain(imps): AccessOf(imps(id)) = VAR

end ImportSet
```

8.3.8 Type Equivalence and Assignability, Parameter Compatibility

This section gives functions that determine equivalence and assignability of types and parameter compatibility.

EquivType determines when two types are considered to be equivalent from the point of view of context conditions. There is also a "validity predicate" called *EQV* that determines further type equivalence requirements that are specified in Turing's formal semantics. The *EQV* predicate enforces run-time constraints, such as the requirement that equivalent arrays must have equal bounds. Any check involving computed values, such as array bounds, is enforced by validity predicates rather than by context conditions. Together, *EquivType* and *EQV* define type equivalence as specified by the Turing Report. Similarly, the *Assignable* function given here together with the *ASN* validity predicate determine assignability as specified by the Turing Report.

The *EquivType* and *Assignable* functions are actually operators of the type *TyDef*. Throughout this section, we will use the notation:

```
                    tyTagA is tyTag (tyA),
                    tyTagB is tyTag (tyB)

EquivType (tyA : TyDef , tyB : TyDef ): Boolean =df
   % EquivType determines when actual parameters can be passed to
   % VAR formal parameters and is used in defining assignability.

   % First is the special case of string(*)
   (RootType (tyA) = String & RootType (tyB ) = String
   & (tyTagA = StringStar or tyTagB = StringStar ))

   or % General case, requiring same type tags
   (tyTagA = tyTagB      % For example, both types may be arrays
   &
   if   tyTagA in {Int,
                   Real,
                   Boolean }          then true

   elsif tyTagA = Subrange            then EquivType (Root (tyA ), Root (tyB ))
                                         % The check for equal bounds is
                                         % done by validity predicates

   elsif tyTagA = Array               then EquivType (IndexOf (tyA ), IndexOf (tyB ))
                                         & EquivType (ElementOf (tyA ),
                                             ElementOf (tyB ))

   elsif tyTagA = String              then true  % But string and string(n ) are
                                            % not equivalent for any n

   elsif tyTagA = StringN             then true  % The check for equal lengths is
                                            % done by validity predicates

   elsif tyTagA = Set                 then EquivType (BaseOf (tyA ), BaseOf (tyB ))

   elsif tyTagA in {Pointer,
                    Opaque,
                    Forward}          then NameOf (tyA ) = NameOf (tyB )

   elsif tyTagA in {Enum,
                    Record,
                    Union }           then NameOf (tyA ) = NameOf (tyB )
                                         & NameOf (tyA ) ≠ NullId
                                         % Two unnamed types (arising from unnamed
```

% function result types or unnamed union
% tag types) are not equivalent.

elsif $tyTag_A = Collection$ **then false** % Never assign or pass
% collections

end if)

Assignable (ty_A: *TyDef*, ty_B: *TyDef*): *Boolean* $=_{df}$
% Type ty_B is assignable to ty_A if the two are equivalent types or
% if ty_A is *Real* and ty_B is *Int*.
EquivType (*RootType* (ty_A), *RootType* (ty_B))
or ($tyTag_A = Real$ & $tyTag_B = Int$)

CompatibleParams (*formals*: *Formals*, % Formal parameters
$\langle E_1, \ldots, E_m \rangle$: **seq of** *E*, % Actual parameter expressions
c: *Context*): *Boolean* $=_{df}$
% Returns true if each formal's type is compatible with its
% corresponding actual's type

$n = m$ % Same number of formals and actuals
& $\forall i$: % For each formal/actual pair
if $syTag(sy_{fi}) = Constant$ **then** *CompatibleConstParams*
elsif $syTag(sy_{fi}) = Variable$ **then** *CompatibleVarParams*
elsif $syTag(sy_{fi}) = Function$
or $syTag(sy_{fi}) = Procedure$ **then** *CompatibleSubpgmParams*
end if
where
$\langle\langle id_{f1}, sy_{f1}\rangle, \ldots, \langle id_{fn}, sy_{fn}\rangle\rangle$ **is** *formals*, % Defines n, id_{fi}, sy_{fi}

ty_{fi} **is** $tyOf(sy_{fi})$, % Type of the formal

CompatibleConstParams **is**
Assignable (ty_{fi}, ty_i)
& ($isDynamicType(ty_i) \Rightarrow isDynamicType(ty_{fi})$),

CompatibleVarParams **is**
isProduction (E_i ::= Ref_i)
& *isProduction* (Ref_i ::= id_i $selectors_i$)
& *EquivType* (ty_{fi}, ty_{ai})
& $syTag(sy_{ai}) = Variable$
& $AccessOf(c, id_i) = VAR$
& ($isDynamicType(ty_{ai}) \Rightarrow isDynamicType(ty_{fi})$),

CompatibleSubpgmParams **is**
  $isProduction\,(E_i ::= Ref_i)$
  $\&\ isProduction\,(Ref_i ::= id_i\ selectors_i)$
  $\&\ syTag\,(sy_{ai}) = syTag\,(sy_{fi})$ % Both fcns or both procs
  $\&\ EquivFormals\,(FormalsOf\,(sy_{fi}), FormalsOf\,(sy_{ai}))$
  & **if** $syTag\,(sy_{fi}) = Function$
    then $EquivType\,(ResultType\,(sy_{fi}), ResultType\,(sy_{ai}))$
    end if,

ty_i **is** $cc\,(E_i, c)$,
    % Type of an expression that is an actual

sy_{ai} **is** $cc\,(id_i\ selectors_i, c)$,

ty_{ai} **is** $tyOf\,(sy_{ai})$, % Type of a reference that is an actual
    % Note that ty_i is the type of the expression
    % that is the actual so $ty_i = RootType\,(ty_{ai})$

$EquivFormals\,(formals_A : Formals, formals_B : Formals) : Boolean =_{df}$
  % Returns true if the types of each pair of formal parameters
  % are equivalent. *EquivFormals* is used by the function
  % *CompatibleParams* in determining if a
  % subprogram can be passed as an actual parameter.

  $m = n$ % Same number of formals in each list
  $\&\ \forall\, i$: % For each pair of formals
   $(syTag\,(sy_{Ai}) = syTag\,(sy_{Bi})$
   & **if** $syTag\,(sy_{Ai})$ **in** $\{Constant, Variable\}$ **then**
      % Constant or *VAR* parameter
      $EquivType\,(ty_{Ai}, ty_{Bi})$
    elsif $syTag\,(sy_{Ai}) = Function$ **then** % Fcn as parameter
      $EquivFormals\,(FormalsOf\,(sy_{Ai}), FormalsOf\,(sy_{Bi}))$
      $\&\ EquivType\,(ResultType\,(sy_{Ai}), ResultType\,(sy_{Bi}))$
    elsif $syTag\,(sy_{Ai}) = Procedure$ **then** % Proc as parameter
      $EquivFormals\,(FormalsOf\,(sy_{Ai}), FormalsOf\,(sy_{Bi}))$
    end if)
  where
  $\langle\langle id_{A1}, sy_{A1}\rangle, \ldots, \langle id_{Am}, sy_{Am}\rangle\rangle$ **is** $formals_A$, % Defines m, id_{Ai}, sy_{Ai}
  $\langle\langle id_{B1}, sy_{B1}\rangle, \ldots, \langle id_{Bn}, sy_{Bn}\rangle\rangle$ **is** $formals_B$ % Defines n, id_{Bi}, sy_{Bi}

8.4 Rules Defining Context Conditions

Section 8.3 has given the ADL type definitions that are used to represent objects in Turing programs. Section 8.4 will now give rules, written in ADL, that specify the static legality of each syntactic construct of Turing. Together, these type definitions and rules (in Sections 8.3 and 8.4) constitute the formal definition of Turing's context conditions.

We will give a rule for each production in Turing's abstract context-free syntax (see appendix) that defines its static legality. Each rule is a function that maps to a boolean or to a type representing the object characterized by the production. If a rule produces false or fails to produce a value, the construct is considered to be illegal (does not satisfy Turing's context conditions). Otherwise, the construct is considered to be legal.

Each production has an associated rule (a function). We say the production *denotes* its corresponding function. For example, the context condition for expression E is written is $cc\,(E\,,\,c\,)$, where c is a context. In this example, the function maps E with c to a type definition (*TyDef*) that represents the type of E.

The presentation of the rules is organized into nine sections (8.4.1 through 8.4.9). The non-terminals with result types covered by these sections are listed in the following table.

Section	Non-Terminal	Result Type for Rule
8.4.1	*Program, S*	*Boolean*
8.4.2	*Decl*	*Context*
	Pervasive	*Mode (PERVASIVE or nonPERVASIVE)*
8.4.3	*T* (type)	*TyDef*
	fields	**map** *Ident* **of** *TyDef*
8.4.4	*Stmt*	*Boolean*
	ForRange	*TyDef*
8.4.5	*Stmt* (**get** and **put**)	*Boolean*
	GetItem, *PutItem*	*Boolean*
	ExpnOrStar	*Boolean*
8.4.6	*E* (expression)	*TyDef*
8.4.7	*Ref*	*SyDef*
	Selectors, *Selector*	*SyDef*
8.4.8	*Decl* (subprogram)	*Context*
	ResultSpec	⟨*Ident*, *TyDef*⟩
	ParameterList	*Formals*
	ParameterDecl	*Formals*

	ParameterType	*TyDef*
	Imports, *ImportItem*	⟨*Context*, *ImportSet*⟩
	Body	*Boolean*
8.4.9	*Decl* (module)	*Context*
	Exports	*Context*

References versus expressions. As can be seen from this table, the result of a reference *Ref* is a symbol definition *SyDef* while the result of an expression *E* is a type definition *TyDef*. There is potential for confusion between references and expressions that will be discussed in terms of this example:

var $A, B: 1..10$

...

$A := B$

The *Stmt* non-terminal expands to produce an assignment statement, which has the form *Ref*:=*E*. This implies that in this example assignment, *A* is a *Ref* while *B* is an *E*. The context condition rule for reference *A* produces a symbol definition whose type is 1..10. By contrast, the rule for expression *B* produces an integer type definition (*Int*). The question is, why do *A* and *B* seem to have different types, when the two are declared using the same type 1..10. The answer to this question is that the type of an expression such as *B* is the *root* type of the corresponding reference. So, when *B* is a reference, its type is 1..10, but when it is an expression, its type is *Int*. (In other words, the left-hand value's type is the declared type 1..10, but the right-hand value's type is the root type *Int*.) This difference between references and expressions is formally specified in the context condition rules for *Ref* and *E*. One of the reasons for this difference is that the type of reference *B* specifies the set of values (1..10) that can be assigned to *B*, while the type of expression *B* specifies the class of operations (integer +, –, *, etc.) that apply to *B*'s value.

Abbreviations. A set of abbreviations will be used to shorten the context condition rules and to make them easier to read:

ty_E	is $cc(E, c)$,	$tyTag_E$	is $tyTagOf(ty_E)$,
ty_0	is $cc(E_0, c)$,	$tyTag_0$	is $tyTagOf(ty_o)$,
ty_1	is $cc(E_1, c)$,	$tyTag_1$	is $tyTagOf(ty_1)$,
ty_i	is $cc(E_i, c)$,	$tyTag_i$	is $tyTagOf(ty_i)$,
ty_{ij}	is $cc(E_{ij}, c)$,	$tyTag_{ij}$	is $tyTagOf(ty_{ij})$,
sy_{ref}	is $cc(Ref, c)$,	$syTag_{ref}$	is $syTagOf(sy_{ref})$,
ty_{ref}	is $tyOf(sy_{ref})$,	$tyTag_{ref}$	is $tyTagOf(ty_{ref})$,
sy_{id}	is $syOf(c, id)$,	$syTag_{id}$	is $syTagOf(sy_{id})$,
ty_{id}	is $tyOf(sy_{id})$,	$tyTag_{id}$	is $tyTagOf(ty_{id})$,

		$syTag_{sy}$	**is** $syTagOf\,(sy)$,
ty_{sy}	**is** $tyOf\,(sy)$,	$tyTag_{sy}$	**is** $tyTagOf\,(ty_{sy})$,

$access_{id}$ **is** $AccessOf\,(c, id)$,

$mode_{id}$ **is** $ModeOf\,(c, id)$

As an example of the use of these abbreviations, consider the rule for the subtraction operator (see Section 8.4.6):

RHS for *E*	**CONTEXT CONDITION** $cc\,(RHS: E, c: Context): TyDef$
$E_1 - E_2$	**if** $isNumeric\,(ty_1)$ & $isNumeric\,(ty_2)$ **then** $NumericType\,(ty_1, ty_2)$ **elsif** $EquivType\,(ty_1, ty_2)$ & $tyTag_1 = Set$ **then** ty_1 **end if**

This rule requires both operands to be numeric or to be of equivalent set types. Without the use of abbreviations, the same rule contains repetitive terms, which detract from readability:

$E_1 - E_2$	**if** $isNumeric\,(cc\,(E_1, c))$ & $isNumeric\,(cc\,(E_2, c))$ **then** $NumericType\,(cc\,(E_1, c), cc\,(E_2, c))$ **elsif** $EquivType\,(cc\,(E_1, c), cc\,(E_2, c))$ & $tyTagOf\,(cc\,(E_1, c)) = Set$ **then** $cc\,(E_1, c)$ **end if**

8.4.1 Context Conditions for Programs

This section gives context conditions for programs and declaration/statement lists. Here are the context conditions for *Program*.

RHS for *Program*	**CONTEXT CONDITION** $cc\,(RHS: Program, c: Context): Boolean$
S	$cc\,(S, c)$

The context for a *program* is the predefined context $c_{predefined}$. We now give the context conditions for the non-terminal S, which expands to a sequence of declarations and statements.

RHS for *S*	**CONTEXT CONDITION** *cc (RHS : S , c : Context): Boolean*
Decl S	*cc (S , cc (Decl , c))*
Stmt S	*cc (Stmt , c) & cc (S , c)*
empty	~∃ *id* : % Unresolved fwd declared subpgms (*LocallyDeclared (c , id)* & $mode_{id}$ = *fwdSubPgm*) & ~∃ *id* : % Unresolved fwd imported subpgms (*LocallyDeclared (c , id)* & $access_{id}$ = *inaccessible* & $syTag_{id}$ = *Procedure*) % All forward imported subprograms are % treated as procedures & ~∃ *id* : % Unresolved fwd collection types (*LocallyDeclared (c , id)* & $access_{id}$ = *inaccessible* & $syTag_{id}$ = *Type*)

A sequence of declarations and statements is terminated by the *empty* case. Any forward declarations in the declaration and statement sequence must be resolved (redeclared non-forward) by the end of the sequence. The rule for *empty* checks that no local forward declarations remain unresolved in the context.

8.4.2 Context Conditions for Declarations

This section gives context conditions for *Decl* (Turing declaration). The reader may wish to look at the example representations of declared items in "Representing Context" (Section 8.3.5) while studying these rules.

RHS for *Decl*	**CONTEXT CONDITION** *cc (RHS : Decl , c : Context): Context*
const *Pervasive* *id* [:*T*] := *E*	**assert** *Assignable (ty , ty_E) & ~isDynamicArray (ty_E)* **result** *Declare (c , id , sy , mode , readOnly)* **where** *sy* **is** *Constant (ty_E , compTime),* *ty* **is** *cc (T , c , id),* *compTime* **is** *isScalar (ty)*

  & *CompileTimeExpn* (*E*, *c*),
 mode **is** *cc* (*Pervasive*)

const *Pervasive*
 id:*T* := **init** (...)

assert *tyTagOf* (*ty*) **in** {*Array*, *Record*, *Union*}
  & *CompileTimeInit* (**init** (...), *c*)
result *Declare* (*c*, *id*, *sy*, *mode*, *readOnly*)
where
 sy **is** *Constant* (*ty*, ~*compileTime*),
 ty **is** *cc* (*T*, *c*, *id*),
 mode **is** *cc* (*Pervasive*)

var {id_i}
 [:*T*] [:= *E*]

assert *Assignable* (*ty*, ty_E) & ~*isDynamicArray* (ty_E)
% Note context-free syntax ensures that
% *T* and *E* are not both omitted
% Declare each id_i
result *Declare* (*c*, id_i, *sy*, *nonPERVASIVE*, *VAR*)
where *sy* **is** *Variable* (*ty*),
 ty **is**
 if *isProduction* ([:*T*] ::= :*T*)
 then *cc* (*T*, *c*, *id*),
 else ty_E
 end if

var {id_i}
 :*T* := **init** (...)

assert *tyTagOf* (*ty*) **in** {*Array*, *Record*, *Union*}
 & *CompileTimeInit* (**init** (...), *c*)
% Declare each id_i
result *Declare* (*c*, id_i, *sy*, *nonPERVASIVE*, *VAR*)
where *sy* **is** *Variable* (*ty*),
 ty **is** *cc* (*T*, *c*, *id*),

var {id_j}:
 array {E_{iL} .. E_{iU}} **of** *T*

assert $\forall$ *i* : (*EquivType* (ty_{iL}, ty_{iU})
 & $tyTag_{iL}$ **in** {*Int*, *Enum*}
 & *CompileTimeExpn* (E_{iL}, *c*))
  % Declare each id_j
result *Declare* (*c*, id_j, *sy*, *nonPERVASIVE*, *VAR*)
where *sy* **is** *Variable* (*ty*),
 ty **is** *Array* ($\langle u_1, \ldots, u_n \rangle$, *cc* (*T*, *c*, id_1)),
 u_i **is** *Subrange* (ty_{iL}, *CompileTimeExpn* (E_{iU}, *c*))

var {id_i}:
 collection of *T*

assert *notInSubprogram* % Declare each id_i
result *Declare* (*c*, id_i, *sy*, *nonPERVASIVE*, *VAR*)
where

notInSubprogram **is**
$Closed(c) \Rightarrow (syTagOf(SymbolOfContext(c))$ **not in** $\{Function, Procedure\})$,
sy **is** $Variable(Collection(cc(T, c_{coll}, id_1), id_i))$,
% Context c_{coll} for type T includes all
% the collections (id_i)
c_{coll} **is** $Declare(c, id_i, sy_{coll}, nonPervasive, VAR)$,
sy_{coll} **is** $Variable(Collection(dummyTy, id_i))$
% Dummy symbol definitions for all the
% collections (id_i), used in type T

var $\{id_i\}$:
collection of
forward $id_{forward}$

assert *notInSubprogram* % Declare each id_i
result $Declare(c_{forward}, id_i, sy_i, nonPERVASIVE, VAR)$

where
notInSubprogram **is** ...as above... ,
sy_i **is** $Variable(Collection(Forward(id_{forward}), id_i))$,
$c_{forward}$ **is** $Declare(c, id_{forward}, Type(Forward(id_{forward})), nonPERVASIVE, inaccessible)$

The following two functions are used in the context conditions for collection subscripting, for **new** and **free** statements, and for import lists.

$CollectionMatchesPointer(c: Context, id: Ident, RHS: Ref): Boolean =_{df}$
$tyTag_{id} = Collection$
$\& \ tyTag_{ref} = Pointer$
$\& \ NameOf(ty_{id}) = NameOf(ty_{ref})$

$FwdCollectionResolved(c: Context, id: Ident): Boolean =_{df}$
$tyTagOf(ElementOf(ty_{id})) = Forward \Rightarrow$
$AccessOf(c, NameOf(ElementOf(ty_{id}))) \neq inaccessible$

We now give the context conditions for **bind** declarations. An identifier introduced in a variable binding is declared with the attributes of the associated reference, which must name a (part of) a variable. This declaration does not take effect until the end of the bind list. The bound identifier has access *VAR* if **var** is specified, otherwise it has access *readOnly*. We check that the identifier is not being bound to a collection, nor is it being bound with a stronger access than the reference presently has. The identifier being bound must not be visible in the surrounding context. After the new identifiers are declared in the context, access to the root identifiers of the bound references is weakened using *DecreaseAccess*: for a **var** bind, the root id becomes inaccessible, for a non-var bind, the root id becomes *readOnly*.

RHS for
Decl

CONTEXT CONDITION
$cc\,(RHS : Decl,\ c : Context) : Context$

bind
$\{Var_i\ id_{iA}$ **to** $Ref_i\}$

assert $isProduction\,(Ref_i ::= id_{iB}\ selectors_i)$
  $\&\ syTagOf\,(sy_{iB}) = Variable$
  $\&\ tyTag_{iB} \neq Collection$
  $\&\ access_{iA} \leq accessOf\,(c,\ id_{iB})$
% Decrease access for each id_{iB}
result $DecreaseAccess\,(c_{iA},\ id_{iB},\ access_{iB})$

where
sy_{iB} **is** $cc\,(id_{iB}\ selectors_i,\ c)$,
c_{iA} **is** % Declare each id_{iA}
  $Declare\,(c,\ id_{iA},\ sy_{iB},\ nonPERVASIVE,\ access_{iA})$,
$access_{iA}$ **is**
  if $isProduction\,(Var_i$ ::= **var**)
  then *VAR*
  else *readOnly*
  end if,
$access_{iB}$ **is**
  if $isProduction\,(Var_i$ ::= **var**)
  then *inaccessible*
  else *readOnly*
  end if

We now give context conditions for declarations of named types. If the type name is not visible in the parameter context, bind it as a type, with the specified type value. Otherwise, if the type name is visible as a forward collection type (indicated by access *inaccessible* and tyTag *Forward*) at the same level (*LocallyDeclared*) in the parameter scope, then resolve this declaration with the type specified here.

RHS for
Decl

CONTEXT CONDITION
$cc\,(RHS : Decl,\ c : Context) : Context$

type *Pervasive id*: *T*

if $\sim Visible\,(c,\ id)$
then $Declare\,(c,\ id,\ sy,\ cc\,(Pervasive),\ readOnly)$
elsif *forwardTypeNeedsResolution*
then $Resolve\,(c,\ id,\ sy,\ cc\,(Pervasive),\ readOnly)$
end if
where
sy **is** $Type\,(cc\,(T,\ c,\ id))$,
forwardTypeNeedsResolution **is**
  $access_{id} = inaccessible$

& $LocallyDeclared(c, id)$
& $tyTag_{id} = Forward$

We now give the context conditions for *Pervasive*; this non-terminal appears in constant and type declarations.

RHS for *Pervasive*	**CONTEXT CONDITION** *cc (RHS : Pervasive): Mode*
pervasive	*PERVASIVE*
empty	*nonPERVASIVE*

8.4.3 Context Conditions for Type Specifications

This section gives context conditions for T (Turing type specifications) as well as for *Fields*. The *DistinctIdents* function is used to check for distinctness among field names, parameter names, subprogram names and function result names.

$$DistinctIdents(idSet_1 : \textbf{set of } Ident, \ldots, idSet_n : \textbf{set of } Ident) =_{df}$$
$$\forall\, i, j: idSet_i * idSet_j \neq empty \Rightarrow i = j$$

Here are the context conditions for T. We include an *Ident* parameter in the following rule to allow us to uniquely name type specifications for enumerated types, records and unions.

RHS for T	**CONTEXT CONDITION** $cc(RHS: T, c: Context, typeId: Ident): TyDef$
int	*Int*
real	*Real*
string	*String*
string (E)	**assert** $tyTag_E = Int$ & $CompileTimeExpn(E, c)$ **result** *StringN* % **string(*)** is handled with subpgm parameters
boolean	*Boolean*
$E_1 .. E_2$	**assert** $EquivType(ty_1, ty_2)$ & $tyTag_1$ **in** $\{Int, Enum\}$ & $CompileTimeExpn(E_1, c)$

& *CompileTimeExpn* (E_2, *c*)
result *Subrange* (ty_1, *compileTime*)

enum($id_1, \ldots, id_n$)

DistinctIdents ($\{id_1\}, \ldots, \{id_n\}$)
result *Enum* ($\{id_1, \ldots, id_n\}$, *typeId*)

array $T_1, \ldots, T_n$ **of** T_{n+1}

assert $\forall\, i$: *isIndex* (*cc* (T_i, *c* , *typeId*))
% Rule for subranges enforces non-dynamic array
result *Array* ($\langle$*cc* (T_1, *c* , *typeId*), ... , *cc* (T_n, *c* , *typeId*)$\rangle$,
cc (T_{n+1}, *c* , *typeId*))

Ref

assert $syTag_{ref}$ = *Type*
result ty_{ref}

set of *T*

assert *isIndex* (*cc* (*T* , *c* , *typeId*))
result *Set* (*cc* (*T* , *c* , *typeId*))

pointer to *id*

assert $tyTag_{id}$ = *Collection*
result *Pointer* (*id*)

record
Fields
end record

Record (*cc* (*Fields* , *c*), *typeId*)

union *Ident* : *T* **of**
{**label** $\{E_{ij}\}$: $Fields_i$ }
end union

assert *isIndex* (*cc* (*T* , *c* , *typeId*))
& (*isProduction* (*Ident* ::=*id*) ⇒
DistinctIdents ({*id* }, *fieldIds*))
& $\forall\, i, j$:
(*EquivType* (ty_{ij}, *RootType* (*cc* (*T* , *c* , *typeId*)))
& *CompileTimeExpn* (E_{ij}, *c*)
& *DistinctIdents* ($fieldIds_1, \ldots, fieldIds_n$))
result *Union* (*fieldMap* , *typeId* , *tagIdent* , *cc* (*T* , *c* , *typeId*))

where
$fieldMap_i$ **is** *cc* ($Fields_i$, *c*),
fieldMap **is** $fieldMap_1 + \ldots + fieldMap_n$,
$fieldIds_i$ **is** **domain**($fieldmap_i$),
fieldIds **is** $fieldIds_1 + \ldots + fieldIds_n$,
tagIdent **is**
if *isProduction* (*Ident* ::=*id*)
then *id*
else *nullId*
end if

We now give context conditions for *Fields*.

RHS for *Fields*	**CONTEXT CONDITION** $cc(RHS: Fields, c: Context)$: **map** *Ident* **of** *TyDef*
$\{id_{i1}, \ldots, id_{nR}: T_i\}$	**assert** $DistinctIdents(\{id_{11}\}, \ldots, \{id_{nR}\})$ % Map each identifier to its respective type **result** $\langle\langle id_{11}, cc(T_1, c, id_{11})\rangle, \ldots, \langle id_{nR}, cc(T_n, c, id_{n1})\rangle\rangle$

8.4.4 Context Conditions for Statements

This section gives context conditions for statements. The following notation is used for assertions and invariants:

> $assertionBoolean_E$ **is**
> % Use a context for E in which **init** constants
> % are accessible
> $tyTagOf(cc(E, AssertionContext(c))) = Boolean$

Here are the context conditions for *Stmt*.

RHS for *Stmt*	**CONTEXT CONDITION** $cc(RHS: Stmt, c: Context)$: *Boolean*
$Ref := E$	% Assignment statement $isProduction(Ref ::= id\ Selectors)$ & $syTag_{ref} = Variable$ & $access_{id} = VAR$ & $Assignable(ty_{ref}, ty_E)$ & $\sim isDynamicArray(ty_{ref})$
Ref	% Call to a procedure $syTag_{ref} = ProcedureCall$
assert E	$assertionBoolean_E$
return	$syTagOf(SymbolOfContext(c)) = Procedure$ **or** $\sim Closed(c)$ % Returning from main program
result E	$Assignable(ResultType(SymbolOfContext(c)), ty_E)$
if E_1 **then** S_1	$\forall j: (tyTag_j = Boolean$

{**elsif** E_i **then** S_i} [**else** S_n] **end if**	& $cc(S_j, LocalContext(c, \sim loopNesting)))$
case E **of** {**label** {E_{ij}}: S_i} **end case**	$tyTag_E$ **in** {*Int*, *Enum*} & $\forall\, i, j$: $(EquivType(ty_{ij}, ty_E)$ & $CompileTimeExpn(E_{ij}, c)$ & $cc(S_i, LocalContext(c, \sim loopNesting)))$
begin S **end**	$cc(S, LocalContext(c, \sim loopNesting))$
new *id*, *Ref*	$isProduction(Ref ::= id_{ptr}\ Selectors)$ & $syTag_{id} = Variable$ & $access_{id} = VAR$ & $syTag_{ref} = Variable$ & $AccessOf(c, id_{ptr}) = VAR$ % The following two functions are defined % with collection declarations & $CollectionMatchesPointer(c, id, Ref)$ & $FwdCollectionResolved(c, id)$
free *id*, *Ref*	... (same as for **new** *id*, *Ref*) ...
tag *Ref*, *E*	$syTag_{ref} = Variable$ & $tyTag_{ref} = Union$ & $isProduction(Ref ::= id\ Selectors)$ & $access_{id} = VAR$ & $Assignable(TagType(ty_{ref}), ty_E)$
loop [**invariant** *E*] *S* **end loop**	$assertionBoolean_E$ & $cc(S, LocalContext(c, loopNesting))$
exit [**when** *E*]	$tyTag_E = Boolean$ & $NestedInLoop(c)$
for *Ident*: [**decreasing**] *ForRange* [**invariant** *E*] *S* **end for**	$isIndex(cc(ForRange, c))$ & *invariantBoolean* & $cc(S, LocalContext(c_{id}, loopNesting))$ **where** c_{id} **is** **if** $isProduction(Ident ::= id)$ **then** $Declare(c, id,$ $Constant(cc(ForRange, c), \sim compileTime),$ $nonPERVASIVE, readOnly)$ **else** c

end if
invariantBoolean **is**
$tyTagOf\,(cc\,(E\,,AssertContext\,(c_{id}))) = Boolean$

The context conditions for *ForRange* are now given.

RHS for *ForRange*	**CONTEXT CONDITION** $cc\,(RHS: ForRange\,,\, c: Context): TyDef$
Ref	**assert** $syTag_{ref} = Type$ **result** ty_{ref}
$E_1 \,..\, E_2$	**assert** $EquivType\,(ty_1,\, ty_2)$ & $tyTag_1$ **in** $\{Int\,, Enum\}$ **result** $Subrange\,(ty_1,\, \sim compileTime)$

8.4.5 Context Conditions for Input/Output

This section gives the context conditions for **put** and **get** statements. We use $access_{IO}$ to check that the **get** and **put** statements have **var** access to the *IO* module:

$access_{IO}$ **is** $AccessOf\,(c\,, IO)$
% Implicit accessibility to *IO* module

The *IO* module is an implicit module supporting input/output; this module is considered to be imported **var** into any subprogram or modules using input/output. The use of $access_{IO}$ is artificial in that it is not possible to import the *IO* module in an actual Turing program.

RHS for *Stmt*	**CONTEXT CONDITION** $cc\,(RHS: Stmt\,,\, c: Context): Boolean$
put [: *E*,] $\{PutItem_i\}$ [..]	$tyTag_E = Int$ & $access_{IO} = VAR$ & $\forall\, i: cc\,(putItem_i,\, c)$
get [: *E*,] $\{GetItem_i\}$	$tyTag_E = Int$ & $access_{IO} = VAR$ & $\forall\, i: cc\,(GetItem_i,\, c)$

We now give context conditions for *PutItem*.

RHS for *PutItem*	**CONTEXT CONDITION** $cc\,(RHS: PutItem\,,\, c: Context): Boolean$
$E_1\,[\,: E_2\,]$	$tyTag_1$ **in** $\{Int\,, Real\,, String\}$

	& $tyTag_2 = Int$
$E_1 : E_2 : E_3$ [: E_4]	$tyTag_1$ **in** {*Int*, *Real*} & $tyTag_2 = Int$ & $tyTag_3 = Int$ & $tyTag_4 = Int$
skip	**true**

We now give context conditions for *GetItem*.

RHS for *GetItem*	**CONTEXT CONDITION** *cc* (*RHS* : *GetItem*, *c* : *Context*): *Boolean*
Ref	*isProduction* (*Ref* ::= *id Selectors*) & $syTag_{ref} = Variable$ & $access_{id} = VAR$ & *tyTagOf* (*RootType* (ty_{sy})) **in** {*Int*, *Real*, *String*}
Ref: *ExpnOrStar*	*isProduction* (*Ref* ::= *id Selectors*) & $syTag_{ref} = Variable$ & $access_{id} = VAR$ & *tyTagOf* (*RootType* (ty_{sy})) = *String*
skip	**true**

We now give context conditions for *ExpnOrStar*, which is used for format specification in **get** statements.

RHS for *ExpnOrStar*	**CONTEXT CONDITION** *cc* (*RHS* : *ExpnOrStar*, *c* : *Context*): *Boolean*
E	$tyTag_E = Int$
*	**true** % Star format item specifies to read entire line

8.4.6 Context Conditions for Expressions

This section gives context conditions for Turing expressions.

RHS for *E*	**CONTEXT CONDITION** *cc* (*RHS* : *E*, *c* : *Context*): *TyDef*
integerLiteral	*Int*

realLiteral	*Real*
stringLiteral	*String*
booleanLiteral	*Boolean*
$E_1 + E_2$	**if** $isNumeric(ty_1)$ & $isNumeric(ty_2)$ **then** $NumericType(ty_1, ty_2)$ **elsif** $EquivType(ty_1, ty_2)$ & $tyTag_1$ **in** $\{String, Set\}$ **then** ty_1 **end if**
$E_1 - E_2$	**if** $isNumeric(ty_1)$ & $isNumeric(ty_2)$ **then** $NumericType(ty_1, ty_2)$ **elsif** $EquivType(ty_1, ty_2)$ & $tyTag_1 = Set$ **then** ty_1 **end if**
$E_1 * E_2$	... same as $E_1 - E_2$ ...
E_1 **mod** E_2	**assert** $isNumeric(ty_1)$ & $isNumeric(ty_2)$ **result** $NumericType(ty_1, ty_2)$
$E_1 ** E_2$	... same as E_1 **mod** E_2 ...
E_1 / E_2	**assert** $isNumeric(ty_1)$ & $isNumeric(ty_2)$ **result** *Real*
E_1 **div** E_2	**assert** $isNumeric(ty_1)$ & $isNumeric(ty_2)$ **result** *Int*
E_1 [**not**]= E_2	**assert** ($isNumeric(ty_1)$ & $isNumeric(ty_2)$) **or** ($EquivType(ty_1, ty_2)$ & $isScalar(ty_1)$) **or** ($EquivType(ty_1, ty_2)$ & $tyTag_1$ **in** $\{String, Set\}$) **result** *Boolean*
$E_1 > E_2$	**assert** ($isNumeric(ty_1)$ & $isNumeric(ty_2)$) **or** ($EquivType(ty_1, ty_2)$ & $isScalar(ty_1)$ & $tyTag_1$ **not in** $\{Boolean, Pointer\}$) **or** ($EquivType(ty_1, ty_2)$ & $tyTag_1$ **in** $\{String, Set\}$)

	result *Boolean*
$E_1 >= E_2$	... same as $E_1 > E_2$ ...
$E_1 < E_2$	... same as $E_1 > E_2$ ...
$E_1 <= E_2$	... same as $E_1 > E_2$ ...
$+E$	**assert** $isNumeric(ty_E)$ **result** ty_E
$-E$	**assert** $isNumeric(ty_E)$ **result** ty_E
not E	**assert** $tyTag_E = Boolean$ **result** *Boolean*
E_1 **and** E_2	**assert** $tyTag_1 = Boolean$ & $tyTag_2 = Boolean$ **result** *Boolean*
E_1 **or** E_2	... same as E_1 **and** E_2 ...
$E_1 => E_2$	... same as E_1 **and** E_2 ...
E_1 [**not**] **in** E_2	**assert** $tyTag_2 = Set$ & $EquivType(ty_1, RootType(BaseOf(ty_2)))$ **result** *Boolean*
Ref	**assert** $syTag_{ref}$ **in** $\{Constant, Variable\}$ & $tyTag_{ref} \neq Collection$ **result** $RootType(ty_{ref})$
Ref([**all**])	**assert** $syTag_{ref} = Type$ & $tyTag_{ref} = Set$ **result** ty_{ref}
Ref(* [$-E$])	**assert** $syTag_{ref}$ **in** $\{Constant, Variable\}$ & $tyTagOf(RootType(ty_{ref})) = String$ & $tyTag_E = Int$ **result** *String*
$Ref(Pos_1 .. Pos_2)$	**assert** $syTag_{ref}$ in $\{Constant, Variable\}$ & $tyTagOf(RootType(ty_{ref})) = String$ & $IsProduction(Pos_i ::= [*-] [E_i])$ & $tyTag_i = Int$ **result** *String*

8.4.7 Context Conditions for References

This section gives context conditions for *Ref* (a Turing reference). A *Ref* expands uniquely to *id selectors*.

RHS for *Ref*	**CONTEXT CONDITIONS** *cc* (*RHS* : *Ref* , *c* : *Context*): *TyDef*

id Selectors	% A reference is an identifier followed by selectors
	assert ($syTag_{id}$ = *Module* & *procOrProcCall*) ⇒
	   $access_{id}$ = *VAR*
	   % Exported procedures can only be called
	   % from *VAR* modules
	result sy_{sels}
	
	where
	sy_{sels} **is** *cc* (*Selectors* , sy_{id}, *c*),
	procOrProcCall **is** *syTagOf* (sy_{sels}) **in**
	     {*Procedure* , *ProcedureCall* }

We now give the context conditions for *Selectors*.

RHS for *Selectors*	**CONTEXT CONDITION** *cc* (*RHS* : *Selectors* , *sy* : *SyDef* , *c* : *Context*): *SyDef*
Selector Selectors	*cc* (*Selectors* , sy_{sel}, *c*) **where** sy_{sel} **is** *cc* (*Selector* , *sy* , *c*)
empty	*sy*

We now give the context conditions for the expansion of *Selector* into field selection.

RHS for *Selector*	**CONTEXT CONDITION** *cc* (*RHS* : *Selector* , *sy* : *SyDef* , *c* : *Context*): *SyDef*

. *id*	% Field selection using dot.
	% The symbol preceding the dot must be a module,
	% a type, a variable or a constant. The variable or
	% constant's type must be a record or union.
	if $syTag_{sy}$ = *Module* % moduleId . selectors
	   & *id* **in domain**(*ExportsOf* (*sy*))
	then *syOf* (*ExportsOf* (*sy*)(*id*)) % Exported symbol
	
	elsif $syTag_{sy}$ = *Type* % enumTypeId . enumId
	   & $tyTag_{sy}$ = *Enum*
	   & *id* **in** *EnumIds* (ty_{sy})

then *Constant* (ty_{sy}, *compileTime*)

elsif % Field of record or union
syTag$_{sy}$ **in** {*Constant*, *Variable* }
& *tyTag*$_{sy}$ **in** {*Record*, *Union* }
& (*id* **in domain**(*FieldsOf* (ty_{sy})) **or** *isUnionTag*)
then
if *isUnionTag*
then *Constant* (*TagType* (ty_{sy}), ~*compileTime*)
elsif *syTag*$_{sy}$ = *Constant*
then *Constant* (ty_{field}, ~*compileTime*)
else *Variable* (ty_{field})
end if
where ty_{field} **is** (*FieldsOf* (ty_{sy}))(id)
end if
where *isUnionTag* **is**
tyTag$_{sy}$ = *Union* & *id* = *TagNameOf* (ty_{sy})

We now give the context conditions for the expansion of *Selector* into a parenthesized list of expressions.

RHS for *Selector*	**CONTEXT CONDITION** *cc* (*RHS* : *Selector*, *sy* : *SyDef* , *c* : *Context*): *SyDef*
(E_1, ... , E_n)	% Array subscript, collection subscript, substring, % set constructor, function call, or procedure call **if** *isArraySubscript* **then** *arrayElement* **elsif** *isCollectionSubscript* **then** *collectionElement* **elsif** *isSubstring* **then** *Constant* (*String*, ~*compileTime*) **elsif** *isSetConstructor* **then** *Constant* (ty_{sy}, *compTime*) **where** *compTime* **is** ($\forall$ *i* : *CompileTimeExpn* (E_i, *c*)) **elsif** *isFunctionCall* **then** *Constant* (*ResultType* (*sy*), ~*compileTime*) **elsif** *isProcedureCall* **then** *ProcedureCall*

```
end if

where
isArraySubscript is
  syTag_sy in {Constant, Variable}
  & tyTag_sy = Array
  & n = m
  & ∀ i: EquivType(ty_i, RootType(u_i))
  where ⟨u_1, ... , u_m⟩ is IndexOf(ty_sy),

arrayElement is
  if syTag_sy = Variable
  then Variable(ty_elem)
  else Constant(ty_elem, ~compileTime)
  end if
  where ty_elem is ElementOf(ty_sy),

isCollectionSubscript is
  tyTag_sy = Collection
  & n = 1
  & isProduction(E_1 ::= Ref)
  & CollectionMatchesPointer(c, id_coll, Ref)
  & FwdCollectionResolved(c, id_coll)
  where id_coll is NameOf(ty_sy),

collectionElement is
  Variable(ty_elem)

  where
    ty_elem is
      if tyTagOf(ElementOf(ty_sy)) = Forward
      then tyOf(syOf(c, id_elem))
      else ElementOf(ty_sy)
      end if,

    id_elem is NameOf(ElementOf(ty_sy)),

isSubstring is
  syTag_sy in {Constant, Variable}
  & tyTag(RootType(ty_sy)) = String
  & n = 1
  & tyTag_E = Int,
```

isSetConstructor **is**
  $syTag_{sy} = Type$
  & $tyTag_{sy} = Set$
  & $\forall\, i: EquivType(ty_i, RootType(BaseOf(ty_{sy})))$,

isFunctionCall **is**
  $syTag_{sy} = Function$
  & $CompatibleParams(FormalsOf(sy), \langle E_1, \ldots, E_n \rangle, c)$
  & $\forall\, i$: ~$SideEffect(imps_i)$, % No side effects
    % in procedures passed as parameters
  & $NoAliasingDueToIncreasedAccess(c, transImports)$,
  % See the section on Preventing Aliasing (8.4.10)

isProcedureCall **is**
  $syTag_{sy} = Procedure$
  & $CompatibleParams(FormalsOf(sy), \langle E_1, \ldots, E_n \rangle, c)$
  & $NoAliasingDueToIncreasedAccess(c, transImports)$
  & $NoAliasingDueToParametricSubpgms$
    $(c, imps_1, \ldots, imps_n)$
  & $NoAliasingDueToVarImportOverlap$
    $(c, imps, FormalsOf(sy), \langle E_1, \ldots, E_n \rangle)$
  & $NoAliasingDueToRefImportOverlap$
    $(c, imps, FormalsOf(sy), \langle E_1, \ldots, E_n \rangle)$,
  % See the section on Preventing Aliasing (8.4.10)

transImports **is** *TransitiveImports*(
    $ResolveFwdImports(ImportsOf(sy), c), \langle\, \rangle)$,

$imps_i$ **is** % Imports of i-th parametric subprogram
  if $isProduction(E_i := Ref)$
    & $syTag_{ref}$ **is** $\{Function, Procedure\}$
  then *TransitiveImports*(
    $ResolveFwdImports(ImportsOf(sy_{ref}), c), \langle\, \rangle)$
  else $\langle\, \rangle$ % Parameter not a subprogram
  end if,

imps **is** $transImports + imps_1 + \ldots + imps_n$
  % Includes imports of all parametric subprograms

8.4.8 Context Conditions for Subprograms

This section gives context conditions for the declaration of subprograms. The context conditions given here include some of the most complex parts of Turing, including forward subprograms and import lists. A function subprogram must not have any side-effects; this restriction is enforced by checking that the function has no variable parameters and no (transitive) **var** imports. The subprogram name, parameter names, imports and result name must be disjoint, and, except for imports, these must be distinct from identifiers pervasive in the enclosing context. The body is absent for forward subprogram declarations. Forward importing a subprogram implicitly declares the subprogram name as an inaccessible subprogram, if it is not already visible in this context (if it hasn't previously been forward imported).

RHS for *Decl*	**CONTEXT CONDITION** $cc(RHS: Decl, c: Context): Context$

Forward
FcnOrProc id
ParameterList
ResultSpec
import(*Imports*)
[*Body*]
	assert $DistinctIdents(\{id\}, \{id_{\mathbf{result}}\},$ **domain**$(params)$, **domain**$(imps))$
	& *identsDistinctFromPervasives*
	& ($isProduction(FcnOrProc$ ::= **function**) ⇒ *noSideEffects*)
	& $cc(Body, c_{body}, id)$ % Body is omitted when % **forward** keyword is specified
	result
	if ~$Visible(c, id)$ **then**
	$Declare(c_{forward}, id, sy, mode, readOnly)$
	elsif *importedPreviouslyUsingFwd* **then**
	$Resolve(c_{forward}, id, sy, fwdSubPgm, readOnly)$
	end if
	
	where
	identsDistinctFromPervasives **is**
	% Subprogram name, function result and
	% parameters must be distinct from pervasives
	∀ id_p **in** $(\{id\} + \{id_{\mathbf{result}}\} +$ **domain**$(params))$:
	~$Visible(Close(c, dummySy), id_p)$,
	
	noSideEffects **is**
	% No *VAR* parameters for functions
	(∀ id_p **in domain**(*params*) :
	$syTagOf(params(id_p)) \neq Variable$)
	& ($isProduction(Forward ::= empty)$ ⇒
	% Functions must not import
	% procedures with side effects

$\sim SideEffect(TransitiveImports(imps, \langle \rangle))$,
% See 8.3.7 Representing Import Sets

importedPreviouslyUsingFwd **is**
$mode_{id} = fwdSubPgm$
$\& \; Access_{id} = inaccessible$
$\& \; LocallyDeclared(c, id)$,

params **is** *cc* (*ParameterList*, *c*),

$\langle id_{\mathbf{result}}, ty_{\mathbf{result}} \rangle$ **is** *cc* (*ResultSpec*, *c*),

sy **is** **if** *isProduction* (*FcnOrProc* ::= **function**)
then *Function* (*params*, *imps*,
$id_{\mathbf{result}}, ty_{\mathbf{result}}$)
else *Procedure* (*params*, *imps*)
end if,

mode **is** **if** *isProduction* (*Forward* ::= **forward**)
then *fwdSubPgm*
else *nonPERVASIVE*
end if,

$\langle c_{forward}, imps \rangle$ **is** *cc* (*Imports*, *c*, $\langle \rangle$),
% $c_{forward}$ adds to *c* those subprograms
% imported **forward**

c_{body} **is** % Context for body consists of imports,
% parameters, pervasives, and subprogram name
ImportContext (*imps*,
DeclareFormals (*params*, $c_{visible}$))
where $c_{visible}$ **is** % Pervasives and subpgm name
Declare (*Close* (*c*, *sy*), *id*, *sy*,
nonPERVASIVE, *readOnly*)

We now give context conditions for the declaration of bodies of **forward** subprograms. The declaration of a subprogram body for a previously declared forward subprogram denotes the resolving of the subprogram identifier with a complete set of attributes and a non-forward mode.

The subprogram header must have occurred at the same lexic level as this body declaration (the subprogram name must be *LocallyDeclared*). A body must not be given for a forward imported subprogram before its header has been given (checked by the requirement that the access be *readOnly*).

All forward imports must have been properly declared by the time the body is declared. This is implicitly checked in the process of resolving forward imports to produce the local subprogram body context. Functions must not forward import procedures; we check that no forward import by a function (indicated by an access of *inaccessible*) is bound to a procedure. Furthermore, functions must not have any (transitive) **var** imports; this is checked by the *SideEffect* predicate.

RHS for *Decl*	**CONTEXT CONDITION** $cc(RHS: Decl, c: Context): Context$
body *FcnOrProc id Body*	**assert** *declaredPreviouslyUsingForward* & $(syTag_{id} = Function) =$ *isProduction*(*fcnOrProc* ::= **function**) & $(syTag_{id} = Function) \Rightarrow$ (*noSideEffects* & *noFwdProcImports*) & $cc(Body, c_{body}, id)$ **result** $Resolve(c, id, sy_{id}, nonPERVASIVE, readOnly)$ **where** *declaredPreviouslyUsingForward* **is** $mode_{id} = fwdSubPgm$ & $access_{id} = readOnly$ & $LocallyDeclared(c, id)$, *noSideEffects* **is** $\sim SideEffect(TransitiveImports(imps, \langle$ % Functions must not import % procedures with side effects *noFwdProcImports* **is** $\sim\exists\ id_{imps}$ **in domain**$(Imports(sy_{id}))$: $(syTagOf(sy_{imps}) = Procedure$ & $access_{imps} = inaccessible))$ **where** $\langle sy_{imps}, access_{imps}\rangle$ **is** $(ImportsOf(sy_{id}))(id_{imps})$, *imps* **is** $ResolveFwdImports(ImportsOf(sy_{id}), c)$, % Replace fwd imports by their definitions c_{body} **is** % Context for body consists of imports, % parameters, pervasives, and subprogram name $ImportContext(imps,$ $DeclareFormals(FormalsOf(sy_{id}), c_{visible}))$, **where** $c_{visible}$ **is** % Pervasives and subpgm name $Declare(Close(c, sy_{id}), id, sy_{id},$ $nonPERVASIVE, readOnly)$

We now give context conditions for the result specifications of functions.

RHS for *ResultSpec*	**CONTEXT CONDITION** *cc (RHS : ResultSpec , c : Context)*: ⟨*Ident , TyDef* ⟩
empty	⟨*nullId , dummyTy* ⟩ % Case for procedures
Ident : T	⟨id_{result} , *cc (T , c ,* id_{result})⟩ **where** id_{result} **is** **if** *IsProduction (Ident ::= id)* **then** *id* **else** *nullId* **end if**

We now give context conditions for parameter lists.

RHS for *ParameterList*	**CONTEXT CONDITION** *cc (RHS : ParameterList , c : Context): Formals*
empty	⟨ ⟩ % Empty sequence of formals
ParameterDecl ParameterList	% Distinct parameter names **assert** *DistinctIdents* (**domain**(*cc (ParameterDecl , c*)), **domain**(*cc (ParameterList , c*))) **result** *cc (ParameterDecl , c*) + *cc (ParameterList , c*)

We now give context conditions for parameter declarations.

RHS for *ParameterDecl*	**CONTEXT CONDITION** *cc (RHS : ParameterDecl , c : Context): Formals*
Var $id_1, \ldots, id_n$: *ParameterType*	**assert** *DistinctIdents* ($\{id_1\}, \ldots, \{id_n\}$) **result** ⟨$\langle id_1, s_1\rangle, \ldots, \langle id_n, s_n\rangle$⟩ **where** s_i **is** **if** *isProduction (Var ::=* **var**) **then** *Variable (cc (ParameterType , c ,* id_1)) **else** *Constant (cc (ParameterType , c ,* id_1), ~*compileTime*) **end if**
FcnOrProc id ParameterList ResultSpec	% Subprogram passed as parameter **assert** *DistinctIdents* ({*id* }, {id_{result} }, **domain**(*params*)) **result** ⟨⟨*id , sy* ⟩⟩ **where** *sy* **is** **if** *isProduction (FcnOrProc ::=* **function**) **then** *Function (params , empty ,* id_{result} ,

ty_{result})
else *Procedure* (*params* , *empty*)
end if,

params **is** *cc* (*ParameterList* , *c*),

$\langle id_{\text{result}}, ty_{\text{result}} \rangle$ **is** *cc* (*ResultSpec* , *c*)

We now give context conditions for parameter types.

RHS for *ParameterType*	**CONTEXT CONDITION** *cc* (*RHS* : *ParameterType* , *c* : *Context* , *tyIdent* : *Ident*): *TyDef*
T	*cc* (*T* , *c* , *typeId*)
string(*)	*StringStar*
array E_1 ..*, ... , E_n ..* **of** *T*	**assert** $\forall i$: (*isIndex* (ty_i) & *CompileTimeExpn* (E_i, *c*)) **result** *Array* ($\langle t_1, \ldots, t_n \rangle$, *cc* (*T* , *c* , *typeId*)) **where** t_i **is** *Subrange* (ty_i, ~*compileTime*)
array E_1 ..*, ... , E_n ..* **of string(*)**	**assert** $\forall i$: (*isIndex* (ty_i) & *CompileTimeExpn* (E_i, *c*)) **result** *Array* ($\langle t_1, \ldots, t_n \rangle$, *StringStar*) **where** t_i **is** *Subrange* (ty_i, ~*compileTime*)

We now give context conditions for import lists.

RHS for *Imports*	**CONTEXT CONDITION** *cc* (*RHS* : *Imports* , *c* : *Context* , *imps* : *ImportSet*): ⟨*Context* , *ImportSet* ⟩
empty	⟨*c* , *imps* ⟩
ImportItem Imports	*cc* (*Imports* , c_1, $imps_1$) **where** $\langle c_1, imps_1 \rangle$ **is** *cc* (*ImportItem* , *c* , *imps*)

We now give context conditions for import items. An import list denotes a function from the global context from which the imports are taken and an accumulating *ImportSet* parameter to a (possibly different) global context, reflecting the binding of forward imports as subprograms, together with an *ImportSet* value representing the import list.

An identifier must not be repeated in an import list. A non-forward import must be visible in the given context and must be accessible with access at least as strong as that requested in the import. Only a variable or module can be imported **var**. A forward collection must not be imported.

A forward import is declared as an inaccessible subprogram (here we arbitrarily choose to define it as a procedure); it must be properly declared later in the context as a subprogram. Note that the context-free syntax checks that forward imports occur only in the declaration of forward subprograms.

RHS for *ImportItem*	**CONTEXT CONDITION** $cc(RHS : ImportItem, c : Context, imps : ImportSet) : \langle Context, ImportSet \rangle$
Var id	**assert** $Visible(c, id)$ & id **not in domain**($imps$) % Distinct imports & $access \le access_{id}$ & ($isProduction(Var ::= \textbf{var}) \Rightarrow$ $syTag_{id}$ **in** $\{Variable, Module\}$) & ($syTag_{id} = Variable$ & $tyTag_{id} = Collection) \Rightarrow$ $FwdCollectionResolved(c, id)$) **result** $\langle c, imps + \langle id, \langle sy_{id}, access \rangle\rangle\rangle$ **where** *access* **is** **if** $isProduction(Var ::= \textbf{var})$ **then** *VAR* **else** *readOnly* **end if**
forward *id*	**if** $Visible(c, id)$ & id **not in domain**($imps$) % Distinct imports & $access_{id} = inaccessible$ & $mode_{id} = fwdSubPgm$ **then** $\langle c, imps + \langle id, \langle dummySy, inaccessible \rangle\rangle\rangle$ **elsif** $\sim Visible(c, id)$ & id **not in domain**(imps) % Distinct imports **then** $\langle c_{subpgm},$ $imps + \langle id, \langle dummySy, inaccessible \rangle\rangle\rangle$ **end if** **where** c_{subpgm} **is** $Declare(c, id, Procedure(\langle\, \rangle, empty),$ $fwdSubPgm, inaccessible)$

We now give context conditions for bodies of subprograms. The context parameter is the local subprogram body context, the *Ident* parameter is the name of the subprogram for checking the "end" identifier. The **init** constants are inaccessible (cannot be referenced) except in **post**, **invariant** and **assert** constructs. Here we declare them as constants with access *inaccessible*. They are made temporarily accessible for **post** and other assertions using the *AssertionContext* operator. The result identifier for a function is accessible only in the **post** assertion. Note that the requirement to terminate a function by a **result** statement is enforced elsewhere (by Turing's formal semantics).

RHS for *Body*	**CONTEXT CONDITION** $cc(RHS: Body, c: Context, id_{subpgm}: Ident): Boolean$
[**pre** E_{pre}] [**init** $\{id_i := E_i\}$] [**post** E_{post}] S **end** *id*	$tyTagOf(cc(E_{pre}, c)) = Boolean$ & $tyTagOf(cc(E_{post}, c_{post})) = Boolean$ & $cc(S, c_{body})$ & $id = id_{subpgm}$ **where** c_{body} **is** % Declare each (inaccessible) **init** constant. % These can be accessed only in assertions. *LocalContext* (*Declare* (c, id_i, *Constant* (ty_i, *CompileTimeExpn* (E_i, c)), *nonPERVASIVE*, *inaccessible*), ~*loopNesting*), c_{post} **is** % Make function result identifier as well % as **init** constants accessible to E_{post} **if** *syTagOf* (*SymbolOfContext* (c)) = *Function* **then** *Declare* (*AssertionContext* (c_{body}), $id_{\mathbf{result}}$, $sy_{\mathbf{result}}$, *nonPERVASIVE*, *readOnly*) **else** *AssertionContext* (c_{body}) **end if**, $id_{\mathbf{result}}$ **is** *ResultId* (*SymbolOfContext* (c)), $sy_{\mathbf{result}}$ **is** *Constant* (*ResultType* (*SymbolOfContext* (c)), ~*compileTime*)

8.4.9 Context Conditions for Modules

This section gives context conditions for modules. The invariant clause, if present, must appear before the declarations of exported subprograms. We check that no exported identifier is declared as a subprogram in the invariant context (c_1). All forward declarations must be resolved by the end of the context (this is checked by: $cc(S_2, c_1)$).

RHS for *Decl*	**CONTEXT CONDITION** *cc (RHS : Decl , c : Context): Context*
module id_{module} **import**(*Imports*) **export**(*Exports*) [**pre** E_1] S_1 [**invariant** E_2] S_2 [**post** E_3] **end** *id*	**assert** $cc\,(S_1, c_{import})$ & $cc\,(S_2, c_1)$ & $tyTagOf\,(cc\,(E_1, c_{import})) = Boolean$ & $tyTagOf\,(cc\,(E_2, c_1)) = Boolean$ & $tyTagOf\,(cc\,(E_3, c_2)) = Boolean$ & $id_{module} = id$ & *invariantAppearsBeforeExportedSubpgms* **result** *Declare* (c , id_{module} , *sy* , *nonPERVASIVE* , *VAR*)

where
sy **is** *Module* (*cc* (*Exports* , c_2, *EmptyContext*), *imps*),
$\langle c_{forward}, imps \rangle$ **is**
  cc (*Imports* , *c* , ⟨ ⟩), % $c_{forward}$ not used
  % Note $c_{forward}$ is same as c here since context-free
  % syntax prevents forward imports by modules
c_{import} **is** *ImportContext* (*imps* ,
  Close (*c* , *Module* (⟨ ⟩, *imps*))),
c_1 **is** *ModuleContext* (S_1,
  LocalContext (c_{import}, ~*loopNesting*)),
  % When invariant is omitted, S_1 is empty
c_2 **is** *cc* (S_2, c_1),
invariantAppearsBeforeExportedSubpgms **is**
 isProduction (*Exports* ::= {*Opaque* id_i })
 ⇒ (~∃ *i* : % No exported id_i such that...
  (*Visible* (c_1, id_i)
  & *AccessOf* (c_1, id_i) = *readOnly*
  & *syTagOf* (*syOf* (c_1, id_i)) **in**
   {*Function* , *Procedure* }))

The *ModuleContext* function is used to create the c_1 context in a module body without checking for unresolved forward declarations (which may be resolved in S_2).

ModuleContext (*RHS* : *S* , *c* : *Context*): *Context* $=_{df}$
 if *isProduction* (*S* ::= *empty*)
 then *c*

 elsif *isProduction* (*S* ::= *Decl* S_1)
 then *ModuleContext* (S_1, *cc* (*Decl* , *c*))

 elsif *isProduction* (*S* ::= *Stmt* S_1)

```
then
  if cc (Stmt, c)
  then ModuleContext (S1, c)
  end if
end if
```

We now give context conditions for export lists. An export list denotes a function of two parameters: the context inside a module after all local module declarations, together with a context used to accumulate the export context value. The function result is a context containing just the exported identifiers. If all the identifiers are exportable from the module's context, and if any that are exported **opaque** are bound as types in the module's context, then the identifiers are bound in the export context with the symbols they have in the exporting module context. Types exported as opaque are bound in the export context as special *Opaque* type values.

RHS for *Exports*	**CONTEXT CONDITION** $cc\,(RHS: Exports,\ c: Context,\ c_{export}: Context)$ $: Context$
empty	c_{export}
Opaque id Exports	**assert** *LocallyDeclared* (c, id) & $syTag_{id}$ **in** {*Constant*, *Type*, *Function*, *Procedure* } & (*isProduction* (*Opaque* ::= **opaque**) ⇒ $tyTag_{id} = Type$) **result** $cc\,(Exports, c, c_{id})$ **where** c_{id} **is** % This prevents re-export of same identifier *Declare* $(c_{export}, id, sy, nonPERVASIVE, readOnly)$, *sy* **is** **if** *isProduction* (*Opaque* ::= **opaque**) **then** *Type* (*Opaque* (id, ty_{id})) **else** sy_{id} **end if**

8.4.10 Preventing Aliasing

This section gives functions that disallow aliasing [Cordy 84] in the context conditions for calls to subprograms. Aliasing may potentially occur in subprogram calls in four ways that are disallowed by the following four functions. Only the first of these applies to function calls. All four apply to procedure calls. A fifth source of aliasing arises from possible overlap among procedures' reference parameters. Since this possibility is sometimes determined by computed values of subscripts, the check for it is deferred to semantics, where it is prevented by the *DISJ* (disjoint) validity predicate. The four functions are used in the rules for subprogram calls (*isFunctionCall* and *isProcedureCall*) in Section 8.4.7.

NoAliasingDueToIncreasedAccess
    (c : *Context*, *transImports*: *ImportSet*): *Boolean* $=_{df}$
    % A call must not increase access to an identifier
    $\forall$ *id* **in domain**(*transImports*) :
        ($Visible(c, id) \Rightarrow AccessOf(transImports(id)) \le access_{id}$)

NoAliasingDueToParametricSubpgms
    (c : *Context*, $imps_1$: *ImportSet*, ... , $imps_n$: *ImportSet*): *Boolean* $=_{df}$
    % No overlap among imports of parametric subpgms
    $\forall\, i, j$:   % For each pair of parameters
        $\forall$ *id* **in domain**($imps_i$) * **domain**($imps_j$) :
            % No common *VAR* imports
            $(AccessOf(imps_i(id)) = VAR) \Rightarrow (i = j)$

NoAliasingDueToVarImportOverlap (c : *Context*, *imps*: *ImportSet*,
    formals: *Formals*, $\langle E_1, \dots, E_n\rangle$: **seq of** E): *Boolean* $=_{df}$
    % *VAR* parameters must not overlap imports
    $\forall\, i: isVarParameter_i \Rightarrow noImportOfId_i$
    where
    $isVarParameter_i$ **is** $syTagOf(sy_i) = Variable$,
    $\langle\langle id_{f1}, sy_1\rangle, \dots, \langle id_{fm}, sy_m\rangle\rangle$ **is** *formals*,
        % This defines each sy_i in terms of *formals*
    $noImportOfId_i$ **is**
        $isProduction(E_i ::= Ref_i)$
        & $isProduction(Ref_i ::= id_i\ Selectors_i)$
        & id_i **not in domain**(*imps*)

NoAliasingDueToRefImportOverlap (c : *Context*, *imps*: *ImportSet*,
    formals: *Formals*, $\langle E_1, \dots, E_n\rangle$: **seq of** E): *Boolean* $=_{df}$
    % Reference parameters must not overlap imports
    $\forall\, i: isRefParameter_i \Rightarrow readOnlyOrNoImportOfId_i$

where
isRefParameter$_i$ **is**
  ~*IsScalar* (*tyOf* (sy_i)) **or** *isOpaqueRefParam*$_i$,
isOpaqueRefParam$_i$ **is**
  tyTagOf (*tyOf* (sy_i)) = *Opaque*
  & ~*IsScalar* (*tyOf* (*tyOf* (sy_i))),
$\langle\langle id_{f1}, sy_1\rangle, \ldots, \langle id_{fm}, sy_m\rangle\rangle$ **is** *formals*,
  % This defines each sy_i in terms of *formals*
readOnlyOrNoImportOfId$_i$ **is**
  isProduction (E_i ::= Ref_i)
  & *isProduction* (Ref_i ::= id_i $Selectors_i$)
  & (id_i **not in domain**(*imps*)
    or *AccessOf* (*imps* (id_i)) = *readOnly*)

8.4.11 Compile-Time Expressions

This section gives functions that determine whether expressions (or initializing values) are considered to be compile-time values.

CompileTimeExpn (*E* : *Production*, *c* : *Context*): *Boolean* $=_{df}$
  isLiteral **or**
  CompileTimeSetConstructor **or**
  CompileTimeIntExpn **or**
  CompileTimeNamedConstant **or**
  CompileTimeOrdOrChr **or**
  CompileTimeCatenation

where

isLiteral **is**
  isProduction (*E* ::=*integerLiteral*) **or** *isProduction* (*E* ::=*realLiteral*) **or**
  isProduction (*E* ::=*stringLiteral*) **or** *isProduction* (*E* ::=*booleanLiteral*),

CompileTimeSetConstructor **is**
  % Set constructors with compile-time elements
  % are compile-time
  isProduction (*E* ::=*Ref*([**all**])) **or**
  (*isProduction* (*E* ::=*Ref* ({E_i}))
    & $tyTag_E$ = *Set*
    & $\forall$ *i* : *CompileTimeExpn* (E_i, *c*)),

CompileTimeIntExpn **is**
% The integer operators +, –, *, **div**, and **mod** are compile-time
% if their operands are compile-time expressions
$((isProduction(E ::= +E_1)$ **or**
$isProduction(E ::= -E_1))$
$\& \ CompileTimeExpn(E_1, c)$
$\& \ tyTag_1 = Int)$
or $((isProduction(E ::= E_1 + E_2)$ **or**
$isProduction(E ::= E_1 - E_2)$ **or**
$isProduction(E ::= E_1 * E_2)$ **or**
$isProduction(E ::= E_1 \textbf{ div } E_2)$ **or**
$isProduction(E ::= E_1 \textbf{ mod } E_2))$
$\& \ tyTag_1 = Int \ \& \ tyTag_2 = Int$
$\& \ CompileTimeExpn(E_1, c) \ \& \ CompileTimeExpn(E_2, c)),$

CompileTimeNamedConstant **is**
% Compile-time named constants are
% so marked in their symbol definitions
$isProduction(E ::= Ref)$
$\& \ syTag_{ref} = Constant$
$\& \ isCompileTime(sy_{ref}),$ % *isCompileTime* is field of *sy*

CompileTimeOrdOrChr **is**
% *chr* and *ord* are compile-time with compile-time operands
$isProduction(E ::= Ref)$
$\& \ isProduction(Ref ::= id \ Selectors)$
$\& \ isProduction(Selectors ::= (E_1))$
$\& \ (id = "ord"$ **or** $id = "chr")$
$\& \ CompileTimeExpn(E_1, c)$

CompileTimeCatenation **is**
% String catenation is compile-time with
% compile-time operands
$isProduction(E ::= E_1 + E_2) \ \& \ tyTag_1 = String \ \& \ tyTag_2 = String$
$\& \ CompileTimeExpn(E_1, c) \ \& \ CompileTimeExpn(E_2, c),$

CompileTimeInit (*InitVal* : *Production*, *c* : *Context*): *Boolean*
% All parts of **init**(...) must be compile-time
$isProduction(InitVal ::= \textbf{init} \ (\{initPart_{Ai}\} \ ))$
$\& \ (isProduction(initPart_{Ai} ::= E_i) \Rightarrow$
$(\forall i : cc(E_i, c) \ \& \ CompileTimeExpn(E_i, c)))$
$\& \ (isProduction(initPart_{Ai} ::= \textbf{init} \ (\{initPart_{Bi}\} \ )) \Rightarrow$
$CompileTimeInit(initPart_{Bi}, c))$

8.5 Assumptions and Observations

This section gives assumptions made about the syntax of Turing, areas of incompleteness in the context condition definition, and observations about this definition.

8.5.1 Assumptions Made by the Definition

The definition of context conditions, as given in this chapter, assumes that certain syntactic transformations have been carried out on Turing programs. First, we assume that subprogram import lists are given explicitly even though the Turing Report makes them optional. Second, we assume each identifier appearing in a program is made unique by prefixing it with the names of all the closed scopes (modules and subprograms) surrounding the definition of the identifier. This allows us to use identifiers as unique labels for enumerated, record and union types. Third, we assume that any module or subprogram that uses the **get** or **put** statements explicitly **var** imports a special module called ''IO'', of which **get** and **put** are assumed to be procedure entries. This assumption simplifies detection of side effects in functions that perform input or output.

None of these assumptions are part of the Turing language defined by the Report. However, it would be easy to specify a set of syntactic transformations to convert strings satisfying Turing's context-free grammar into the form assumed above.

8.5.2 Incompleteness of Turing's Formal Context Conditions

The context condition definition presented here omits the following contextual restrictions described in the Turing Report.

(1) The export of opaque types from modules is incompletely handled here. According to the Report, only the name of an opaque type is available for purposes of type checking outside the exporting module. This definition allows access to the structure of opaque types through exported constants and subprograms that are defined in terms of opaque types.

(2) We do not explicitly define the context conditions for the predefined subprograms of Turing. Rather we take the context of a program to be a predefined scope called $c_{predefined}$ which contains bindings of all the predefined names to their attributes. The predefined functions *eof* and *intstr* and predefined attributes *upper* and *lower* have optional parameters. These optional parameters are not supported by this definition.

(3) We do not check that **init** value lists used to initialize array, record and union constants and variables are componentwise assignable to the array, record or union type. Array and union initialization depend on expression semantics to compute index ranges and to select union alternatives based on a tag value. Note that these initializations are not checked by the semantics definition either.

8.5.3 Observations

Turing's context conditions are lengthy and complicated for several reasons related to the design objectives for the language:

(1) The language syntax was consciously designed to reject a large class of erroneous programs at the syntactic level, mainly through syntactic type checking.

(2) Context conditions enforce the scope rules of Turing. The rules determine the binding of names to objects and the allowed referencing of these names. For example, scope rules enforce the information hiding properties of modules. They also restrict access to variables that have been bound to using the Turing **bind** construct (to prevent aliasing), to **init** constants and to **forward** objects that cannot be referenced in most contexts until they have been fully declared.

(3) Assumptions made by the formal semantics, such as the absence of expression side effects and syntactic aliasing, are enforced by context conditions.

(4) Context conditions provide support for efficient implementation. For example, they prevent records from having fields whose size cannot be determined until run-time.

We conclude by evaluating how appropriate the definition style used here is in meeting the goals set for the formal definition of Turing syntax. In the introduction to the chapter, we listed the goals as: clarity, consistency and completeness. In addition to these goals, the formal definition of syntax is intended to: (a) assist programmers by answering questions about the language, (b) serve as a guide for implementors and assist them in developing correct implementations of the language, (c) assist the designers of the language.

We believe that this definition is suitable for use as a reference manual by programmers, although we expect that most questions arising in the course of everyday programming will be resolved by referring to the Report. To facilitate cross referencing between the Report and the formal definition of context conditions, the context condition definition follows the organization used in the Report's presentation. Mnemonic names in the formal definition were chosen to correspond to the terminology used in the Report.

The mathematical concepts applied in the definition are well within the grasp of a person with training in computer science. With a modest investment of time a conscientious programmer should be able use this definition as an accessible source of precise information in situations where the Report's description is inadequate.

This definition provides a solid basis for implementation of context condition checkers for Turing. The formality of the definition eliminates the ambiguity that plagues informal definitions. It would be relatively easy to construct a prototype implementation based on an operational interpretation of the definition itself. A more conventional implementation could be built following the modular organization suggested by the types and rules of the definition. Types could be implemented as modules and rules could be implemented as subprograms that take a representation of the abstract syntax as a parameter value. See [Rosselet 84] for a more thorough treatment of implementation. The notation used to define context conditions contains only simple mathematical objects, such as sets and sequences, a factor that should help in proving the correctness of a conventional compiler implementation.

Formalizing a language definition forces a careful examination of many pathological situations that might otherwise escape a designer's attention. This definition provided only marginal assistance in the language design effort — in the form of exposing ambiguity and incompleteness in the design and in the Report. However, this definition was developed after most of the design decisions for Turing had already been made, and after most of the language had been implemented. Had the formal definition preceded implementation, the effort to formally describe the language would have been a more important factor in the design process.

Chapter 9

Formal Semantics: The Meaning of Turing Programs

1 Introduction

The syntax of the Turing language has been formally defined by giving its lexical syntax, context-free syntax, and context conditions. Any string of characters that satisfies Turing's syntax is considered to be a Turing program. We will now formally define the semantics of Turing. In other words, we will give the meaning of each Turing program. Before studying this formal definition, the reader may wish to review the language's informal definition, given in the Turing Report.

The primary goals for the formal definition of Turing's semantics are clarity, consistency and completeness. The definition is designed to be easily understood by a Turing programmer or by a Turing implementer. Its formalisms are chosen to be of immediate help in the development of correct Turing programs and Turing implementations. By the mathematical nature of this definition, it is independent of any particular implementation of Turing. The only notable features of Turing whose semantics are not given are the predefined subprograms.

The language defined here is Ideal Turing, which by definition never suffers resource exhaustion; integer operations never overflow, stacks are unbounded, real number precision is infinite, and so on. However, the section called Implementation Constraints explains how to deal with the inevitability of finite resources in Turing implementations.

The definition assumes a familiarity with mathematical concepts such as predicate calculus, set theory, axiomatization of integers, and so on. The operations of Turing (such as real addition, set union, and boolean conjunction) are exactly those of mathematics.

Any potential failure in evaluating an expression (such as division by zero) is prohibited by explicit validity predicates. When these predicates are true, we are guaranteed that expressions in Turing programs have their usual mathematical meaning.

9.1.1 Organization of the Definition

The definition of Turing's formal semantics is organized into four parts as shown in Figure 9.1.

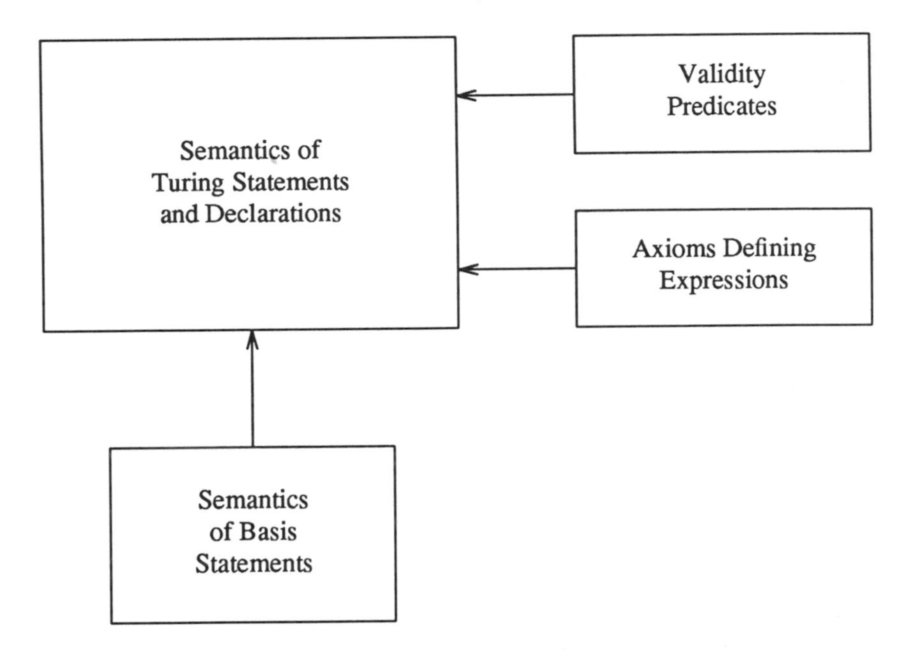

Figure 9.1 Organization of Semantic Definition of Turing

The first and central part defines Turing's statements and declarations. This part, when stripped of its surrounding English explanations, is about four pages long. Each Turing statement or declaration is defined by transforming it to basis statements (or to already defined Turing statements or declarations). The second part defines the ten basis statements; these are very simple statements which together are sufficient for defining all Turing statements and declarations. The formal definition of this basis in terms of weakest preconditions is about a dozen lines long.

The third part consists of the seven validity predicates, which determine when it is meaningful to evaluate an expression or to execute a statement. For example, the EXPN (expression) validity predicate is false when applied to an array reference with an out-of-bounds subscript. When stripped of surrounding English explanations, the definition of these predicates is about four pages long.

The fourth part consists of the formal definition of expressions. Ideally, this part would give an axiomatization of all expressions that can appear in Turing programs. However, since most Turing types, such as booleans, integers and reals, inherit their meaning from mathematics, these axioms are not actually given. Axioms defining records and arrays are given, because axioms for these are less well known. This axiomatization could have been omitted because Turing's records and arrays have the same meaning as comparable features in languages such as Pascal. Turing's unions and collections were purposely designed to have the same axioms as records and arrays.

To illustrate this organization, we give the definition of the semantics of Turing's assignment statement:

$$sem(x := e) \quad =_{\mathrm{df}} \quad ASSERT\ EXPN(e)\ \&\ ASN(T_x, e);\, x \leftarrow e$$

The *sem* function (given in the central part) defines the Turing statement $x := e$ by transforming it to basis statements (*ASSERT*, $\leftarrow$, and semicolon). The basis statements use validity predicates (*EXPN*, which requires e to be valid, and *ASN*, which requires e's value to be within the range of x's type T_x). The meaning of expression e is determined by axioms.

These definitions assume that syntactic checks, defined formally by context conditions, have eliminated potential sources of side effects. These checks also eliminate potential sources of aliasing except those eliminated by the *DISJ* validity predicate. In general, the term *syntactic checks* will refer to restrictions imposed by Turing's lexical and context-free grammars and context conditions.

9.1.2 Novel Aspects

The formal language semantics given here is novel in a number of ways, as will be listed in this section. Because of these novel aspects, this formal semantics may serve as an object of study for those interested in programming language design, formalization of language semantics and formal specification techniques.

Foremost, this semantics emphasizes clarity and easy understandability across a wide audience of computer professionals. To understand the semantic definition of Turing statements, declarations and validity conditions, the reader needs only to know programming in languages like Algol and Pascal. He or she does not need to have mastered specialized notations such as denotational semantics or weakest preconditions. Consequently, this definition can be of immediate use to Turing programmers and Turing implementors.

A key aspect of the understandability of the semantics arises from its modularity, in other words, from its clear division into the four parts shown in Figure 9.1.

The semantics given here is more complete than that given in most formal language definitions. For example, it has been common to omit the formalization of input/output, whereas Turing's rather extensive input/output features are formalized here. It has also been common to ignore floating point and problems of resource exhaustion. This semantics is notable for providing a clean approach to the formalization of floating point and arithmetic with bounded sets of values. This degree of completeness is intended to assure that Turing programs that are proven correct should in practice actually accomplish their specified goals.

The semantics given here takes the *axiomatic* approach in that the basis statements are defined using weakest preconditions. This use of weakest preconditions is novel in its extension to triples of predicates in order to give the semantics of exit and return statements.

This semantics can alternatively be considered to be *operational*. An appendix formalizes this operational approach and demonstrates that weakest preconditions can be defined operationally rather than by postulation. This establishes the precise relationship between the operational and axiomatic semantics of Turing. When a language is defined only axiomatically, it is difficult to know if an implementation of the language satisfies its formal semantics. The operational approach gives the language implementor a direct method for translating Turing programs into actions to be carried out by a computer. This directness suggests methods of proving the correctness of the code generator of a Turing compiler.

The treatment of potential run-time failures, such as division by zero, is particularly clear in this definition. All potential failures are formalized in terms of validity predicates that appear in the *ASSERT* statements that are used in defining Turing's statements and declarations. Each validity predicate is a function that is formalized by a table that specifies its value in terms of a boolean expression.

The treatment of both pointers and unions is particularly clear in this formalization. The invention of a *pointer set* for each collection variable provides a simple formal technique for prohibiting the use of dangling pointers. The definition of Turing's **tag** statement leaves no doubt that resetting a union's tag implies the loss of the values of all other fields in the union. Too often, details of this sort have been omitted in other language formalizations.

9.1.3 Notation

In the definition of Turing semantics, lower case keywords will correspond to Turing statements while upper case will correspond to basis statements. We will use the following notation:

x is an identifier
$Q[x : e]$ is predicate Q with free variable x replaced by e
$x . s$ is identifier x followed by selector sequence s.
A selector sequence consists of component selectors, which are array or collection subscripts and record or union field selectors.

$x(s : e)$ is the value of x with its s component replaced by the value of expression e
$c\ .\ ps$ is the set of all pointers to existing elements of collection c
T_r is the type of reference r
UNINIT (T) is the uninitialized value for type T, and is not a value in type T
EXPN (e) is true when expression e is valid
REF (r) is true when reference r is valid
TYP (T) is true when type T is valid
ASN (T_r, e) is true when e can validly be assigned to the type of r
EQV (T_1, T_2) is true when types T_1 and T_2 are equivalent
DIST (L) is true when all expressions in set L are distinct
DISJ (U, V) is true when references in set V are pairwise disjoint and each reference in U is disjoint from references in V.

The seven functions *EXPN, REF, TYP, ASN, EQV, DIST* and *DISJ* are validity predicates; they are defined formally in a later section. The following syntactic notation is used:

[item] means the item is optional
{ item } means zero or more copies of the item

We will use standard mathematical notation that is not necessarily allowed in Turing expressions; for example, $x \geq 1$ means *x*>=1, and $0 \leq n \leq 20$ means 0<=*n* & *n*<=20.

9.2 Basis Statements

Before giving the semantics of Turing's statements and declarations, we will define the ten basis statements. These statements will first be given an informal operational semantics, and then a formal, axiomatic semantics. The entire set of Turing statements and declarations will be defined in terms of this basis.

9.2.1 Informal Semantics of the Basis

This section gives an informal operational description of the ten statements in the basis; the next section gives their axiomatic semantics. The first six basis statements are particularly simple:

1.	*CONTINUE*	The null (or skip) statement
2.	*PICK(x, s)*	Assign to x any value from non-empty set s
3.	*IF e THEN S1* *ELSE S2* *END IF*	Choose *S1* or *S2* based on e

4.	*S1;S2*	*S1* followed by *S2*
5.	*ABORT*	Program failure with immediate halt
6.	*CHAOS*	Program failure with arbitrary continuation

The following auxiliary statements are defined in terms of these first six basis statements:

$x \leftarrow e$ $=_{df}$ *PICK* $(x, \{x\})$ Assignment of value e to x
FAIL $=_{df}$ *IF CHECKING THEN ABORT ELSE CHAOS END IF*
ASSERT e $=_{df}$ *IF e THEN CONTINUE ELSE FAIL END IF*

The *PICK* statement is the only nondeterministic statement in the basis. In the definition of Turing it is used in only four places: in the definition of ← (unchecked assignment, which is deterministic), in the definition of the **new** statement, in the definition of unchecked variable initialization, and in the definition of the random number generation procedures (which are not formalized here).

ABORT and *CHAOS* are used only in defining *FAIL*; they do not appear in further definitions. *CHECKING* is a constant that is true when Turing execution is to be faithful. The essence of faithful execution is that every failure results in an immediate abortion. (See the Turing Report for a discussion of checking and faithful execution.)

The first six basis statements may be a sufficient basis for a target language that does not support loop exits or procedure returns. To handle exits and returns, which are the "structured *GOTO*s" of Turing, we define four more basis statements:

7. *BLOCK S END BLOCK*
   Bracketing to support exiting from *S*
8. *SUBPROG S END SUBPROG*
   Bracketing to support returning from *S*
9. *EXIT* Terminate (jump to end of) enclosing *BLOCK*
10. *RETURN* Terminate (jump to end of) enclosing *SUBPROG*

A *BLOCK* is executed sequentially to its end unless an *EXIT* or *RETURN* is encountered; an *EXIT* causes a jump to the end of the nearest enclosing *BLOCK*. A *SUBPROG* is analogous except *RETURN* is the statement producing a jump to *END*. Note that the body *S* of a *BLOCK* is executed only once (not repetitively). We assume that a syntactic check guarantees that *EXIT* only occurs inside a *BLOCK*. The main program is assumed to be nested in a *SUBPROG*; this implies that a *RETURN* from the main program causes termination.

As will be seen, a loop with body *S* is considered to be equivalent to many copies of *S* followed by *FAIL* in a block, i.e., *BLOCK S; S; ... S; FAIL END BLOCK*. Loop termination occurs when *EXIT* is encountered in one of the copies of *S*. The *FAIL* in the block occurs after indefinitely many occurrences of *S*; this expresses the formal intent that infinite loops are prohibited. Conceptually, a nonterminating loop eventually fails when encountering *FAIL* at the end of the block.

A call to a procedure is considered to be equivalent to a copy of the procedure's body (surrounded by *SUBPROG* and *SUBPROG END*) with appropriate assignments to and from parameters. This copying of loop and procedure bodies can be considered to be done dynamically (as needed), so only a finite number of copies is required.

The semantics of Turing will be given by transforming all its statements and declarations into basis statements; this can be called *transformational* semantics. Alternatively, it can be considered to be *axiomatic* semantics because the basis is defined here formally by weakest preconditions. We can also call it *basis* semantics, because the basis can easily be defined by an alternate technique, such as formal operational semantics.

9.2.2 Formal Semantics of the Basis

This section gives a formal semantics of the basis using weakest preconditions. See [Hehner 84], [Gries 81] or [Dijkstra 76] for a coverage of weakest preconditions. An alternate definition of basis, given in terms of formal operational semantics, is given in an appendix.

We traditionally write $wp(S, q)$ to denote the weakest predicate that must be true before S is executed, in order to guarantee that S establishes predicate q. This notation assumes that S can terminate cleanly only one way: by executing to its end. In Turing, a statement can terminate cleanly three ways: by continuing (executing to its end), exiting, or returning, as in this example:

```
if a > b then exit
elsif a = b then return
else a := a + 1
end if
```

If $a > b$, this statement exits and is expected to establish its exiting predicate (Q_e), if $a = b$, it returns and is expected to establish its returning predicate (Q_r), and otherwise it adds 1 to a and is expected to establish its continuing predicate (Q_c). We introduce an extended version of the wp notation that maps a triple of postconditions (Q_c, Q_e, Q_r) to a triple of preconditions (P_c, P_e, P_r):

$$wp(S, (Q_c, Q_e, Q_r)) = (P_c, P_e, P_r)$$

We write Q for (Q_c, Q_e, Q_r) and P for (P_c, P_e, P_r), so this can be written as

$$wp(S, Q) = P$$

For example, the *CONTINUE* and *ABORT* statements have these definitions in terms of wp:

$$wp(CONTINUE, (Q_c, Q_e, Q_r)) =_{\mathrm{df}} (Q_c, Q_e, Q_r)$$
$$wp(ABORT, (Q_c, Q_e, Q_r)) =_{\mathrm{df}} (\mathbf{false}, Q_e, Q_r)$$

In every case, $P_e = Q_e$ and $P_r = Q_r$, because any *EXIT* or *RETURN* in a statement preceding S necessarily must establish the same exiting/returning predicate as does S. Therefore, we will shorten our *wp* definitions so that only P_c is defined. For example, the definitions of *CONTINUE* and *ABORT* are shortened to:

$$wp(CONTINUE, Q)_c =_{df} Q_c$$
$$wp(ABORT, Q)_c =_{df} \mathbf{false}$$

Since *wp* semantics does not distinguish possible failure from definite failure, *CHAOS* has the same *wp* definition as *ABORT*:

$$wp(CHAOS, Q)_c =_{df} \mathbf{false}$$

The *PICK* statement requires Q_c to be true for every value in set s:

$$wp(PICK(x,s), Q)_c =_{df} \forall\, x \textbf{ in } s: Q_c$$

Statement sequences ($S1; S2$) are defined analogously to the traditional *wp* definition:

$$wp(S1; S2, Q)_c =_{df} wp(S1, wp(S2, Q))_c$$

The *IF* statement is defined analogously to the traditional *wp* definition:

$$wp(IF\ e\ THEN\ S1\ ELSE\ S2, Q)_c =_{df}$$
$$e \Rightarrow wp(S1, Q)_c\ \&\ \sim e \Rightarrow wp(S2, Q)_c$$

The *wp* for *BLOCK* requires contained *EXITs* to establish the *BLOCK*'s continuing predicate Q_c, while *SUBPROG* requires contained *RETURNs* to establish Q_c:

$$wp(BLOCK\ S\ END\ BLOCK, Q)_c =_{df} wp(S, (Q_c, Q_c, Q_r))_c$$
$$wp(SUBPROG\ S\ END\ SUBPROG, Q)_c =_{df} wp(S, (Q_c, Q_e, Q_c))_c$$

A statement preceding *EXIT* (or *RETURN*) must establish Q_e (or Q_r):

$$wp(EXIT, Q)_c =_{df} Q_e$$
$$wp(RETURN, Q)_c =_{df} Q_r$$

Note that the *wp* for *EXIT* and *RETURN* effectively ignores the continuation postcondition Q_c, because neither statement allows continuation to the textually following statement.

This completes the *wp* definitions of the ten basis statements. The appendix that defines the formal operational semantics of the basis shows that these *wp* definitions can be derived as theorems.

Since the basis is defined using weakest precondition's, one can in principle use the *wp* methodology of correct program development with Turing. However, the basis can as well be defined other ways, for example, operationally as is done in an appendix. As a result, the formal semantics of Turing is understandable without mastering *wp* concepts.

Using the definitions of $\leftarrow$, *FAIL* and *ASSERT* given above, we can easily prove:

Lemma: $wp(FAIL, Q)_c$ = **false**
$wp(ASSERT\ e, Q)_c = e \,\&\, Q_c$
$wp(x \leftarrow e, Q)_c = Q_c\ [x: e]$

We assume that failure never occurs in a basis statement except by an explicit *FAIL*. This means that the basis has partial semantics, i.e., it does not give a reasonable meaning to invalid constructs such as division by zero or use of uninitialized variables. By contrast, Turing semantics are total; this totality is accomplished by "guarding" each potentially invalid construct by an *ASSERT*. The *ASSERT* effectively translates any invalid construct into an explicit *FAIL*. The *ASSERT* expressions are composed of validity predicates.

9.3 Semantics of Turing Statements and Declarations

We will now give, in order, the semantics of variable and constant declarations, bind declarations, simple statements, input/output, loops, procedures, functions and modules. Each construct is defined by giving an equivalent construct that consists of only basis statements or previously defined constucts.

This method of definition used here is somewhat less formal than that used in giving the formal definition of Turing's context conditions. Here we rely, to a certain degree, on the reader's ability to recognize a construct, and we do not give a formal definition of the syntax of these constructs. This relaxation in the degree of formalism allows us to omit details which would complicate the definition, and which, it is hoped, are obvious to the reader.

9.3.1 Variable and Constant Declarations

We will generally ignore questions of scope of names by use of this assumption: each separately declared identifier is assumed to be unique. When names are repeated (due to copies of loop/procedure bodies), each use of an identifier is correlated with the nearest preceding declaration of that identifier within the same body. This is a simple version of the usual Algol scope rules. The semantics we give for declarations simply specifies that type definitions must be valid (*TYP* is the type validity function). Explicit initialization in a declaration is treated as an assignment (assignment is defined in the next section). When checking is specified and variable x is declared without explicit initialization, it is considered to be set to an "uninitialized value" by the *UNINITIALIZE* routine:

UNINITIALIZE(x) $=_{df}$ *IF CHECKING THEN* $x \leftarrow UNINIT(T_x)$
ELSE PICK(x, UNIV)
END IF

UNIV is the universe of possible values, which includes $UNINIT(T_x)$. The *UNINITIAL-*

IZE routine is used in declarations, in the **new** statement, and in the **tag** statement. We now give the semantics of Turing declarations:

DECLARATION *S*	**SEMANTICS** *sem(S)*
type [**pervasive**] $x : T$	*ASSERT TYP(T)*
var x: T	*ASSERT TYP(T); UNINITIALIZE(x)*
var x: $T := e$	**var** x: T; $x := e$
var $x := e$	**var** $x : T_e := e$
var x_1 $\{, x_i\}$: T	**type** t: T; **var** x_1: t $\{$; **var** x_i: t $\}$
var x_1 $\{, x_i\}$: $T := e$	**var** x_1 $\{, x_i\}$: T; $x_1 := e$ $\{; x_i := e\}$
var x_1 $\{, x_i\}$ $:= e$	**var** x_1 $\{, x_i\}$: $T_e := e$
const [**pervasive**] x [$:T$] $:= e$	**var** x [$:T$] $:= e$
var x: **collection of** T	*ASSERT TYP(T);* $x \leftarrow x(ps : U())$ (This initializes x . ps, the set of pointers to x's active elements, to U(), the empty set)
var x: **collection of forward** T	$x \leftarrow x(ps : U())$

For declarations of non-collections, the semantics effectively transforms more complex forms (lower in the above list) to less complex forms (higher in the list). The definition of **const** as **var** is justified because syntactic checks guarantee that there can be no modification to **const** values. T_e is the *root* type of expression e; as defined by the Turing Report, this implies that (1) if e has an integer value then T_e is **int** and (2) if e has a string value then T_e is **string** (in spite of the fact that e may have the form of a variable declared using an integer subrange or limited length string).

Turing allows the initializing expression e to be an **init** construct, **init**($e_1\{, e_i\}$), in the declarations of arrays, records, and union types. An **init** clause can be formalized as either a sequence of assignment statements or as a new form of expression. We will not carry out this formalization.

9.3.2 The Bind Declaration

In Turing, (a part of) a variable can be given a new name using a **bind** declaration. The definition of procedure calls treats passing of **var** and non-scalar parameters as binds. Each binding can be considered to be implemented by value-result. Since Turing bans aliasing, the binding can as well be implemented by reference, which is generally more efficient. Aliasing due to binding is prevented by the requirement that items being bound must be disjoint. All non-**var** items in a **bind** are treated like u and all **var** items like v:

DECLARATION S	SEMANTICS *sem(S)*
bind u to U, **var** v to V; S	*ASSERT REF(U)* **and** *REF(V);* *ASSERT DISJ(U, V);* **var** $u: T_U$; $u \leftarrow U$; **var** $v: T_V$; $v \leftarrow V$; **const** $t_j := e_j$; S'; $V' \leftarrow v$

In this definition, S is the scope of the identifiers u and v. T_U and T_V are the declared types of variables U and V (not their root types). The set of constants t_j record the values of all subscripts e_j in reference V. Reference V' is the same as V except that t_j instead of e_j are used as subscripts; as a result, a binding to an array or collection element is not affected by subsequent changes to the subscripting expressions in V. S' is the same as S except that each each exit or return (or result) from S is preceded by the statement $V' \leftarrow v$. The assignments $u \leftarrow U$, $v \leftarrow V$, and $V' \leftarrow v$ use $\leftarrow$ instead of := because the right side need not be initialized. Syntactic restrictions guarantee that the value of u cannot change during its scope (in statement S).

If there are no exits/returns terminating the **bind** and U and V contains no subscripts, then $DISJ(U, V)$ becomes manifest and the semantics simplifies to:

DECLARATION S	SEMANTICS *sem(S)*
bind u **to** U, **var** v **to** V; S	*ASSERT DISJ* (U, V); **var** $u: T_U$; $u \leftarrow U$; **var** $v: T_V$; $v \leftarrow V$; S; $V \leftarrow v$

9.3.3 Statements other than Input/Output, Loops and Procedure Calls

This section gives the definition of all Turing statements except input/output, loops and procedure calls. The reader is reminded that these definitions assume that syntactic checks, such as disallowing assignment of strings to integer variables, have been enforced.

STATEMENT *S*	**SEMANTICS** *sem(S)*
$x := e$	*ASSERT EXPN(e)* & $ASN(T_x, e)$; $x \leftarrow e$
$x . s := e$	$x := x(s : e)$
assert *e*	*ASSERT EXPN(e); ASSERT e*
if *e* **then** *S* 1 **else** *S* 2 **end if**	*ASSERT EXPN(e);* *IF e THEN S1* *ELSE S2* *END IF*
begin *S* **end**	*S* (This assumes declared identifiers are distinct)
if *e* **then** *S* **end if**	**if** *e* **then** *S* **else** *CONTINUE* **end if**
if e_a **then** S_a **elsif** e_b **then** S_b {**elsif** e_i **then** S_i} [**else** S_c] **end if**	**if** e_a **then** S_a **else if** e_b **then** S_b {**elsif** e_i **then** S_i} [**else** S_c] **end if** **end if**
case *e* **of** **label** L_{11} { ,L_{1j} } : *S* 1 {**label** L_{i1} {,L_{ij} } : *Si* } **label:** *Sc* **end case**	*ASSERT EXPN*(L_{ij}) & *DIST*(L_{ij}); **if** $e = L_{11}$ {**or** $e = L_{1j}$} **then** *S* 1 {**elsif** $e = L_{i1}$ {**or** $e = L_{ij}$} **then** *Si* } **else** *Sc* **end if**
case *e* **of** **label** L_{11} {,L_{1j}}: *S* 1 {**label** L_{i1} {,L_{ij}}: *Si* } **end case**	**case** *e* **of** **label** L_{11} {,L_{1j}}: *S* 1 {**label** L_{i1} {,L_{ij}}: *Si* } **label:** *FAIL* **end case**

tag x, e	$UNINITIALIZE(x)$; $x\ .\ t := e$ (where t is the union's tag field)
tag $x\ .\ s, e$	**var** $y : T_{x\ .\ s}$; **tag** y, e; $x\ .\ s := y$

new c, x	$PICK(x, U(\textbf{all}) - c\ .\ ps)$;
	 if $x \neq nil(c)$ **then**
	 $c\ .\ ps \leftarrow c\ .\ ps + U(x)$;
	 $UNINITIALIZE(c(x))$
	 end if
	 (U(**all**) is the set of all pointers to c,
	 $c\ .\ ps$ is the set of pointers to c's
	 existing elements, and
	 $U(x)$ is the singleton set containing x)

new $c, x\ .\ s$	**var** y: **pointer to** c; **new** c, y; $x\ .\ s := y$
free c, x	$ASSERT\ REF(c(x))$; $c\ .\ ps := c\ .\ ps - U(x)$; $x := nil(c)$ (This checks that x is in $c\ .\ ps$ before removing x from $c\ .\ ps$ and setting x to nil)
free $c, x\ .\ s$	**var** $y := x\ .\ s$; **free** c, y; $x\ .\ s := y$

We will now make certain observations about these statement definitions. Assignment to part of a structured value can be proved to have this weakest precondition:

Lemma: $\text{wp}(x\ .\ s := e, Q)_c = (REF(x\ .\ s)\ \&\ ASN(T_{x\ .\ s}, e)\ \&\ Q[x : x(s : e)])$

There is a common pattern for handling changes to components of structured values. As can be seen in the definition of assignment, **tag**, and **new**, the simpler case of changing an entire variable is handled first; then the case of component changes is given in terms of the simpler case. This pattern will be used again in defining the **get** statement.

The requirements that case labels must be valid and distinct ($EXPN(L_{ij})$ & $DIST(L_{ij})$) can be enforced at compile time, because syntactic checks require case labels to be manifest.

The definition of the **tag** statement implies that all fields other than the tag field are uninitialized. This clearly shows that even if a **tag** statement resets the tag field to its current value, all other fields are lost.

An implementation of the **new** statement returns the pointer value $nil(c)$ when there is no space to allocate another collection element. This possibility is shown in the definition of **new** in that the chosen (PICKed) pointer value can be $nil(c)$. The **new** and

free statements are defined to maintain *c . ps* as the set of pointers to active elements of *c*. The *REF* validity predicate requires that in any reference *c* (*p*), *p* must be a member of *c . ps*. Since *c . ps* cannot be written in a Turing program, it need not be directly implemented.

The semantics of Turing statement sequences (semi-colon) is not given explicitly because it is identical to that of the basis. Note that the only basis statements used so far in our definition of Turing are the first six: *CONTINUE, PICK, IF*, semicolon and *ABORT/CHAOS* (via *FAIL*).

9.3.4 Loops

As mentioned before, a loop is considered to be equivalent to many copies of its body nested in a *BLOCK*. There is a final *FAIL* that specifies the requirement for eventual termination.

STATEMENT *S*	SEMANTICS *sem(S)*
exit	*EXIT*
exit when *e*	**if** *e* **then exit end if**
loop *S* **end loop**	*BLOCK S* END BLOCK* where $S^* =_{df} \lim_{n \to \infty} S^n$ $S^0 =_{df} FAIL$ $S^{n+1} =_{df} S ; S^n$

for *x*: *a* .. *b*
S
end for
	var *a1* := *a*;
	const *b1* := *b*;
	if *a1* <= *b1* **then**
	loop
	const *x* := *a* 1;
	S;
	exit when *x* = *b* 1;
	a 1 := *succ* (*a* 1)
	end loop
	end if

Turing's decreasing **for loop** is the same as the increasing **for loop**, except <= is replaced by >= and *succ* by *pred*.

We have thus far ignored loop invariants. We can treat a loop invariant as an assert statement, so

loop invariant I ; S **end loop**

is equivalent to

loop assert I ; S **end loop**

There is an alternative method of handling loop invariants, which will now be briefly outlined, but not covered in any detail. This method extends the syntax of Turing to allow a loop bound, as shown here:

```
loop
  invariant I;
  bound B ;
  S
end loop
```

The invariant and bound expressions are not restricted to be Turing expressions; in other words, they can use any mathematical notation. The invariant I must be true at the beginning of each iteration. The bound B must be non-negative at these same times, and must decrease with each iteration. This guarantees loop termination; the value of B gives a bound on the remaining number of loop iterations.

9.3.5 Procedures

The declaration of a procedure requires the types of its formal parameters to be valid:

DECLARATION *S*	**SEMANTICS** *sem(S)*

procedure
  $p(k: T_k, u: T_u,$ **var** $v: T_v)$
    import (...)
  S
end p
	ASSERT $TYP(T_k)$ & $TYP(T_u)$
	  & $TYP(T_v)$

We have shown one scalar constant (non-var) parameter k, one nonscalar constant parameter u, and one variable parameter v; these represent any number of parameters. The semantics of procedure calls will reflect the fact that Turing is designed to allow parameters u and v to be passed by reference. The semantics of the Turing **return** statement is not given explicitly because it is identical to the basis *RETURN*.

If p is a non-recursive procedure with formal parameters k, u and v and body S, then a call to p with actual parameters K, U and V is defined as:

$$p(K, U, V) =_{df} CALL(p, K, U, V)$$

where

$$CALL(p, K, U, V) =_{df} \quad \begin{array}{l} \textbf{const}\ k: T_k := K; \\ ASSERT\ ASN(T_u, U)\ \&\ EQV(T_v, T_V); \\ \textbf{bind}\ u\ \textbf{to}\ U,\ \textbf{var}\ v\ \textbf{to}\ V; \\ SUBPROG\ S\ END\ SUBPROG \end{array}$$

The **const** declaration implies that scalar non-**var** parameters can be passed by value; it also implies parameter compatibility checks. The *ASSERT* checks the parameter compatibility of U to u and V to v. The **bind** implies that U can be passed by reference (or by value) and that V can be passed by reference (or by value-result). If S contains no **return** statements, the final line, *SUBPROG S END SUBPROG*, reduces to simply S.

If U does not contain subscripts, then there is no difference between scalar and non-scalar non-**var** parameters; in this case we can consider U to be an instance of K. If neither U nor V contains subscripts, the possibility of aliasing disappears in that *DISJ* becomes manifest. In this case, we can avoid the complexity of **bind**, and *CALL* can be expressed more directly as:

$$CALL(p, K, V) = \quad \begin{array}{l} \textbf{const}\ k: T_k := K; \\ \textbf{var}\ v: T_v;\ ASSERT\ EQV(T_v, T_V); \\ ASSERT\ DISJ(V); \\ v \leftarrow V; \\ SUBPROG\ S\ END\ SUBPROG; \\ V \leftarrow v \end{array}$$

If p is recursive, the definition of a call remains correct from an operational point of view. However, it must be refined for *wp* semantics in order to guarantee that recursion eventually terminates. From an intuitive point of view, this refinement replaces each procedure call by the corresponding procedure body. This replacement is repeatedly carried out for recursive procedures. Eventually, deeply nested calls are replaced by *FAIL* statements. These deeply nested *FAIL* statements guarantee bounded depth recursion. We will now define this refinement formally.

We will assume that the procedures of a program are named p_1, p_2, up to p_n. We now define the general case (recursive or non-recursive) of a call to procedure p_i:

$$p_i(K, U, V) =_{df} \lim_{n \to \infty} p_i^n(K, U, V)$$

where

$$p_i^0(K, U, V) =_{df} FAIL$$

$$p_i^{n+1}(K, U, V) =_{df} CALL(p_i, K, U, V)[p_j : p_j^n]$$

We used the notation $CALL(p_i, K, U, V)[p_j : p_j^n]$ to mean that in $CALL(p_i, K, U, V)$ each p_j is to be replaced by p_j^n.

We can consider that the definition of $p_i(K, U, V)$ grows a nesting of expanded (copied) procedure bodies. The growth is seeded with a null ($FAIL$) version of each body, called $p_i^0(K, U, V)$, then the growth repeatedly adds surrounding procedure bodies, called $p_i^n(K, U, V)$. The value of n effectively gives the allowed depth of subprogram calls at that particular level of nesting. It is straightforward to show that when p_i is non-recursive, this generalized definition of call reduces to the previously given non-recursive case.

We have thus far ignored **pre**/**post** and their associated **init** clause. We can treat **pre** and **post** as assertions and **init** as a **const** declaration, so that given

> **procedure** p (...)
>   **pre** P **init** $x_i := e_i$ **post** Q
> S
> **end** p

the definition of $CALL$ is expanded to be

$CALL(p, K, U, V) =_{df}$ **const** $k : T_k := K$;
$ASSERT\ ASN(T_u, U)\ \&\ EQV(T_v, T_V)$
bind u **to** U, **var** v **to** V;
assert P;
const $x_i := e_i$;
$SUBPROG\ S\ END\ SUBPROG$;
assert Q

There is an alternative method of handling procedure calls, which will now be briefly outlined, but not covered in any detail. This method extends the syntax of Turing to allow a procedure bound. With this extension, the syntax for procedures becomes:

> **procedure** p (...)
>   **pre** P
>   **init** $x_i := e_i$
>   **post** Q
>   **bound** B
> S
> **end** p

The precondition P must be true at procedure entry and Q must be true when returning. Bound B is an integer expression whose value must be non-negative at entry and must decrease with each recursive call. When **pre**/**post** are present, we consider that they give the meaning of the procedure. Any procedure body that satisfies them and decreases the bound while keeping it non-negative is considered to implement the specification. The rest of the program should depend on the specification and not on the particular procedure body.

9.3.6 Functions

Declarations of Turing functions imply a check that the types of the formal parameters and the result are valid:

DECLARATION *S*	**SEMANTICS** *sem(S)*

function $f(x: T_x)\ r: T_r$
  import(...)
  S
end f
	$ASSERT\ TYP(T_x)\ \&\ TYP(T_r)$

We will consider that x represents any number of parameters. Turing functions are syntactically prohibited from having side effects and from having variable parameters.

A call to f with actual parameter b, written $f(b)$, creates the value of return variable r by executing

$$x := b\,;\ Sf$$

where

$$Sf =_{\text{df}} SUBPROG\ \textbf{var}\ r: T_r;\ S;\ FAIL\ END\ SUBPROG$$

The assignment $x := b$ requires b to be valid and assignable to T_x. This assignment implies that function parameters can be passed by value. The *FAIL* statement enforces the restriction that a function must be terminated by a **result** statement, and not by falling off the end of the function. The semantics of the **result** statement occurring within function f is:

STATEMENT *S*	**SEMANTICS** *sem(S)*
result e	$r := e\,;\ RETURN$

The *RETURN* is a *GOTO* to the end of *Sf* (to the end of the *SUBPROG*).

The remainder of this section gives the semantics of a function call $f(b)$ by giving (1) the validity predicate for the call, written $EXPN(f(b))$, and (2) the relation between the function's value and its parameter(s), written $AXIOM(f(x))$. This material may be skipped on first reading.

For non-recursive, deterministic function f (as above), *EXPN* and *AXIOM* are defined as:

$$EXPN(f(b)) =_{\text{df}} wp(x := b\,;\ Sf,\ \textbf{true})$$
$$AXIOM(f(x)) =_{\text{df}} wp(Sf,\ r' = r)\,[r':f(x)]$$

For example, suppose f is the mx function:

```
function mx(x1, x2: int) r: int
  if x1 > x2 then result x1
             else result x2
```

end if
end *mx*

Then *mx*'s validity predicate and axiom are:

$$EXPN(mx(x1,x2)) = (INITIALIZED(x1) \;\&\; INITIALIZED(x2))$$
$$AXIOM(mx(x1,x2)) = ((INITIALIZED(x1) \;\&\; INITIALIZED(x2)) \Rightarrow (x1 > x2 \Rightarrow f(x1,x2) = x1 \;\&\; x1 \le x2 \Rightarrow f(x1,x2) = x2))$$

The Turing language has syntactic restrictions guaranteeing that each function is repeatable, meaning equal arguments and imported values necessarily produce equal results. However, a function can still be non-deterministic in the sense that its specification can allow a set of results; it remains true that a particular implementation of the function will deliver repeatable results. If function f calls non-deterministic functions, the axiom must be generalized to:

$$AXIOM(f(x)) = \sim wp(Sf, r' \neq r)\,[r' : f(x)]$$

The double negation in this axiom corresponds to the following idea. The final value r' is related to parameter and imported values in all the ways in which it cannot be guaranteed that at the end r' will differ from r. If f uses only deterministic features, the axiom reduces to the previous version.

If f_i is the i-th function occurring in a program and if f_i is recursive, $AXIOM(f_i(x))$ remains as above, but we must generalize $EXPN$:

$$EXPN(f_i(b)) = \lim_{n \to \infty} wp(x := b;\, Sf_i^n, \mathbf{true})$$

where

$$Sf_i^0 =_{\text{df}} FAIL$$

$$Sf_i^{n+1} =_{\text{df}} Sf_i\,[f_j : f_j^n]$$

This construction is similar to the one used to define recursive procedures. It grows a nested set of function and procedure bodies, by starting with null bodies (*FAIL*). Each surrounding body encloses bodies of the next lower order of body. The number n effectively determines the maximum allowed depth of subprogram call at that particular level of nesting. We can derive this alternate formulation of $EXPN(f_j(b))$:

Lemma: $EXPN(f_i(b)) = (EXPN(b) \;\&\; ASN(T_x, b) \;\&\; PRE(f_i)[x : b])$

where $PRE(f_i) =_{\text{df}} \lim_{n \to \infty} wp(Sf_i^n, \mathbf{true})$

Consider this example of a recursive function:

```
function fact(x: int) r: int
  if x = 0 then result 1
        else result x *fact (x-1)
  end if
end fact
```

For the *fact* function we get:

$$EXPN(fact(x)) = (INITIALIZED(x) \ \& \ x \geq 0)$$
$$AXIOM(fact(x)) = (INITIALIZED(x) \Rightarrow (x = 0 \Rightarrow fact(x) = 1 \ \& \ x \neq 0 \Rightarrow fact(x) = x * fact(x-1)))$$

9.3.7 Modules

The Turing module construct is a syntactic packaging that serves to hide information, i.e., to control scope of names. Since this definition of Turing semantics assumes that all declared identifiers are distinct, we can ignore this packaging. The semantics of modules requires the module invariant to be true following module initialization and at the beginning and end of execution of each exported subprogram.

DECLARATION *S*	SEMANTICS *sem(S)*

module *m*
  import(...) **export**(...)
  pre *P*
  S 1
  invariant *I*
  S 2
  post *Q*
end *m*
	assert *P* ;
	S 1;
	S 2′;
	assert *I* & *Q*

S2' is the same as S2, except each body *Sx* of an exported subprogram is replaced by **assert** *I* ; *Sx* ; **assert** *I* . Alternatively, we could define that S2' is the same as S2, except invariant *I* is added as a conjunct in the pre and post assertions of each exported subprogram. If any of **pre** *P* , **invariant** *I* or **post** *Q* are omitted, the corresponding predicate (*P* , *I* , or *Q*) is taken to be simply true.

9.3.8 Input/Output

Turing's **get** and **put** statements provide a variety of convenient input/output constructs. The formalization of these statements is straightforward but long. The reader may wish to skip this section on first reading; before reading this section it may be wise to review the Turing Report's informal definition of input/output.

We treat each input or output stream as a string and use Turing's string operations (substring, catenate and length) to manipulate these strings. We assume that streams (and hence strings) can be quite long. The definitions we give will not generally be acceptable by a Turing implementation, which will probably limit the length of strings to *strmax* (commonly 255 characters).

Each stream is considered to have a stream number. The t-th stream is called $str(t)$. We can consider that *str* is an array of strings. When the stream number is omitted in a **get** or **put** statement, a default is assumed. We will assume that these defaults are always explicitly given (in spite of the fact that the Turing programmer can access these default streams only by omitting their numbers, and never by explicitly giving a number).

A stream is always in one of three exclusive states: open for **get**, open for **put**, or not open. The *open* predefined procedure, which will not be formalized, changes the state of a stream. The default output stream is always open for **put** and the default input stream is always open for **get**. *OPENGET(t)* is true when $str(t)$ is open for **get**, and *OPENPUT(t)* is true when $str(t)$ is open for **put**. In this section we will use the notation:

newline = "\n"
tab = "\t"
blank = " "
formfeed = "\f"
creturn = "\r"
quote = "\""

In the definition of the put statement, p_i represents an output item:

STATEMENT *S*	**SEMANTICS** *sem(S)*
put:t, p_1 {,p_i }	*ASSERT EXPN(t) & OPENPUT(t)*; $str(t) := str(t) + conv(p_1)$ { $+conv(p_i)$ } + *newline*

If the **put** statement ends with dot-dot (..) then the final *newline* is omitted. Each output item p_i is converted to a string by *conv* before being catenated onto the output stream. In the following table, which defines *conv*, the symbols i, s and r are integer, string and real expressions, respectively.

ITEM *p*	**CONVERTED ITEM** *conv(p)*
skip	*newline*
s	s

$s : w$	*s + repeat(blank, w-length(s))*
i	*intstr(i, 0)*
$i : w$	*intstr(i, w)*
r	*realstr (r, 0)*
$r : w$	*realstr (r, w)*
$r : w : fw$	*frealstr (r, w, fw)*
$r : w : fw : ew$	*erealstr (r, w, fw, ew)*

The functions *intstr, realstr, frealstr,* and *repeat* are predefined functions of Turing; they are defined informally in the Turing Report. Syntactic checks guarantee that each **put** item is a string, integer or real, and that it is a real for the last two forms of **put** items.

We begin the definition of the **get** statement by breaking it up into statements with only one **get** item (g_i):

STATEMENT *S*	**SEMANTICS** *sem(S)*
get: t, g_1 {,g_i}	**get:** t, g_1 {; **get:** t, g_i}

Each get item has one of these four forms:

(a)	**skip**	Skip white space
(b)	v	Skip white space then read next token
(c)	v : *	Assign rest of line to v
(d)	$v : n$	Assign up to n characters to v

Syntactic checks guarantee that v is a variable reference, that v's root type is **int, real** or **string** in form (b), and that v's root type is **string** in (c) and (d).

If the input variable contains a component selector, we simplify to a form of **get** without selectors:

STATEMENT *S*	**SEMANTICS** *sem(S)*
get:t, x . s [:*fmt*]	**var** y : $T_{x\,.\,s}$; **get** :t, y [:*fmt*]; x . s := y

The *fmt* format item is either * or n.

Turing's predefined function *eof*(t) is defined to mean *length*(*str*(t))=0. Our definition of the **get** statement will use the function *isWhiteSpace* (s), which is defined to mean:

s = *newline* **or** s = *blank* **or** s = *tab* **or** s = *formfeed* **or** s = *creturn*

We will also use procedures called *skipWhiteSpace, findTokenEnd,* and *findLineEnd* and a function called *convToken*, which will be defined below. We now give the semantics of getting a single variable without component selectors:

STATEMENT *S*	**SEMANTICS** *sem(S)*
get: *t* **, skip**	*ASSERT EXPN(t) & OPENGET(t);* *skipWhiteSpace(str(t))*
get: *t* **,** *v*	**get:** *t* **, skip;** **var** *j* **: int;** *findTokenEnd(str(t), j);* %This can fail *v := convToken (str (t)(1 .. j),* T_v*);* *str (t) := str (t) (j+1 .. *)*

get: *t* **,** *v* **: ***	*ASSERT EXPN(t) & OPENGET(t) &*
	  ~eof(t);
	var *j* **: int;**
	findLineEnd(str(t), j);
	v := str (t) (1 .. j); %Fails if *j* > upper(v)
	*str(t) := str(t) (j+1 .. *);*
	if *~eof(t) & str(t)(1) = newline* **then**
	  *str(t) := str(t) (2 .. *)*
	end if

get: *t* **,** *v* **:** *n*	*ASSERT EXPN(t) & OPENGET(t);*
	ASSERT EXPN(n) & n ≥ 0;
	var *j* **: int;**
	findLineEnd(str(i), j);
	if *length(str(t)) > j &*
	  str(t) (j+1) = newline **then**
	  j := j+1
	end if
	j := min(j, n);
	v := str (t) (1 .. j); %Fails if *j* > upper(v)
	*str(t) := str(t) (j+1 .. *)*

The procedures used in defining **get** are now defined.

PROCEDURES	**SEMANTICS** *sem(S)*

skipWhiteSpace(u)	**loop**
	  exit when *length(u)=0*
	      or *~isWhiteSpace (u (1));*
	  *u := u (2 .. *)*
	end loop

findTokenEnd(u, j)

```
ASSERT length(u)>0;
if u(1) = quote then
  j := 2;
  loop
    ASSERT j ≤ length(u);
    exit when u(j) = quote;
    if u(j) = "\\" then
      j := j+1
    end if
    j := j+1
  end loop
else
  j := 1;
  loop
    exit when j = length(u)
      or isWhiteSpace(u(j+1));
    j := j+1
  end loop
end if
```

findLineEnd(u, j)

```
j := 0;
loop
  exit when j = length(u)
    or u(j+1) = newline;
  j := j+1
end loop
```

The function *convToken* is defined by this table:

ROOT TYPE T_v	**CONVERSION** *convToken(tok,* T_v*)*
int	*strint(tok)*
real	*strreal(tok)*
string	**if** *tok(1) = quote* **then** *convStrLit(tok(2..*-1)* **else** *tok*

The *convStrLit* function replaces each extended character (such as \t) by its corresponding value (such as tab).

We have given the semantics of Turing's entire set of input/output constructs; the definition is not complex, but it is long. The definition could, of course, be shortened by omitting many forms. For example, if the only form of input/output were single character **get** or **put**, then the semantic definition would be extremely simple. However, Turing is defined for convenience of usage, and this sort of simplification would not be in the spirit of the language.

9.4 Validity Predicates

The semantics of Turing are given in terms of basis statements, expressions defined by axioms, and validity predicates that specify when constructs can be meaningfully evaluated or executed. This section defines the seven validity predicates: *EXPN*, *REF*, *TYP*, *ASN*, *EQV*, *DISJ* and *DIST*. With the exception of user supplied assertions, these are the only predicates appearing in basis *ASSERT* statements. These predicates correspond to Hehner's [84] meaning predicates, Dijkstra's [76] domain predicates, and the legality assertions in Euclid [Lampson 77, Elliot 82].

The checks implied by validity predicates are analogous to syntactic checks, such as preventing a string from being assigned to an integer. Turing is designed to enhance reliability and efficiency by maximizing the degree to which syntactic checks can detect errors. Syntactic checks are sometimes called compile-time checks, because they are designed to be enforced by a compiler.

Turing is designed so that syntactic checks can be carried out without evaluating the expressions in Turing programs. Any check involving values of expressions is enforced by a validity predicate. These predicates are sometimes called run-time checks or constraints, because in principle they are carried out at run-time. However, two of them (*EQV* and *DIST*) are actually manifest, meaning that all expressions they contain are manifest (compile-time) expressions. It is expected that most Turing compilers will check *EQV* and *DIST*, issue warnings when they are violated, and generate code to fail when the run-time check of the predicate is to be executed. This implies that distinctness (*DIST*) of case and union labels and type compatibility (*EQV*) of var parameters can always be checked at compile time. Beware that even though such tests are manifest, they are still considered to be run-time checks rather than syntactic checks.

Most of Turing's type compatibility checks are enforced syntactically. The remaining checks, which involve expression values, are carried out by *EQV* and *ASN*. Since *EQV* is manifest, the only required run-time type compatibility check is *ASN*, which guarantees that assigned integers, enumerated values and strings are within the ranges of their target types.

Most validity predicates disallow constructs that are clearly meaningless, such as division by zero and subscripts out of bounds. However, some checks are more a matter of taste in language design. For example, the *TYP* predicate requires that $a \le b$ in the subrange type a .. b; it would have been possible to require instead that $a \le succ(b)$, which would allow empty subranges. Empty subranges were disallowed in Turing because they are commonly an indication of a programming error and because they require special handling, for example, when they are subscript ranges.

A validity predicate accepts a syntactic object, such as an expression, and converts it to another syntactic object, namely, a boolean expression. As an example, consider *EXPN*$(25+x/y)$. *EXPN*'s argument is the *syntactic form* $25+x/y$ (and not the *value* of $25+x/y$). *EXPN* maps this form to boolean expression that is true when x and y are initialized and y is nonzero:

$$EXPN\,(25{+}x\,/y) = (INITIALIZED\,(x)\ \&\ INITIALIZED\,(y)\ \&\ y \neq 0)$$

The right side is a function of x and y and is true when $25{+}x\,/y$ can be meaningfully evaluated.

9.4.1 Valid Reference Predicate (REF)

The first validity predicate we define is *REF*. It takes as an argument a reference, which is an identifier followed by component selectors (array or collection subscripts and record or union field selectors). The reference can be assigned to and is sometimes called a *left hand value*. Given the syntactic checks of Turing, the only ways a reference can be invalid are: a subscript may be invalid or not locate an array/collection element and a union field may be selected when the union's tag is not properly set. A reference, being a target of assignment, does not need to be initialized. The *REF* predicate is defined as:

REFERENCE r	**VALIDITY PREDICATE** $REF(r)$
$a\,(b_1, b_2, \cdots)$ (subscripting array)	$REF(a)\ \&\ EXPN(b_i)\ \&\ LOWER_i \leq b_i \leq UPPER_i$ ($LOWER_i$ .. $UPPER_i$ is range of i-th subscript of a)
$c\,(p)$ (collection c with pointer p)	$EXPN\,(p)\ \&\ p$ **in** $c\ .\ ps$ ($c\ .\ ps$ is the pointer set of c, i.e., the set of all pointers to active elements of c)
$u\ .\ x$ (non-tag field x of union u)	$REF\,(u)\ \&\ u\ .\ t$ **in** $LABELS\,(u\ .\ x)$ (where $u\ .\ t$ is the tag of u, and $LABELS\,(u\ .\ x)$ is the set of labels of field x)
$r\ .\ x$ (field x of record r or tag x of union r)	$REF(r)$
x (identifier x)	**true** (checked syntactically)

Since a collection c cannot appear in an array, collection or union, the predicate $REF(c)$ is identically true. We have abbreviated predicates such as $L_i \leq b_i \leq U_i$ by omitting the quantification over i.

9.4.2 Valid Expression Predicate (EXPN)

We now consider the *EXPN* predicate. The purpose of *EXPN* is to guarantee that the expression it is applied to can be meaningfully evaluated. We will now elaborate on this idea. Let *EVAL* be the function that accepts an expression *e*, together with values of variables and constants used in *e*, and produces the value of *e*. In implementation terms, *EVAL* produces a machine-oriented value, usually a bit string, that represents *e*'s value. In axiomatic terms, *EVAL* can be thought of as manipulating expression *e*, using expression axioms, attempting to reduce *e* to an explicit (unsimplifiable) constant. If *EVAL* cannot produce a meaningful value, it instead produces a special value called *failure*. We assume that our expression axioms can never reduce an expression to *failure*, so, for example, the expression 6/0 cannot be axiomatically reduced to any value. This postulate relates *EXPN* and *EVAL*:

$$EXPN(e) \Rightarrow EVAL(e) = e$$

This means that if *e* is valid, then *e* can be evaluated, and the resulting value can be axiomatically proven to be equal to the original expression e (with values given for referenced variables and constants). For example, if *e* is 6+2, we get

$$EXPN(6+2) \Rightarrow EVAL(6+2) = (6+2)$$
$$\textbf{true} \Rightarrow 8 = (6+2)$$
$$8 = (6+2)$$
$$\textbf{true}$$

EXPN applied to 6+2 yields true, while *EVAL* applied to 6+2 yields 8. The axioms defining integers are used to reduce 8=(6+2) to true. As a second example, if *e* is 6/0 we get

$$EXPN(6/0) \Rightarrow EVAL(6/0) = (6/0)$$
$$\textbf{false} \Rightarrow failure = (6/0)$$
$$\textbf{true}$$

EXPN applied to 6/0 yields false, while *EVAL* applied to 6/0 yields *failure*. We assume that the axioms for expressions provide no way of reducing 6/0 to a value (or to *failure*). By the rules of predicate calculus, the next to last predicate reduces to true even though it contains the term 6/0. These rules are commutative, so for example, (**true or** 6/0=7) is equal to (6/0=7 **or true**) which equals (**true**).

Although Turing's boolean operators are conditional (the right side is not evaluated if the left determines the result), our postulate states that when they are valid they follow the rules of predicate calculus. In the definition of *EXPN* for the boolean binary operators, the right operand is required to be valid only when the left does not determine the result of the operator.

For an expression to be valid, its contained references that are to be evaluated must be valid; the three occurrences of *REF* (a) in the definition of *EXPN* specify this requirement. The value of scalar reference a must be initialized to be valid. The definition of *EXPN* uses *INITIALIZED* (a) to mean $a \neq UNINIT(T_a)$ where $UNINIT(T_a)$ is a special value not contained in the root type of T_a. Note that a nonscalar (array, record, set, union or collection) is not required to be initialized. We will not list substrings that use * to represent string length; we assume that * is rewritten as *length(s)*, for example, $s(*)$ is rewritten as $s(length(s))$.

EXPRESSION e	**VALIDITY PREDICATE** $EXPN(e)$
$a \ \& \ b$	$EXPN(a) \ \& \ (a \Rightarrow EXPN(b))$
a **or** b	$EXPN(a) \ \& \ (\sim a \Rightarrow EXPN(b))$
$a \Rightarrow b$	$EXPN(a) \ \& \ (a \Rightarrow EXPN(b))$
a/b, a **div** b, a **mod** b	$EXPN(a) \ \& \ EXPN(b) \ \& \ b \neq 0$
$a ** b$ (a, b **int**)	$EXPN(a) \ \& \ EXPN(b) \ \& \ b \geq 0 \ \&$ ($a \neq 0$ or $b \neq 0$)
$a ** b$ (a **real**, b **int**)	$EXPN(a) \ \& \ EXPN(b) \ \& \ (b \leq 0 \Rightarrow a \neq 0)$
$a ** b$ (a **int or real**, b **real**)	$EXPN(a) \ \& \ EXPN(b) \ \& \ (b \leq 0 \Rightarrow a > 0) \ \& \ (b > 0 \Rightarrow a \geq 0)$
$a+b$, $a-b$, $a*b$	$EXPN(a) \ \& \ EXPN(b)$ (For set operations, conjoin $EQV(T_a, T_b)$)
$a>b$, $a<b$, $a=b$, $a \leq b$, $a \geq b$	$EXPN(a) \ \& \ EXPN(b)$ (For set operations, conjoin $EQV(T_a, T_b)$)
$+a$, $-a$, $\sim a$	$EXPN(a)$
a **in** b, a **not in** b	$EXPN(a) \ \& \ EXPN(b) \ \& \ LOWER \leq a \leq UPPER$ ($LOWER$ .. $UPPER$ is set's manifest base type)
$T(a_1 \{, a_i\})$ (T is set type name)	$EXPN(a_i) \ \& \ LOWER \leq a_i \leq UPPER$ ($LOWER$ .. $UPPER$ is set's manifest base type)
T(**all**), $T()$ (T is set type name)	**true**
$a(b \ .. \ c)$ (substring of a)	$EXPN(a) \ \& \ EXPN(b) \ \& \ EXPN(c) \ \& \ b \geq 1 \ \& \ b \leq length(a) \ \& \ c-b+1 \geq 0$
$a(b)$ (substring of a)	$EXPN(a) \ \& \ EXPN(b) \ \& \ 1 \leq b \leq length(a)$
a (scalar reference a)	$REF(a) \ \& \ INITIALIZED(a)$ where

	$INITIALIZED(a) =_{df} a \neq UNINIT(T_a)$
a (nonscalar reference a)	$REF(a)$
$f(a)$ (function call)	$EXPN(a)$ & $ASN(T_x, a)$ & $PRE(f)[x:a]$ (precondition $PRE(f)$ of f must be true with actual parameter a substituted for formal parameter x; see 9.3.6)
0, 3.14, "a", ... (all explicit constants)	**true** (all explicit constants are valid)
$a(s : c)$ (replacement of a's component s by c)	$REF(a . s)$ & $ASN(T_{a.s}, c)$

The final item in this definition, $a(s : c)$, is used in the giving the semantics of Turing, but is syntactically prohibited in Turing programs.

9.4.3 Valid Type Predicate (TYP)

Most checking to verify that Turing types are valid is carried out by syntactic checks. The only remaining checks, which are enforced by the *TYP* predicate, involve the values of expressions. *TYP* requires that expressions in types are valid, that $a \leq b$ in a .. b, and that union labels are distinct and compatible with the tag's type. All these checks are manifest except the check that $a \leq b$ in the declaration of a dynamic array.

TYPE T	**VALIDITY PREDICATE** $TYP(T)$
int, real, boolean	**true**
a .. b	$EXPN(a)$ & $EXPN(b)$ & $a \leq b$
string, string(*)	**true**
string(a)	$EXPN(a)$ & $a \geq 1$
array T_i **of** U	$TYP(T_i)$ & $TYP(U)$ (Note: upper bounds of * are always valid)
record $x_{ij} : T_i$ **end record**	$TYP(T_i)$

union *tag* : U **of** **label** L_{ij} : x_{ij} : T_i [**label** : x_{nj} : T_n] **end union**	$TYP(U)$ & $TYP(T_i)$ & $EXPN(L_{ij})$ & $DIST(L_{ij})$ & $ASN(U, L_{ij})$ (Labels L_{ij} must be distinct and assignable to U)
collection of T	$TYP(T)$
collection of **forward** x	**true** (validity of type x is checked at its declaration)

9.4.4 Assignable Predicate (ASN)

The *ASN* predicate is used to guarantee that values are within the range of the target type. The only case in which this predicate is nonmanifest is the check that integer and enumerated values are within their target subranges and strings are no longer than their target types. All other assignability checks, such as for sets and records, can be enforced at compile time.

TARGET TYPE T	ASSIGNABLE PREDICATE $ASN(T, e)$
int	**true**
a .. b	$a \le e \le b$
real	**true**
boolean	**true**
enum(... **)**	**true**
string	**true**
string(a**)**	$length(e) \le a$
string(*)	$length(e) \le upper(s)$ (where s is the formal parameter with type string (*))
set of a .. b	EQV(**set of** a .. b, T_e)
array ... **of** ...	EQV(**array** ... **of** ..., T_e)
record ... **end record**	**true** (checked syntactically)
union ... **end record**	**true** (checked syntactically)

9.4.5 Type Equivalence Predicate (EQV)

EQV is a manifest validity predicate that is used, for example, to guarantee that **var** parameters are compatible and that sets combined by set operators have equivalent base types. The manifestness of *EQV* follows from the syntactic requirements that: lengths of string types must be manifest or star, subrange lower bounds must be manifest, dynamic arrays cannot be assigned, and dynamic array formal parameter upper bounds must be given as star. It follows that all type equivalence checks can be enforced at compile time. *EQV* is defined as:

TYPE T_1	TYPE T_2	EQUIVALENCE PREDICATE $EQV(T_1, T_2)$
$a_1 .. b_1$	$a_2 .. b_2$	$a_1=a_2$ & $b_1=b_2$
string(a_1)	**string**(a_2)	$a_1=a_2$
array T_i **of** T	**array** U_i **of** U	$EQV(T_i, U_i)$ & $EQV(T, U)$

All other cases of $EQV(T_1, T_2)$ arising in Turing are true. *EQV* is symmetric, i.e., $EQV(T_1, T_2)=EQV(T_2, T_1)$.

9.4.6 Disjointness Predicate (DISJ)

DISJ is a validity predicate that prevents aliasing by guaranteeing that references in binds and parameter lists do not overlap. *DISJ* is used directly only once, in the definition of bind. It is also used indirectly in defining procedure calls.

DISJ has two arguments, U and V; these are sets of references. *DISJ* is true when the references in V are pairwise non-overlapping and each reference in U does not overlap a reference from V.

$$DISJ(U, V) =_{df} (\forall i, j: i \neq j \Rightarrow \sim OVERLAP(V_i, V_j))\ \&$$
$$(\forall k, j: \sim OVERLAP(U_k, V_j))$$

A pair of items is considered to overlap if they have equivalent prefixes up to the end of one of them. For example, *x.a(4).g* and *x.a(4)* overlap. This idea is now formalized in the definition of the *OVERLAP* predicate, whose only purpose is to define *DISJ*.

ITEMS r_i, r_j	OVERLAP PREDICATE $OVERLAP(r_i, r_j)$
$x_1 . s_1, x_2 . s_2$	$x_1=x_2$ & $OVERLAP(s_1, s_2)$ (same leading or field identifiers x_1 and x_2)
$(a_j) . s_1, (b_j) . s_2$	$a_j=b_j$ & $OVERLAP(s_1, s_2)$ (equal subscripts or equal pointers a_j and b_j)

s_1, (null item)	**true** (overlap occurs when the prefixes match up to the end of one or both items)
(null item), s_2	**true** (as above)

Since passing of non-scalar parameters to procedures is treated as a **bind**, an item may be a string expression, such as $s + t$; such expressions are considered not to overlap any other item.

9.4.7 Distinctness Predicate (DIST)

DIST is a manifest validity predicate used to guarantee that the labels of a case statement or union type are distinct. It is defined as:

$$DIST(L_{ij}) = \forall\, i, j : i \neq j \;\Rightarrow\; L_i \neq L_j$$

where L_{ij} represents a set of (label) values indexed by i and j.

This completes the definition of validity predicates; we now consider the axiomatization of Turing's data types.

9.5 Axioms Defining Expressions

The expressions that appear in Turing programs are defined, in principle, by sets of axioms. In other words, the meaning of each Turing expression is defined axiomatically. These axioms allow a person to reason formally about Turing expressions, and they allow mechanical proof systems to deal with Turing programs.

Most of Turing's data types, such as booleans, integers and real numbers correspond exactly to the same concepts in classical mathematics. These types have been extensively studied; it is not our purpose to develop new formalisms for describing them. Rather, in most cases, we will simply refer to existing axiomatizations. We consider that these axioms are not properly part of the semantics of Turing, but rather are inherited from mathematics.

An axiomatization of a type begins by defining the well-formed formulas (*wff*'s) of the given type. In our terminology, this is done by giving the *syntax* of the formulas of interest. We will avoid the term *wff*, and will refer simply to *formulas*, which are assumed to be well formed.

Axioms are given that define the *semantics* of these formulas. These axioms can be thought of as rules for manipulating formulas to produce other formulas. If a formula can be reduced (manipulated to become) the formula **true**, then it is called a theorem. For example, if $x > 2$ is true, then the formula ($x > 2$ **or** $z = 21$) can be proven to be true (to be a theorem), using this axiom: given any true formula t and any formula a, the formula (t **or** a) is true. Throughout this treatment of axioms, we will be following the approach Hehner [84] used in defining his PRO language.

We shall briefly consider, in order, the axiomatization of:

Propositional calculus
Predicate calculus
Integers
Real numbers
Enumerated types
Sets
Arrays and records
Collections and pointers

The second item, predicate calculus, is considered because quantification is used in defining Turing, although it never appears in expressions in Turing programs.

9.5.1 Propositional Calculus

Propositional calculus defines formulas involving boolean values (**true** and **false**) and boolean operators (~, &, **or**, ⇒). In other words, it defines the boolean type.

The use of axioms to define a type is nicely illustrated by Hehner's definition of booleans. His axioms are as follows, where t and t' are true predicates, f and f' are false predicates, and a is any predicate.

true	~**false**
$\sim f$	$\sim(\sim t)$
t & t'	$\sim(f$ & $a)$
t **or** a	$\sim(a$ & $f)$
a **or** t	$\sim(f$ **or** $f')$
$a \Rightarrow t$	$\sim(t \Rightarrow f)$
$f \Rightarrow a$	$\sim(t=f)$
$t=t'$	$\sim(f=t)$
$f=f'$	

The definition of Turing's boolean expressions, when they are valid, is given exactly by propositional calculus. There is a potential source of confusion that arises due to the possibility that operands of boolean operators may be invalid. Consider the following examples:

(1) $6/0 = 6/0$
(2) $6/0 = 13 \Rightarrow 4 < 5$

Using propositional calculus, we can prove that both of these formulas are true. The first is true because syntactically identical phrases are considered equal. The second is true because ($a \Rightarrow t$) is **true** for any true formula t.

This does *not* mean that these two formulas evaluate to true when they appear in a Turing program. Each expression in a Turing program is guarded by a validity predicate that is false when the expression is invalid. The expression 6/0 = 6/0 has a false validity predicate, which effectively causes program failure; see the section called Validity Predicates for details.

9.5.2 Predicate Calculus

Predicate calculus defines existential and universal quantification, for example,

$$\forall x \textbf{ in int: } \exists y \textbf{ in int: } y=x+1$$

We will not provide axioms to define predicate calculus; these can be found in Hehner's book [84].

9.5.3 Integers

Integers have been formalized many times, beginning with Peano's classical work, so integer axioms will not be given here. Godel has proved that any axiomatization of a type as rich as **int** implies that there are true formulas that cannot be proven. Hence there are truths about certain Turing programs which can never be proven.

We shall assume that meaningless constructs, such as 6/0, cannot be reduced by the axioms to simpler forms. Thus, the axioms do not introduce a *failure* value corresponding to meaningless expressions.

Although **int** can be axiomatized, it cannot be completely supported by an implementation of finite size. Hence, Ideal Turing, which we are defining here, is like a Turing machine in that it must be thought of as a mathematical engine with unbounded resources. See the section called "Implementation Constraints" for a formalization that handles Turing programs that are limited to a bounded subrange of the integers.

9.5.4 Real Numbers

We will not axiomatize real numbers, but will rely on their meaning from classical mathematics. This meaning implies infinite precision. For example, all the following are considered to be true, for any valid real x and y:

(1) $(x/y)*y = x$ (for $y \neq 0$)
(2) $sqrt(x)**2 = x$ (for $x \geq 0$)
(3) $sin(x)**2 + cos(x)**2 = 1$

As with integers, we cannot implement the real type with bounded resources.

Real numbers are even less tractable than integers. Even if we are given a mathematical engine with unbounded resources, such as a Turing machine, we cannot carry out arithmetic for irrational numbers. Instead, we will consider that there is a mathematical oracle who evaluates real expressions. This oracle is not finitely implementable. See the section called "Axioms for Floating Point" for a formalization of a finite approximation of real numbers.

9.5.5 Enumerated Types

Turing's enumerated types are essentially bounded subranges of the integers, with explicit constants (literals) given in the type declarations. They will not be formalized here.

9.5.6 Strings

Turing's string type is the same as a sequence in classical mathematics, with the extension that in Turing, subsequences can be selected from sequences. Strings are sequences made up of characters. The set of characters is expected to be chosen by an implementation to be either ASCII or EBCDIC. This choice determines the ordering (<, >, ...) among characters and hence among strings; the EBCDIC ordering differs from ASCII. Hence a program proven correct for ASCII will not necessarily be correct for EBCDIC and vice versa.

Since strings are a more exotic type than, say, integers, we will give axioms defining them. We will write c to represent a sequence containing one character, for example, "a" or "%", and *null* to represent the string "" of length zero. A string literal is considered to be a catenation of its characters, e.g., "XYZ"="X"+"Y"+"Z". We will use s and t to represent strings and m and n to represent integers. The first six axioms define catenation (+) and substrings with a single integer selector, e.g., $s(n)$.

(1) $length(null) = 0$
(2) $length(c) = 1$
(3) $length(s+t) = length(s)+length(t)$
(4) $length(s) = 1 \Rightarrow s(1)=s$
(5) $(1 \leq n \leq length(s)) \Rightarrow ((s+t)(n)=s(n))$
(6) $(length(s) < n <= length(s+t)) \Rightarrow ((s+t)(n)=t(n\text{-}length(s))$

Axioms 5 and 6 allow a form of substring, $(s+t)(n)$, which is syntactically disallowed in a Turing program, but is mathematically clear. The next three axioms define substrings with two integer selectors, e.g., $s(m\,..\,n)$.

(7) $(1 \leq n \leq length(s)+1) \Rightarrow s(n\,..\,n-1)=null$
(8) $s(n\,..\,n) = s(n)$
(9) $s(m\,..\,n) = s(m) + s(m+1\,..\,n)$

The next axiom defines when two strings are considered equal, in terms of length and character equality.

(10) *(s = t) = (length(s)=length(t) &*
(length(s) = 0 **or**
s(1)=t(1) & s(2 .. length(s))=t(2 .. length(t))))

The final axiom defines ordering among strings, in terms of character ordering.

(11) $(s > t) = (s \neq null$ &
$(t = null$ **or**
$s(1) > t(1)$ **or**
(s(1)=t(1) & s(2..length(s))>(2..length(t))))

The other comparison operators are defined in terms of > and =, for example, $(s \geq t) = (s > t$ **or** $s = t)$. The use of * in a substring selection is assumed to be replaced by the string's length, e.g., *s(1 .. *–1) = s(1 .. length(s)–1)*.

9.5.7 Sets

A set type in Turing is particularly simple, because it ranges over a bounded base type, e.g., 2..10. As a result, formal difficulties with sets, such as Russell's paradox, are avoided. We will not axiomatize the set type.

The classical mathematical set notation $\{e_1, e_2, \cdots e_n\}$ is written in Turing as $T(e_1, e_2, \cdots e_n)$ where T is the name of a set type whose base type contains $e_1, e_2, \cdots$ and e_n. The notation T(**all**) represents the set of all items in T's base type, and $T()$ is an empty set. Following Pascal, Turing uses this notation for sets:

in	Set membership
+	Set union
*	Set intersection
–	Set difference
≤	Subset
≥	Superset

Sets are used in defining the **new** and **free** statements, where U represents the type: **set of pointer to** x. Although this type cannot be written in a Turing program, it is mathematically clear.

9.5.8 Arrays and Records

Arrays and records have structured values, whose components can be individually accessed. The meaning of these types is exactly the same as in other languages such as Pascal. We have used the notation $x\ .\ s$ to mean the selection of x's component s and $x(s{:}e)$ to mean the value of x except with its s component replaced by e.

We define $x\ .\ s$ and $x(s{:}e)$ by these two axioms:

$$s_1 = s_2 \Rightarrow v(s_1{:}\ e)\ .\ s_2 = e$$
$$s_1 \neq s_2 \Rightarrow v(s_1{:}\ e)\ .\ s_2 = v\ .\ s_2$$

The notation $s_1 = s_2$ means, component selector by component selector, subscripts in s_1 and s_2 are equal, and field selector identifiers are identical. To handle component selectors consisting of several parts, we introduce this additional axiom.

$$v(s_1\ .\ s_2{:}\ e) = v(s_1{:}\ v\ .\ s_1(s_2{:}\ e))$$

The *REF* and *EXPN* validity predicates require array subscripts to be in their declared ranges and e in $v(s{:}\ e)$ to be assignable to the type of $v\ .\ s$.

9.5.9 Unions

The union type has been designed so that its semantics are given exactly by the axioms for arrays and records. The *REF* predicate allows access only to those fields that are selected by the current tag value. The definition of the **tag** statement effectively uninitializes all fields except the tag.

9.5.10 Collections and Pointers

Collections have been designed so that they are exactly defined by the axioms for arrays and records. The reader may wish to review the informal definition of collections and pointers in the Turing Report before studying this section.

There is a special pointer value *nil(c)* for each collection c which does not locate any element of c. We consider that *nil(c)* is a literal, so any substitution for c does not replace the c in *nil(c)*.

We consider that each collection c has an implicit field $c\ .\ ps$, where ps stands for *pointer set.* At any point in a Turing program, $c\ .\ ps$ represents the set of pointers to existing elements of c. The definition of collection declarations and of the **new** and **free** statements guarantees that *nil(c)* is not a member of $c\ .\ ps$.

The *REF* validity predicate requires that p is in $c\ .\ ps$ for any reference $c(p)$. The **new** and **free** statements are defined such that $c\ .\ ps$ is kept up to date. The type of $c\ .\ ps$ is **set of pointer to** c; this type is called U. Type U cannot be declared in a Turing program, but is mathematically clear. The type **pointer to** c contains an infinite number of elements; we will avoid axiomatizing this type by considering it to be the same as **int**. Syntactic restrictions prevent pointers from participating in integer arithmetic. We can consider that *nil(c)* is a particular integer value, such as zero.

9.5.11 Uninitialized Values

We consider that each type *T* has associated with it a value called *UNINIT* (*T*), which is not a value in *T*. When checking is specified, a declaration effectively initializes a variable of type *T* to the value *UNINIT* (*T*), unless the declaration includes explicit initialization; see "Variable and Constant Declarations". If *T* is a structured value, then any component selection on its uninitialized value yields the component's uninitialized value. For example, if *v* is an uninitialized integer array and *i* is a valid subscript for *a*, then the value of *v* (*i*) is *UNINIT* (**int**).

The *EXPN* validity predicate implies that a scalar value must not be accessed unless it is initialized. However, passing a reference to a **var** parameter is not considered to be an expression access and does not require initialization.

Nonscalar values, such as arrays and records, can be partially initialized. The *EXPN* validity predicate allows nonscalars as a whole to be accessed, whether initialized or not. For example, it is allowed to assign an uninitialized array or to pass it to a non-**var** parameter; see ''Validity Expression Predicate.''

There is a potential source of confusion related to uninitialized values. Suppose *i* is an **int** variable. Consider the predicate ($i \leq 0$ **or** $i \geq 0$), which means the same as (*i* **in int**). Since *i*'s type is **int**, we may be tempted to conclude that the predicate is true. Since *i* can have a value outside of **int**, notably, *UNINIT* (**int**), this conclusion is not warranted. If this statement appears in a Turing program:

assert $i \leq 0$ **or** $i \geq 0$

then it is defined to mean

ASSERT $i \neq$ *UNINIT* (**int**) & ($i \leq 0$ **or** $i \geq 0$)

9.6 Implementation Constraints

Up to this point, the definition of the semantics of Turing has assumed that resources to execute a Turing program are unlimited. In other words, we have been defining Ideal Turing, which never suffers from resource exhaustion. This section faces the question of how to cope with the inevitability of finite resources. The reader may wish to review the section of the Turing Report on ''Implementation Constraints on Integer, String and Real Types'' before reading this section. We will discuss, in order, axiomatization of floating point operations, handling limited ranges of values, and usage of time and space.

9.6.1 Axioms for Floating Point

Implementations of Turing will commonly choose to approximate the real type using floating point. We will now show how floating point operations can be axiomatized. Let o_f be the floating point approximation to the mathematical real operator o_m, where o is one of the real operators +, –, *, /. We assume that o_m has already been defined by axioms giving the semantics of mathematically exact real operations. We define o_f by these two axioms.

$$x \; o_m \; y = 0 \Rightarrow x \; o_f \; y = 0$$

$$x \; o_m \; y \neq 0 \Rightarrow abs(((x \; o_m \; y) - (x \; o_f \; y)) \,/\, (x \; o_m \; y)) < rreb$$

The relative round-off error bound *rreb* is an implementation defined constant. The Turing Report recommends that $rreb \leq$ 1e–14. Axioms for floating point predefined functions and exponentiation (**) are similar, but may use multiples of *rreb* to reflect the lower degree of precision in these operations. Analogously, explicit real constants, such as 0.1, are not in general exactly representable in floating point, and should be specified using *rreb*. When reasoning about programs implemented using floating point we must use these axioms rather than the axioms defining mathematically exact real operations.

These axioms are nondeterministic in the sense that a result may lie anywhere in a range of values. Hence, floating point results may vary from implementation to implementation. However, in a particular implementation, results must be repeatable; otherwise mathematical identities such as $x +_f y = x +_f y$ will fail to be true.

9.6.2 Bounded Expression Validity Predicate (BEXPN)

This section shows how the *EXPN* validity predicate can be expanded to handle limited ranges of computed values. With this expansion, the weakest precondition for a Turing program will contain terms whose truth guarantees that overflow cannot occur.

The Turing Report gives recommended minimal ranges of values to be supported by Turing implementations, in terms of implementation constants such as *minint, maxint* and *maxstr*. For each integer value i, the range is $minint \leq i \leq maxint$; it is recommended that $minint \leq -(2{**}31-1)$ and $maxint \geq (2{**}31-1)$. For each string s, the limit is $length(s) \leq maxstr$; it is recommended that $maxstr \geq 255$. It is assumed that each real value r is represented as a significant digits part f and an exponent e, where $r = f * radix{**}e$, *radix* is the number base, and f is normalized ($f \neq 0 \Rightarrow 1/radix \leq abs(f) < 1$. The Report recommends that e should range over an equivalent base 10 range of at least –38 .. 38. This range implies a corresponding exponent range of *minexp* .. *maxexp* given in terms of *radix*. The resulting constraint on each real value r is $minexp \leq getexp(r) \leq maxexp$, where *getexp* is a function that retrieves r's exponent e.

We will now expand the *EXPN* predicate to enforce non-overflow of computed values. The expanded predicate, called *BEXPN* (bounded expression validity predicate), is defined as follows:

$$BEXPN(i) =_{df} EXPN(i) \,\&\, minint \le i \le maxint$$
$$BEXPN(s) =_{df} EXPN(s) \,\&\, length(s) \le maxstr$$
$$BEXPN(r) =_{df} EXPN(r) \,\&\, minexp \le getexp(r) \le maxexp$$
$$BEXPN(b) =_{df} EXPN(b)$$

where i is any integer expression, s is any string expression, r is any real expression and b is any other expression (such as boolean or enumerated). With *BEXPN*, we postulate

$$BEXPN(e) \Rightarrow BEVAL(e)=e$$

This means: if *BEXPN* is true of any expression e, then its evaluation (called *BEVAL*) using bounded ranges is guaranteed to produce a value that satisfies the axiomatic definition of expression e.

The definition of *BEXPN* effectively requires an implementation to evaluate expressions in a particular order, to avoid introducing spurious overflows due to expression re-ordering; if a particular implementation re-orders expressions, we cannot rely on *BEXPN* to prevent overflow.

9.6.3 Time/Space Usage

The time/space usage of a Turing program is very sensitive to implementation techniques, so it is difficult to provide a general formalization of it. However, we will suggest an approach that may be useful for a class of implementations.

The essence of the approach is to use auxiliary variables to record time/space usage:

TIME	- amount of execution time used
SPACE	- amount of data space in use
MAXSPACE	- maximum amount of data space used

We assume these are initialized to zero. We expand the definition of the semantics *(sem)* of each statement or declaration to include appropriate assignments updating these three variables.

To enforce a bound on time/space usage, we add these conjuncts to the postcondition of a Turing program.

$$TIME \le TIMELIMIT \,\&\, MAXSPACE \le SPACELIMIT$$

The precondition of the entire program will contain terms whose truth guarantees that *TIME* will not exceed *TIMELIMIT* and *MAXSPACE* will not exceed *SPACELIMIT*.

9.7 Observations about Formal Semantics

By way of conclusion, certain observations will be made about the shortcoming of this formal language semantics and its use in the development of correct programs.

9.7.1 Shortcomings of this Semantics

As might be expected in an undertaking as ambitious as formalizing a language the size of Turing, not all aspirations were equally well attained. This section lists certain shortcomings of this semantics.

One worrisome aspect arises from the treatment of loops and recursive subprograms. These were formalized in terms of limits. These limits can be considered to be limits of predicates (see [Hehner 84]). The trouble with this approach is that the treatment of unbounded nondeterminism is not satisfactory [Boom 82, Back 79]. For example, this loop written in Ideal Turing is expected to terminate for all initial values of i, but the limit of predicates approach predicts termination only for non-negative i:

```
loop
  if i > 0 then i := i-1
  elsif i = 0 then exit
  elsif i < 0 then randnat(i)
  end if
end loop
```

(This example is based on a similar program in [Dijkstra 76].) The *randnat* procedure non-deterministically picks i to be any random natural number, and can be implemented as:

```
procedure randnat(var i : int)
  var x : real
  rand(x)   % Pick real x in range 0.0 to 1.0
  if x = 0 then i := 23   % Any positive value is ok
      else i := round (1/x)
  end if
end randnat
```

The nettlesome question of whether unbounded nondeterminism is computationally meaningful is left for others to ponder. In Turing, unbounded nondeterminism arises in two places: in the *rand* predefined function and in the formalization of floating point, which allows any (repeatable) result in a specified region surrounding the mathematically exact result.

This semantics omits the formalization of Turing's real random number generation procedures and thereby sidesteps important but difficult questions about the meaning of randomness.

Another shortcoming of the treatment of loops and recursion is illustrated by this program:

> **loop**
>   **put** *"Green"*
>   **put** *"Red"*
> **end loop**

This is an infinite loop that can be thought of as the control for a traffic light, repeatedly turning the light green then red. The formal semantics for Turing follows Dijkstra [76] in requiring the termination of all loops. This formal requirement unfortunately violates the intention that such loops should execute by indefinitely repeating their bodies. The formal enforcement of finite termination of recursive subprogram calls is effected by **bound** expressions, whose values remain non-negative, and decrease with each recursive call. The definition of these subprogram bounds is rather informal here, and perhaps deserves more detailed attention.

A related shortcoming has to do with partial results up to a failure. For example, the weakest precondition formalization of Turing specifies that the following program has the same meaning as any program that eventually fails:

> **put** *"Hi"*
> **put** *"Ho"*
> **put** *1/0*

The operational approach by contrast captures the intention that *Hi* and *Ho* are to be output before the program fails due to division by zero.

This semantics has been greatly simplified by the assumption of no side effects and no aliasing. This assumption is justified in that any violation of it can be automatically detected, and is prohibited by context conditions together with validity conditions. It is also justified because these violations make a Turing program harder to understand. However, Turing implementations commonly allow these violations (after warnings). The result is that offending programs have an operational meaning, but this meaning is not given by the formal semantics.

Although a reasonable approach has been given here to handling most questions of resource exhaustion, one thorny question remains. This has to do with finiteness of the run-time stack that most implementations of Turing use. Guaranteeing that this stack will not overflow requires intimate knowledge of the particular implementation, so this question has remained unanswered here.

Questions of performance and time/space efficiency can be formalized in a relatively straightforward way because Turing has been explicitly designed for direct implementation on existing hardware. However, only tentative suggestions have been given here toward addressing these questions.

The scope of names in Turing programs has been handled relatively informally. The two rules that define scope are as follows. Each user declaration is assumed to introduce a unique identifier. Recursive subprograms require resolution of each identifier to the nearest preceding declaration of the identifier. These two rules are clear enough and are perhaps the right level of formality for the human reader. However, a more formal approach is clearly possible.

The semantics of Turing given here is not formal at the level of allowing mechanical interpretation. A mechanically interpretable semantics is desirable in that it could be automatically checked for well-formedness and could be tested to see if it satisfies our intuition. However, this level of formalization seems to be attainable only at a cost in notational complexity and human understandability, and has not been carried out here.

9.7.2 Correctness Methodology

Turing has been designed so that it can be axiomatically formalized, and this semantics demonstrates the attainment of this goal. This goal has included the aspiration of supporting formal correctness proofs of Turing programs and use of constructive approaches to program construction, as introduced by Dijkstra [76].

The use of Turing with a formal programming methodology can be simplified by constraining certain language features, for example:

(1) Disallowing subscripting in **bind** and in reference parameters.
(2) Disallowing **return** statements and allowing **result** statements only at the ends of functions.
(3) Allowing **exit** only when it is the first or last statement of a loop.

These restrictions simplify the meaning of **bind** and procedure calls. They also eliminate the formal complications due to exiting or returning in the middle of a construct. With these simplifications, *wp* rules should be derived for each Turing statement or declaration in the restricted language. Procedure call rules in the style of Gries [81] should be derived. With these simplifications, an approach such as that taken by Gries [81] is immediately applicable to Turing.

Appendix A

Soul of the Turing Language

(Published in Computerworld, May 14, 1984)

An intensive 12-month effort at the University of Toronto has produced the new general purpose programming language called Turing. During this period the team, working at the University's Computer Systems Research Group, produced compilers for the IBM 3033 and the VAX, wrote the Turing Report, published a textbook on the language, and developed a mathematical specification to eliminate possibilities of ambiguities in the language. Computerrwrld asked Prof. Ric Holt, one of the language designers, to describe: What does it take to develop a new language? What are the personal stories behind the technical efforts? What sort of environment leads to technical innovation? Here is his story.

A quiet summer. It is summer 1982; Jim Cordy and I are enjoying a bit of a lull. Our development project, leading to the systems programming language Concurrent Euclid, is receiving a warm acceptance. Universities are using it in advanced courses and companies are using it for production software. But lulls are not a way of life around the Computer Systems Research Group, where people jokingly quip, "If it works, it's obsolete." Frantic activity is more the norm, and a new project is brewing.

More powerful than Pascal. Prof. Tom Hull wants to know how the University is going to teach computer science using interactive systems. Programming has been taught for a decade at Toronto using batch processing with PL/I (actually SP/k and PL/C), so Tom suggests developing an interactive PL/I system for the VAX. I disagree. To me,

PL/I is a "fatal disease," a complex mess, a necessary evil that was useful for introducing structured programming in the seventies. In PL/I you write I=J=2; and no one can guess what it means (it compares J to 2 and sets I to 1 or 0). You write 25+1/3 and you get either an overflow or the wrong answer. No, I argue, it is time for something better.

Why not use Pascal, I urge, with its elegance and available compilers. Hull says: No, a language is needed that is more powerful than Pascal. With Wirth's definition of Pascal, he points out, the students can't write matrix multiplication; they can't use exponentiation. They can't even write a "put message" procedure. Pascal, has long been my favorite language, but besides Tom's complaints, I worry that its input/output and string manipulation are too clumsy; they cause students to concentrate on details rather than mastering programming principles. Still Pascal seems the best available choice.

Tom asks why don't we use Euclid. It is a fair question, because I have been loudly preaching the advantages of Euclid for producing modular, efficient and highly reliable programs. But, I explain, although Euclid is lovely, it was designed for systems programming, not for general purpose programming. This explanation bothers me. After all, Euclid *is* a good language. Is it possible, I wonder, to mold Euclid into a general purpose language?

Easier than BASIC. Meantime, my son Adam, ten years old, has learned to use BASIC on our home computer. He creates mesmerizing swirls of color on the screen, as well as making the thing talk and play music. I explain to Adam that BASIC is crude, that programming in BASIC is like trying to swim in spaghetti and meatballs. I decide it is time to set Adam on the road to Correct Programming. I decide to teach him Pascal. So together, we develop the Pascal program that prints Hello. There, I say, isn't that nice? Adam is not impressed. Why, he asks impatiently, do you have to type all that just to print Hello. Well, I explain, there is one line to say it's a program, one line to say it has a beginning, one line to say print Hello, and one line to say it has an end. "Four lines to say Hello??", he asks, "In BASIC you just type one line". I am getting ready to launch a discussion on the virtues of structure, top down programming, etc., but it seems that Pascal and I have lost credibility in the eyes of our ten year old audience.

I can't help thinking that Adam is right. The fact is, BASIC excels at minuscule programs, and many programs are minuscule, especially student programs. But BASIC programs longer than about a page tend to be mind scramblers — not a good thing for the serious programmer and certainly not a good thing for the student. Is it possible, I wonder, to have a language that is easier than BASIC, for small programs, and yet more powerful than Pascal?

Hatching the chicken and egg. The University receives a gift from IBM: a 3033 computer (370 architecture). This means the University cannot standardize on VAX interactive software. There is no compatible software that we can use on both the 3033 and the VAX. This situation provokes me into proposing a new language.

I ask Jim Cordy: what about creating a new language to run on these two architectures (370 and VAX). He points out that even if we designed the language and developed the compilers, it would be of no use without a textbook. Prof. Pat Hume and I have co-authored several books, so I ask him if he would work with me on a textbook for the new language. He expresses some interest, but points out that a textbook is of no use without classes to use it. So, I ask Al Borodin, Department Chairman, what are the chances of switching to the new language. He thinks this might be possible, but points out that the department could not consider a new language without a textbook and solid compilers.

So this is a chicken and egg problem; how does one simultaneously create both chicken and egg (compiler and textbook)? Will anyone use them anyway? Certainly there is no chance of acceptance unless the product is clearly better than other options. Even if it is better, some people feel strongly that the University should not be an "island," that it should not use a language unless it is widely accepted.

With a Machiavellian twinkle in my eye, I tell Jim and Pat that Al thinks the department can be expected to use the new language. I tell Jim and Al that Pat and I will get the book done; I tell Al and Pat that Jim and I will take care of the language and compiler. Pat and I go to our publisher, Reston, and convince them to publish our yet to be written textbook, for a not yet designed language, supported by not yet developed compilers for an uncommitted Computer Science audience. Jim and I submerge ourselves in a four month non-stop debate which our secretaries believe is an ongoing feud, but which is actually our way of designing a language.

Language goals. We want to produce a better language, with good compilers, for use in classes next year (for September 83). The language must be easy to use and learn, but it is not to be just a teaching language, because then it would never gain wide acceptance. It must incorporate the state of the art, the hard-won software wisdom of the seventies: modules with "information hiding," complete but optional run-time checking, precise language specification as in denotational semantics, and program verification supported by proof rules.

It must obey the "no surprise" rule, meaning users should not write a statement like I=J=2; and have it produce, without warning, an unexpected result. The language and compiler must help the user create reliable programs, detecting bugs early in the development cycle, rather than leaving lurking bugs in production programs. The language must support highly efficient programs, so that users are not tempted to sacrifice reliability and use low level languages such as Assembler or C. The language must be easy to compile — after all, we are to produce two compilers, for the VAX and 370, within the year.

By Christmas 82, Jim and I produce an acceptable draft of the Turing Language Report, whose early versions have been alternatively blessed and cursed by the "hackers."

The hackers. Mark Mendell has developed a reputation as a super hacker, a programmer par excellence, turning Unix inside out if necessary to solve system problems, producing a Concurrent Euclid code generator in two months for the nearly incomprehensible Intel 432 object-oriented architecture. He retires each evening to read an armload of science fiction paperbacks. Jim and I know we will have to rely on Mark to produce the code generator for the new compiler. Steve Perelgut is a newcomer. He has worked on Bell Northern Research's Protel compiler. It falls to Steve to program the stickiest part of the compilers. He is the person who gets cajoled, coerced and "volunteered" into developing the semantic analysis pass of the compilers. The danger with semantic analysis is that the language incorporates new concepts: anti-aliasing and elimination of expression side effects. It falls to Steve to create the required software magic to support these concepts in the compiler. Jim and I worry about Steve, because his part is crucial and yet he is a bit of an unknown. Steve's response to our worries is to ask when we want what done, to finish it on time, to ask again, and to finish again.

The mood of the project is contagiously enthusiastic. We eat lunch regularly at various Chinese restaurants and unwittingly entertain other eaters with loud jargon-filled arguments about import lists, the format of token streams, grokking transitively imported modules, and booting to the 370.

Sharpest software tools. We have the best tools available. We have Unix with file flogging utilities. We use S/SL, University of Toronto's compiler writing system. It allows us to produce a scanner in a few days and a parser in a few more days. Yes, they initially have some bugs, but these are easily spotted and fixed. Yes, the scanner and parser are a bit slow, but there will be time to speed them up later. The bulk of the compiler is written in Concurrent Euclid; this allows us to isolate implementation details in modules, to get extensive compile time checking, as well as checked execution during testing. As much as possible, we recycle parts of the Concurrent Euclid compiler, using them to create the compiler for the new language.

YACC complains. We have ignored Unix's parser generator, YACC, because we feel it cannot produce a production quality parser for our compilers. We are intrigued by the fact that YACC can automatically detect bugs (ambiguities) in the grammar of a language. So we enlist Philip Matthews, who has been doing research on program semantics, to see if YACC will accept our language's grammar. He produces a BNF grammar for the new language and feeds it to YACC. YACC develops indigestion and rejects the grammar. We point accusing fingers at YACC; it refuses to change its mind, claiming that our grammar is ambiguous. In the end we see that YACC is right. Delighted with YACC's computer generated complaint about the new language, Jim and I re-design the syntax for the troublesome language constructs, and YACC finally blesses our language.

Baptizing the language. It is January 1983. Pat says the language deserves a decent name. We have been calling it "New Euclid." He says it is not just a new version of Euclid, it is a new development, a happy departure, a University of Toronto invention. OK, I say, but all the good mathematicians have been used up: Pascal and Euclid are taken. We ponder calling it Von Neuman, but we decide no one can spell that. We ask ourselves: How about something that relates it to T and U as in the University of Toronto; that is how the name Turing came to mind. That seems right: a language named after Alan M. Turing, one of the pioneering geniuses of Computer Science.

I tell Mark and Steve, who respond with undisguised disgust. Yuck is what they say. They closet themselves briefly and emerge with an alternate name: Jarvis. (Jarvis is a street in Toronto that is known for street walkers.) When I persist with the name Turing, they retaliate by changing our internal documentation to call the language Jarvis. I suspect the name Jarvis lives in hidden crevices in the compiler, but officially the language is baptized "Turing."

The Matthews Plan. In Fall 82 I meet with Philip Matthews and Alan Rosselet. Alan is doing Ph.D. research on the formal definition of context constraints, such as type checking in programming languages. We have a long discussion about the need for the absolutely precise definition of all details about programming languages. Philip proposes that, if Turing is to be a better language, then it must have a mathematically precise definition. I agree in principle, but am doubtful about whether we have time or resources to produce the definition. Philip outlines his goal, which we come to call the Matthews Plan. It requires (1) a regular grammar to specify the language's lexical structure, (2) a context-free (BNF) grammar for its syntax, (3) an ADL program (ADL is a notation invented by Rosselet) to define static constraints such as type checking, and (4) proof rules to give meaning to the concept of program execution. Thus was begun the project to mathematically specify the language.

Three major thrusts. We now have three major concurrent projects stemming from the Turing Language Report. These are: the compilers, the textbook and the formal definition (the Matthews Plan). These turn out to be effective proving grounds for the newborn language; the careful study of the language required by these three helps us to iron out inconsistencies, incompleteness and ineptitudes in the original language design.

Hume drops the "skip". Pat Hume is writing a chapter of the Turing textbook. He finds that every example "put" statement ends with the word skip. He considers this foolish. He reacts by removing every "skip" in the chapter. The result is a nice chapter, containing nice programs for a language that isn't Turing. I complain that a textbook for the wrong language is not going to help much. He complains that it is ridiculous to say "skip" every time you print anything. Of course he is right. Jim and I retire to debate vociferously about how to get rid of "skip". It takes a month to settle on a good solution. With "skip" eliminated, an entire Turing program to print Hello is reduced to the single line: put "Hello". There is not even a line number; it is simpler then BASIC. Pat is happy and so is Adam.

Meeting the schedule. In January 1983 the compiler project begins in earnest, starting as soon as the language is reasonably well defined. I tell Al Borodin (and anyone else who will listen) that we expect to have a compiler for the 370/3033 to prototype in September 83 classes, but possibly we might have it ready for May 83 summer classes.

I have a schedule drawn on the left side of my blackboard that shows when each part of the compiler must be completed in order to prototype Turing in May summer classes. Schedules for software projects are a private joke for me, because I've drawn them for many projects, but I've never seen one followed. With Turing it is different. Each piece neatly falls into place at its prescribed time.

After working on the compiler for two months, it occurs to us that the summer classes can be taught on a VAX. The VAX compiler would be faster to produce because (1) we are using a VAX to support our compiler development and (2) the VAX has a cleaner instruction set than the 370. All of the compiler is written in a machine independent language (Concurrent Euclid); the Turing compiler is identical for the 370 and the VAX except for its code generation pass. So we switch our target machine from the 370 to the VAX, and continue developing the compiler.

Come May we have completed most of the Turing compiler for the VAX. It does not yet support some advanced features. It still has some known bugs. It is largely untested. What to do? Use it, of course.

Summer of 83. By May 83 Pat Hume and I have a usable draft of 14 chapters of the Turing textbook. It has been produced using the computer, so we run off a copy and have it locally bound for summer classes. It will take us a few more months to reach the point where we can computer typeset the entire book and hand the camera ready copy to the publisher.

The compiler team is smugly proud of its raw, new VAX Turing compiler, so we congratulate ourselves with a five course feast of Peking duck. Our new unwritten schedule is simple: by September we are to have a rock solid compiler for the VAX and a new but usable compiler for the 370.

We ask Steve Tjiang to join the compiler team. He agrees to spend the summer creating the code generator for the 370, while Steve Perelgut and Mark expand the compilers to handle the remaining language features, speed up the compiler, trim its size, and fix its bugs.

Steve Tjiang is well known to us as the undergraduate who explains things to graduate students. In September 83 he will go to Stanford to become a graduate student himself. Our only worry about him is that he sometimes creates programs that only he is capable of understanding. He encounters a stumbling block: the assembler on the 370 generates wrong code for some constructs. Undaunted, he finds the source code for the assembler, corrects it and carries on. We worry momentarily about the fact that our correct assembly language produced by our correct Concurrent Euclid compiler will not be correctly assembled at other installations. We decide to ignore the problem.

September 83. With the arrival of students for Fall 83 classes, the VAX version of the Turing compiler is well proven. More important: it has been enthusiastically received by students and professors. The Computer Science Department is visibly excited at the prospect of using the new language.

The textbook has been typeset and is in the bookstore. The 370 version of the compiler is complete, but largely untested. Three thousand University of Toronto students begin using the language on four VAXes and the IBM 3033.

I learn that courses other than introductory programming have adopted the new language. The course on data structures is using Turing's modules, dynamic arrays, pointers, and union types and finding them superior to data structuring features in PL/I and Pascal.

In November, Bill Buxton announces that Turing is so much easier to teach than PL/I that he is two weeks ahead of his teaching schedule.

Lecture at IBM. Some of us at the University are invited to give lectures to the Toronto IBM Laboratory, which does compiler work. In my lecture I explain how the Turing compiler was developed. The question I get is: what are the management protocols for approving this sort of development project at the University? I am confused by the question and reply: I guess we do not have any management protocols. He explains that for him, gaining approval for a project of this magnitude, involving the creation of a language with compilers and user documentation, would consume more resources then the University consumed on the entire Turing project. It occurs to me that the Turing people (language designers, compiler implementors, book writers and formal definers) have been eating, breathing and sleeping the language for a year.

Is the world ready for it? We feel we have a better language and a better compiler, but we wonder: is the world ready for it? We are encouraged when the publisher (Reston) begins producing Turing T shirts to promote the book. The Toronto newspaper picks up the story; this leads to a radio interview on Turing, which leads to more media coverage.

We carefully package the VAX compiler for external distribution. We begin development of a Turing compiler for IBM PC compatibles, scheduled for May 84 completion. We begin developing an interpretive Turing programming environment for home computers. Maybe the world *is* ready for a better language. We think so, so just in case, we are making Turing ready for the world.

Appendix B

A Theorem about Lexical Sequences

This appendix considers the question of whether Turing's lexical structure is ambiguous. We prove that if a string satisfies the principle of maximal scan, then there is only one way to divide it into lexical units. However, if the string violates the principle of maximal scan, then in some cases it is possible to divide the string into tokens in two different ways.

To explain the exceptional case first, consider the following string.

"5...10"

Two token sequences corresponding to this string are

≪"5.", "..", "10"≫

and

≪"5", "..", ".10"≫.

Luckily, neither of these two token sequences satisfies the context-free syntax, so this string can not appear in a Turing program.

Now consider the case when the string does satisfy the principle of maximal scan, or more correctly, when a sequence of lexical units corresponding to the string satisfies the principle. In this case, as the following theorem shows, there is only one sequence of lexical units that corresponds to the string, and thus there is only one way to divide the string up into tokens and separators. (In the following we use functions called *cat* and *prefix* that are defined in Chapter 6.)

Theorem. Let s be a string, and let t_1 and t_2 be sequences of lexical units that satisfy the principle of maximal scan. If $cat(t_1)=s$ and $cat(t_2)=s$, then t_1 and t_2 are equal.

Proof. We will assume that t_1 and t_2 are not equal and derive a contradiction.

If t_1 is the empty sequence $\langle\rangle$, then by the definition of *cat*, $cat(t_1)$ $(= s)$ is the null string. Since the null string is not a lexical unit, if s is the null string, then t_2 must also be an empty sequence. Thus if one of t_1 or t_2 is the empty sequence, they both must be.

Otherwise, assume neither t_1 nor t_2 are the empty sequence, and let e_1 and e_2 be the first elements of t_1 and t_2, respectively, that differ. First note that e_1 must be a prefix of e_2, or e_2 must be a prefix of e_1 (that is, they can not have different characters in the same position), for otherwise the results of catenating the elements of the sequences together would differ. So the only way e_1 and e_2 can differ is if one is shorter than the other.

Without loss of generality, assume e_2 is longer than e_1, and let c be the first character in t_2 that is not in t_1. Because the results of concatenating the elements of the sequences together must be the same, c must also be the first character of the element following e_1 in t_1.

Now consider whether $prefix(e_1+\text{'}c\text{'})$ is true or not. If it is true, then t_1 does not satisfy the principle of maximal scan, contradicting the assumption of the theorem. But if $prefix(e_1+\text{'}c\text{'})$ is false, then there is no way to extend $e_1+\text{'}c\text{'}$ to be a lexical unit, and thus e_2 is not a lexical unit, and t_2 is not a sequence of lexical units. Thus e_1 and e_2 must be equal, and so t_1 and t_2 must also be equal. This concludes the proof.

Appendix C

Translating Extended Context-Free Syntax Into Standard Notation

This appendix shows how to translate extended context-free syntax, used in defining Turing, into traditional notation. Our notation extends the traditional notation in three ways:

(1) brackets indicate optional sequences,

(2) braces indicate repeatable sequences, and

(3) a separate table gives the precedence for operators.

However, any set of production rules using these three extensions can be translated into an equivalent set of production rules that does not use these extensions. This translation can be performed as follows.

(1) If "item" denotes a sequence of tokens, non-terminals, brackets, and braces, then replace any occurrence of

[item]

by the non-terminal *optionalItem* (where *optionalItem* is a name not used elsewhere), and add the following rule to the set of productions.

An *optionalItem* is one of:

a. item

b.

Here and below if the line after a label is blank, then the sequence is empty.

(2) Similarly, replace any occurrence of

{ item }

by the non-terminal *repeatedItem* (where again *repeatedItem* is a name not used elsewhere), and add the following rule.

A *repeatedItem* is one of:
 a. *repeatedItem* item
 b.

(3) And if –, +, and * are three infix left-associative operators which can replace *infixOp*, and – also represents a prefix operator which can replace *prefixOp* in a rule such as the following:

An *expn* is one of:
 a. *literal*
 b. *prefixOp expn*
 c. *expn infixOp expn*

and if the precedence of these four operators is, from highest (tightest binding) to lowest,

prefix – (highest)
*
+, infix – (lowest)

then the following rules express this precedence.

An *expn* is one of:
 a. *expn + term*
 b. *expn – term*
 c. *term*

A *term* is one of:
 a. *term * signedLiteral*
 b. *signedLiteral*

A *signedLiteral* is one of:
 a. *– literal*
 b. *literal*

Appendix D

Abstract Context-Free Syntax for Turing

The formal definition of Turing's context conditions uses an abstract context-free syntax, which is given below. This is like the standard (or concrete) context-free syntax for Turing except that details that are of no concern to context conditions are eliminated. Turing's context conditions assume that various syntactic restrictions specified by the more detailed standard context-free syntax are satisfied by the program in question.

Program	::=	*S*
S	::=	*Decl S*
	|	*Stmt S*
	|	*empty*
Decl	::=	**const** *Pervasive id* [:*T*] := *InitVal*
	|	**var** $\{id_i\}$ [: *T*] [:= *InitVal*]
	|	**var** $\{id_i\}$: **array** $\{E_{iL}..E_{iU}\}$ **of** *T*
	|	**var** $\{id_i\}$: **collection of** *T*
	|	**var** $\{id_i\}$: **collection of forward** *id*
	|	**bind** $\{Var_i\ id_i$ **to** $Ref_i\}$
	|	**type** *Pervasive id*: *T*
Pervasive	::=	**pervasive**
	|	*empty*

```
T          ::= int
             | real
             | string
             | string (E)
             | boolean
             | E1 .. E2
             | enum (id1 .. id2)
             | array T1 .. T2 of T
             | Ref
             | set of T
             | pointer to id
             | record
                  Fields
               end record
             | union Ident : T of
               {label {Eij}: Fields_i}
               end union

Fields     ::= {id_i1, ... , id_iR : T_i}

Stmt       ::= Ref:=E
             | Ref
             | assert E
             | return
             | result E
             | if E1 then S1
                  {elsif E_i then S_i}
                  [else S_n]
               end if
             | case E of
                  {label {Eij}: S_i}
               end case
             | begin S end
             | new id, Ref
             | free id, Ref
             | tag Ref, E
             | loop
                  [invariant E]
                  S
               end loop
             | exit [when E]
```

| **for** *Ident* : [**decreasing**] *ForRange*
  [**invariant** *E*]
  S
end for

ForRange ::= *Ref*
| E_i .. E_2

Stmt ::= **put** [:*E* ,] {$PutItem_i$} [..]
| **get** [:*E* ,] {$GetItem_i$}

PutItem ::= E_1[: E_2]
| E_1: E_2: E_3 [: E_4]
| **skip**

GetItem ::= *Ref*
| *Ref* : *ExpnOrStar*
| **skip**

ExpnOrStar ::= *E*
| *

E ::= *integerLiteral*
| *realLiteral*
| *stringLiteral*
| *booleanLiteral*
| $E_1 + E_2$
| $E_1 - E_2$
| $E_1 * E_2$
| E_1 **mod** E_2
| E_1 ** E_2
| E_1 / E_2
| E_1 **div** E_2
| E_1 [**not**]= E_2
| $E_1 > E_2$
| $E_1 >= E_2$
| $E_1 < E_2$
| $E_1 <= E_2$
| $+E_1$
| $-E_1$
| **not** E_1
| E_1 **and** E_2
| E_1 **or** E_2

	|	E_1 => E_2
	|	E_1 [**not**] **in** E_2
	|	*Ref*
	|	*Ref* ([**all**])
	|	*Ref* (*[−*E*])
	|	*Ref*(Pos_1 .. Pos_2)
Ref	::=	*id Selectors*
Selectors	::=	*Selector Selectors*
	|	*empty*
Selector	::=	. *id*
	|	(E_1, ... , E_n)
Decl	::=	*Forward FcnOrProc id ParameterList ResultSpec* **imports** (*Imports*) [*Body*]
	|	**body** *FcnOrProc id* *Body*
ResultSpec	::=	*empty*
	|	*Ident* : *T*
ParameterList	::=	*empty*
	|	*ParameterDecl ParameterList*
ParameterDecl	::=	*Var* id_1 , ... , id_n: *ParameterType*
	|	*FcnOrProc id ParameterList ResultSpec*
ParameterType	::=	*T*
	|	**string** (*)
	|	**array** E_1 .. E_2 **of** *T*
	|	**array** E_1 .. E_2 **of string** (*)
Imports	::=	*Var id*
	|	**forward** *id*
Body	::=	[**pre** E_{pre}] [**init** {id_i := E_i}] [**post** E_{post}] *S* **end** *id*

Decl ::= **module** id_{module}
import (*Imports*)
export (*Exports*)
[**pre** E_1]
S_1
[**invariant** E_2]
S_2
[**post** E_3]
end *id*

Exports ::= *empty*
| *Opaque id Exports*

The remaining rules are implicit in the formal definition of Turing's context conditions. These rules appear in the *isProduction* construct in context conditions.

InitVal ::= **init** ({*initPart*})

initPart ::= E_i
| **init** ({*initPart*})

Ident ::= *id*
| *empty*

Forward ::= **forward**
| *empty*

Var ::= **var**
| *empty*

FcnOrProc ::= **function**
| **procedure**

Opaque ::= **opaque**
| *empty*

Pos ::= [*–] [*E*]

Appendix E

Formal Operational Semantics for Basis Statements

A formal operational approach to programming language semantics is given. It is used to define the ten basis statements that underly the formal semantics of the Turing programming language. This approach is operational in that it gives the state by state progression characterizing the execution of a program consisting of basis statements. This progression closely models the execution of programs on existing computers. The approach is called *next state semantics.*

This approach is introduced for several reasons. First, it demonstrates that the operational semantics for a language like Turing can be clearly and briefly formalized. Secondly, it demonstrates that Turing's formal semantics can be considered to be either axiomatic (when the basis is defined using weakest preconditions) or operational (when the present definition is used). Finally, as will be shown after the definition, *wp* semantics can be defined in terms of (or derived from) operational semantics, rather than being postulated.

We assume that there is a set of variables, named $x, y, \cdots$, and that the values of these variables taken together define the state v of the computation. A particular variable x can assume a value from the set Σ_x. For example, if x is a scalar variable in Turing and checking is specified, then $\Sigma_x = T_x + \{UNINIT(T_x)\}$. In other words, x is either uninitialized or has a value in its declared type T_x. For nonscalars such as arrays, Σ_x includes partially initialized values. When checking is omitted, Σ_x may contain implementation dependent bit patterns. The overall state space Σ is the cross product of the individual variable's state spaces:

Definition: $\Sigma = \Sigma_x * \Sigma_y * ...$
where $x, y, \cdots$ are the program variables.

Next we define the status of a completed computation. The status indicates whether a computation ends by an abort, by an exit, by a return, or normally by reaching the end of the statement being executed.

Definition: $STATUS =_{df} \{CONTINUE, EXIT, RETURN, ABORT\}$

In next state semantics, each statement S is considered to be a total function mapping from an initial state to a set of pairs:

$$S : \Sigma \rightarrow 2**(\Sigma^* \times STATUS)$$

Σ^* is the set of sequences of states from Σ. $(\Sigma^* \times STATUS)$ is the set of pairs of sequences and statuses. Each pair is *(trace, status)* where *trace* is a sequence of states and *status* is a member of *STATUS*. The idea is that the statement is started in a particular state; its execution causes a sequence of state changes recorded by *trace*. The *status* indicates how the execution terminates. Since the execution can be nondeterministic, we have a set of *(trace, status)* pairs.

To provide an expressive notation, we will write

$$v \; S \; (trace, status)$$

to mean

$$(trace, status) \textbf{ in } S(v)$$

This can be read as: when started in state v, statement S can generate the *trace* of states, terminating with the specified *status*.

We will use the following notation:

t1 + *t2* is the catenation of traces *t1* and *t2*
t(*) is the last state in trace *t*

We will abbreviate *CONTINUE* as *CONT*. We will write e (for expression e) to mean the expression with v's constituent values $(x, y, ...)$ substituted for the corresponding identifiers in e.

We now define the ten basis statements in terms of next state semantics.

v S (trace, status)	**DEFINITION OF** *v S (trace, status)*
v *CONT* *(trace, status)*	$trace = \langle v \rangle \;\&\; status = CONT$
v *PICK*(x, s) *(trace, status)*	$\exists\, e$ **in** $s: trace = \langle v(x{:}e) \rangle \;\&\; status = CONT$
v IF e THEN S1 *ELSE S2* *END IF (trace, status)*	$e \Rightarrow v\, S1\, (trace, status)$ & $\sim e \Rightarrow v\; S2\, (trace, status)$

v S1; S2 (trace, status)	*(∃ t1, t2:* *trace = t1 + t2 &* *v S1 (t1, CONT) &* *t1(*) S2 (t2, status))* **or** *(v S1 (trace, status)* *& status ≠ CONT)*
v ABORT (trace, status)	*trace = ⟨v⟩ & status = ABORT*
v CHAOS (trace, status)	*trace* **in** Σ^* *& status* **in** *STATUS* (No constraints on computation)
v BLOCK S END BLOCK *(trace, status)*	*status=CONT &* *(v S (trace, CONT)* **or** *v S (trace, EXIT))* **or** *((status=RETURN* **or** *STATUS=ABORT) &* *v S (trace, status))*
v SUBPROG S END SUBPROG *(trace, status)*	*(status=CONT &* *(v S (trace, CONT)* **or** *v S (trace, RETURN))* **or** *((status=EXIT* **or** *STATUS=ABORT) &* *v S (trace, status))*
v EXIT (trace, status)	*trace=⟨v⟩ & status=EXIT*
v RETURN (trace, status)	*trace=⟨v⟩ & status=RETURN*

Since all Turing statements and declarations are defined in terms of these ten basis statements, we have now effectively given a formal operational semantics of Turing.

We will show how axiomatic semantics, such as weakest preconditions, can be defined in terms of next state semantics. Since Turing has three ways of terminating a statement (not counting aborting), each statement effectively has three postconditions. We will write

$$(P_c, P_e, P_r) = wp(S, (Q_c, Q_e, Q_r))$$

to mean that S is to establish Q_r if it returns, Q_e if it exists and Q_c if it continues, and that for the statement preceding S, P_c must be true for continuation, P_e when exiting and

P_r when returning. We will write Q to represent the triple of predicates:

$$Q = (Q_c, Q_e, Q_r)$$

Similarly, $P = (P_c, P_e, P_r)$. We will use a subscript of c, e or r to select one of the three predicates in a triple; for example, $wp(W, Q)$ is a triple, so $wp(W, Q)_c$ is its c component.

In defining wp, we will use notation such as $Q_c[v: t(*)]$ to mean the truth value of predicate Q_c when its variables $v=(x, y, \cdots)$ are substituted for by the corresponding values of $t(*)$; recall that $t(*)$ is the final state in trace t. We now define wp in terms of operational semantics:

Definition: $wp(S, Q) =_{\text{df}} (P_c, Q_e, Q_r)$
where $P_c =_{\text{df}} \forall\, t \textbf{ in } \Sigma^*: \neg(v\ S\ (t, ABORT))\ \&$
$(v\ S\ (t, CONT) \Rightarrow Q_c[v: t(*)])\ \&$
$(v\ S\ (t, EXIT) \Rightarrow Q_e[v: t(*)])\ \&$
$(v\ S\ (t, RETURN) \Rightarrow Q_r[v: t(*)])$

This definition specifies that the statement preceding S is required to establish the same exit condition Q_e and return condition Q_r as S. It states that v must not lead to an abort, that Q_c must be true in every continuing state $t(*)$, that Q_e must be true in every exiting state $t(*)$, and that Q_r must be true in every returning state $t(*)$.

Since the exit and return preconditions of all statements are the same as their corresponding exit and return postconditions, the only interesting precondition is for continuing (P_c). We will now develop as theorems the weakest precondition P_c of each of the ten basis statements.

The following theorem, which can be proven by inspection of the preceding definitions, gives the continuing precondition P_c for four basis statements.

Theorem: $wp(CONT, Q)_c = Q_c,$
$wp(EXIT, Q)_c = Q_e,$
$wp(RETURN, Q)_c = Q_r,$
$wp(ABORT, Q)_c = \textbf{false}$

By observing that *CHAOS* can abort, we can prove:

Theorem: $wp(CHAOS, Q)_c = \textbf{false}$

It is also easy to prove that:

Theorem: $wp(BLOCK\ S\ END\ BLOCK, Q)_c = wp(S, (Q_c, Q_c, Q_r))_c$
$wp(SUBPROG\ S\ END\ SUBPROG, Q)_c = wp(S, (Q_c, Q_e, Q_c))_c$

In Turing, an *EXIT* never terminates a *SUBPROG*, so the exit precondition of the *SUBPROG* statement can be ignored.

The only remaining basis statements are *IF*, *PICK* and semicolon. We now state corresponding theorems for them without proof.

Theorem: $wp(IF\ e\ THEN\ S1\ ELSE\ S2\ END\ IF, Q)_c = (e \Rightarrow wp(S1, Q)_c\ \&$
$\sim e \Rightarrow wp(S2, Q)_c)$

Theorem: $wp(PICK(x, s), Q)_c = \forall\ x$ **in** $s: Q_c$

Theorem: $wp(S1; S2, Q)_c = wp(S1, wp(S2, Q))_c$

The important thing to observe is that these theorems are equivalent to the *wp* definitions of the ten basis statements given in the axiomatic semantics of Turing. There, the *wp* of each basis statement was postulated. Here, we postulate the operational semantics and prove *wp* as theorems.

Appendix F

Available Implementations of Turing

As of January, 1987 there exist both a compiler and an interpreter for Turing. The compiler is written in Concurrent Euclid and the interpreter is written in Turing. The compiler and interpreter currently operate on IBM PC compatibles, IBM mainframes, Vax, and SUN/68000. There is also a programming environment that integrates the compiler and interpreter with a full screen editor, written in Turing. There is an implementation of Turing Plus written in Turing Plus, that translates to either 68000 machine code or to C source code. Work on these implementations has taken place at the Computer Systems Research Institute of the University of Toronto and, with the move of J.R. Cordy to Queen's University (Kingston) work is also being done there. This software is available from:

Holt Software Associates Inc.
Suite 305
203 College St.
Toronto, CANADA M5T 6P9
(416) 978-6985

Bibliography

Aho, A.V., Ullman, J.D. *Principles of Compiler Design.* Addison-Wesley.

Back, R.-J. Semantics of unbounded nondeterminism. Tutkimuksia - Research Reports, Computing Centre, University of Helsinki, 1976.

Barnard, D.T. Hierarchic Syntax Error Repair, Ph.D. thesis, Department of Computer Science, University of Toronto, March 1981.

Bekic, H., Bjorner, D., Henhapl, W., Jones, C. B., Lucas, P. A formal definition of a PL/I subset. Parts I and II, Technical Report TR25.139, IBM Vienna Laboratory, December 1974.

Boom, H.J. A weaker precondition for loops. ACM Transactions on Programming Languages, Vol 4., No. 4, October 1982.

Bjorner, D., Oest, O.N. *Towards a Formal Description of Ada.* Springer-Verlag, 1980.

Branquart, P., Louis, G., Wodon, P. *An Analytical Description of CHILL, the CCITT High Level language.* Springer-Verlag, 1982.

Brinch Hansen, P. *Programming a Personal Computer*. Prentice-Hall, 1982.

Cooper, D. *Standard Pascal, Reference Manual*. Norton, 1983.

Cordy, J.R. Compile-Time detection of aliasing in Euclid programs. *Software-Practice and Experience* 14, 8, pp. 755-768, August 1984.

Demers, A., Donahue, J. Revised Report on Russell. Report TR79-389, Department of Computer Science, Cornell University, 1979.

Dijkstra, E.W. Guarded commands, nondeterminism, and formal derivation. *Comm. ACM 18*, pp. 453-57, August 1975.

Dijkstra, E.W. *A Discipline of Programming*. Prentice-Hall, 1976.

Donahue, J.E. *Complementary Definitions of Programming Language Semantics*. Lecture Notes in Computer Science, Springer-Verlag, New York, 1976.

Elliot, D. On proving the absence of execution errors. Ph.D. thesis, Department of Computer Science, University of Toronto (also Technical Report CSRG-141), March 1982.

Fischer, C.N., LeBlanc, R.J. Efficient implementation and optimization of run-time checking in Pascal, in *Proceedings of a Conference on Language Design for Reliable Software*, SIGPLAN Notices 12, 3, 1977.

Gannon, J.D., Horning, J.J. *Language Design for Programming Reliability*. IEEE Transactions on Software Engineering, June 1975.

Goguen, J.A., Thatcher, J.W., Wagner, E.G. An initial algebra approach to the specification, correctness and implementation of abstract data types. In *Current Trends in Programming Methodology*, Vol.4, ed. R.T.Yeh, 80-149, 1978.

Gries, D. *The Science of Programming*. Springer-Verlag, New York, 1981.

Guttag, J.V., Horowitz, E., Musser D.R. Abstract data types and software validation. *Communications of the ACM* 21, 12, pp. 1048-1064, December 1978a.

Guttag, J.V., Horning, J.J., The algebraic specification of abstract data types. *Acta Informatica*, 10:1, 27-52, 1978b.

Guttag, J.V., Horning, J.J., Preliminary report on the Larch shared language. Technical Report CSL-83-6, Xerox PARC, December 1983.

Habermann, A.N. Critical comments on the programming language Pascal. *Acta Informatica 3*, pp. 47-57, 1973.

Hehner, E.C.R. *The Logic of Programming*. Prentice-Hall International Series in Computer Science, 1984a.

Hehner, E.C.R. Predicative Programming. *Comm. of the ACM* 27, 2, 1984b.

Hoare, C.A.R. Proof of correctness of data representations. *Acta Informatica* 1, pp. 271-281, 1972.

Hoare, C.A.R., Wirth, N. An axiomatic definition of the programming language Pascal. *Acta Informatica* 2, pp. 335-355, 1973a.

Hoare, C.A.R. *Hints on Programming Language Design*. Computer Science Department, Stanford University, Stanford, December 1973b.

Hodges, A. *Alan Turing: the Enigma*. Simon & Schuster, New York, 1983.

Hoffman, C., O'Donnell, M. Programming with equations. *ACM Transactions on Programming Languages and Systems*, 4:1, 83-112, 1982.

Holt, R.C., Wortman, D.B., Barnard, D.T., Cordy, J.R. SP/k: a system for teaching computer programming. *Comm. of the ACM* 20, 5, pp. 301-309, May 1977.

Holt, R.C., Wortman, D.B. A model for implementing Euclid Modules and prototypes. *Transactions on Programming Languages and Systems*, vol. 4, no. 4, pp. 552-562, October 1982a.

Holt, R.C., Cordy, J.R. , Wortman, D.W. An introduction to S/SL: syntax semantics language. *ACM Transactions on Programming Languages and Systems* 4, 2, pp. 149-178, April 1982b.

Holt, R.C., Cordy, J.R. The Turing language report. Technical Report CSRG-153, Computer Systems Research Institute, University of Toronto, December 1983.

Holt, R.C. Turing: an inside look at the genesis of a programming language. Computerworld 18, 20, May 1984a.

Holt, R.C., Hume, J.N.P. *Introduction to Computer Science using the Turing Programming Language.* Reston, Prentice-Hall Publishing Co., Reston, Virginia, 1984b.

Hull, T.E., Abrham, M.S., Cohen, M.S., Curley, A.F.X., Hall, C.B., Penny, D.A., Sawchuk, J.T.M. Numerical Turing. *ACM SIGNUM Newsletter* vol. 20, no. 3, pp. 26-34, July 1985.

Hume, J.N.P., Holt, R.C. *Structured Programming using PL/I and SP/k.* Reston Publishing Co. (now Prentice-Hall), Reston, Virginia, 1975.

ISO *Specification of the Computer Programming Language Pascal*, International Standards Organization, 1981.

Ichbiah, J. et al. Rationale for the design of the Ada programming language, ACM Sigplan Notices, vol. 14, no 6, June 1979.

Kernighan, B.W. Why Pascal is not my favorite programming language. Computer Science Technical Report 100, Bell Laboratories, July 1981.

Lampson, B.W., Horning, J.J., London, R.L., Mitchell, J.G., Popek, G.J. Report on the programming language Euclid. ACM SIGPLAN Notices 12, 2, February 1977. (The revised language is described in report CSL-81-12, Xerox Palo Alto Research Center, October 1981.)

London, R.L., Guttag, J.V., Horning, J.J., Lampson, B.W., Mitchell, J.G., Popek, G.J. Proof rules for the programming language Euclid. *Acta Informatica* 10, 1978, pp. 1-26.

MacLane, S., Birkhoff, G. *Algebra.* Macmillan Publishing Co., New York, second edition, 1979.

Martin, A.J. A general proof rule for procedures in predicate transformer semantics. *Acta Informatica* 20, pp. 301-313, 1983.

Miller, G.A. *The magic number seven, plus or minus two: some limits on our capacity for processing information*, Psychological Review 63, 81-97, 1956.

Nakajima, R., Yuasa, T. *The IOTA Programming System.* Springer-Verlag, Lecture Notes in Computer Science 160, 1983.

O'Donnell, M. *Equational Logic as a Programming Language*. MIT Press 1985.

Parnas, D.L. Information distribution aspects of design methodology. *Proceedings of IFIP Congress 71*, North-Holland, pp. 339-344, 1971.

Polak, W. Compiler Specification and Verification. Lecture Notes in Computer Science No. 124, Springer Verlag, Berlin Heidelberg New York, 1981.

Popek, G.J., Horning, J.J., Lampson, B.W., Mitchell, J.G., London, R.L. Notes on the design of Euclid. Proceedings of the ACM Conference on Language Design for Reliable Software, published in ACM SIGPLAN Notices 12, 3, pp. 11-18, March 1977.

Rosselet, A. Definition and implementation of context conditions for programming languages. Technical Report CSRG-162, Computer Systems Research Institute, University of Toronto, July 1984.

Scott, D., Strachey, C. Towards a Mathematical Semantics for Computer Languages. in *Computers and Automation*, John Wiley and Sons, New York, 1972.

Soloway, E., Bonar, J., Ehlich, K. Cognitive Strategies and Looping Constructs: An Empirical Study. *Comm. ACM* vol. 26, no 11, pp. 853-60, November 1983.

Stoy, J.E. *Denotational Semantics*. MIT Press, Cambridge, Mass., 1977.

Tennent, R.D. The denotational semantics of programming languages. *Comm. ACM* vol. 19, no 8, August 1976.

Tennent, R.D. A denotational definition of the programming language Pascal. Programming Research Group, University of Oxford, 1977.

Weinberg, G.M. *The Psychology of Computer Programming*. Van Nostrand, New York, 1971.

Welsh, J., Sneeringer, W.J., Hoare, C.A.R. Ambiguities and insecurities in Pascal. *Software - Practice and Experience* 7, 6, pp. 685-696, November 1977.

Wirth, N. *On the design of programming languages*. Information Processing Programming Methodology, North-Holland, Amsterdam, 1974.

Wirth, N. *Programming Languages: What to Demand and How to Assess Them.* Institut fur Informatik, Eidgenossiche Technishe Hochschule, Zurich, March 1976.

Wulf, W., London, R., Shaw, M. An introduction to the construction and verification of Alphard programs. *IEEE Transactions on Software Engineering*, SE-2, no. 4, December 1976.

Wulf, W., Shaw, M. Global variables considered harmful. ACM SIGPLAN Notices 8, 2, pp. 28-34, February 1973.

Index

A

abbreviation, in context condition
definition 184
abbreviation (see also short form) 12
ABORT **222**, 222, 223, **224**, 280, 281, 282
abs 95
absolute value 95
abstract context-free syntax 145, 157, 160, 183, **273**
abstract data type 26
acceptability 35
access 147
  representing 167
  to field union 32
  unconstrained 24
Access (accessibility) type in ADL 147, 160, **167**
AccessOf **170**, 185, 193
access 153
$access_1$ 173
$access_{id}$ 185
$access_{io}$ 194
actual parameter 56, 72
Ada 9, 12, 13, 30, 37, 38, 124
Adam 262
addition 89, 142, 217
address 64, 74
adjacency 25
ADL 3, 114, 124, 146, **149**, 150, 183, 265
  as a functional programming language 149
  basic concepts 150
  rules 157, 158
  types **152**, 159
  types, to represent Turing objects 146, 160
Aho, A.V. 113
aids to implementor 124
airtight formal definition 37
Algol 133, 219
Algol scope rule 225
algorithm, graph 9
algorithm, numeric 9
aliasing 20, 29, 31, 35, 47, 54, 57, 74, 75, 80, 124, 125, 146, 147, 148, 211, 215, 227, 264
  context conditions for 211
  no 258
  preventing 80, 148, **211**
all **93**, 144, 244, 252, 276
allocation, dynamic (see also **new**) 30
alternative, otherwise 68, **83**
ambiguity 123, 215
ambiguous 264, 269
analysis, semantic 146
analytic definition 128
and 143
and 89, **91**, 104, 275
anti-aliasing 125
APL 20, 32
approach, axiomatic 220

approximation of real number 251
arctan 95
arctand 95
arctangent 95
argument (see actual parameter)
argument, command line 85
arithmetic, complex 78
arithmetic, pointer 19
array 91, 100, 214, 219, **253**
  assignment 66
  dynamic 35, 37, 38, 41, 57, 63, 66, 68, 70, 164, 191, 247
  subscript 199
  uninitialized 254
array 104, 136, 162, 187, 191, 206, 245, 273, 274, 276
Array 162, **163**, 180, 191, 200, 206
arrayElement 199, **200**
arrayType 65, **66**, **136**
artificial intelligence 5
ASCII 3, 101, 102, 112, 128, 129, 251
ASN 179, 221, 228, 232, 241, 245, 246
aspect, cultural psychological 18
aspect, novel 219
assert 43, 81, 82, 139, 147, 158, 192, 208, 228, 274
ASSERT 220, **222**, 225, 226, 228, 241
assert, in ADL 158
assertion 43, 44, 192, 241
  invariant 44
  legality 241
assertionBoolean$_E$ 192, 193
AssertionContext **173**, 208
assignability **69**, 147
assignability 179
assignable **70**, 253
  predicate *ASN* 246
Assignable **164**, 179, **181**, 186, 187, 192, 193
assignment statement **82**, 192, 219, 228
assignment
  array 66
  nondeterministic 221
  tag 68
  unchecked 222
associate left-to-right 143
assumptions, by context condition 214
attribute 98
attribute grammar 148
automata, finite 113
automatic detection of errors 15
automatic garbage collection 9
available implementation 285
axiom 4, 149, 150, 152, 248
  for floating point 255
AXIOM 234, **235**
axiomatic
  approach 220
  definition of operator 149
  semantics 3, 29, 38, **115**, 116, 119, 121, 125, 146, 223, 281
  type definition 145
  type definition, in ADL 152
Axiomatic Denotational Language 3, 146, **149**
axiomatically 145
axiomatization 219, 248
  of integer 217
axioms defining expressions 248

B

back slash character 59
Backus, J.W. 133
Backus-Naur Form 133
banning loop 28
banning variable 28
Barnard, D.T. ii, 14
base type 252
  of set 66
BaseOf **163**, 197, 201
BASIC 1, 8, 9, 10, 15, 24, 34
  easier than 10, 262

basis
  formal semantics of 223
  informal semantics of 221
  semantics 223
  statement 115, 218, **221**, 224, 230, 279, **280**, 281, 283
before use, declaration 34
begin (see also declaration and statement) 16, 41, 81, **83**, 110, 140, 193, 228, 274
Bekic, H. 30
Bell Northern Research ii, 263
BEVAL 256
BEXPN **255**, 256
bind 47, **64**
bind 80, 81, 110, 135, 167, 169, 188, 189, 248, 259, 273
  construct 57
  context conditions for 189
  declaration 227
binding, of name to object (see declaration, bind)
Bjorner, D. 30
blank 127
  padding 92
blank 237, 238
BLOCK **222**, **224**, 230, 281, 282
block, **begin** 41
BNF 113, 133, 265
Body 184, **208**, **276**
body, procedure 72, 138
body, subprogram 55
boldface 133, 134
boldface 60, 127
boolean 219
  conditional operator 91
  explicit constant 59
  expression 249
  negation 143
  operator **91**, **249**
  value 249
boolean 65, 136, 161, 190, 245, 274
Boolean 161, **163**, 180, 196
booleanExpn 142
booleanLiteral 196, 212, 275
Borodin, A. 263, 265
bound 231, 233, 258
bound, lower 98
bound, upper 41, 99, 247
boundary, line 59
bounded expression validity predicate 255
bounded set 220
brace **133**, 271
bracket 133
bracketed comment 59
Branquart, P. 30
break statement (see **exit**)
Brinch Hansen 7
bug, lurking 17, 19, 20, 24, 263
bugs inevitable 17
Buxton, Bill 266
by reference 64, 74, 227, 232
by value 74, 232

C

C 9, 12, 13, 17, 21, 22, 31, 263, 285
c 158
C's of formal specification, three 27, 122
calculus, predicate 217, 249, **250**
calculus, program 27
calculus, propositional 249
call 150
  by-reference 64, 74, 227, 232
  by-value 74, 232
  function 88, 89, 199, 234
  procedure 56, 72, 199, 223, **232**, 233, 247
  subprogram 211
  validity predicate for 234
CALL 232

capitalization 43
carriage return 110, 127
cartesian product (see record, tuple)
cascaded selection 43
case 103, 140, 193, 228, 274
case
  label 229
  lower 109
  selector range 32
  sensitivity 109
  upper 109
caseStatement 81, **83**, 139, **140**
cat 269
catenation 39, 60, 89, 94, 95, 142, 154, 213, 251
cc 112, 114, 158
CE (Concurrent Euclid) 4, 38
ceil 96
cfs 112, 113
challenge, intellectual 26
change Turing 109
CHAOS **222**, **224**, 281, 282
char type (see **string**)
character 251
  back slash 59
  carriage return 110
  collating sequence 101
  new line 87
  non-white-space 86
  oriented input 86
  set 111
  white space 127
check
  compile-time 241
  run-time 53
  subscript 21
  syntactic 219, 241
checking 44, 58, 222, 279
  complete 21
  full 21
  run-time 39, 263
  strong type 20
  type 20, 38, 265
CHECKING **222**, 225
chicken 262
children 10
  teaching 38
Chill 30
Chinese restaurant 264
Chomsky, N. 133
chopping floating point 108
chr 94, **96**, 101, **129**, 213
CI 118
circular import 177
CL 118
clarity 27, 28, **122**, 124, 146, 148, 215, 217, 219
  maximum 19
classroom 16
clause, **elsif** 43
clause, **where** 155
clean syntax 53
clean termination 223
close 84, 100
Close **169**, 177
Closed 172
$Close_1$ 173
CLU 9
cluster 48, 54
code optimization 34
coherence 35
collating sequence, character 92, 96, 101, 251
collection 30, 44, **63**, 99, 109, 110, 199, 253
  cyclic 63
  declaration 62
  element reference 30, 45, 88, 199, 253
  forward 207
  garbage 9, 35
  read-only 80
  self-referencing 69
collection 54, 135, 162, 169, 187, 226, 273

Collection 162, **163**, 181, 188, 189, 191, 200
collectionDeclaration 61, **63**, **135**, 139
collectionElement 199, **200**
collectionId 137
CollectionMatchesPointer **188**, 193, 200
colon 13
COM 118
command line argument 85
command, Dijkstra guarded 28, 52
comment 40, **59**, 112, 127
  bracketed 59
  end-of-line 59
  executable 44
common sense 18
commutative 243
comparison of record 34
comparison operator 91
compatibility with Pascal 29
compatibility, parameter 70, 147, **179**
compatibility, type 70, 146, 241
compatible, IBM PC 1
CompatibleConstParams 181
CompatibleParams **175**, **181**, 182, 201
CompatibleSubpgmParams 182
CompatibleVarParams 181
compilation, feedback-free 34
compilation, separate 9
compile-time 54
  check 241
  expression **93**, 148, **212**, 241
  integer expression 93
compiler 20, 33, 34, 216, 266, 285
  correctness 27, 116
  ideal 118
  one-pass 34
  portable 34
  requirement for 118
  transporting 34
CompileTime **163**, 165, **166**, 193
CompileTimeCatenation 212, **213**
CompileTimeExpn 65, 136, 137, 138, 140, **142**, 190, 191, 193, 208, **212**
CompileTimeInit 187, **213**
CompileTimeIntExpn 212, **213**
CompileTimeNamedConstant 212, **213**
CompileTimeOrdOrChr 212, **213**
CompileTimeSetConstructor 212
complementary definition 122
complete 219
  checking 21
completeness 27, **122**, 146, 215, 217
complex arithmetic 78
complex language 38
complex object 24
complexity
  controlling 24
  in formalism 28
  language 125
  managing 26
  minimizing 8
  of formal specification 28
  program 17, 24
component selector 238, 253
componentSelector **88**, **142**
compromise 7
computer 12
  personal 5
Computer Systems Research Group 261
Computer Systems Research Institute 285
Computerworld 261
concern, separation of 26
concise expressive notation 11
conciseness 12
concrete syntax (see also context-free syntax) 273
concurrency 9, 38
Concurrent Euclid 4, 17, 25, 116, 261, 264, 266, 285
condition, context 112, **114**, 114, **145**, 157, 183, 214, 217
condition, **post** 44, 50
condition, **pre** 44

condition generator, verification 116
conditional 243
  boolean operator 91
  operator, in ADL 151
conditions, rules defining context 183
conjunction 89, **91**, 217
consistency 27, **122**, 123, 146, 215, 217
  notational 13
const 61, 135, 165, 186, 226, 273
  pervasive 168
constant 41, 54, 80
  compile-time 42
  declaration 61, 186, 225
  explicit 54, 59, 89, 93, 112, 245
  explicit boolean 59
  explicit integer **59**, 129
  explicit real **59**, 129, 255
  init 173, 208
  literal 54
  manifest 54
  named 54, 93, 213
  nonmanifest 54
  nonscalar parameter 231
  run-time 42, 54
  scalar parameter 231
  signed 59
  unsigned 59
Constant 165, **166**, 168, 186, 187, 193, 197, 199, 200
constantDeclaration **61**, 61, **135**
constraint
  implementation 31, 58, **106**, **254**
  implementation message 118, 119
  language 58, **106**
  language message 118, 119
  run-time 58
  run-time language 118
  validity 58
construct
  bind 57
  error-prone 18, 53
  frequently used 103
  high frequency 11
  ill-used 17
  init 226
  invalid 225
  meaningless 116, 250
constructive 124
constructor operator, in ADL **151**, 152, 156, 163, 166, 169, 174, 176
constructor, set 49, **93**, 144, 199, 212
CONT 280, 282
context 147
context condition 112, **114**, 114, **145**, 157, 183, 214, 217
  definition, parts of 145
  definition, design goals 146
  for declaration 186
  for expression 195
  for input/output 194
  for module 208
  for program 185
  for reference 198
  for subprogram 202
  for type specification 190
  definition overview 146
  rules, index to 183
Context 158, 161, **169**
context sensitive syntax 112, 114, **145**
Context type in ADL 147, **168**
context, initial 159
context, representation of in ADL 168
context-free
  abstract syntax 145, 157, 183, **273**
  extended syntax 271
  structure 113
  syntax 111, 112, **133**, 145, 157, 207, 217
CONTINUE **221**, 223, **224**, 280
control, scope 25
controlled visibility 25
controlling complexity 24
conv 237
convenience 53
  of use 10
convenient I/O 38

conversion
  function 42
  implicit 90
  type function 96
convStrLit 240
convToken 238, 239, **240**
Cooper, D. 27
Cordy, J.R. i, 5, 35, 211, 261, 285
correct program development 224
correctness
  compiler 27, 116
  methodology 259
  program 17, 27, 28, 116, 257
  proof 38, 116, 149
cos 95
cosd 95
cosine 95
creturn 237, 238
cultural
  framework 18
  psychological aspect 18
  recognizability **12, 19**
Curley, A.F.X. ii, 5
cycle, program development 19
cyclic collection 63
$c_{predefined}$ 159, 185, 214

D

dangling
  else 16
  pointer 32, 33, **63**
  uninitialized pointer 30
data type, abstract 26
DBU (declaration before use) 34
deallocation of storage (see **free**)
DECIMAL, FIXED precision 23
Decl 158, 183, 184, **186**, **189**, **202**, 204, **209**, **273**, 273, **276**, **277**
declaration **61**, 61, 81, **147**, 186
  before use 34
  bind 227
  collection 62
  constant 61, 225
  context conditions for 147, 168, **186**
  context-free syntax 135
  representation of in ADL 165, 168
  semantics of 225
  subprogram 82
  type 65
  variable 15, 62, 225
declaration **135**, 139
declarationOrStatement **81**, **139**
declarationOrStatementInMainProgram **61**, **135**
declarationOrStatementInModule **78**, **139**, 139
DeclarationsAndStatements 76, **81**, 82, 138, **139**, 140
Declare 168, **169**, 186, 187
DeclareFormals **174**, 203, 204
$Declare_1$ 173
DecreaseAccess 169, **170**, 188, 189
$DecreaseAccess_1$ 173
decreasing 83, 84, 141, 193, 230, 275
  for 104
default 12, 13
  input stream 84, 94
defaultew 98
defaultfw 98
Defense, U.S. Department of 38
defining expressions, axioms 248
defining context conditions, rules 183
definition
  ADL type 146
  airtight formal 37
  complementary 122
  executable 149
  formal 2, 3, 26, 217
  informal 2, 217
  of expressions, formal 219
  of Turing, formal 111

denotational 145, 157
  rule 145
  rule, for context conditions 157
  Scott-Strachey semantics 115
  semantics 149, 219, 263
Department of Defense, U.S. 38
deproceduring (see function call)
dereferencing (see collection element reference)
descent, recursive 113
descriptor, run-time 35
design goal 1, **7**
design, programming language **7**, 216, 219
designers, use of formal definition 215
designing for formalization 30
detailed scrutiny 125
detection of errors 15
deterministic 50
  function 234
development, correct program 224
development cycle, program 19
diagnostic treatment of error 14
difference 142, 252
  set 89
Digital VAX 1, 5, 108
Dijkstra, E.W. 4, 27, 52, 223, 241, 257, 258, 259
Dijkstra guarded command 28
dimension 99
direct importing 80
directly implementable 31
disaster 18, 53
discard information 24
discriminant (see **tag, union**)
discriminated union (see **union**)
DISJ 211, 219, 221, 227, 232, 241
disjoint 211, 221
displacement of field 35
DIST 221, 241, 246, **248**
distinct 221
DistinctIdents **190**, 191, 192, 202, 205
distinctness predicate 248
distribution, uniform 99
div 89, 90, 160, 196, 213, 244, 275
divide-and-conquer 24, 26
division 89, 90, 142, 143
  by zero 91, 116, 218, 220, 225
do statement (see **loop**)
dollar 42
domain 154
domain 155
domain predicate 241
Donahue, J.E. 122
dot operator 67, 68, 69, 78, 82, 88, 198
dot-dot 237
duck, Peking 266
dummySy 164, **167**, 207
dummyTy **164**, 205
dynamic allocation (see also **new**, collection) 30, 44
dynamic array 35, 37, 38, 41, 57, 63, 66, 68, 70, 164, 191, 247
dynamic string 65, 70, 74
dynamic type 164

E

E 183, **195, 275**
early warning 19
ease of learning **10**, 124
easier than BASIC 10, 262
easily overlooked error 18
EBCDIC 3, 101, 102, 112, 128, 129, 251
effect 31
  no remote 21
  side 20, 29, 41, 51, 54, 56, 57, 74, 75, 85, 124, 146, 149, 202, 214, 215, 258, 264
efficiency 28, **31**, 53, 124, 146
  estimate 32
  run-time 146
efficient implementation 215

efficient program 263
egg 262
elegance, rule of 8
ElementOf **163**, 200
elision, in ADL 149, **157**
Elliot, D. 241
else 82, 103, 140, 228, 274
  dangling 16
ELSE 222
elsif 43, 82, 103, 140, 151, 193, 228, 274
embedded computers 38
empty 153, 154
  set 252
  subrange 241
empty 158
EmptyContext **169**, 209
EmptySet 150, 151, 152, 156
end 38, 138, 139, 140
end if 16, 40
end of
  file 86
  line 60
  line comment 59
  string 59
engineering 12
  software 9
enjoyment 35
entire program 159
enum 46, **66**, 136, 161, 191, 274
Enum 146, 161, **163**, 180, 191, 198
enumerated 70, 214
  type 45, 88, 249, **251**
  value 93
enumeratedType 65, **66**, **136**, 137
enumeration, in ADL 153
EnumIds **163**, 198
environment 147
  programming 34, 285
eof 86, 87, **94**, 214, 238, 239
eos **59**, 86, 96, 107
equal 18, 22, 89, 92, 143, 252
  not 143
equality 93
equational axioms, defining data type 150
equivalence
  name 41
  predicate *EQV*, type 247
  structural 41
  type **69**, 147, 148, **179**, 247
equivalent 175, 221
  prefix 247
  type 41, 181
EquivFormals **175**, **182**
EquivType **163**, 179, **180**, 182, 185, 187, 190, 191, 193, 194, 196, 197, 200
EQV 179, 221, 232, 241, **246**, **247**
erealstr **97**, 238
error
  automatic detection of 15, 20
  diagnostic treatment of 14
  early warning of 19
  easily overlooked 18
  handling of 13, 14, 16
  high frequency 17
  human 17
  isolation of 19, 21
  low frequency 18
  lurking bug 17, 19
  minimizing severity of 17
  misspelling 15
  poor handling of 22, 24
  programming 17
  relative round off 108
  run-time 19
  semantic message 119
  severity of 17
  syntax 14, 19
  syntax message 118
  treatment of 14
error-prone construct 18, 53
escape 59
estimate efficiency 32
Euclid 1, 5, 7, 9, 15, 17, 30, 116, 241, 262, 264

Euclid, Concurrent 4, 17, 25, 38, 116, 261, 264, 266, 285
Euclid, New 5, 264
evaluate 151
evaluation, order of 90
evaluation, using axioms in ADL 150
excellence, standard of 26
exception handling 9, 32
exception handler, PL/I's 28
executable comment 44
executable definition 149
execution
  fail-stop 21
  faithful 1, **21**, 26, 31, 32, 33, 38, 44, 118, 222
  mode of 32
  unchecked 120
exhaustible resources 3
exhaustion, resource 3, 31, 52, 63, 123, 217, 220, **254**, 258
exhaustion, resource message 118, 119
existential quantification 250
exit 83
  loop 83
exit 81, 103, 114, 139, 193, 230, 259, 274
EXIT **222**, **224**, 230, 280, 281, 282
exit when 103
exits/returns 227
exp 96
expectation 14
experience, teaching 16
expert 12
explicit constant 54, 59, 89, 93, 112, 245
  boolean 59
  integer **59**, 129
  real **59**, 129, 255
explicitConstant 89, **142**
explicitStringConstant 142, 144
explicitUnsignedIntegerConstant 142, 144
explicitUnsignedRealConstant 142, 144
expn **60**, **88**, 135, 138, **142**
EXPN 117, 218, 221, 228, 234, **235**, 241, 242, 243, **244**, 253, 254, **255**, 256
ExpnOrStar 183, **195**, **275**, 275
exponent 129
exponent part 59
exponent, infinite range 106
exponentiation 9, 37, 38, 89, 90, 109, 143
exponentWidth 85, 97, **141**, 141
export 56, 139, 162, 166, 209, 236, 277
Export 184
export, context conditions for 210
export list 25, 56
exported procedure 82
Exports **210**, 210, **277**
ExportsOf **166**, 198
exposed, problem 125
expression 88, 148, 184
  axioms defining 248
  boolean 249
  bounded validity predicate 255
  compile-time **93**, 148, **212**, 241
  context condition for 148, **195**
  context-free syntax 142
  difference from reference 184
  formal definition of 219
  initializing 62, 226
  invariant 79
  post 79
  pre 79
  regular 113
  run-time 94
  validity predicate EXPN 243
expressive notation 11
expressive power 53
extended context-free syntax 271
extension, language 124
external 3, 108
external subprogram 110
extraneous verbiage 11

F

factorial 107, 236
FAIL **222**, 225, 234, 235
fail-stop execution 21
fail-stop implementation 21
failure **243**, 250
  run-time 220
faithful execution 1, **21**, 26, 31, 32, 33, 38, 44, 118, 222
faithful implementation 58, 117
false **59**, 88, 142, **249**
FcnOrProc 205, **277**
features of Turing 37
feedback, from user 14
feedback-free compilation 34
field 88
  displacement of 35
  ghost 35
  selection 153, 154, 198
  selector 220, 242
  tag 229, 242
  union, access to 32
  width 10, 12
Fields 183, **274**
FieldsOf 163
figure, significant part 59
file (see also input, output, **get**, **put**, *open*) 40, 100
  end of 86
  sequential 84
findLineEnd 238, **240**
findTokenEnd 238, 239, **240**
finite automata 113
finite map, in ADL 154
finite memory 31
finite resource 217, 254
Fischer, C.N. 32, 34
FIXED DECIMAL precision 23
flexible array (see dynamic array)
floating point 58, 107, 123, 220, 254, 255, 257
  axiom for 255
  chopping of 108
floor 96
fluent reader 18
fmt format 238
for 42, **84**, 103, 109, 141, 193, 230, 275
  decreasing 104
form 111
  short 12, 39, 60, **103**, 110
  shortened by usage 11
formal 53, **147**
  definition 2, 3, 26, 217
  definition, airtight 37
  definition, goals for 146
  definition of expression 219
  definition of Turing 111
  intractability 30
  operational semantics 125, 223, 279
  parameter 56, 147, 174, 234, 247
  semantic definition 1
  semantics 28, 44, **217**, 218, 279
  semantics of basis 223
  specification, complexity of 28
  specification, three C's of 27
  specification technique 219
  var parameter 69, 72
Formal 155, 161, **174**
formalism, mathematical 27
formalization 125
  designing for 30
  language 125
Formals type in ADL 147, **174**
FormalsOf **166**, 201
format, *fmt* 238
format, star 195
formfeed 127
formfeed 237, 238
formula, well-formed 248
ForRange **84**, **141**, 183, 193, **194**, **275**
forStatement 81, **83**, 140, **141**
Fortran 8, 15, 22, 31
forward 147
  collection 207

declaration 34
import 202, 204
procedure 76, 168
subprogram 76, 125, 202
forward 34, 55, 61, 63, 69, 72, 74, 109, 110, 135, 137, 138, 162, 169, 176, 188, 203, 207, 226, 246, 273, 276, 277
Forward 162, **163**, 169, 180, 200, **277**
ForwardFcnOrProc 276
forwardImportList **74**, 137, **138**
fractionWidth 85, 97, **141**, 141
framework, cultural 18
frealstr **97**, 98, 109, 238
free 44, 63, 80, 81, 140, 193, 229, 252, 274
free variable 150
free-format 39
frequency of errors 17, 18
frequently used construct 11, 103
frills syntax, no **11, 19**
full checking 21
function 41, 56, 72, 85, 100, 234
call 88, 89, 199, 234
conversion 42
definition, in ADL 155
deterministic 234
generic 9
id 138
mathematical 95
next state 115
non-deterministic 235
parametric 48
predefined 94
recursive 236
sem 115, 219
string 94
type conversion 96
function 72, 104, 165, 203, 204, 234, 277
Function 165, **166**, 201, 203, 205
functional notation 155
functional programming language 149
functionality 19
FwdCollectionResolved **188**, 193, 200, 207
fwdSubpgm **167**, 186, 203, 204, 207

G

Gannon, J.D. 7, 17, 20
gap, minimize 28
garbage 23
garbage collection 9, 35
GCD 104
general purpose language 8
general taxation 32
generality **8**, 35, 124
generalized input/output 9
generation, random number 257
generative definition 128
generator, pseudo-random number 50
generator, verification condition 116
generic function (polymorphism) 9
generic package 38
geometry, turtle 11
get 75, **84**, 87, 94, 104, 122, 183, 194, 214, 229, **239**, 238, 275
getexp 255, 256
GetItem **86, 141**, 183, 194, **195, 275**
$GetItem_i$ 275
getStatement 81, **86**, 140, **141**
ghost field 35
GLM 2
global goal 35
global variable 24, 25
goal, design 7
goal, global 35
goals, language 263
Godel 250
Good Lord's Machine 2
Gordian knot 14

GOTO (see also **exit, return**) 19, 234
  structured 222
graceful treatment of errors 14
Graham, T.C.N. ii
grammar (see also syntax)
  attribute 148
  context-free 113
graph algorithm 9
gratuitous non-determinism 28
greater than 92, 143
Gries, D. 27, 223, 259
guarded command 28, 52
Guttag, J.V. 116

H

Habermann, A.N. 38
hacker 263
handler, PL/I's exception 28
handling of errors 13, 14
handling of exceptions 9, 32
handling, poor error 22, 24
Hansen, Brinch 7
hardware, underlying 32
header, program 38, 39
heap (see also collection) 52
Hehner, B.A. ii
Hehner, E.C.R. ii, 4, 27, 116, 223, 241, 249, 250, 257
HI 11, 31
hiding, information **25**, 48, 215, 263
high frequency error 17
high frequency construct 11, 103
history of Turing 4
Hoare, C.A.R. ii, 7, 38
Hodges, A. 5
Holt Software Associates 285
Holt, R.C. i, 2, 5, 8, 9, 10, 34, 37, 109, 113, 150, 261
Horspool, R.N. ii
Hull, T.E. ii, 5
human error 17
Hume, J.N.P. ii, 5, 10

I

I 118
I-before-E 15
I/O, convenient 38
IBM 262
  Laboratory 266
  mainframe 285
  PC 1, 34, 267, 285
  system 370 1, 5, 34, 108
Ichbiah, J. 7
id **60**, 144
  function 138
ideal compiler 118
Ideal Turing 2, 4, **106**, 217, 250
Ident 277
identifier 54, 59, 112
  predefined 105
  result 75
  uniqueness of 214
identifier 144
identity 89, 143
if 82, 103, 140, 192, 228, 274
IF **221, 224**, 228, 280, 283
if operator, in ADL 151
ifStatement 81, 82, 139, **140**
ill-used construct 17
imperative language 31
implementability 35
implementable, directly 31
implementation **34**, 124, 149, 215, 217, 255
  available 285
  constraint 31, 58, **106, 254**

constraint message 118, 119
efficient 215
fail-stop 21
faithful 58, 117
interpretive 146
non-checking 58, 68
requirement for 118
simplification of 146
implementor 146
aids to 124
use of formal definition 215
implication 89, **91**, 110, 143
implicit conversion 90
import
circular 177
direct 80
forward 202, 204
indirect 80
read-only set 178
representation of in ADL 175
var 75
import 35, 74, 75, 110, 138, 165, 166, 169, 176, 209, 236, 277
Import 184
import list 25, 55, 75, 76, 122, 147, 214
context conditions for 206
ImportContext 170, **177**, 203, 204
ImportItem 184, 206, **207**
importList **74**, 137, **138**, 139
Imports **206, 276**
ImportSet **147**, 155, 161, 175, **176**, 206
ImportsOf 166
in 89, **93**, 143, 155, 156, 244, 252, 276
In 150, 151, 152, 156
inaccessible 64, 81, 170, 173
subprogram 207
Inaccessible 167
inaccessible 147, 169, 176, 178, 179, 186, 188, 189, 203, 204, 207, 208
include **102**, 108
inclusion, source 102
inclusive or 89, **91**, 143
incomplete 122
incompleteness 214
inconsistency 29, 31, 38
index 40, **94**
index type **65**, 66, 84, 164
IndexOf **163**, 200
indexType 66, 136, **137**
indirect importing 80
inevitable, bugs 17
inexhaustible resource 31
infinite
exponent range 106
loop 258
precision 106
range of value 31
infixOp 272
infixOperator 89, 142
informal 53
definition 2, 217
semantics of basis 221
information hiding **25**, 48, 215, 263
information, discard 24
information, loss 24
init 62, 76, 123, 135, 138, 167, 187, 213, 226, 233, 276, 277
constant 173, 208
value list, for array, record, union 214
initial context 159
initial value 40
initialization 225
nonscalar 123
variable 20, 222
initialized 23, 46, 100
INITIALIZED 117, 243, **245**
initialized, partially 254, 279
initializing expression 62, 226
initializingValue **62**, **135**
initPart 277
InitVal 273, **277**
input 84
character-oriented 86
context condition for 148, 194
context-free syntax for 139

default stream 84, 94
line oriented 86, 238
token oriented 86, 238
input/output 139, **148**, 194, 219, 237, 262
context condition for 194
generalized 9
insecurity 38
Insert 150, 151, 152, 156
int 65, 70, 106, 136, 161, 190, 245, 274
Int 161, **163**, 180, 190, 195
integer 219, 249, 250
axiomatization of 217
compile-time expression 93
explicit constant **59**, 129
pseudo random 99
integer **129**, 129, 144
integerLiteral 195, 212, 275
integrate 48
intellectual challenge 26
intelligence, artificial 5
intentions 15
intractability, formal 30
interaction 24
unforeseen 26
interactive interpreter 10
interactive programming 54
International Standards Organization 4, 29
interpretation, mechanical 259
interpreter 10, 31, 33, 34, 146, 285
requirement for 121
intersection 89, 142, 154, 252
intreal 70, 90, **96**
introductory programming 16
intstr 42, **96**, 109, 214, 238
intuition 7
invalid construct 225
invariant 173, 192, 208
loop 231
invariant 43, 82, 83, 84, 109, 139, 140, 141, 193, 208, 209, 231, 236, 274, 275, 277
assertion 44
expression 79
IO module 194, **214**
iron 40
isArraySubscript 199, **200**
isCollectionSubscript 199, **200**
isCompileTime 166
isDynamicArray **164**, 186, 187, 192
isDynamicType **164**, 181
isFunctionCall 199, **201**, 211
isIndex **164**, 191, 193
$isInLoop_1$ 173
isLiteral 212
isNumeric **164**, 185, 196, 197
ISO 4, 29
isolation, error 19, 21
isolation, textual 25
$isOpaqueRefParam_i$ 212
isProcedureCall 199, **201**, 211
isProduction **159**, 277
$isRefParameter_i$ 212
isScalar **164**, 186
isSetConstructor 199, **201**
isSubstring 199, **200**
isWhiteSpace **238**, 240
italic 134

J

Jarvis 264
Johnson, S.C. 134

K

Kernighan, B.W. 4, 9, 38
keyword 11, **105**, **112**, 127, 129
kilogram weight 15

Kingston 5
Kingston, Queen's University 285
Kleene-star operator 128
knowledge, reading 12

L

label 153, 241, 248
  value 68
  case 229
label 46, 67, **83**, 103, 137, 140, 191, 193, 228, 274
LALR(1) production rule 134
Lampson, B.W. 5, 241
language
  complex 38
  complexity 125
  constraint 58, **106**
  constraint message 118, 119
  design **7**, 216, 219
  error prone construct 18
  extension 124
  formalization 125
  functional 149
  general purpose 8
  goals 263
  imperative 31
  PRO 249
  run-time constraint 118
  semantics 219
  specification 27
  strongly typed 88
  structured 10
  subset 10
  teaching 8
law of substitution 51
learning, ease of **10**, 124
Lee, E.S. ii
left-hand value 184, 242
left-to-right, associate 143
legality assertion 241
legality, static **145**, 157, 183
length 154
  maximum 35, 39, 65, 70, 99
  string, varying 37, 38
length 92, **94**
less than 143
LessEq 168
levels of mastery 10
lex 112, 113, 131
lexemes 112
lexical sequences 269
lexical structure **112**, 112, **127**, 265
lexical syntax 145, 217
lexicalUnit 129
lifetime, of variable (see scope)
limit 108
  of predicates 257
limited precision 123
limited, resource Turing 4
line
  argument, command 85
  boundary 59
  character, new 87
  end of 60
  header 39
  oriented input 86, 238
linked list 45
LISP 20, 32, 149
list, **export** 25, 56
list, **import** 25, 55, 75, 76, 122, 147, 214
list, linked 45
literal constant 54
ln 96
LocalContext **170**, 170, 173, 193, 208, 209
$LocalContext_1$ 173
locality, principle of 25
localization 21
LocallyDeclared **171**, 186, 203, 210
logic of programming 116
Logo 8, 11
loop **83**, **230**, 258

banning 28
exit 83
for 42
infinite 258
invariant 231
termination 222
with-exit 28
loop 103, 140, 193, 230, 274
loopNesting **170**, 193
loopStatement 81, 82, 139, **140**
loss, no information 24
low frequency error 18
lower bound 98
lower case 109
lower **98**, 109, 214
LR(1) 109
LR(k) 34, 113
lurking bug 17, 19, 20, 24, 263

M

Machine, Good Lord's 2
machine, Turing 250
mainframe, micros to 34
mainframe, IBM 285
maintenance, program 17, 19, 24
Malton, A.J. ii
manage complexity 26
manifest 241
constant 54
manipulation, string 31, 262
manipulation, text 9
manual, reference 215
map 154, 174, 176
map type, in ADL 147, 154
mastery, levels of 10
matching operator 155, 156
matching production 159
mathematical
formalism 27
function 95
nature 217
notation 53
oracle 251
precision 26
set 128
subprogram 31
mathematics 12
matrix multiplication 262
Matthews, P.A. i, 5, 116, 264, 265
Matthews Plan 26, 265
max **95**, 155
maxexp **107**, 108, 255, 256
maximal scan 106, 112, 128, **131**, 269
maximize utility 8
maximum 95
clarity 19
string length 35, 39, 65, 70, 99
maxint **107**, 108, 123, 255
maxscan 131
MAXSPACE 256
maxstr **107**, 108, 255, 256
meaning 217
of Turing program 217
predicate 241
meaningless construct 116, 250
mechanical interpretation 259
member 89
membership 143, 154, 252
memory, finite 31
Mendell, M.P. ii, 5, 263
MergeImports 177
message
implementation constraint 118, 119
language constraint 118, 119
resource exhaustion 118, 119
semantic error 119
syntax error 118
methodology, correctness 259
micros to main frame 34
Miller, G.A. 24

min 95
minexp **107**, 108, 255, 256
minimal, recommended range 255
minimize complexity 8
minimize gap 28
minimizing frequency of errors 17
minimum 95
minint **107**, 108, 255, 256
mismatched parentheses 14
misplaced semicolon 14
misspelling error 15
mod 89, **90**, 91, 143, 196, 213, 244, 275
mode 100
  of execution 32
ModeOf **171**, 185
$mode_1$ 173
$mode_{id}$ 185
Mode type in ADL 147, 160, **167**
modification 109
Modula 9, 25, 37, 38
modular type 148
modularity 219
module 9, 24, 25, 37, 48, 54, 55, 56, **78**, 82, 109, 116, 137, **148**, 152, 184, 236, 263
  context condition for 148, 208
  context-free syntax 137
  IO 194
module 139, 166, 168, 209, 236, 277
Module **166**, 166, 168, 198, 207
ModuleContext **209**, 209, 210
moduleDeclaration 61, **78**, 135, **139**
moduleId **137**, 137
modulo 90
Molle, M. ii
more powerful than Pascal 9, 262
multiplication 89, 142
  matrix 262
mutually recursive 76
mx 234

N

name equivalence 41
name, parameter 202
named constant 54, 93, 213
named type 69
namedType 65, **69**, 84, 136, **137**, 137, 141
nameless tag 33
NameOf 163
Naur, P. 133
negation 89, 143
NestedLoop 173
net, safety 32
Neuman, Von 264
new 44, 52, 63, 68, 80, 81, 140, 193, 222, 229, 252, 274
New Euclid 5, 264
new line character 87
newline 127, 237, 238, 239, 240
Newton, D. ii
next state function 115
next state semantics 279, 281
nil 99, 229, 253, 254
nil pointer 52
no aliasing 258
no frills syntax **11**, **19**, 37
no information loss 24
no parameter 72
no remote effect 21
no surprise rule 18, 20, 22, 23, 24, 263
no unpleasant surprise 18
NoAliasingDueToIncreasedAccess 201, **211**
NoAliasingDueToParametricSubpgms 201, **211**
NoAliasingDueToRefImportOverlap 201, **211**
NoAliasingDueToVarImportOverlap 201, **211**
non-white space character 86
non-checking implementation 58, 68

non-constructor operator, in ADL **151**, 152
non-determinism, gratuitous 28
non-deterministic function 235
non-overlapping 64, 247
non-pervasive 147
non-recursive procedure 231
non-terminal 133
  expansion rule, in ADL 157
non-var parameter 41, 69
nonConstructor 163, 166, 170
nonConstructor 152, 156, 174, 177
nondeterminism 49
  unbounded 257
nondeterministic 255
  assignment 221
  statement 222
nondiscriminated variant record 33
nonmanifest constant 54
nonPERVASIVE **167**, 187, 190, 193, 203
nonscalar 75, 101, 244
  constant parameter 231
  initialization 123
  type 65
nonterminals 60
normalized 107
Norvell, T. ii
not 89, **91**, 104, 143, 196, 275
not equal 143
not in 93
not= 89
notation 128, 220
  concise expressive 11
  functional 155
  syntactic **60**, 221
  traditional **12**, 23, 24
notational consistency 13
novel aspect 219
null 63, 221
nullary operator 153
nullId 205
number
  approximation of real 251
  generator, pseudo-random 50
  generation, random 257
  real 249, **250**
  real, pseudo random 99
  stream 84, 100, 237
numdigits **107**, 108
numeric algorithm 9
numeric operator 90
Numeric Turing 5
numeric type 164
NumericType **164**, 185, 196

O

object, complex 24
obvious efficient implementation 32
of 136, 137
omission 125
one page rule 24
one-pass compiler 34
opaque 69, **71**, 78, 139, 162, 166, 210, 277
Opaque 162, **163**, 180, 210, **277**
opaque type 26, 84, 125, 214
open 40, 84, **100**
OPENGET **237**, 239
OPENPUT 237
operand 150
operation 150
  matching 156
operational 2, 37, 220
  semantics **115**
  semantics, formal 125, 223, 279
operator 105
  boolean **91, 249**
  comparison 91
  conditional boolean 91
  constructor 151
  dot 67, 68, 69, 78, 82, 88
  if 151

matching 155
non-constructor 151
nullary 153
numeric 90
precedence of 133
set 93
string 92
OperatorOf 155, 156, 163, 167
optimization, code 34
option 12, 13
optionalItem 271
or 89, 275
or, inclusive 89, **91**, 143
oracle, mathematical 251
ord 66, 94, **96**, 101, 213
order of evaluation 90
order of precedence 89
ordering 251, 252
of strings 92
otherwise alternative 68, **83**
output 84
context conditions for 148, 194
context-free syntax 139
overflow 32, 33, 52, 91, 217, 255, 256
stack 32
overlap 247
OVERLAP 247
overlapping 80
overloaded 154
overlooked, easily error 18
overrideName 108

P

package 48, 78
generic 38
padding, blank 92
page rule, one 24
paradox, Russell's 252
parameter 72, 150, 232
actual 56, 72
compatibility 70, 147
compatibility, context conditions 179
context conditions for 205
formal 56, 147, 174, 234, 247
formal, **var** 69, 72, 241
name 202
non-var 41, 69
none 72
nonscalar constant 231
passing 108
reference **73**, 80
scalar constant 231
subprograms as 48
value 73
variable 231
ParameterDecl 183, **205**, **276**
parameterDeclaration **73**, **138**, 138
parameterized type 9
ParameterList 183, 203, **205**, **276**
ParameterType **74**, **138**, 184, 205, **206**, **276**
parametric function 48
parametric procedure 75
parametric subprogram **73**, 80, 201, 211
parentheses 11
mismatched 14
redundant 15
Parnas, D.L. 25, 48
parse tree 157
parser 264
part, exponent 59
part, significant figure 59
partial result 258
partial semantics 225
partially initialized 254, 279
Pascal 1, 4, 9, 11, 12, 15, 16, 17, 21, 22, 23, 24, 25, 29, 30, 31, 37, 219, 261
compatibility with 29
inconsistency 38
insecurity 38
more powerful than 9, 262

shortcomings of 28
super 37
passing, parameter 108
pay for what you use 32
PC 5
IBM 1, 34, 267, 285
Peano 250
Peking duck 266
Perelgut, S.G. ii, 5, 263
performance transparency 32
performance, program 19
personal computer 5
pervasive 75, 109, 147, 167
pervasive 61, 65, 104, 136, 167, 190, 273
PERVASIVE **167**, 190
Pervasive 167, 183, 186, 187, **190**, **273**
phrase structure 111, 157, **133**
PICK **221**, 222, **224**, 229, 280, 283
PL/C 4, 261
PL/I 4, 8, 9, 11, 12, 14, 16, 17, 22, 23, 30, 38, 124, 261
PL/I's exception handler 28
Plan, Matthews 26
Plus, Turing 5, 9, 38, 285
point, floating 58, 107, 123, 220, 254, 255, 257
pointer 30, 44, **68**, 91, 253
arithmetic 19
dangling 32, 33, **63**
nil 52
set 220, 221, 229, 253
to 137
uninitialized, dangling 30
pointer **68**, 162, 191, 229, 274
Pointer 162, **163**, 180, 188, 191
pointerType 65, **68**, 136, **137**
Polak, W. 27
poor error handling 22, 24
Popek, G.J. 7
portable compiler 34
Pos 277
post 43, 76, 138, 139, 173, 208, 209, 233, 236, 276, 277
condition 44, 50
expression 79
postcondition 119
triple 223
postulation 220
power, expressive 53
powerful than Pascal, more 9, 262
Pratt, T.W. ii
pre 43, 76, 138, 139, 155, 173, 209, 233, 276, 277
pre condition 44
pre expression 79
precedence 90, 133, **143**, 271
precedence, order of 89
precision 5, 217
FIXED DECIMAL 23
infinite 106
limited 123
mathematical 26
precondition 44, 119, 155
in ADL 155
triple 223
weakest **116**, 219, 223, 281
pred 66, **94**, 230
predefined
context 185
function 94
identifier 105
procedure 99
subprogram 122, 214, 217
predicate 223
assignable *ASN* 246
bounded expression validity 255
calculus 217, 249, **250**
call validity 234
distinctness 248
domain 241
limits of 257
meaning 241
transformer 3
triple 223

type equivalence *EQV* 247
valid expression *EXPN* 243
valid reference *REF* 242
valid type *TYP* 245
validity **117**, 119, 179, 218, 220, **241**, 250
prefix 131
equivalent 247
prefix 269
prefixOperator **89**, 89, 142, **143**
preventing aliasing 80, **211**
principle 7
of locality 25
print statement (see **put**)
PRO language 249
problem exposed 125
procedural language 31
procedure 56, 72
body 72, 138
call 56, 72, 199, 223, **232**, 233, 247
exported 82
forward 76, 168
non-recursive 231
parametric 75
predefined 99
recursive 232
procedure 104, 165, 166, 168, **231**, 277
Procedure 165, **166**, 168, 198, 201, 203, 207
ProcedureCall 81, **82**, 139, **140**, **166**, 166, 192, 198, 199
production 21, 157, 183
rule 133
denotation of in context conditions 183
matching in ADL 159
proficient reasoning 28
program **61**, **147**
calculus 27
complexity 17, 24
context conditions for 147, **185**, 185
context-free syntax 135
correct development 224
correctness 27, 257
development cycle 19
efficient 263
entire 159
header 38
in a functional language 149
maintenance 17, 19, 24
meaning of 217
performance 19
reliability 16
reliable 263
specification 27
understandability 17
verification 263
program 135
Program 159, 183, **185**, **273**
Program *S* 158
programmer 146
use of formal definition 215
programming
environment 34, 285
errors 17
in a functional language 149
interactive 54
introductory 16
language design 219
logic of 116
system 262
systems 38
progression, state by state 279
PROLOG 32
proof of correctness 38, 116
proof of equality using axioms in ADL 150
proof rule 116, 263, 265
propositional calculus 249
prove 151
ps 221, 226, 230, 253
pseudo random integer 99
pseudo random real number 50, 99
psychological aspect 18
psychological study 18, 24
purpose, general language 8

purpose, similar 13
put 75, **84**, 85, 94, 104, 122, 141, 183, 194, 214, **237**, 275
PutItem 84, **85**, 85, 183, **194**, **275**
PutItem$_i$ 275
putStatement 81, **84**, 140, **141**

Q

quantification 149
existential 250
universal 250
Queen's University 5, 285
quote 237, 240

R

radix **107**, 108, 255
rand 50, **99**
randint 50, **99**
randnat 257
randnext 50, 99
random number generation 257
random integer, pseudo 99
random real number, pseudo 99
randomize 99
randseed 50, 100
range 154
case selector 32
infinite exponent 106
infinite value 31
recommended minimal 255
subscript 32
RD 119
read statement (see **get**)
read-only 64, 79, 80, 147
collection 80
import set 178
variable 55
readability 19
reader, fluent 18
reading knowledge 12
readOnly **167**, 176, 186, 187, 188, 189, 193, 203
readOnlyOrNoImportOfId$_i$ 212
real 219
approximation of 251
explicit constant **59**, 129, 255
number 249, **250**
number, pseudo random 99
type 255
real 58, 65, 106, 136, 161, 190, 245, 274
real 129
Real 129, 144, 161, **163**, 180, 190, 196
realLiteral 196, 212, 275
realstr **98**, 109, 238
reasoning, proficient 28
recognizability, cultural **12**, **19**
recognizing token 106
recommended minimal range 255
record **67**, 70, 91, 100, 146, 154, 198, 214, 219, 242, **253**
comparison of 34
nondiscriminated variant 33
variant 19, 30, 32, 33, 54, **67**
record **67**, 137, 162, 165, 191, 245, 274
Record 162, **163**, 180, 191, 199
recordType 65, **67**, 136, **137**
recursion 258
recursive
descent parser 113
function 236
mutually 76
procedure 232
subprogram 177, 258
redeclaration 55, 61
redundancy 20
redundant parentheses 15
Ref 183, 191, 192, 195, **198**, 274, 275, **276**
REF 221, 227, 229, 230, 241, **242**, 253

reference **88**, 89, **148**
call by 64, 74, 232, 227
context condition for 148, **198**, 198
context-free syntax 142
difference from expression 184
manual 215
parameter **73**, 80
valid predicate REF 242
reference 184
reference 142
referent, uniform 45
registration, vehicle 46
regular expression 113
relative round off error 108
reliability **17**, 24, 53, 124
reliable program 263
remainder 89, 90, 143
remote symptom 19
remote, no effect 21
rename 57
renaming 47
repeat **95**, 238
repeat statement (see **loop**)
repeatability 49
repeatable 107, 235, 255, 257
repeatedItem 272
repetition of statements (see **loop**)
Report, Turing 2, **53**, 121, 145, 214, 217, 261, 265
representation of in ADL
access 167
context 168
formal 174
import set 175
mode 167
program 160
symbol 165
type 161
requirement for
compiler 118
implementation 118
interpreter 121
run-time 119
Resolve **172**, 204
ResolveFwdImports **178**, 201, 204
resource
exhaustion 3, 31, 52, 63, 123, 217, 220, **254**, 258
exhaustion message 118, 119
finite 217, 254
inexhaustible 31
limited Turing 4
restaurant, Chinese 264
Reston 263
result
follows from specification 26
identifier 75
in ADL 158
partial 258
type 75, 172
result 42, 72, 81, 84, 103, 139, 158, 192, 234, 259, 274
ResultId **166**, 208
ResultSpec 183, 203, **205**, 205, **276**
ResultType **166**, 182, 192, 208
return 42, 72, 81, 82, 84, 103, 139, 192, 231, 232, 259, 274
RETURN **222**, **224**, 234, 280, 281, 282
return, carriage 110, 127
RHS 158
RI 119
right-hand side 157
right-hand value 184
RJ 120
RL 119
RN 120
root 62
square 95
type **70**, 83, 86, 95
Root 163
RootType **164**, 197, 200, 201
Rosselet, J.A. i, 3, 114, 116, 146, 149, 215, 265
round **96**, 109
round off, relative error 108
rounded 97

Rowley, P.L. ii
rreb **108**, 108, 255
rule **7**, 147, 183
  ADL 157
  Algol scope 225
  context conditions 183
  directly implementable 31
  error isolation 21
  for non-terminal expansion in ADL 157
  no surprise 18, 20, 22, 23, 24, 263
  of elegance 8
  of substitution 29
  of thumb 7
  one page 24
  production 133
  proof 116, 263, 265
  scope 25
RUN 118
run-time
  checking 39, 53, 263
  constant 54
  constraint 58
  descriptor 35
  expression 94
  failure 220
  language constraint 118
  requirement for 119
  stack 258
  support 31
  value 62
Russell's paradox 252

S

S 158, 183, 185, **186**, **226**, **227**, **228**, **230**, **273**, 273
safe, type 68
safety net 32
sat **119**, 120
scalar 73, 100, 164
  constant parameter 231
  type 65
scan, maximal 112, 128, **131**, 269
scanner 113, 128, 264
scanning, maximal 106
scope 55, 61, 84, 147, 225, 258
  Algol rule 225
  control 25
  rule 25
Scott, D. 115
Scott-Strachey denotational semantics 115
scrutiny, detailed 125
security 54
select statement (see case)
selection, cascaded 43
selection, field 153, 154, 198
Selector 183, **198**, **199**, **276**
selector
  case range 32
  component 238, 253
  field 220, 242
  sequence 220
Selectors 276
self-referencing collection 69
sem function **115**, 219, **226**
semantic analysis 146
semantic error message 119
semantics 111, **115**, 217, 248
  axiomatic 3, 29, 38, **115**, 116, 119, 121, 125, 223, 281
  basis 223
  denotational 115, 219, 263
  formal 28, 44, **217**, 218, 279
  formal operational 125, 223, 281
  language 219
  next state 281
  of declarations 225
  of statements 225
  of informal basis 221
  operational 3, **115**

partial 225
Scott-Strachey denotational 115
shortcomings of 257
static 145
total 225
transformational 223
semantics, next state 279
semicolon 11, 12, 16, 18, 38, 39, 109, 135, 230
misplaced 14
sense, common 18
sensitive, context syntax 112, 114, **145**
sensitivity, case 109
separate compilation 9
separate, spaces words 18
separation of concern 26
separator **59, 127, 129**
seq 154
sequence 152, **154**
character collating 101
collating 92, 96, 251
in ADL 154
selector 220
token 127
lexical 269
sequential file 84
set 48, 100, 109, 152, **153**, 249
base type of 66
bounded 220
character 111
constructor **49, 93**, 144, 199, 212
data type, axiomatic specification of in ADL 150
difference 89
empty 252
in ADL 153
operator 93
pointer 220, 221, 229, 253
read-only import 178
representing import 175
theory 217
type 49, **252**
set 66, 136, 162, 191, 274
Set 150, 152, 156, 162, **163**, 180, 201
setConstructor 89, **93**, 142, **144**
setType 65, **66, 136**
severity of error 17
short form 12, 39, 60, **103**, 110, 134
shortcomings of Pascal 28
shortcomings of semantics 257
shortens, usage form 11
side effect 20, 29, 41, 51, 54, 56, 57, 74, 75, 85, 124, 146, 149, 202, 214, 215, 258, 264
side, right-hand 157
SideEffect **179**, 201, 203, 204
sign 95
sign, warning 28
signed constant 59
significant figure part 59
similar purpose 13
similar syntax 13
simplicity 28
simplification, of expression using axioms in ADL 151
simplify 151
sin 95
sind 95
sine 95
skip 265
statement 221
skip 85, 86, 87, 141, 195, **237, 238, 239**, 275
skipWhiteSpace 238, **239**, 239
small fast implementation 34
SNOBOL 32
software engineering 9
Soloway, E. 28
soul of Turing 261
source inclusion 102
SP/k 4, 8, 10, 14, 15, 261
space 256
character, non-white 86
state 279
white 86, 106, 110, 127
SPACE 256

SPACELIMIT 256
spaces separate words 18
spaghetti 262
special symbol **105**, 112
specification
formal, complexity of 28
formal, three C's of 27
language 27
program 27
results follow from 26
technique, formal 219
type, context condition for 190
square root 95
S/SL 34, 113, 114, 150, 264
stack 56
overflow 32
run-time 258
stamp, time 33
standard of excellence 26
Standards, International Organization 4
standardType **65**, 65, **136**
star 13, 92, 109, 112
format 195
stars, triangle of 39
state by state progression 279
state space 279
state, next function 115
state, next semantics 281
statement 13, 61, **81**, 81, **82**, 139, **148**, 228, 248
assert 82
ASSERT 220
assignment **82**, 192, 219, 228
basis 115, 218, **221**, 224, 230, 279, **280**, 281, 283
begin 83
context conditions for 148, 192
context-free syntax 137
exit **83**, 114, 170
for **84**, 109
free 83
get 84
new 52, **83**
nondeterministic 222
null 221
put 84
result 42, 43, 72, 82, 234
semantics of 225
skip 221
tag 33, 67, 80, **84**, 100, 220, 253
statement 135, **139**, 139
static legality **145**, 157, 183
static semantics 145
static type checking 20
STATUS 280
Stmt 158, 183, **192**, 194, 273, **274**, **275**
storage allocation (see **new**, collection)
str 237
Strachey, C. 115 stream 34, 40, 84, 94, 237
stream number 84, 100, 237
stream, default input 84, 94
streamNumber 84, **141**
string 42, 100
dynamic 65, 70, 74
end of 59
function 94
manipulation 31, 262
maximum length 39, 65
operator 92
ordering of 92
temporary 35
type 251
varying length 37, 38
string 65, 70, 136, 161, 190, 245, 274
string 144
String 161, 180, 190, 196
string(*) 74, 138, 161, 180, 190, 206, 276
stringLiteral 196, 212, 275
StringN 146, 147, 161, **163**, 180, 190
StringStar 161, **163**, 206
strint 86, **97**, 240
strong type checking 20, 22
strongly typed language 88
strreal **98**, 240

struct declaration (see **record**)
structural equivalence 41
structure, context-free 113
structure, lexical **112**, 112, **127**, 265
structure, phrase 111, 157
structured GOTO 222
structured language 10
structured value 229
student 16
study, psychological 18, 24
SUBPROG **222**, **224**, 232, 234, 281, 282
subprogram 24, 56, **72**, 82, 109, 137, **148**, 183
  as parameter 48
  body 55
  body, context conditions for 208
  call 211
  context condition for 148, **202**, 202
  context-free syntax 137
  declaration 82
  external 110
  forward 76, 125, 202
  inaccessible 207
  mathematical 31
  parametric 48, **73**, 75, 80, 201, 211
  predefined 122, 217
  recursive 177, 258
subprogramBody **76**, 137, **138**, 138
subprogramDeclaration 61, **72**, 135, **137**, 139
subprogramHeader **72**, 108, 137, **138**
Subrange 162, **163**, 180, 187, 191, 194, 206
subrange, empty 241
subrangeType 65, **66**, **136**, 137
subroutine (see subprogram)
subscript 220, 242
  array 199
  check 21
  range 32
subscripting 88
subset 89, 252
substitution, law of 51
substitution, rule of 29
substring 13, 42, 43, 89, **92**, 142, **143**, 199, 251
substringPosition 92, 143, **144**
subtraction 89, 142, 154
  map 154
succ 66, **94**, 230
SUN/68000 1, 34, 285
super Pascal 37
superset 89, 252
support, run-time 31
surprise rule, no 18, 20, 22, 23, 24, 263
surprise, unpleasant 13, **18**
switch statement (see **case**)
SyDef **147**, 153, 160, 165, **166**, 168
symbol table 168
symbol, representation in ADL 165
symbol, special **105**, 112
SymbolOfContext 170, **172**, 208
symptom, remote 19
syn **111**, 112, 114, 115, 121, 132
syntactic
  check 219, 241
  notation **60**, 221
  transformation 214
  trivia 11
  variable 133
syntax **111**, 111, 145, 217, 248
  abstract context-free 145, 157, 183, **273**
  clean 53
  concrete 273
  context sensitive 112, 114, **145**
  context-free 111, 112, **133**, 145, 157, 207, 217
  error 14
  error message 118
  extended context-free 271
  lexical 145, 217
  no frills **11**, **19**, 37
  similar 13
syOf 171
system programming 38, 262

syTagOf **167**, 184, 185
$syTag_{id}$ 184
$syTag_{ref}$ 184
$syTag_{sy}$ 185
sy_{id} 184
sy_{ref} 184

T

T 183, **190**, **274**
tab 127
tab 237, 238
table, symbol 168
tag 33, 62, 68, 81, 88, 140, 193, 229, 274
  assignment 68
  field 229, 242
  nameless 33
tag statement 33, 67, 80, **84**, 100, 220, 253
TagNameOf **163**, 199
TagType 163
taxation, general 32
teacher 16
teaching 53
  children 38
  experience 16
  language 8
technique, formal specification 219
temporary, string 35
Tennent, R.D. 38, 157
terminal 133
termination, clean 223
termination, loop 222
terminology 54
test, Turing 5
testing 21
text manipulation 9
textbook, Turing 27
textual isolation 25
then 140
theorem 248
theory, set 217
three C's of formal specification 27
thumb, rules of 7
time 256
  stamp 33
TIME 256
TIMELIMIT 256
Tjiang, S.W.K. ii, 5, 266
token **60**, 86, **112**, **127**, **129**, 133
  oriented input 86, 238
  recognizing 106
  sequence 127
Toronto, University of 4, 5, 8, 34, 261, 264, 266, 285
total semantics 225
toy 8
trace 280
trade off 7, 35
tradition, violation of 12
traditional notation **12**, 18, 23, 24
transfer, type function 96
transformation, syntactic 214
transformational semantics 223
transformer, predicate 3
TransitiveImports 176, **177**, 201, 203, 204
TransitiveROImports 178
transparency, performance 32
transporting compiler 34
treatment of errors 14
tree, parse 157
triangle of stars 39
triple postcondition 223
triple precondition 223
triple, predicate 223
trivia, syntactic 11
true **59**, 88, 142, **249**
trunc 90
truncate 22
tuple, in ADL 154
Turing 1, 264
  change 109

- features of 37
- formal definition of 111
- machine 250
- program, meaning of 217
- resource limited 4
- soul of 261
- test 5
- textbook 27

Turing, Alan M. 5, 264
Turing, Ideal 2, 4, **106**, 217, 250
Turing, Numeric 5
Turing Plus 5, 9, 38, 285
Turing Report 2, **53**, 121, 145, 214, 217, 261, 265
turtle geometry 11
TyDef **146**, 160, 161, 162, **163**, 179
TyDef type, in ADL 161
tyOf **163**, 184, 185
TYP 221, 225, 226, 231, 241, 245, 246
type 62, **148**
- abstract data 26
- ADL 146, **152**, 159
- assignability, context conditions 179
- base 252
- checking 20, 38, 265
- compatibility 70, 146, 241
- conversion function 96
- context condition 148, 190
- context-free syntax 136
- declaration 65
- declaration, context conditions for 189
- dynamic 164
- enumerated 45, 88, 249, **251**
- equivalence **69**, 147, 148, **179**, 247
- equivalence predicate EQV 247
- equivalence, context conditions for 179
- equivalent 41, 181
- index **65**, 66, 84, 164
- map 147
- modular 148
- named 69
- nonscalar 65
- numeric 164
- opaque 26, 125, 214
- parameterized 9
- real 255
- representation of in ADL 160, 161
- result 75, 172
- root **70**, 83, 86, 95
- safe 68
- scalar 65
- set 252
- set, base of 66
- specification, context conditions for 190
- string 251
- transfer function 96
- union-like 153

type 136, 152, 165, 168, 189, 226, 273
- *Set* 156

Type 165, **166**, 168, 198
typed language, strongly 88
typeDeclaration 61, **65**, 135, **136**
typeId 69, **137**, 137
typeSpec **60**, 74, 135, **136**, 136, 137, 138
typing, strong 22
tyTagOf **163**, 185
tyTag 180, 184, 185
ty 184, 185

U

U 229, 253
U.S. Department of Defense 38
unambiguous 113
unbalanced **if** 151
unbounded 217
- nondeterminism 257

unchecked 32
- assignment 222
- execution 21, 32, 120

unconstrained access 24
undefined 151
undefined value, in ADL 158
underflow 91
underlying hardware 32
understandability 28, 219
    program 17
understanding 19
unforeseen interaction 26
uniform distribution 99
uniform referent 45
uninit 33
UNINIT 221, **225**, 245, 254, 279
uninitchar **59**, 86, 96, 107
UNINITIALIZE 226
uninitialized 279
    array 254
    dangling pointer 30
    value 33, **100**, 221, 225, **254**
    variable 15, 32, 33, 117
UNINITIALIZED **225**, 229
union 30, 33, 45, 68, 70, 80, 91, 100, 142, 153, 198, 214, 217, 242, 248, 252, **253**
    field access 32, 33
union 46, **67**, 137, 162, 191, 246, 274
Union 162, **163**, 180, 191, 199
union-like type, in ADL 153
unions 54
unionType 65, 67, 136, **137**
unique identifiers 214
UNIV 225
universal quantification 250
University of Toronto 4, 5, 8, 34, 261, 264, 266, 285
University, Queen's 5, 285
Unix 264
unpleasant surprise 13
unpleasant, no surprise 18
unresolved 178
unsigned constant 59
upper bound 41, 99, 247
upper case 109
upper **98**, 109, 214
usage shortens form 11
use, convenience of 10
use, declaration before 34
use, pay for what you 32
used, frequently construct 103
useful **119**, 121
    redundancy 20
user feedback 14
utility, maximize 8

V

vagueness 125
valid 117
    expression predicate *EXPN* 243
    reference predicate *REF* 242
    type predicate *TYP* 245
validation 149
validity
    constraint 58
    predicate **117**, 119, 179, 218, 220, **241**, 250
    predicate for call 234
    predicate, bounded expression 255
value
    absolute 95
    boolean 249
    call by 74, 232
    enumerated 93
    infinite range of 31
    init 214
    initial 40
    label 68
    left-hand 184, 242
    parameter 73
    right-hand 184
    run-time 62
    structured 229
    uninitialized **100**, 221, 225, **254**

value-result 227
var 55, 74, 135, 138, 165, 167, 168, 187, 207, 226, 273, 277
declaration, context conditions for 187
formal parameter 69, 72
import 75
parameter 241
VAR 147, **167**, 187, 189
Var 167, **277**
variable 54
banning of 28
declaration of 15, 62, 225
default value 15
free 150
global 24, 25
initialize 20, 222
parameter 231
read-only 55
syntactic 133
uninitialized 15, 32, 33, 117
Variable 165, **166**, 168, 187, 193, 197, 200
variableBinding **64**, 81, **135**, 139
variableDeclaration 61, **62**, **135**
variableReference 64, 82, 86, **88**, 135, 139, **142**
variant record 19, 30, 32, 33, 54, **67**
nondiscriminated 33
varOrForward **74**, **138**
varying length string 37, 38
VAX, Digital 1, 5, 34, 108, 261, 265, 285
vehicle registration 46
vehicleRecord 67
verbiage, extraneous 11
verbose 38
verification 54
condition generator 116
of Turing implementation 149
program 263
violation of tradition 12
visibility 55
controlled 25
Visible **170**, 170, 171
Von Neuman 264
architecture (see implementation)

W

Wait, J.W. ii
warning sign 28
warning, early 19
weakest precondition **116**, 219, 223, 281
Weber, I.S. ii
weight, kilogram 15
Weinberg, G.M. 7
well-formed formula 248
Welsh, J. 29, 38
wff 248
when 81, 103, 139, 193, 230, 274
where clause 155
while statement (see **loop**)
white space 86, 106, 110
character 127
width, field 10, 12
widthExpn 85, 86, 87, **141**, 141
Wirth, N. 7, 262
with 47
with Pascal, compatibility 29
word 112
wordiness 37
words, spaces separate 18
wordy 38
workstation, SUN/68000 1
wp 116, 117, 223, 224, 259, 279, 282, 283
write statement (see **put**)
Wulf, W. 24, 25

Y

YACC 134, 264
you pay for what you use 32

Z

zero division 116